CONTENTS

IMPROVISATION AND SOCIAL AESTHETICS

Improvisation, Community, and Social Practice
A NEW SERIES EDITED BY DANIEL FISCHLIN

Books in this new series advocate musical improvisation
as a crucial model for political, cultural, and ethical dialogue and action—for imagining and creating alternative ways of knowing and being in the world. The books
are collaborations among performers, scholars, and
activists from a wide range of disciplines. They study the
creative risk-taking imbued with the sense of movement
and momentum that makes improvisation an exciting,
unpredictable, ubiquitous, and necessary endeavor.

IMPROV- ISATION AND SOCIAL AESTHET- ICS

GEORGINA BORN, ERIC LEWIS, AND WILL STRAW, EDS.

Duke University Press   Durham and London   2017

Printed and bound by CPI Group (UK) Ltd, Croydon, CR0 4YY
Typeset in Charis by Tseng Information Systems, Inc.

Library of Congress Cataloging-in-Publication Data
Names: Born, Georgina, editor. | Lewis, Eric, [date] editor. |
Straw, Will, [date] editor.
Title: Improvisation and social aesthetics / Georgina Born,
Eric Lewis, and William Straw, eds.
Other titles: Improvisation, community, and social practice.
Description: Durham : Duke University Press, 2017. | Series:
Improvisation, community, and social practice | Includes
bibliographical references and index.
Identifiers: LCCN 2016045052 (print) |
LCCN 2016048372 (ebook)
ISBN 9780822361787 (hardcover : alk. paper)
ISBN 9780822361947 (pbk. : alk. paper)
ISBN 9780822374015 (e-book)
Subjects: LCSH: Improvisation (Music)—Social aspects. |
Music—Social aspects. | Aesthetics—Social aspects. |
Arts and society.
Classification: LCC ML3916.I47 2017 (print) |
LCC ML3916 (ebook) | DDC 781.3/6—dc23
LC record available at https://lccn.loc.gov/2016045052

Cover art: The Art Ensemble of Chicago and Cecil Taylor,
1984. Photo by Guy Le Querrec/Magnum Photos.

Duke University Press gratefully acknowledges the Social
Sciences and Humanities Research Council of Canada for
its support of the Improvisation, Community, and Social
Practice (ICASP) project, at the University of Guelph, which
provided funds toward the publication of this book.

ACKNOWLEDGMENTS

This volume has its origins in a conference held at McGill University in March 2010 under the auspices of the research area Improvisation and Social Aesthetics within a larger research program entitled Improvisation, Community, and Social Practice (ICASP). A multi-institutional network of projects funded by Canada's Social Sciences and Humanities Research Council, with major concentrations at the University of Guelph, the University of British Columbia, and McGill University, ICASP ran from 2007 to 2014. While based in Canada, ICASP encompassed collaborations with many international scholars and other research projects.

The 2010 conference, itself called Improvisation and Social Aesthetics, was a vibrant and successful experimental event that brought together a number of participants in the ICASP research area with other Canadian and international scholars working on improvisation and social aesthetics in relation to music and a range of other art and performance forms. The conference was co-sponsored by ICASP and the Schulich School of Music at McGill; it was organized by Lisa Barg and Eric Lewis. All participants in the conference have chapters in this volume, with the exceptions of Amelia Jones and Jason Stanyek (who declined to contribute) and Will Straw (who is, however, a co-editor). We thank our contributors, as well as those who participated in the conference, for their commitment to this exciting and creative collective project.

The process of producing this edited collection benefited from the work of two invaluable assistants—Tracey Nicholls (also a contributor to this volume) and Eric Murphy—as well as from the assistance of Daniel Fischlin, the series editor, and the suggestions of the two anonymous readers for Duke University Press. We thank them all for their support and help.

WHAT IS SOCIAL AESTHETICS?

Georgina Born, Eric Lewis, and Will Straw

Although the social sciences directed their attention toward the production, circulation, and consumption of art from at least the early twentieth century, the dominant academic discourse on art and aesthetics for a long time has been, and in some quarters continues to be, an expression of neo-Kantian and neo-Humean philosophies. While the details and the value of both Kant's and Hume's aesthetics continue to be debated, it is fair to say that both theories, in different yet related ways, have neglected the ways in which one's location and embeddedness in a particular culture and social milieu affect one's aesthetic judgments, the role that such social location might play in aesthetics, and questions of whether and how social experience might itself be immanent in aesthetic experience.[1] Instead, both traditions have looked to what they consider to be universal human capacities and cross-cultural generalities to elucidate the sources of aesthetic pleasure and judgment. Such a focus on the perceptual and cognitive aspects of aesthetic experience and belief—and, in particular, the attempt to treat them as human capabilities that transcend culture, time, and place—has led to a focus on such issues as the existence or nature of aesthetic connoisseurship and the possible objectivity of aesthetic evaluation, as well as to attempts to isolate a distinctive aesthetic attitude and even a distinctive aesthetic mode of perception. In this respect, such aesthetic theories are atomic in that they elevate individual agents and their mental beliefs and perceptual capacities as the primary concern.[2]

The result is that the historical roots of aesthetics as a distinct field of inquiry has precluded any potential development of a social aesthetics, and this has occurred for two broad reasons. First, the Kantian claims that "pure" judgments of beauty follow from a disinterested feeling of pleasure, coupled with the purposeless nature of art as art, would seem to rule out of court any consideration of the social in aesthetics. Second, the normative Humean claim that the proper theory of taste entails concurrence of aesthetic judgments among all aesthetic "experts" presumes that aesthetics can and should be neutral with regard to social status, position, history, and function. The influence views such as these had (and in some quarters continue to have) on demarcating the boundaries of the aesthetic are responsible for the absence of any consideration in prior theories both of what a social aesthetics might represent and of the diverse forms it might take. The chapters that follow explore and develop a number of distinct yet mutually resonant formulations of a social aesthetics, a social aesthetics that, in part by virtue of its rejection of the universality implied by this early history, is per force plural and varied. What ties these approaches together is a rejection of the claim, however grounded, that one can or should disentangle the social, in all its varied modalities, from experiences and conceptions of the aesthetic. In this sense, art objects and events are thought to transcend their narrow material, temporal, and spatial boundaries and to participate vitally, richly, and vigorously in the larger socio-material assemblages within which they are created, circulated, and consumed — within which they and the subjects of aesthetic experience that they elicit and encounter together live their lives.[3]

Early aesthetic theories, and subsequent theories indebted to them, have helped to explain much about our aesthetic worlds, including differences and similarities between our beliefs about artworks and their effects on us, as well as our experiences of and interactions with other kinds of objects. Yet at the same time, the failure of such models of aesthetic inquiry to engage from the outset with the social and cultural dimensions of our aesthetic lives has resulted in theories that are peculiarly barren of nuance, unable to understand actual aesthetic attitudes, and blind to how such social relations as those pertaining to class, race, ethnicity, religion, gender, sexuality, or nationality, and the histories and power relations in which they are entwined, as well as the socialities animated by art objects and events, inflect aesthetic experience — often in ways that precisely deny that they are so inflected.

Recognition of the powerfully social nature both of aesthetic judgment and of aesthetic experience not only suggests that more than just the philosopher's normal toolkit needs to be brought to bear in the analysis of aesthetics (i.e., the philosopher's concern with conceptual analysis, logical argumentation, and the impact of a given theory on related theories). It suggests also that sociological, anthropological, and cultural-historical research should inform future investigation into and theorization of the aesthetic (Born 2010c; Bourdieu 1984). Aesthetics as a field of inquiry, in this view, needs to move beyond the individual or atomic and toward the social or molecular, interrogating, for example, such pervasive social and cultural processes as the role of aesthetic experience in the formation of affective alliances (Straw 1991) or aggregations of those affected by art and music (Born 2011). It needs to consider the many ways in which individual aesthetic judgments are influenced by social processes and pressures that may be fluid or rigid and enduring. It needs to address how social entities themselves—social groups, populations, cultural institutions, disciplinary formations, governments—adopt, invent, forge, promote, and/or police certain aesthetic tendencies and positions. And it needs to register and theorize how particular socialities and social relations can themselves "get into," partake in, and animate aesthetic imagination and experience.

In this light, the notion of a "social aesthetics" can be seen *both* as a broadening of the traditional subject matter of aesthetics (i.e., individual beliefs about art objects, the cognitive and perceptual processes behind them, and the ontology of art objects that underlie such attitudes) and, emphatically, as a critique of it. A social aesthetics is, then, less concerned with demarcating a class of aesthetically valuable objects than it is with explaining how and why a given set of objects or experiences—those associated with, say, Beethoven or Bird, Brancusi or Beuys, Beach Boys or Blackalicious—is judged to be valuable, or its value contested, by some social group or other, or is taken to be the entangled locus of social-aesthetic experience. By rejecting what is often seen as a Kantian view of the functionlessness of art, a social aesthetics argues for, and investigates the details of, the many ways in which our interactions with art participate in or serve an array of political orientations and social and cultural processes: from signaling our membership in and commitment to particular social identities (Marxist, African American, queer, and so on) or culturally imagined communities (punk, psytrance, death metal, and so on), to reifying, contesting, or modeling alternatives to existing social formations. These concerns lead the contributors to this book to focus on the aesthetic orientations of entities that are larger than the individual—to examine, for example, the diverse ways in which institutions or elite social groups may codify their power and prestige through certain aesthetic commitments or aesthetically informed practices, but equally the manner in which social groups and collective projects as well as individual artists can develop or promote aesthetic practices that are intended to counteract prevailing cultural norms, dominant social mores or political discourses, or that may become a locus for enacting alternative social relations.

One might think, therefore, that there are few points of contact between traditional aesthetics and a social aesthetics—that a social aesthetics is concerned with anything but the aesthetic. But this would be a mistake in two ways, as the chapters in this volume attest—first, because a social aesthetics continues to realize the reality and the importance of aesthetic pleasures and displeasures, while recognizing that discussions, theories, and conflicts about aesthetic judgments will at the same time often signal, consciously or unconsciously, either a commitment to or a questioning of given social identifications and political positions; and second, because a social aesthetics questions the utility of the very separation of the categories "aesthetic" and "social" when analyzing the nature of artistic objects and processes and the aesthetic experiences they elicit—a stance most obviously relevant, but not limited, to the performing arts (music, theater, dance, performance art, sound art, and so on).

Far from saying that aesthetic judgments are unimportant, then, a social aesthetics argues that they are much more important and less confined than has been realized by traditional aesthetics, in that they are judgments that we may employ to demarcate ourselves from others, to glorify or vilify others, to help define the communities in which we claim membership and to which we claim allegiance, as well as to imagine and experiment with new socialities and social identifications at the limits of present arrangements. To embrace a social aesthetics, then, is to believe that aesthetics matters in ways far beyond those previously assumed, for a social aesthetics recognizes that our aesthetic pronouncements and embodied experiences are saturated with social meaning, are routinely enrolled to serve multiple social and cultural purposes, and are as much about the subjects of aesthetic experience as they are about aesthetic objects. Indeed, in this sense a social aesthetics both depends on and augurs a relational, historically situated conception of aesthetic subject and object (Born 2009, 80–81; cf. Paddison 1993, 216). At the same time, by arguing that the sensory, perceptual, and embodied modes of experience at the heart of aesthetic theory should be grasped as immanently encultured and social,[4] a social aesthetics ushers in novel and long-overdue means of analyzing aesthetic experiences themselves.

The recognition that the social, broadly construed, is an ineliminable part of aesthetic experience and that we cannot isolate or purify the objects of aesthetic appreciation from their social entanglement serves also to broaden the class of objects toward which aesthetic theory might be turned. This broadening has been witnessed across the humanities and social sciences since the 1970s, as popular culture and music, noncanonical forms of visual culture, mass-media content, and so-called para-literatures have taken their place within university curricula and in the research activities of scholars across these fields. Indeed, it is these developments that ushered in from the 1970s the new interdisciplinary fields of cultural and media studies. Admittedly, this is a shift that remains unsteady and ambivalent: media and popular-culture texts and artifacts are still not accorded the same status and value in elite academic circles as the objects of the traditional humanities, and admission of interest in any social dimension of culture often remains a trigger for fears and accusations of that grave sin, sociological reductionism. Nonetheless, with these openings, the boundaries of what constitutes an artwork have come to be seen as more porous than previously believed. No longer are art objects thought to consist solely of a distinct class of entities, produced under certain conditions, for certain reasons, and usually by a prescribed class of art creators. This expansion of the range of cultural phenomena deemed worthy of cultural analysis has been accompanied by a recognition of the fluid, often contradictory ways in which social processes, conventions, and norms shape aesthetic objects, just as aesthetic discourses can in turn shape social processes and even sociocultural institutions (Born 1995, 2004). Yet this broadening of the objects of cultural analysis has commonly *not* been accompanied by a concern with the aesthetic per se. Rather, for decades the kinds of textual analysis that prevailed in film, media, and cultural studies took its bearings from ideology critique, certain Foucauldian orientations, psychoanalytic theories, and formal or narrative analysis—theories and methodologies from which questions of the aesthetic are invariably absent. At the time of this writing, for example, the challenge of conceptualizing the aesthetic in relation to media, especially new media, remains at the cutting edge of media studies. Thus, while efforts to characterize the interconnections between the aesthetic and the social *should* have been central to key currents in cultural theory in recent decades—from semiology, Anglo-American cultural studies, and film and media studies to the sociology of culture and analyses of cultural production—they have been halting. From the social-science side, Pierre Bourdieu's sociology of art and culture is indicative,[5] for despite his sustained commitment to theorizing cultural production, Bourdieu (1984) produced mainly a negative critique of aesthetics.[6]

The main exception in this history is the anthropology of art, in which social and cultural analysis has been accompanied by a conviction that matters of aesthetic and affective experience, as well as "form and the relative autonomy of form" (Morphy and Perkins 2006, 18), lie within its scope (see, e.g., Coote and Shelton 1992; Layton 1991). A great deal of work in the anthropology of art has been concerned with charting indigenous art systems and their aesthetic discourses, often by exploring their difference from Western romantic and modernist idioms. Form and aesthetics, then, have been central problematics, despite continuing controversy about whether the concept of the aesthetic can legitimately be employed cross-culturally as an analytical category.[7]

In parallel with these developments in the academy, since the early 1960s a spate of artistic and musical movements developed—among them Fluxus, happenings, and installation and intermedia art—that drew attention to the ways in which social relations and social situations can participate in aesthetic phenomena or contribute to aesthetic experience, a trajectory that culminated recently in the upsurge of curatorial, art-critical, and art-theoretical writings and debates that erupted around the concept of relational aesthetics.[8] It is in the wake of these movements within art and music over the past half-century that a further step in the conceptual apparatus underpinning a social aesthetics has become necessary, because together these movements foster the recognition not only that art and music are conditioned and shaped by wider social and cultural processes, but also that art and music themselves have the potential both to influence social processes and to put into practice, model, enact, and experiment with novel socialities and social relations of diverse kinds. In this light, recent anthropologies and sociologies of art and music have proposed that the relationship between art or music and the social should be conceptualized in terms of bidirectional influences or mutual mediation (Born 2005, 2011, 2012; DeNora 2003, 2010; Hennion 1993, 2003). In short, just as social (and economic and political) conditions and processes shape art and music, so do art and music shape social (and economic and political) life.

It is worth dwelling a little longer, however, on the historical developments alluded to in the previous paragraph, for the emergence of an array of post-formalist, socially inflected artistic movements since the 1960s went along with a widespread rejection of the very idea of the aesthetic on the part of those propounding what was pointedly termed "anti-aesthetic" art, of which conceptual art is generally taken to be the vanguard (Skrebowski 2009). Indeed, for Peter Osborne (2013, 37), art from the mid-1960s entailed a "struggle over art's relationship to [the] aesthetic," a "campaign . . . at once anti-institutional and the bearer of an alternative institutionalization, following the temporal logic of artistic avant-gardes." This campaign "so fundamentally transformed the field of practices . . . recognized as 'art' . . . as to constitute a change in art's 'ontology' or very mode of being. The new, postconceptual artistic ontology that was established [was] 'beyond aesthetic'" (37). Against this background, for some commentators, the present swell of interest in relational aesthetics should be understood as a belated, possibly tamed (and perhaps even ironic) recuperation of elements of the earlier, more socially critical stances enunciated by key strands of 1960s and post-1960s art. Hence, Luke Skrebowski (2009) argues compellingly that the systematic conceptual art associated with the artist and theorist Jack Burnham, as well as with Hans Haacke, Daniel Buren, Michael Asher, Marcel Broodthaers, and others, should be understood genealogically as a precursor of later socially oriented art movements, in particular what became known as institutional critique,[9] as well as relational aesthetics.

Judith Rodenbeck (2011; see also n. 9) contends, in turn, that today's relational aesthetics and participatory art form part of a genealogy, previously unrecognized, that should encompass not only such ancestors as John Cage's 4'33" of 1952, Marcel Duchamp's lecture, "The Creative Act" of 1957, and Umberto Eco's concept of the "open work" of 1962, but also, above all, Allen Kaprow's invention of happenings and the advent of the Fluxus movement. Running through Rodenbeck's genealogy are emphases on participation, the everyday, and the "actively critical, experimental, and fundamentally *social*" nature of these art practices (xiii). As she continues, both happenings and Fluxus events were "radically material, immersive, hybrid, and performative; they were funky, amateurish, and [again] fundamentally social. . . . [Moreover] both happenings and Fluxus events were devised as critiques of the dealer-gallery-museum system" (250–51). Indeed, for Rodenbeck, it was these movements and their "engagements with process" that engendered the "twinned performative, immaterial, hybrid projects of conceptual and systems art" (250–51). Benjamin Buchloh (1990) argues similarly that conceptual art originates in an "aesthetics of administration" where, in Skrebowski's (2009, 29) words, "'administration' is understood as a direct mimicry of the operating logic of late capitalism and its positivist instrumentality." Buchloh traces the "aesthetics of administration" from roots in Joseph Kosuth's conceptual work through its extension in Haacke's and Buren's critiques of "the social institutions from which the laws of positivist instrumentality and the logic of administration emanate in the first place" (Skrebowski 2009, 30). Whatever stance one takes on these complex and entangled genealogies, commentators appear to agree on the amnesia evident in the fact that the earlier era and its "fundamentally social" practices demand a "historical perspective that [the proponents of relational aesthetics have] willfully rejected" (Rodenbeck 2011, 247).

In light of these genealogical rereadings, we might observe that the politically and socially inflected movements from the 1960s to the 1980s—happenings, Fluxus, conceptual art, and post-conceptual developments such as institutional critique—were engaged at the same time in both radically expanding and emptying out, to the extent of its absolute negation, the then prevailing concept of the aesthetic. Given that it did not seem an option to recast the notion of the aesthetic to encompass either the social, participatory, and "lifelike" aspects of 1960s art or its "low theater, cheap entertainment" and carnivalesque (Rodenbeck 2011, 251) qualities, it seems that the term was generally abandoned, along with its formalist and essentialist baggage, rather than revised in that era. Equally striking, however, is the softening evident in a recent return to the notion of the aesthetic in art theory and criticism, perhaps in part because of its neglect by key lineages of cultural theory for decades, a return of the repressed that entails a freeing up and an overcoming of the earlier rigid dualisms in which formalism was equated with the aesthetic and post- or anti-formalism with its negation. No doubt, this book—one of whose key terms, "social aesthetics," originally arose independently of the lineages just outlined[10]—is another, convergent emanation of the wider current interest in re-theorizing the aesthetic for post-formalist and post-conceptual conditions.[11] But the aim of the chapters gathered here is not to rehabilitate or return to old conceptions of the aesthetic or simply to register the bankruptcy of the old terms and dualisms. It is instead to make progressive conceptual leaps toward a radically enlarged, productively denatured conception of the aesthetic that is suited to contemporary practices, as well as to those earlier practices and genealogies that are being recovered by writers like Skrebowski and Rodenbeck—a conception of the aesthetic as immanently social.[12]

A social aesthetics can therefore be seen as expanding the traditional bounds of aesthetics in two counter-movements. It takes into account the social conditions bearing on experiences of and judgments about art objects, including how these conditions inform the creation, dissemination, reception, and import of such judgments. At the same time, a social aesthetics enlarges or dissolves the very boundaries that have previously defined art, musical, and performance processes and events themselves, showing not only how they are mediated by wider social conditions and institutions but also how they are immanently social and may in turn proffer—or better *em-practise*—novel realms of social experience, new modes of sociality.[13] The domains of art, music, and performance therefore cross-fade with the social, in this way eroding the inflexible categorization of what constitutes aesthetic experience and its art or musical objects characteristic of earlier aesthetic theories. The essays in this collection take both of these directions, sometimes at once. On the one hand, they unpick the social and political conditions bearing on aesthetic experiences, objects, and practices; on the other hand, they direct attention to the social relations and social dynamics immanent in art, musical, and performance works and practices as aesthetic events.

In addition to expounding a social aesthetics, a second theme is central to this collection: that of the relation between a social aesthetics and improvisation. The aforementioned aspects of social aesthetics make it particularly appropriate to an analysis of improvisatory art, since improvisation, regardless of its medium, has often been conceived by both its practitioners and its theorists as being intimately inflected by the social formations in which it is created and as being, in aesthetically relevant ways, a social practice in itself. Improvised art is often created partially as a social commentary—perhaps on an existing art scene, perhaps on a wider set of social or political issues (see, e.g., Heble 2000; Jones 1963; Monson 2007); while, crucially, the artwork itself—the "object of aesthetic appreciation" in traditional aesthetics—entails, more obviously than in the non- or less improvised arts, processes of social interaction. In other words, there are both social and historical reasons and aesthetic reasons for why the improvised arts can be seen as a key conduit for the development of a social aesthetics.[14] First, and with particular regard to improvised music, improvisation is often seen as a response and a corrective to the normative ontology of Western art music, in which experience of the "work" comes to us embedded in a rigid hierarchy descending from composer through performer to audience (Goehr 1992). From this perspective, the very act of improvising enacts an alternative to, and embodies a critique and rejection of, the social relations—the particular musical division of labor—constructed by the Western art music tradition, and is in this critical respect an act not only of social commentary but, potentially, of social experimentation.[15] Of course, one may consider the account of hierarchical relations between composition and improvisation that grounds this analysis both historically mistaken and musically and conceptually misguided—as, for example, Nicholas Cook does in his chapter in this volume.

Second, and less controversial, group improvisation involves essentially dialogical engagements between the improvisers, so that they are compelled to communicate with one another, all parties receiving, negotiating, responding to, and attempting to create meaningful (musical or performance) utterances and gestures in real time.[16] The precise way this dialogue unfolds has often been portrayed as the primary locus of the aesthetic distinctiveness of improvisation (Monson 1996), but—the pivotal point—the dialogical aesthetic practice is also, immanently, a social interaction. In other words, and most obviously with respect to music (but also, as several chapters aver, in the other performance arts), improvisation cannot but emprac- tise or manifest a social aesthetics. Again, while music-making techniques that do not foreground improvisation can themselves enact or inflect social processes, and invariably also involve dialogue among performers (Schutz 1964), differences in degree perhaps do, in this case, result in a difference in kind. Music-making practices centered on scores and their interpreta- tion, and powered by individual author-composers, have for decades at- tracted the primary attention of the disciplines of musicology, music theory, and music analysis, generating copious textual exegeses from a variety of theoretical perspectives. Not until the improvisatory arts and their asso- ciated social aesthetics receive sustained attention of the sort initiated by the chapters that follow will we be in a position from which critically to judge how and to what degree the improvisatory arts differ from the non- improvisatory, and what sort of distinction, if any, can be drawn between the social entanglement of and the socialities engendered by these two meta-artistic formations.[17]

The essays in this collection speak to and complement one another in assorted ways, from obvious affinities such as the art form they investigate or the theoretical paradigms they use, through the forms of mediation they examine or the particular points of contact between the social and the aes- thetic on which they focus. All of the contributors are aware of the dangers that arise from the very outset in discussing improvisation, whose defini- tion and limits remain contested.[18] Rather than attempt to define improvi- sation in any pure or essential terms, all of the essays identify an improvi- sational moment or aspect of the practices they examine. In this sense, they are all acutely aware that the very notion of improvisation is itself contested ground—aesthetically and socially—and that distinct practitioners and communities, with their particular histories and concerns, characterize and theorize improvisation differently. What emerges is a wide-ranging series of accounts not just of how the social and the aesthetic relate within the context of particular improvisatory arts, but also of how the very notion of an improvisatory art is a product of specific aesthetic and social conditions—conditions that often pull in contradictory directions and that may themselves be the sites of potent contestation.

Attempts to offer a definitive account of improvisation quickly encounter the very different senses that the term has accrued in relation to particular media and art forms, their cultures of production, and their communities of practice. Improvisation in the cinema, for example, may be taken to center on the activity of actors, of technicians (such as those controlling cameras or sound-recording devices), or of audiences, or on those elements of everyday life (such as crowds or moving vehicles) whose behavior, captured on film, is unplanned and unanticipated. In the visual arts, abstract expressionism in general, and action painting more specifically, is often said to be paradigmatic of improvisation, while in music jazz is usually considered the form that most obviously brings improvisation to the fore. Yet the connections here between the cultures of improvisation at play are far from straightforward. In the popular imagination, Jackson Pollock's middle-period drip paintings are said to be visual analogues of bebop, with its casting aside of many harmonic rules, its free invention of melody, and its reckless energy.[19] These features of be-bop are often seen as paradigmatic of the emphasis on personal agency in jazz improvisation, the fact that jazz solos are a product of the improviser's own decisions and are an expression of his or her individual creative voice. Yet at the same time, drip painting by its very nature breaks the intentional bonds between artist and canvas, as the precise pattern of paint is to a large degree a result of chance. So improvisation in jazz is understood as a highly personal and intentional practice, while action painting is analyzed as improvisational yet lacking this grounding in artistic intentionality—in fact, as rejecting it.

It is, then, the differences in how the term "improvisation" may be employed, and the ways in which practices, discourses, and cultures of improvisation diverge or are in tension, that are of greatest interest, since they point to the radically contingent nature of improvisation as it is understood and empractised, and as it has developed historically in relation to specific artistic media. Thus, in jazz, improvisatory elements are commonly taken to be grounded in the music's highly intentional nature and its embeddedness

in and continuation of a particular musical history, while in abstract expressionism, both intentionality and history are downplayed with an emphasis
instead on the unconscious and the act of creation. Neither account is false,
but any attempt to place them both under some unifying concept is bound
to obscure more than it illuminates—at the same time as ignoring actual
artistic and social practices and discourses. In attending to these traditions,
we learn more about the historically path-dependent nature of such practices and discourses of improvisation—notably, why jazz has been thought
to be improvisatory, why action painting was seen as a painterly cognate to
jazz, and how a particular school of free improvisation problematizes these
connections—than we reveal about any sort of essence of improvisation applicable across media, art forms, and cultures. At this point, we turn to an
overview of the chapters, grouped according to key themes and affinities in
analysis and outlook.

Part I: The Social and the Aesthetic

In distinctive ways, the four chapters in the book's opening part all address improvisation and social aesthetics primarily in relation to music—
or, in one case, music and machines. Improvisation studies in the field of
music labor under the long history of a musicology that has been directed
almost exclusively toward Western art music, as well as fixated primarily on
the analysis of orthodox musical scores, and the inevitable Platonism concerning musical works that follows.[20] The substance or content of music is
equated with music's notatable or scoreable parameters, and as a corollary
the aesthetic properties of music have by and large been assumed to be exhausted by those properties that can be scored.[21] Improvisation has invariably ended up defined negatively: as a musical practice lacking characteristics of composed music.[22] The rise of both the New Musicology and popular
music studies in the 1980s, with their common engagement with the social
relations and political circumstances in which music is produced and received, signaled a willingness to turn scholarly attention toward so-called
popular and vernacular musics.

In this historical light, from multiple directions within the study of cultural production, Georgina Born (2010c) has observed, we find calls for a
theoretical rethinking of the relationship between art and/or music and the
social. Her chapter opens by remarking how difficult it has proved, nonetheless, to develop an approach adequate to conceptualizing how the social
enters into the aesthetic operations of both music and art; indeed, music and

art, she argues, set some of the most general and obdurate interdisciplinary challenges to the humanities and social sciences in this regard, and improvisation poses them particularly acutely. In parallel, Born notes a crisis within anthropological and social theory over the past two decades centered on the need to reconceptualize the social—or "sociality"—itself, suggesting that attending to music and art can advance these wider debates focused on re-theorizing the social. Born then clarifies a number of ways in which the social is put into practice and conceptualized in several lineages of contemporary art practice and commentary, from the relational aesthetics of Nicholas Bourriaud (2002), through the experimental institutional interventions of the Artist Placement Group, to the avowedly activist nature of socially engaged art. She follows the art theorist Claire Bishop (2004) in her important challenge to Bourriaud: as Bishop asks, if art is engaged in producing social relations, then the question is, "What types of relations are being produced, for whom, and why?" In this way, Born highlights the need to develop conceptual tools adequate to the task of disentangling and identifying the distinctive forms of sociality produced by art and musical practices so as to avoid their elision, foster a more acute appreciation of both their singularity and their mutual interrelations, and enable fertile comparisons to be drawn between contemporary art and improvised music.

Turning to music, Born shows how the primary way in which a social aesthetics has been identified is in relation to the immediate "microsocialities" of musical practice and performance, which tend to be idealized and to occlude several additional ways that music, and the aesthetic experiences that it engenders, mediate and are mediated by social processes. To advance beyond the preoccupation with music's microsocialities, in the main body of the chapter Born proposes an analytical framework centered on four planes of the social mediation of music. She then takes this framework to improvised music, in which the articulation of the four planes is manifest in richly reticulate socialities, while drawing comparison between the varieties of social aesthetics in contemporary art and those evident in improvised music. Born addresses two improvised music ensembles to exemplify the modes of analysis opened up by her framework: the Association for the Advancement of Creative Musicians (AACM), an African American musicians' collective founded in Chicago in 1965, and, particularly, the practices of one of its core groups, the Art Ensemble of Chicago; and the Feminist Improvising Group, an experimental, all-woman European ensemble working at the borders of improvised music and performance art founded in London in 1977 (in which Born herself played cello and bass guitar). In an era in which post-formalist music, art, and interdisciplinary practices are vastly expanding the very nature and definition of "art," "music," "performance," and "work," Born suggests, it is imperative to develop subtler categories of analysis with regard to how variously the social enters into and transforms, and may in turn be transformed by, the aesthetic.

In chapter 2, Nicholas Cook assails the still common notion that improvisation and work performance should be conceived as totally opposed "others," showing that a focus on performance as a social phenomenon can reveal their similarities and how they are, in effect, interpenetrating practices. Taking Corelli's Violin Sonatas as a case study, he argues that there is no categorical distinction between the performance of works and improvisation: all score-based performance involves the deconstruction, or situated interpretation, of preexisting structures, while, conversely, all improvisation involves reference to, or the elaboration of, preexisting schemata. One result of this is that the notated musical work is itself revealed to be a socially and historically contingent construction that emerges out of the interactions of musicians whose collective creativity produces the meaning seen retroactively to reside in the musical work. The consequence of this analysis is to relocate the generator of aesthetic experience from the supposedly inherent qualities of musical works to the social interactions that constitute their performances as such interactions are orchestrated by scores. Meaning emerges from the only partially predictable engagements between individuals, historically conditioned circumstances, and an open range of stimuli or signifiers that may be auditory, kinesthetic, visual, or cultural—or, indeed, that may belong, in principle, to any humanly perceptible medium.[23] Aesthetic ideologies, Cook contends, are what power the false dichotomies set up between improvisation and work performance, just as they overlook the socialities at play in musical work performance, instead concentrating narrowly on the features of scores. Only once we return performance to the center of aesthetic analysis, even when considering Western art music, according to Cook, will we be in a position to compare and contrast the socialities at play in both improvisational and work-performance settings and, in particular, to recognize commonalities between these forms of social aesthetics.

Chapter 3, by Ingrid Monson, asks us to guard against another sort of a priori, generalizing assumption—namely, that the relationship between improvised music and political movements for black equality in the United States is easily transferred to other improvising communities concerned with issues of cultural identity and politics. Her chapter takes a comparative perspective on the relationship between improvisation, the aesthetic, and the social by contrasting the development of an Afro-modernist aesthetic politics in American jazz improvisation of the 1950s and 1960s with the concept and process of *sensibilisation* in the contemporary musical aesthetics of Mali. Both musical traditions are highly improvisational and virtuosic, but each articulates the connections between social, ethical, religious, and musical currents in different ways. In American jazz of the 1950s and 1960s, the linking of aesthetics and the social involved the connection of explicitly modernist aesthetic values—among them originality, formal experimentation, and vanguardism—to the political and cultural struggle for civil rights and black power in a white-majority nation. In Mali, the idea of sensibilisation as an important and valorized activity on the part of popular artists involves the imperative to educate broad audiences about major issues of social, political, ethical, and medical concern through lyrics and performance styles that raise awareness through a combination of contemporary information and traditional modalities of expression. Rather than take a critical stance on nationalism, many Malian artists give it a positive orientation by exhorting the populace to place their skills and labor in the service of developing the country and its international profile. Race was the primary social formation examined and articulated in the social aesthetics of American jazz in the 1950s and 1960s; gender, health, and economic aspirations provide the central themes articulated by the social aesthetics of contemporary Mali.

Monson's comparative analysis is salutary in showing how the aesthetics of improvisation can mediate a variety of relationships to the social, as well as diverse political priorities. It also warns against assuming at the outset what such a relationship might be. Moreover, Monson's essay productively anatomizes two classic types of the relationship between the aesthetic and the social: in the modernist terms in which aesthetic gestures are understood to be inherently negational of the larger social and political order, and in the "functional" terms in which long-valued performance idioms are taken to be the bearers or carriers of a wider, positive, and transformative politics.

Taken together, Cook's and Monson's essays serve as useful guides for anyone studying improvised music, warning against assuming from the outset improvisation's unique and pure status—itself often a product of romantic or essentialist accounts of improvisation's emancipatory political potential—and reminding us that careful historical and ethnographic research on particular scenes and eras of improvisation are necessary if we are to avoid a "one size fits all" account of the social aesthetics of improvisation. Born's chapter, in turn, offers a rich blueprint for future research by urging us to attend to how the four planes of social mediation that she identifies enter into social-aesthetic experience. Her framework also highlights the distinctive ways in which the multifaceted socialities enacted by improvised practices both operate within particular social, cultural, and historical conditions and have the potential strenuously to contribute to their transformation.

In chapter 4, George Lewis adds another crucial dimension by raising the need for a detailed and nuanced historical account of the relationships between improvisation, social aesthetics, and the variable status of the human within assemblages of people and machines. While the dominant drift in studies of technology-based artistic expression has often been in the direction of a dehumanization, in which people come to be seen as nodes in networked relations, Lewis traces the countervailing tendency to endow machines with characteristics that are conventionally human. The call, in certain computer-music improvisation practices, to "let the network play" expresses the conviction that machines themselves possess attributes conventionally regarded as human, such as subjectivity, affectivity, autonomy, and individuality—indeed, that networked machines should be conceived of as "quasi-subjects." Lewis's genealogy of these practices challenges the long-standing, almost unquestioned humanism of theories of improvisation, while also participating in the broader enterprise, observable across a broad swath of recent writing in aesthetics, of rewriting the history of relational aesthetics. For critic-historians such as Bishop, Bourriaud's account of relational aesthetics is insufficiently attentive to conceptual and post-conceptual art practices from the 1960s onward; but Lewis's corrective finds a different point of departure. Key ideas about the "sociality" of artistic expression may be found, Lewis suggests, in landmark works that rethink the relationship between humans and machines. These works include the cybernetics of Gregory Bateson and Norbert Weiner, and the insights of Gordon Pask into the ways in which machines learn. They include also such works as the Little Computer People experiments of Rich Gold and David Crane, in which the interactions between humans and computers are marked by attention and affection rather than primarily by instrumental transactions from which any sense of social relations and human mutuality are absent. While the overarching direction in studies of human-computer interaction has been toward imagining forms of shared consciousness, Lewis's richly textured history points to the ideal of a common human-machine sociality analogous to that which is often claimed for practices of musical improvisation.

Part II: Genre and Definition

In traditional philosophical aesthetics, categories of art such as "painting" or "sculpture" affect the aesthetic primarily by establishing properties that are considered standard, variable, or counter-standard for members of that category, and it is the particular combination of such properties that determines the aesthetic value of the artwork in question.[24] Yet such categories are often presented as if they were determined solely by consideration of the media at play—for example, paint applied in two dimensions, sound, or three-dimensionally sculpted solids—and the specificity of the categories is deemed to stop at the level of such media. The reasons for this approach in traditional aesthetics are complex, but much headway can be made in understanding them once it is realized that this project is at its heart ontological and a direct outgrowth of other historical taxonomic enterprises that also focused on the materiality and gross form of the entities under consideration—whether they were zoological categories or the periodic table. In this approach, the autonomy of the various arts, and the hierarchical relationships assumed to exist between them, were considered to be based on the medium associated with each art form and the unique potential for crafting each medium that they afforded.

Genre theory, which initially emerged out of a similar program in relation to the literary arts (Frow 2005), came with time to shed its natural scientific and taxonomic ontological skin. From the early 1980s, particularly under the influence of film theory (Altman 1981, 1987, 1996; Neale 1980, 1990), the analysis of genre developed in less formalist directions and became increasingly focused on how genre categories are themselves intimately entangled in social processes, from the production and marketing operations of the media and culture industries and their attempted construction of reliable audiences, to the responses of actual viewers—where the latter process can entail both the reproduction of existing social identity formations and the forging of new coalitions or articulations between such social formations (Brackett 2005, 2016; Born 2005, 2011). Commitment to a certain artistic, literary, or musical genre (abstract expressionism, free verse, death metal) can be understood, then, both as expressing a constellation of social commitments and as partially constitutive of such commitments.

In this light, the chapters by David Brackett and Eric Lewis examine the dual aesthetic and social processes at work in the constitution and evolution of musical genres, investigating, in particular, the social dimensions of disputes about genre—dimensions often obscured by the overtly aesthetic language in which they are conducted. Brackett uncovers the complex history of the creation and reception of what may appear to be just a "novelty item" in Count Basie's catalogue (although it was his biggest hit): the track "Open the Door, Richard!" By examining the history of Basie's version alongside that of others, Brackett reveals a series of complex social and political battles that were set in motion concerning the whole notion of "popular music" and who could, or should, lay claim to this meta-genre. As Brackett argues, genres are invariably embroiled in plays of power and prestige, struggles in which social relations and aesthetics are intertwined but in which the evolving connections between the social and the aesthetic, as they fuel the formation and transformation of genres, are rarely publicly acknowledged. He uncovers how the concept of improvisation was understood in the particular historical situation surrounding "Open the Door, Richard!" and how improvisation figured into the distinctions made between different genres of music and their social connotations. In this way, Brackett establishes the often hidden ways in which the real or perceived presence or absence of improvisation can influence the social meanings attributed to, as well as the social constituencies reached by, particular musical genres.

Brackett emphasizes that what was at stake in the "battle" between popular music and jazz in the genre constellations of this era concerned at its core issues of racial identity and of the representation of nonwhite others in music—issues that turned on and stirred up the inflammatory perception that music encoded social identities and social relationships. This is a theme picked up by Lewis, in chapter 6, in his discussion of the practices, reception, and commentary surrounding the music of the AACM in Paris in 1969. The Association's works were often received against a backdrop of black radical politics and interpreted in such terms. Lewis shows how the members of the AACM refused to limit their music to membership of one musical genre; indeed, going further, he argues that they consciously problematized the genre membership of their own works, in this way forcing critics and audiences to question the genre designations at play. By doing so, Lewis contends, the members of the AACM were "aesthetically thickening" their works, while at the same time guarding against any assumption that there was a single social (antiracist) agenda behind their music. Lewis therefore extends Brackett's claim that genres bring social relations and musical sounds into mobile interrelations by suggesting that the AACM transformed the socially charged debates about the genre membership of their music into an aesthetic value. In this way, the AACM members took a stand against both aesthetic and social essentialism, as well as against any social reductionism in the interpretation of their music and practice. Arguably, Lewis suggests, they were at the same time resisting and articulating alternatives to the forms of racial essentialism to which they were often subjected.

Chapter 7, by Darren Wershler, adopts a quite different approach to genre in the contemporary arts. It addresses what is at stake in the contestation of genres and, particularly, those that foreground improvisation, arguing that such contestation comes focally to how the nature and location of creativity are understood. Wershler asks whether there is such a thing as "uncreative" improvisation, and if so, how it would operate. Pointing to the pervasive backdrop of modernist assumptions concerning the nature and value of creativity in the arts, Wershler suggests that uncreative improvisation may well be able to animate and articulate social critique more effectively than those kinds of improvisation that continue to take creativity as the hallmark of the artistically transgressive.

To develop his arguments, Wershler focuses on the work of the writer and artist Kenneth Goldsmith, particularly in his capacity as a disc jockey for the free-form New Jersey radio station WFMU. It has become increasingly common for critics, theorists, and practitioners to invoke the DJ as the paradigmatic authorial figure in contemporary culture, a figure taken to engage in practices of selection and combination of preexistent elements from the archive as a wellspring of new cultural forms (e.g. Bourriaud 2005; cf. Oswald 2006). What often remain uninterrogated, however, are a number of modernist formulations lying behind this valorization, in particular the view that creativity, novelty, and even "true art" are the inherently valuable results of the DJ's inspired curations and manipulations. Wershler argues that since the 1950s, when business culture began to claim creativity for itself, the arts have seen a corresponding movement into the deliberately boring and the uncreative. Against this background, he suggests, novelty and creativity can no longer signify in the manner that modernist thinking presupposes. Wershler examines a variety of Goldsmith's on-air performances in light of his writings on the subject of uncreativity to reexamine key terms in the discourse around improvisation and creativity. Goldsmith's oeuvre is shown to be worthy of consideration precisely because it works explicitly with categories that many practitioners and critics extolling the virtues of improvisation and improvisatory creativity exclude: the uncreative and the useless. Goldsmith's work, Wershler contends, intervenes in the ways in which ideas of the creative and creativity circulate within contemporary culture, moving between discourses that are, variously, legal, entrepreneurial, technology-centered, and aesthetic in character.

Part III: Sociality and Identity

The third part of the book is concerned with two dimensions of a social aesthetics: on the one hand, with the particular types of social relations that take shape in collaborative improvised practices as they relate to—and potentially critique or reimagine—the standard social arrangements, or division of labor, and the dominant institutional forms that support art, film, or music making; and, on the other hand, with how certain lived categories of social identity and social difference—those relating, for example, to sexuality, gender, race, or class—"get into" improvised practices and may also be transformed by those practices. The chapters therefore engage not only with issues of social identity as they are mediated by an aesthetics of improvisation, but also with improvisation as a locus for the generation of social relations—including the inherent potential for experimentation, and for the cultivation of interpersonal empathy, in those relations.

In chapter 8, Lisa Barg begins her essay on Billy Strayhorn, best known as the longtime arranger for Duke Ellington, with a fruitful question: "What socialities are involved in the aesthetic practices of arranging?" As her analysis shows, improvisation may serve as a potent site for the articulation of historically marginalized identities, in part through the forms of intimacy and negotiation that improvisation typically necessitates. Barg focuses on Strayhorn's works as a vocal arranger, arguing that these collaborations both paralleled and articulated his status as a gay, but largely closeted, African American man. Strayhorn's dissident sexual identity required that he work in the shadows, as a collaborator, in a distanced but empathetic space from which his musical voice could merge with and give shape to the voices of others. The very act of arranging, it might be suggested, is itself a difficult, almost a "queer," practice, given traditional musicological categories, inasmuch it situates or insinuates itself ambiguously within the composer-conductor-performer division of labor central to Western art music. Barg shows how the "queerness" of arranging as an aesthetic enterprise, particularly given its ambiguous relationship to both the scored and the improvisatory elements of Ellington's music, marked it as an ideal social location from which to enact queer labor.

Strayhorn's collaborations with singers in the activity of vocal arranging opened up spaces of interpersonal dialogue, but they were not (or not always) spaces of transparent and full communication. As Barg shows, Strayhorn's own "queer" identity moved between presence and absence, manifesting itself subtly in musical inflections and transgressions. While the music that resulted from these partnerships is easily read as proof of successful collaborations, it is more usefully grasped as having been produced through complex negotiations in which Strayhorn's "sonic empathy" was key even if it often went unrecognized.

In her afterword to the anthology *Black Popular Culture*, Michele Wallace (1998, 345) offered a dissent from the ways in which music had come fully to circumscribe what she called "the parameters of intellectual discourse in the African-American community." Among other things, Wallace called for greater attention to the histories and accomplishments of African American visual cultures. In chapter 9, Tracey Nicholls does not set music against the visual arts. Instead, she centers her essay on the role played by improvisation in the often overlooked visual-art criticism of the African American cultural theorist bell hooks. Nicholls argues that hooks's theory of the visual arts is grounded in an ethics of love that is informed by her appreciation of jazz and of the plurality of creative voices that improvisatory arts such as jazz both presume and place in dialogue.

One key reason for the neglect of hooks's writings on art, Nicholls suggests, is her emphasis on the aesthetics of ordinary craft objects, often created by individuals who stand outside the institutionally sanctioned art worlds. From the perspective of dominant art discourses, such individuals and their art are marked as deviant. The art objects they produce are often viewed as "mere" arrangements, put together to serve practical purposes (e.g., quilts); such art objects therefore occupy an ambiguous space between that of autonomous artworks and wholly functional things. The improvisatory, in this kind of art making, is most evident in the use of discarded, fragmented, and everyday materials. For Nicholls, drawing on hooks, salvage art, mosaic forms, and graffiti art all involve ways of drawing on everyday environments in order to bring aesthetic value to such environments and thus participate in processes of empowerment. Moreover, the vernacular space of art making is one in which the possibility of participation is extended to ever increasing numbers of people, refuting the social and cultural closures inherent in the institutionalization of the arts and music, just as the ongoing improvisation of novel and hybrid artistic forms challenges the exclusionary conceptions of artistic legitimacy that prevail in the art world.

Complementing the previous two chapters, chapter 10, by Marion Froger, examines an often forgotten moment in the history of improvisatory art practices. In the early 1960s, the filmmakers who made up the French New Wave turned to improvisation in a number of ways. To arrive on a film set (or a real street) with a camera and a minimal script was to leave oneself open to the unpredictable unfolding of real-life events, which filmmakers might follow or in which they might intervene. In this respect, the fiction films of the New Wave drew on principles of unscripted spontaneity that had already proved revolutionary in the field of documentary film. At the same time, by allowing actors to improvise their dialogue, filmmakers such as Jean-Luc Godard produced situations in which the relationships between characters on screen developed through processes of adjustment and negotiation similar to those that mark relationships in real life.

As Froger makes clear in her detailed study of responses to these films, improvisation raised the question of social relations at multiple levels. For craftspeople working in the mainstream film industry, improvisation represented a challenge to long-standing protocols and trade union agreements in which professional roles were clear, dialogue and camera angles were planned in advance, and a polished quality was the ultimate objective. With their disregard for such protocols, the improvising filmmakers of the New Wave were viewed widely as self-indulgent, privileged upstarts. The changes in profilmic practice were, then, dual: improvisation on screen engendered novel social relations, which in turn fueled, and were entangled with, aesthetic changes; while experimentation with professional roles also amounted to a challenge to the established division of labor in filmmaking. At the same time, audiences might respond to improvisatory practices in at least two distinct ways. From one perspective, improvising was a gesture of generosity on the part of filmmakers, who invited viewers to enter into something akin to their own social worlds and to watch intimate relationships take shape before the camera. From another perspective, improvisation was a gesture of disdain toward audiences, who found themselves excluded from the seemingly frivolous interactions of an in-group accused of lacking any sense of professional or artistic responsibility. Froger shows how the controversies and critical dissension that surrounded New Wave films were often based on judgments of filmmakers' relationship to society at large. Had these filmmakers produced a new, inclusive cinema that simultaneously challenged decaying industry structures and outdated aesthetic codes while embracing audiences in new and democratic ways? Or were they simply the bearers of a generational self-centeredness marked by contempt for audiences and disdain for a craft and a profession seen as having exhausted itself?

Part IV: Performance

The three chapters in this final part of the collection all focus in distinctive ways on how a social aesthetics might be conceived primarily in relation to performance. In addition, Susan Kozel and Winfried Siemerling both address how new technologies, when employed in the creation of art, can mediate both aesthetic and social change. More specifically, they demonstrate how social limitations often seen to be inherent in the very technology at hand can be transcended in aesthetically productive ways via diverse improvisatory gestures. Siemerling's chapter focuses on the practice of "turntablism" and, in particular, the use of hip hop by the Canadian poet and writer Wayde Compton to channel and rearticulate local black history and diasporic subjectivities. Siemerling argues that Compton's precise ways of employing turntablism and the spoken word operate both as a mode of performance and as a means by which to present and remix very specific aspects of black British Columbian history in nuanced terms. He contends that this is the case despite the common complaint against turntablism specifically, and against bricolage art more generally, that such cut-and-paste methods occlude cultural specificity and lack the ability to mediate any content with real cultural depth and specificity. Siemerling shows how Compton manages to transcend such charges through his highly improvisatory use of turntablism grounded in the signifying tradition,[25] in which repetition with a signal difference is considered a crucial means by which personal and community narratives can be both retained and modified to speak to new, pressing social concerns. In this way, the chapter enables us to understand Compton's artistic choices as contributions to a transformative, improvisational social aesthetics that is transcultural in its reach yet articulates a very particular and local sense of social identity and community.

In chapter 12, Kozel addresses how a social aesthetics attuned to the senses might be developed in relation to contact improvisation in dance, with particular attention to touch—between audience members and performers, and between dancers as mediated through mobile technologies. Kozel's interest is in interpreting the aesthetics of dance improvisation through a variant of phenomenology to reveal "the dynamic ebb and flow of states of encounter of all the participants," in which everyone is, in some sense, a performer. To do this, Kozel focuses on the interplay between improvisation and intercorporeality in two dance events—one of them, IntuiTweet, entailing reflexive analysis of a collaborative dance and media project, employing the networked digital space of Twitter and SMS messaging, in which she was herself involved. With reference to Rancière's (2009a) framing of aesthetics as a reconfiguration of perception, as well as Derrida's (2005) interest in the place of the anaesthetic in the aesthetic, Kozel highlights how the interactions immanent in these dance improvisations point to the social as innately inter-corporeal—where, through the late work of Merleau-Ponty, inter-corporeality is understood as a field of multiple embodied exchanges.

The first dance event, *Small Acts*, centered on "undecided situations" constructed for audience members as they followed dancers moving through a series of rooms and corridors, producing ambiguous transformations with the effect that audience members shifted between being spectators and participants. Through this fluid movement—across spaces and roles—the rhythm of the event was infused, Kozel suggests, with collective waves of affective anticipation. The fabric of aesthetic experience derived, she argues, from the improvised, anticipatory movements through diverse spaces of performers and audience, so that those who "watched" also contributed their own improvised movements to the event. In contrast, IntuiTweet, an experimental collaboration between three dancer-researchers, points to how social media can enhance and choreograph a social aesthetics. Tasked with noticing moments of their own "movement intuition," the dancers used Twitter to convey to one another what they were sensing and how they were moving at any given moment. When a tweet was received as a text, the dancer was expected to improvise the movement received, enacting a shift in bodily state or repositioning of limbs, and then to respond. This generated a flurry of movement messages, an asynchronous flow of kinesthetic exchanges afforded by the convergence between dance improvisation and social networking. While the contact improvisation in *Small Acts* consisted of inter-corporeal improvisation between audience and performers, in IntuiTweet it was fostered by movement translated into and disseminated as texts and then retranslated and reenacted through a distributed network of bodies. These improvisations, Kozel contends, offer an understanding of the anaesthetic not as the opposite of the aesthetic but as a field of less categorizable qualities of social interaction; at the same time, in Rancière's terms, they create and re-create bonds between people, giving rise to new modes of confrontation or participation.

In contrast to Siemerling and Kozel, Zoë Svendsen is concerned in chapter 13 with the contributions of improvisation to the socialities immanent in theatrical work, and thereby to a social aesthetics—given that theater is "always already relational, always rehearsing the possibility of social communities." She observes that the socialities produced by the spatial and literary codes of the theater are rarely remarked on by theater scholars. She sets out, however, from Michael Fried's infamous call to "defeat theater," since for Fried theater—with its acknowledgment of co-presence in the relation between artwork and audience—is an affront to "modernist sensibility." It is precisely against such a view, Svendsen argues, that a great deal of contemporary theatrical practice has been predicated on theater's inherent "doubleness": "its capacity not only for representing social relations, but also for shaping the [actual] sociality of the occasion." Svendsen traces the history of changing conventions of the social relations of theater, noting, for example, how George Devine, the founder of the Royal Court in London, promoted Friedian artistic autonomy, denying the permeability of social and aesthetic practices specific to theater. But in parallel, she notes those many movements—"from the anti-institutional avant-garde practices of Surrealists, Dadaists, and Futurists, to Brechtian epic, to the socialist theater companies that took theater directly 'to the people'" in Britain between the 1960s and the 1980s—that have experimented in diverse ways with direct social engagements between writers, actors, and audiences.

This history forms the backdrop to Svendsen's reflexive analysis of the place of improvisation within dramaturgical practice today. She notes that although improvisation plays a key role in theater as a socially oriented practice, its provenance is unclear. In some accounts, all acting is taken to be improvisatory; in others, improvisation is equated with values of intuition, immediacy, or spontaneity; in yet others, improvisation stands as a supposed bulwark against theater's reification and commodification. Three case studies allow Svendsen to convey a range of ways in which improvisation can enliven the social aesthetics of theater. The first, *Discombobulator*, highlights through improvisation the violence of a traditional proscenium-arched theatrical space that frames every action as spectacle. The performance thematizes entrapment within an aesthetic structure and the limitations of human agency while inviting the ready, empathic collusion of the audience. *Four Men and a Poker Game* demonstrates, in turn, how improvisation in performance can collapse the distance implicitly posited by the theatrical frame between fictional time and real-time experience in the venue, allowing the performance to converge with actual social engagements between audience and performers. *3rd Ring Out: Rehearsing the Future* goes further, dramatizing the porousness of social and aesthetic relations in theatrical process. Premised on the uncanny parallels between the scenarios provided to the civil servant "players" of nuclear war exercises and the instructions given to actors when improvising in rehearsal, the project rehearses the ethical dilemmas likely to be thrown up by the crises brought about by climate change. Combining performance, game, simulation, and artistic event, *3rd Ring Out* invites audience members both to encounter and to improvise around these ethical dilemmas. The piece elides artistic and social practice in the production of an emergency planning-style event; through research, discussion, and voting, participants shape both dramatic narrative and potential human futures, while the sometimes tense and volatile socialities that arise during the performance problematize the equation of participation with the creation of "community" that is so central to Bourriaud's relational aesthetics.

As a group, the three chapters in part IV reveal the varied, subtle, and often reflexive ways in which new performance techniques traversing theater, dance, music, poetry, and new media propose or presume new relationships between the social and the aesthetic. The chapters point, as well, to the productive role played by improvisation as the historical divisions between artistic disciplines are challenged and as new assemblages of technologies and people are brought into being.

Across different artistic disciplines, improvisation has meant different things, followed distinct (though sometimes intersecting) historical trajectories, and been theorized with varying degrees of complexity. If this seems like an opportune time in which to pursue a more integrated account of improvisation, it is in part because paradigms of performance and improvisation have become so prevalent in social theory today, just as present-day cultural theory is also preoccupied with a set of issues whose pertinence for thinking about improvisation seems clear. Such issues include the status of the creative gesture, the mutability of the performing body, scrutiny of the work concept, and the multiple ways in which social relations may be artistically, dramaturgically, and musically located, constructed, or (re)imagined. Concerns such as these are at the heart of productive new ways of thinking about improvisation, but as this volume demonstrates, they have also animated the common project of a social aesthetics, which necessarily grapples with their fertile entanglement. This entanglement is a thread woven through the chapters in this book, inviting further dialogue and both attesting to and calling for the creation of new modes and spaces of inter- and trans-disciplinary inquiry—in particular, across the humanities and social sciences.

Notes

1. It will not concern us here whether such critiques of Kantian aesthetics are accurate. The single most influential Kantian text concerning aesthetics is his third and final critique, *The Critique of Judgment* (*Kritik der Urteilskraft*), published in 1790. A potted history of the reception and critique of Kant with respect to the aesthetic issues central to this volume would have one focus on the distinction Kant draws, but does not always flag, between free (*frei*) and adherent (*anhangend*) beauty (see esp. section 16 of *The Critique*), and his focus on free beauty, coupled with his claim that music is an example of an art that manifests free beauty. For discussions of this distinction, see Kalar 2006; Lorand 1989; Scarré 1981; Zuckert 2007. This distinction, which suggests a purely formalist aesthetics, was later taken up by Eduard Hanslick, whose influential formalist aesthetics of music in turn became a model for later formalist aesthetics applied to visual art: see Hanslick 1986. For Kant's influence on Hanslick, see Kivy 2009. Kant's theory suggests to many that abstract nonrepresentational art also manifests free beauty and so is open to formalist aesthetic analysis. Of course, the rise of formalist aesthetics more generally, to which social aesthetics in part aspires to be a response and a corrective, parallels the growth of nonrepresentational art as it became characteristic of modernism. A related point of criticism is the Kantian belief, the details of which are open to assorted interpretations, that aesthetic judgments have normative force—that when one makes an aesthetic judgment, it is with the conviction that others should share it—and that, in some sense or other, such judgments have an objective weight. While much philosophical aesthetics in the Anglo-American tradition continues to grapple with Kantian aesthetics, even when critical of it either wholly or in part, Continental philosophical traditions have tended to reject the Kantian paradigm. Indeed, at the risk of overgeneralizing, it is fair to say that Continental aesthetics is unified by its rejection of the Kantian paradigm and, in particular, what is seen as its failure to investigate critically the actual lived conditions under which aesthetic judgments are made, and thus a failure to recognize and note the centrality of the social and political dimensions of our aesthetic lives, which may indeed partially constitute them. Taking such failures seriously has led to the development of aesthetic theories that have emerged hand in hand with new theoretical paradigms in sociological, anthropological, and cultural theory (along with new theories in art history), and that are all the richer for this. For these reasons, among others, anti-Kantian aesthetics tend to focus on how our aesthetic lives operate as parts of greater systems and to argue that the constellations of relations we stand in with respect to other individuals, groups, institutions, and social or political processes must be part of any useful aesthetic inquiry. Perhaps the single most developed criticism of a Kantian paradigm, and one that indicates the productivity of empirical research into the structures and dynamics of the consumption of art and culture, is Bourdieu 1984. In his lengthy introduction, Bourdieu makes clear the anti-Kantian nature of his work and what he sees as shortcomings in the Kantian program.

2. This critical observation has parallels with criticisms of methodological individualism in the social sciences, in that methodological individualism takes social and cultural processes to be explicable primarily in terms of the summation of individual actions and intentions.

3. One important reference for adopting such a general stance in regard to matter and materiality is Bennett 2010. In this volume, we add to this general stance, however, a series of explorations of the particular, especially vital contributions of art objects and events, and the forms of experience they engender, to such socio-material assemblages.

4. The locus classicus of such arguments is the work of the anthropologist Steven Feld: see, among others, Feld 1982, 1988, 1994, 1996.

5. For a critical overview of these developments, including an assessment of Bourdieu's contributions to the sociology of art and culture, as well as the limitations of his work, see Born 2010c. Born's article centers, however, on demonstrating the wider significance and fertility of anthropological approaches to music, art, and performance because of their commitment to addressing, in nonreductive ways, the interrelations between their aesthetic, social, and material dimensions.

6. The most interesting alternative to this negative position in Bourdieu's oeuvre is his dialogue with Hans Haacke, in which he engages sympathetically with an artist the subtlety of whose aesthetic and other decisions are inevitably central to the conversation: see Bourdieu and Haacke 1995.

7. See the debate over the proposition "Aesthetics is a cross-cultural category" in Ingold 1996. The debate moves between, on the one hand, a critique of the cultural-historical specificity of Kantian aesthetic discourses and, on the other, the view that the aesthetic can usefully be employed as an analytical category to sensitize anthropologists to the existence (or nonexistence), and the nature, of "emic" discourses concerning form and sensory experience, pleasure and value.

8. The founding text is Bourriaud 2002; see also Kester 2004. Critical responses include Bishop 2004, 2005; Downey 2007; Foster 2006; Martin 2007. Arguably, the kinds of practices gathered under this debate extend, and participate in, a long line of development from the Fluxus-inspired performance art and happenings of the 1960s, in which the lines between artist and audience were blurred and the site and the events and socialities taking place within it became the focus of aesthetic experience: see, among others, Baas 2011; Friedman 1998; Higgins 2002; Rodenbeck 2011.

9. On the art movement that has become known as institutional critique, see Alberro and Stimson 2009; Fraser 2005; Möntmann 2006.

10. The term "social aesthetics" as employed in this volume, and the project for this book, arose from the Improvisation and Social Aesthetics research group set up in 2007 at the start of the Improvisation, Community and Social Practice major research program funded mainly by Canada's Social Science and Humanities Research Council and based at the University of Guelph, the University of British Columbia, and McGill University. The research group was convened by Georgina

Born and included many of the scholars who have contributed to this volume. The conceptual basis of the book was further developed by a conference held at McGill in 2010 at which all the contributors gave papers.

11. In this vein, and symptomatically, Osborne (2013, 116) has recently written about post-conceptual art as "both aesthetic and conceptual" and about conceptual art itself as "the experience of the impossibility/fallacy of the *absolutization* of the anti-aesthetic."

12. It is striking how for some theorists this conclusion—fueled by the burgeoning art history of the 1960s to the 1990s—is unsustainable, even unthinkable, perhaps due to the haunting specter, particularly for those espousing philosophical aesthetics, of sociological reduction. Having worked through certain social features of post-conceptual art, such as its alternative institutionalization and the collectivization of the "artist-function," Osborne (2013, 48), for example, arrives at six "insights" or characteristics that, he argues, constitute the "condition of possibility of a postconceptual art." But none of the six touch on art's social dimensions, even those that Osborne himself has adumbrated. Instead, they dwell on art's "conceptuality," materiality, and "radically distributive" or "irreducibly relational" nature. Rather than re-theorize art's "ineliminable" aesthetic dimension, Osborne ultimately develops a post-Adornian conception of the aesthetic dimension by equating it with art's "materialization," that is, its "felt, spatio-temporal" presentation—where this excludes from feeling, space, and time any social dimension. Indeed, here and elsewhere, for Osborne the "spatial" (in the guise of the geopolitical, or art's transnationalization or globalization) appears to represent an inadequate stand-in, theoretically, for any diagnosis of art's plural social mediations.

13. The term "empractise" is intended to work against any Cartesian fallacy concerning the nature of dialogism, for the dialogical nature of improvised practices cannot be understood in the terms of cognitive processes that "direct" the performing body or the social processes inherent in dialogism. Rather, the dialogism is a matter of how embodied gestures and responses directly put into practice—that is, empractise—processes and interactions that are at once both aesthetic and social.

14. Two extreme theoretical positions concerning the relationship of musical improvisation (directed toward jazz in both cases) to social and political commentary and action, both of which form the loci of major schools of thought on this issue, are Theodor Adorno's writings on jazz and Jacques Attali's *Noise* (1985). For a useful, though not exhaustive, collection of Adorno's writings on jazz, see Adorno 2002a. The two authors form the poles of a continuum that, at one end, portrays jazz as devoid of any political effectiveness due to its commodified and standardized tendencies, and, at the other end, views jazz improvisation as having the potential to model or perform new forms of social and political relation. The essays in this collection, which address improvisation in a number of media, adopt a range of views gathered toward the latter pole while contending emphatically that any analysis of this propensity cannot be culled from a raw ac-

count of improvisation as a technique or practice, but requires consideration of the social and historical conditions within which particular media, genres and acts of improvisation proceed.

15. For a striking analysis of the construction of a hierarchical relation between composition and improvisation in a non-Western classical musical tradition, see Nooshin 2003.

16. While dialogism is foregrounded in group musical improvisations, it is also characteristic of other forms of improvisation — notably, in dance, theater, and performance art: cf. the chapters by Kozel and Svendsen in this volume.

17. For example, while both a free improvisation ensemble and a string quartet require careful acts of listening, responding, and communicating among their members, in the former case responsibility for the sounds produced resides wholly with each member of the ensemble, while in the latter case the responsibility for many aesthetically relevant decisions resides outside the ensemble, with the composer, thereby being predetermined and imposed. For a contrary view, however, see Benson 2003.

18. But for a productive attempt and an overview, see Bailey 1992.

19. Indeed, it is often claimed that Pollock was a fan of Charlie Parker, listening to him while creating his drip paintings. Yet this is inaccurate: Pollock's interest in jazz was limited to trad and Dixieland. Helen Harrison, curator of the Pollock-Krasner House and Study Center, has lectured on this topic (see https://www.youtube.com/watch?v=3H5hPbb3sPg), as well as on the links often drawn between Pollock and jazz.

20. For discussions and developments of musical Platonism, see Dodd 2007; Kivy 1993a, 1993b; Levinson 1990a, 1990b. For a critical discussion of the history of musical Platonism, see Goehr (1992).

21. It is important to note, however, that many types of music — not all of them centered on improvisation — have been subject to neglect in terms of aesthetic analysis because of the primacy accorded by musicology to those musical parameters that can be readily notated in the orthodox score. Musicology has been slow, then, to respond to a series of developments since the 1950s — experimental music, electronic, electroacoustic and computer music, interactive, site-specific, and installation-based sound art, and electronic popular music — in which musical thought and practice focus on timbral, rhythmic, pitch-based, performance, or conceptual gestures that are difficult to capture in orthodox musical notation, where the ontological distinction between music, sound, and environment may be disturbed, and where the creative possibilities of recording and amplification, live performance and installations are brought aesthetically to the fore.

22. For a seminal analysis of this kind of "othering" of improvisation, but with reference to a non-Western classical music tradition, see, again, Nooshin 2003.

23. For a compatible analysis of how music produces meaning, see Born 1993b.

24. For the classic article on this topic, see Walton 1970.

25. For the most extensive discussion of signifying, see Gates 1988.

I · THE SOCIAL AND THE AESTHETIC

CHAPTER 1

AFTER RELATIONAL AESTHETICS

Improvised Music, the Social, and
(Re)Theorizing the Aesthetic

Georgina Born

What does it mean to speak of a social aesthetics and, in particular, to do so in relation to improvised music? In this mainly conceptual chapter I develop some proposals concerning the relations between improvised music and the social and pursue the implications for retheorizing the aesthetic. I will be concerned with the social mediation of music, where mediation is conceived as a two-way or co-productive process. As we will see, music engenders certain kinds of socialities, yet it also refracts or transforms existing social formations. This conceptual project responds to a series of overlapping movements: the demand issued by scholarship in ethnomusicology, musicology, popular music studies, jazz studies, and sociology of music for progress in theorizing the heterogeneity and the different scales of music's social mediation; the drive in art theory and criticism to take seriously and analyze those facets of recent art practices in which the social features as a dimension of aesthetic experience; and the concern within anthropological and social theory to reconceptualize the social—or "sociality"—itself (Latour 2005; Long and Moore 2012a, 2012b; Strathern 1990). These movements do not exist in isolation: that they are intertwined is evident in the way that ethnography, the method of anthropology, has become involved in contemporary collaborative art (Foster 1995; Rutten et al. 2013; Schneider and Wright 2006, 2010) and music practices (Born 2013a).

Despite this convergence, it has proved surprisingly difficult to develop an approach adequate to the challenge of conceptualizing how the social enters into the aesthetic operations of both music and art. Indeed, music and art set general challenges to social theory in this regard, and improvised music poses them acutely. As I will show, however, it is precisely because of these challenges that music and art, and improvised music in particular, can also be generative and advance the wider debates about theorizing the social. This chapter therefore bears on the conceptual heart of this volume as a whole.

To begin, let us consider a number of symptomatic and contrasting ways in which the social enters into contemporary art practices and critical discourses. The most prominent is the paradigm of relational aesthetics enunciated by the critic and curator Nicholas Bourriaud (2002), often taken to be emblematic in the analysis of present-day art. Relational aesthetics places art's orchestration of socialities at the core of a new conception of the aesthetic. Bourriaud contends, in a programmatic text, that art from the 1990s has revolved around "practices which take as their theoretical and practical point of departure the whole of human relations and their social context," which he equates with the production of a "specific sociability" (16, 113). Relational aesthetics is therefore committed to assessing contemporary art practices "on the basis of the inter-human relations which they represent, produce or prompt" (112). Bourriaud's explanation for this turn concerns the "extraordinary upsurge of social exchanges" given by greater mobility, rapid urbanization, and the expansion of travel and telecommunications since the Second World War. At the same time, pervasive commercialization reaches into human affairs so that "the social bond has turned into a standardized artifact" and "the space of current relations is . . . severely affected by general reification" (9). In reaction, the new practices, which he locates within a genealogy of post-conceptual art, take as their point of departure intersubjectivity, interaction, and proximity, with the effect that "alternative forms of sociability, critical models and moments of constructed conviviality are worked out" (43–54). "Artistic praxis," he contends in a resonant phrase, "appears these days to be a rich loam for social experiments" (9).

In one direction, "the artwork of the 1990s turns the beholder into a neighbour, a direct interlocutor" (Bourriaud 2002, 43); in another direction, the exploration of social bonds takes the form of "recreating socio-professional models," such that the artist takes "the real field of the production of goods and services, and aims to set up a certain ambiguity . . . between the utilitarian function of the objects he is presenting, and their aesthetic function" (35). A precursor of the latter turn, Bourriaud argues, was the Artist Placement Group (APG), which from the late 1960s to the 1980s placed artists in branches of government and industry, an alternative institutional setting to the gallery and exhibition. An example of the former direction for Bourriaud, art as interlocution, is the performance event "Turkish Jokes" in 1994, in which Jens Hanning broadcast funny stories in Turkish through a loudspeaker in a square in Copenhagen, producing "in that split second a micro-community, one made up of immigrants brought together by collective laughter which upset their exile situation," a micro-community "formed in relation to the work and in it." Bourriaud concludes, "Depending on the degree of participation required of the onlooker by the artist, along with . . . the model of sociability proposed . . . , an exhibition will give rise to a specific 'arena of exchange'" (17). Indeed, in his concern with proximity, form, and movement, Bourriaud flirts ambiguously with the antihumanist stance of the theorists of circulation and inter-object relations (Gaonkar and Povinelli 2003; Straw 2010), who find their ancestor in the recently rediscovered sociology of Gabriel Tarde. For Tarde, it is the circulation of entities, affects, and behaviors that creates the very fabric of the social (Barry and Thrift 2007; Born 2010b; Candea 2010).

Bourriaud's argument is engaging, but it is hard to discern any coherence in the manifold social relations and social interactions staged by the practices he describes. Indeed, the diversity of art practices that he relates far outstrips his theoretical credo: it is impossible to reduce what he sets in motion to his oft-cited maxim that the goal of relational aesthetics is "to heal the social bond." Predictably, rather than turn to the disciplines of the social for assistance, he rejects sociology as a source of understanding of the variety of social forms that he adumbrates. Moreover, he dismisses any engagement with the dynamics of difference, conflict, and antagonism that are in part constitutive of the social. Bourriaud's paradigm invites Hal Foster's (2006, 190) pithy criticism of a "happy interactivity: among 'aesthetic objects' Bourriaud counts 'meetings, encounters, events, various types of collaboration between people, games, festivals and places of conviviality.' . . . To some readers such 'relational aesthetics' will . . . seem to aestheticize the nicer procedures of our service economy." Bourriaud's own rendering of the social—as opposed to that of the practices he relates—tends, then, toward reductive idealizations. Claire Bishop (2004, 65), a critic and theorist who has championed participatory art, puts the key challenge acutely: "Bourriaud wants to equate aesthetic judgment with an ethicopolitical judgment of the relationships produced by a work of art. But . . . the quality of the relationships in 'relational aesthetics' are never examined or called into question. . . . If relational art produces human relations, then the next logical question to ask is what types of relations are being produced, for whom, and why?"

Late in his book, Bourriaud (2002, 82) reflects on the criticisms drawn by relational art practices, noting that "they are . . . reproached for deny-ing social conflict and dispute, differences and divergences, and the impos-sibility of communicating within an alienated social space, in favour of an illusory . . . modelling of sociability." As a rejoinder, he states emphatically, "These approaches do not stem from a 'social' or 'sociological' form of art"; rather, the relational exhibition "is an interstice, defined in relation to the alienation reigning everywhere else. . . . . The exhibition does not deny the social relationships in effect, but it does distort them and project them into a space-time frame encoded by the art system" (82). Crucially, he seems here to be arguing that relational art both participates or partakes in wider social relations *and* that it stages a microsocial space apart that may refract or "dis-tort" them. Bishop (2012, 45) makes a similar observation: "By using people as a medium, participatory art has always had a double ontological status: it is both an event in the world, and also at a remove from it."

Bourriaud himself fails fully to theorize this crucial point; he has no vo-cabulary to distinguish between the several modalities of the social that he conflates. But Bishop's "double ontological status" also reduces what is going on. For now, I will point to not two but three social dimensions of the social aesthetics that are immanent in Bourriaud's examples. The first con-sists of the socialities enlivened by Hanning's "Turkish Jokes," a "micro-community" of laughing Turkish immigrants. This indexes a realm of im-mediate, co-present, and affective microsocial relations and interactive associations that are regularly set in motion by the performance arts, as well as by public art and site-specific works (Salter 2010). The second, again shown by Hanning's performance event, consists of art's refraction of wider, preexisting social relations, whether of class, race, ethnicity, gender, or sexu-ality. In this light, Hanning's public art event is one that in Deleuzian terms is crossed by, or evokes, a molar politics of common ethnic-, migration-, and class-based identifications (Patton 2000, 43). And the third consists of how art can intervene in the organizational, institutional, and political-economic forms in which it is embedded or with which it is articulated. It is this third dimension that is exemplified by APG's experimental engagement with, and expansion of, art's institutional spheres. Such practices refract or "distort" a quite different order of the social.

This third dimension deserves a brief exposition. The APG was an orga-nization founded by John Latham with roots in conceptual art which, from the late 1960s, negotiated residencies for artists inside a series of corporations, including Britain's National Coal Board, British Rail, British Steel, the Scottish Office, ICI, and the Esso oil company. The APG's orientation to the social therefore took the form of sustained experimental interventions in institutional processes—processes that were quite independent of the art institutional nexus. The group's artists were charged with becoming involved in the functioning of the corporation, using anything to hand and retaining an "open brief" (Bolt Rasmussen 2009; Metzger 1972; Slater 2001). As Andrew Barry (2013, 90) notes, "The artist was understood . . . as an 'incidental person' whose presence and actions might effect change." The APG did not overtly criticize the institutions with which it worked; nor did it seek to provide alternatives. Instead, it sought to "introduce change in society through the medium of art relative to those structures with 'elected' responsibility for shaping the future—governments, industries and academic institutions" (Barbara Steveni, quoted in Walker 2002, 55). Indeed, one of the APG's principles was that the artist must find an outcome or intervention that was not politically overdetermined. In this sense, the APG's projects manifested Deleuze's minor politics of the emergent, underdetermined by preexisting political formations (Patton 2000). Yet it is worth noting that the APG's politics have often been misunderstood as molar politics by later artists who purported to follow them.[1] At this point, we might draw a link with Peter Bürger's (1984, 49) focus, in his analysis of the historical avant-gardes, on art as institution; in his words, "The European avant-garde movements can be defined as an attack on the status of art in bourgeois society. What is negated is not an earlier form of art . . . but art as an institution that is unassociated with the life praxis of men." Through the APG, then, we glimpse something of the spectrum and the evolution of art's imbrication with institutions: from the critique of art as institution (Alberro and Stimson 2009; Fraser 2005) to experimental institutional intervention without telos.

But a final way in which the social enters recent art contrasts markedly with both the APG and relational aesthetics: it is in the guise of "socially engaged art" (Thompson 2012), politically informed interdisciplinary practices in which "external" social and political realms become the arena within which art stages its interventions. These practices are emphatically intended to influence the "real" world via politicized interventions in larger institutional spheres. This is art motivated by a keen awareness that "living itself exists in forms that must be questioned, rearranged, mobilized, and undone": "living as form" (29). With roots traced to Russian Constructivism, Duchamp, Artaud, Fluxus, Situationism, the "social sculpture" of Joseph

Beuys, and groups such as the Critical Art Ensemble, socially engaged art is a broad and heterogeneous lineage encompassing strategic, often sustained projects that defy discursive boundaries in order to produce "effects and affects in the world" (32). Apparently in a similar vein to relational aesthetics, "participation, sociality, and the organization of bodies in space play a key feature in much of this work" (21). Yet more than relational aesthetics, these practices seek also to engage with judicial and governmental processes, as in the collaborative, prison-based practice of Laurie Jo Reynolds, who calls her work "legislative art" by analogy with Augusto Boal's (1998) "legislative theatre," which in turn is indebted to Paolo Freire (2000). Socially engaged art may also become involved in community activism, as in the two-decades-old experimental housing project and art residency Project Row Houses, animated by the artist Rick Lowe, which rehabilitated a low-income, mainly African American neighborhood in Houston by building a strong base of local participation among residents.

In notable contrast to relational aesthetics, then, rather than seeking to "heal" the general reification or foster consensus, socially engaged art animates encounters and events marked more often by social conflict, "deep discord and frustration" (Thompson 2012, 24). Exemplary here is the infamous installation "Please Love Austria" (2000), devised by the German artist Christoph Schlingensief, which staged a parodic "Big Brother"–style media event in a public square outside the Vienna State Opera House in which real asylum seekers were housed in a shipping container, their activities televised live on the Internet, while the public was asked to vote daily on the least popular detainees, who were returned to a real detention center outside the city. The provocative, parodic, and politically ambiguous installation stimulated heated debate, scandalizing and antagonizing elements of the public.

In avowedly instrumental terms, Nato Thompson (2012, 22) notes that socially engaged art has "become an instructive space to gain valuable skill sets in the techniques of performativity, representation, aesthetics, and the creation of affect." Hence, the stress on methodologies, research, and long-term activism, and the reflexive interest in the forms of the social, are efforts both at shifting the focus away from traditional aesthetic concerns and at enriching and transforming what is meant by the term "aesthetics" (Born 2010c, 198–200). The critical questions to be asked of socially engaged art therefore differ from those raised by relational aesthetics. For the problem is not one of the cultivation of sociality as an end in itself but the opposite: that art and its socialities are mobilized and valorized primarily by reference to given or prior political and social justice ends. As Bishop (2004, 2006) notes, such practices risk negating the specifically aesthetic dimension, reducing "art to a question of the ethically good or bad," as well as making a problematic equation between "forms of democracy in art and forms of democracy in society" (Bishop 2012, 41). Instead, Bishop calls for art that respects its own mediating role, thereby holding "artistic and social critiques in tension" (40).

Contemporary art therefore manifests diverse engagements with the social that can be traced back at least to the 1960s. The art historian Luke Skrebowski (2009, 67) comments that this was a transitional era in which "the art and the social context were of a piece. Indeed, the recognition that art's social context impacts its character constituted a fundamental tenet of the alternative to formalist modernism." In the preceding paragraphs I have distinguished four modalities of the social in recent art and aesthetics, however, with the precise purpose of resisting their reduction to notions of social "context." In analyzing these variants, my aim has been twofold: to show that while the social is increasingly manifest in contemporary art and aesthetics, and theorized as such, it takes distinctive forms that matter and should not be conceptually elided; and, on this basis, to enable fertile comparisons to be drawn in the remainder of this chapter between the varieties of social aesthetics in contemporary art practices and those evident in improvised music.

At this point it is productive to turn to music and the other performance-based arts. A foundational difference is immediately apparent, for it is not difficult to recognize that the social forms an immanent part of performance situations, in music as in the other performance-based arts. That is, specific socialities are created in performance situations among the performers, between performers and audiences, and among audiences (Born 2014). While the guardians of formalism or of the philosophical legacies of German idealism might strive to maintain that music is an art of pure sounding form and that its social manifestations are secondary, they are now matched by writers for whom music's social qualities are considered in various ways intrinsic to aesthetic experience; indeed, this is now arguably an established view in ethnomusicology (Blacking 1974; Keil 1966; Turino 2008) and in popular music studies (Frith 1998). Of course, to highlight the social is not necessarily to override the significance of other components of aesthetic experience. Moreover, the social can be more or less reflexively grasped or foregrounded by musical actors—composers, musicians, listeners—as a dimension of aesthetic experience. Such a reflexive awareness can in turn be more or less experimental or inventive in its orientation.

Strikingly, it is possible to draw a contrast between the evolving concert performance tradition associated with Western art music of the past two centuries and performance in certain lineages of improvised music since the 1960s. In the former tradition, as historians have shown, the social is relatively less foregrounded and is subject to a weak reflexivity. The emergence of this tradition has been traced in the first decades of the nineteenth century by James Johnson (1995, 277), who identifies it with the rise of bourgeois individualism and its manifestation in "intensely subjective" modes of musical experience in which "interior communion met . . . romantic spirituality." Absorbed listening and attention to music's abstract meaning were accompanied by a policing of manners and "anonymous and rule-bound" (233) allegiance to notions of decency and respectability. For the same period, Richard Sennett (2002, 213–14) points to a spate of urban social and architectural transformations allied to a burgeoning obsession with privacy, such that concert life saw the cultivation of silent, self-disciplined, contemplative, and interiorized spectatorship—a bourgeois "act of purification" that, in his compelling phrase, amounted to "a defense against the experience of social relations." For Sennett, intensifying urban processes of individualization and privatization, effecting an erosion of social interaction, were matched by new behavioral norms and by the constitution of new modes of subjectivity suited to the concert and theater. By the late nineteenth century, he concludes, "the whole rationale of public culture had cracked apart" (218). We might say that a defining feature of the ontology of Western art music from the nineteenth century to the present has been a disavowal of music's social mediations (Born 2005, 2013c).

In marked contrast, the lineages of improvised music of the late twentieth century often manifested a heightened reflexivity about the socialities engendered by performance, just as some practitioners set out to engage with the social in inventive ways. If we take the three modalities of the social identified earlier that are elided in Bourriaud's portrayal of relational aesthetics—the co-present socialities set in motion by performance, how these socialities refract wider and preexisting social relations, and how art can intervene in the institutional and political-economic forms in which it is embedded or with which it is articulated—each has found striking expression in certain traditions of improvised music. Regarding the first: improvising musicians have often demonstrated a self-conscious interest in the aesthetic potential or effects of the socialities of performance, including the dialogical and multilateral expressive exchanges enlivened by collective improvisations (Monson 1996). Regarding the second: to different degrees, improvising musicians have shown a concern with how wider, enduring social relations of race, class, and gender enter into and may be reproduced, entrenched, refracted, or reimagined in the socialities of musical performance. And regarding the third: certain practitioners of improvisation have seen an active engagement with institutional forms, primarily those through which their music is produced and distributed, as a necessary or even unavoidable extension of their creative practice. But the fourth modality identified earlier is also evident in the history of improvised music. That is to say, like socially engaged art, improvised music in some of its manifestations has been engaged in catalyzing wider political struggles for social justice and social equality (Fischlin and Heble 2004; Fischlin et al. 2013; G. E. Lewis 2008). I return to amplify these arguments later.

In sum, as with contemporary art, at issue in these several modalities is how improvised music both mediates and can transform the social—by animating novel socialities—and how this music is itself mediated or traversed by wider social formations. In what follows I suggest that to theorize these distinctive modalities, what is required is a heuristic analytical framework centered on music's social mediations as they imbue music's aesthetic operations. This must immediately be qualified, for improvised music is not unique in exhibiting these types of social mediation, which are shared with other musical traditions (Born 2012). However, there is perhaps something singular about improvisation in that improvised performances are marked by and enable degrees of openness, mutuality, and collaboration that are heightened and intensified when compared with the interpretation of scored works, and that necessitate participants' real-time co-creation and negotiation of social-and-musical relationships. From one perspective, then, such performances may become sites for empractising ways of "being differently in the world" based on a "recognition that alternatives to orthodox practices are available" (Fischlin and Heble 2004, 11).[2]

How well positioned are the academic music disciplines to address these questions of music's social mediation? It is striking that when we turn to recent attempts to theorize the relations between music and the social—whether in popular music studies, music sociology, or ethnomusicology—no adequate, encompassing paradigm is on offer. I want to outline two current and symptomatic positions in this regard, both of which are productive but neither of which is sufficient.

First, David Hesmondhalgh's (2005) review of a series of concepts employed in recent years to analyze the nature of collective musical identities: subculture, scene, and tribe. Hesmondhalgh poses them as amounting to the analysis of music's social mediation per se and finds that none of the terms bear the explanatory weight required of them. Instead, he turns to notions of articulation and genre, drawing on the work of such writers as Richard Middleton and Jason Toynbee. The upshot is to argue against any homology model in which music is taken to reflect some prior meta-category such as class, race, or nation and for a differentiated approach to the analysis of music and social identities, although he generates no wider framework. In my view, Hesmondhalgh throws out one important conceptual gain in the shift from subculture to scene: the way that the concept of scene captures music's autonomous capacity to generate specifically musically imagined communities that are irreducible to wider categories of social identity (Born 1993b; Born and Hesmondhalgh 2000; Straw 1991).

A second perspective comes from the work of the music sociologists Tia DeNora and Antoine Hennion—specifically, their theorization of music's mediation of subject-object relations. Expanding on Adorno's analysis, both rightly point to the bidirectional mediation between music and the social. Music, in their distinctive accounts, mediates or co-produces human socialities and subjectivities; in turn, music is itself constituted by human imagination, enmeshed in discourses and practices, and embodied in socio-technical arrangements (cf. Sterne 2003; Theberge 1997). Thus, "Music is active within social life . . . because it offers specific materials to which actors may turn when they engage in the work of organizing social life. Music is a resource—it provides affordances—for world-building . . . Just as music's meanings may be constructed in relation to things outside it, so, too, things outside music may be constructed in relation to music." Music, moreover, can take the lead "in the world-clarification, world-building process of meaning-making, . . . [It] serves as a kind of template against which feeling, perception, representation and social situation are created and sustained" (DeNora 2010, 44). Hennion (2001, 3) contends, in turn, that music "transforms those who take possession of it" so that we can speak of "the co-formation of a music and of those who make and listen to it." While their insistence on the bidirectional nature of mediation is invaluable, in these works Hennion and DeNora tend to reduce the socio-musical universe to the microsocial space of relations and practices favored by ethnomethodological and symbolic interactionist sociologies. For my purposes, too much is occluded by adopting this stance.

Both of these perspectives foreshorten music's social mediation, neglecting other dimensions of the social in play, which are addressed by different areas of scholarship and which demand to be brought together and thought in their complex interrelations. My argument, then, is that music necessitates an expansion of the conceptual framework of social mediation; that if music engenders myriad social forms, it is productive to analyze them in terms of four planes of social mediation. In what follows, I give an overview of the four planes before returning to improvised music.

In the first plane, music produces its own diverse socialities—in the immediate microsocialities of musical performance and practice and in the social relations embodied in musical ensembles and associations. It is this first plane that is most apparent in all the performance arts. In the second plane, music has powers to animate imagined communities, aggregating its listeners into affective alliances, virtual collectivities or publics based on musical and other identifications. In the third plane, music refracts wider social relations, from the most concrete to the most abstract of collectivities—music's instantiation of the nation, of social hierarchies, or of the social relations of class, race, religion, ethnicity, gender, or sexuality. In the fourth plane, music is bound up in the broader institutional forces that provide the basis for its production, reproduction, and transformation, whether elite or religious patronage, market or non-market exchange, public and subsidized cultural institutions, or late capitalism's multi-polar cultural economy. The first two planes amount to socialities, social relations, and social imaginaries that are assembled or affectively constituted specifically by musical practice and musical experience. In contrast, the last two planes amount to wider social relations and institutions that themselves afford or condition certain kinds of musical practice, although these relations and institutions also enter into the nature of musical experience, permeating music's immediate socialities and imagined communities.

Several propositions central to this chapter follow. First, and strikingly, the first two planes—music's microsocialities and imagined communities—are underdetermined by and have a certain autonomy from the last two, music's wider social conditions. Second, all four planes of social mediation enter into the musical assemblage—although they are invariably treated separately in existing discussions of music and the social. Moreover, the four planes are irreducible to one another, yet they are articulated in contingent and nonlinear ways through relations of conditioning, affordance, or causality. It is precisely the mutual mediations of and complex articulations among the four planes that enable musical assemblages to engender certain kinds of socio-musical experience that are also forms of aesthetic experience, as well as offering the potential for experimentation with those diverse modes of social aesthetic experience.

In writing here about four planes of social mediation and of a musical assemblage, I draw on earlier works in which I have proposed that, more obviously than visual and literary media, music has no material essence but a plural and distributed material being and that music's multiple simultaneous forms of existence—as sound, score, discourse, site, performance, social relations, technological media—indicate the necessity of conceiving of the musical object as a constellation. Compared with the visual and literary arts, then, music has to be grasped as an extraordinarily complex kind of cultural object—as an aggregation of sonic, visual, discursive, social, corporeal, technological, and temporal mediations. It should be conceived as an assemblage (Deleuze 1988; Rabinow 2003), where a musical assemblage can be defined as a characteristic constellation of such mediations (Born 2005, 2012). Thus, the properties (or meanings) of music must be cognized in terms of the assemblage—or constellation of mediations—of which it is composed. In its plurality, music has the oxymoronic quality of being at once immaterial (as sound, or code) and multiply material; it might be conceived as the "paradigmatic multiply mediated, immaterial-and-material, fluid quasi-object" (Born 2005, 7), one in which subjects and objects are entangled. I describe this approach to counter any view that by foregrounding an analytics of the social I intend at the same time to privilege a musical humanism; indeed, a central aim of my approach is to combat the limited account of the social and material offered by theorists like Latour, and to argue that it is imperative to rejoin a critical analytics of the social with a nuanced account of mediation and materiality—that is, to proffer a combined analytics of the social-and-material.

Turning to the first plane, the immediate microsocialities engendered by musical performance and practice: what is striking about research in this area is that it is divided between compelling empirical, often ethnographic studies from ethnomusicology, popular music studies, and music sociology (as in the work of DeNora, Hennion, Sara Cohen, Steven Feld, Ruth Finnegan, Jocelyne Guibault, Charles Keil, Ingrid Monson, and many others), and broad theoretical statements. Such theoretical statements invariably draw their inspiration from three sources: the social phenomenology of Alfred Schutz (1964); the post-Foucauldian stance of Jacques Attali's *Noise* (1985), and specifically his final chapter on "Composing"; and the writings of Christopher Small (1998). Common to these three writers is a tendency to idealize the realm of microsocial relations in music through a reductive sociology that metaphysically over-codes social realities. To begin with Small: despite his quasi-ethnographic descriptions of the socialities of rock and folk festivals, rap gigs, and symphony concerts, he arrives at problematic normative generalizations. Thus, he writes,

> What we need to keep in mind is that those taking part in performances of different kinds are looking for different kinds of relationships, and we should not project the ideals of one kind of performance onto another. [But a]ny performance, and that includes a symphony concert, should be judged finally on its success in bringing into existence for as long as it lasts a set of relationships that those taking part feel to be ideal and in enabling those taking part to explore, affirm and celebrate those relationships."[3] (Small 1998, 49)

Schutz and Attali, for their part, offer compelling analyses, yet both entail idealizations. In Attali's (1985, 133) frankly speculative account of "Composing," embedded as it is within a larger historical analysis of music and power, Free Jazz is taken as the model for a "coming order" of music making "exterior to the institutions" in which "creative labor is collective. . . . Production takes the form of . . . collective composition, without a predetermined program imposed upon the players, and without commercialization. [This is] a new practice of music among the people. . . . By subverting objects, it heralds a new form of the collective imaginary, a reconciliation between work and play" (141). A utopian account of improvisation is therefore central to Attali's speculative socio-musical vision.

Schutz is deservedly the most influential of the theorists of the microsocial, and his social phenomenology centers on an analysis of intersubjectivity in music, which he portrays as a paradigm of human communication and relatedness. Schutz (1964) discerns three modes of intersubjectivity in musical performance. The first involves performer and listener, who experience simultaneously "the polythetic steps by which the musical content articulates itself in [music's] inner time" (175). The second involves composer and listener or performer, such that, "although separated by hundreds of years, the latter participate with quasi-simultaneity in the [composer's] stream of consciousness, performing with him (*sic*) . . . the ongoing articulation of his musical thought" (171). Third, Schutz points to the intersubjective relations of musical ensembles in which "each co-performer's action is oriented . . . reciprocally by the experiences in inner and outer time of his fellow" performers (175). Such "tuning-in" involves not merely consciousness, but mutual responses among the co-performers to one another's gestures and expressions "in immediacy" and in shared space (176). While highly suggestive, particularly for improvised practices in which heightened communicative, social, and embodied mutualities are arguably more to the fore than in the collective interpretation of scored music, Schutz's portrayal of the social consolations of live performance results finally in an idealized metaphysics of musical co-presence, one that is consonant both with the discourse of absolute music and with the "audiovisual litany" identified by Jonathan Sterne as central to the history of auditory media (Sterne 2003, 15–19).

In sum, if all three writers idealize the microsocialities of musical practice, this is made possible by how these microsocialities are illusorily "autonomized" by being detached from the larger circuits of social relations in which they are embedded or with which they are articulated. In light of this tendency to focus only on the microsocialities of performance, the task is to rethink music's (and art's) social mediation across the four planes. To indicate the utility of such an approach from a classic study of an African American improvisational music: Charles Keil's (1966) analysis of urban blues in Chicago in the 1960s dwells insistently on how the microsocialities of club-based blues performance (first plane) were entangled in and refracted the wider social relations of race and class to which both musicians and audiences were subject (third plane), while the affective conjoining of these superimposed socialities was achieved, and heightened, through the emotionally charged musically imagined community assembled and animated by the sounds of blues music (second plane). Keil describes how, in the midst of performance, the blues singer Bobby Bland and his band engendered a sociality both between themselves and with their audience. Minute gestures and vocal inflections, humor and innuendo, conjured up social solidarities and collective catharsis in part through constant implicit references to the "stylistic common denominators" (143) that linked blues performance and religious preaching in the lives of black Chicagoans in this era.

Keil's study points to a final dimension of the framework I am proposing: that it participates in a larger project of critical social theory that, in the words of Chantal Mouffe (2000, 125), assumes that "relations of power are constitutive of the social." Thus, rather than conceive of social relations in a pluralistic world as integrative, or as oriented to consensus or community, we should address them as constituted equally by difference, as well as by agonism and antagonism. This is a foundational assumption in what follows. Only by adopting this approach, which depends on empirical work (whether historical or ethnographic) as a basis for critical analysis, is it possible to vault over Schutz and develop a less metaphysical social phenomenology, one that is attentive to the microsocialities of musical practice and performance as they are imbricated with other social relations—other planes of the social.

In light of these theoretical and methodological proposals, how have the socialities and social aesthetics of improvised music been addressed?

Initially, it is intriguing to note how often practitioners' accounts of improvisation focus on the first plane: on the nature of and the potentials immanent in the microsocialities of performance and practice. At the same time, they provide a kind of autoethnography of the social in performance, of improvisation as a crucible of intensified and reflexive social experience, and of improvised performance as commonly also a space of microsocial experiment. Most striking is how—akin to Bourriaud—these qualities of socio-musical experience are spoken of as synonymous with the aesthetic qualities of performance. This is evident in diverse musicians' commentaries reported in Derek Bailey's (1992) pioneering book on improvisation. Perhaps the most characteristic stance is to conceive of improvised performance as fomenting a kind of free and labile movement between individual and collectivity so that individuality becomes a relational moment or state within a larger entity. As Moira Gatens and Genevieve Lloyd (2002, 73), neo-Spinozist philosophers concerned with conceptualizing this labile movement, put it: "For Spinoza, there are collective dimensions to individual selfhood. For him there is no possibility of selfhood in isolation. To be an individual—a determinate self—at all is to be embedded in wider social wholes in which the power of bodies is strengthened or impeded. To be an individual self is to be inserted into economies of affect and imagination which bind us to others in relations of joy and sadness, love and hate, cooperation and antagonism." The philosopher Garry Hagberg (2016) develops a liberal variant of this focus on the relation between individual and collectivity, and one that is specifically attuned to jazz improvisation. Hagberg criticizes what he calls the "social contract model" in which "the collective is no more than a convergence of individuals who, *as individuals first*, choose . . . to join a group that offers [musical] benefits . . . that expand what the individual could create alone." In this account, "the individual, *as individual* (in political and ontological terms), is present and intact from start to finish" and "the entire content of the collective is simply the sum of the individuals combined" (Hagberg 2016, 1–2, italics in the original). Instead, Hagberg develops a notion of "collective" or "group-emergent intention" at the heart of improvising ensembles, which he links to "de-individuation" (9–10). Such "shared intention," he argues, should be understood as "(1) non-summative, (2) irreducible . . . to the individual . . . , and (3) [as] worked out, with limited variations, across the span of its enactment" (5).

A more radical challenge to the individual-collective dualism comes from the anthropologist Marilyn Strathern (1990, 5) in her attempt to supersede the twin reifications—"society" and asocial "individual"—that underpin Durkheimian social theory. For Strathern, such reifications should be abandoned in favor of a processual conception of sociality and a view of persons as both multiple and fully social. Thus, in Melanesia, for example, where she did ethnographic research, "persons are as 'dividually' as they are individually conceived. They contain a generalised sociality within"; while "society" should give way to a conception of social processes as involving "a constant movement . . . from one type of sociality to another" (Strathern 1988, 13–14), where sociality refers in turn to "the creating and maintaining of relationships." Such forms of sociality can result in aggregations of persons that entail either the elimination of difference, presenting "an image of unity . . . created out of internal homogeneity, a process of de-pluralization" or, on the contrary, the elaboration of heterogeneity.

An eloquent concretization of the preoccupation with the relation between individuality and collectivity is provided by Eddie Prévost's reflections on the microsocialities of the influential British improvising group AMM:

> The personalities within the ensemble are clearly defined. They have maintained their integrity. Part of AMM's philosophy . . . is the idea of concurrent commentary: separate voices speaking at the same time, interweaving and interleaving. But each voice is not atomized or individuated. Paradoxically, it may be that individuality can only exist and develop in a collective context. . . . We are part of a movement that has, arguably, remade music. . . . I'm inclined to think of it . . . as a meta-music. One of the generative themes of this meta-music is the relationship between musicians. . . . I doubt if our strong friendships could survive very long without the creative vehicle of AMM. It gives the meaning to our association. (Quoted in Bailey 1992, 129–30)

Other improvisers, in contrast, adopt more mannerist stances on the first plane, the microsocialities of improvised performance, conveying both how the orchestration of these socialities is taken to be immanent in performance aesthetics and how the same microsocialities are conceived of reflexively as a locus of experimentation. In John Zorn's "Game Pieces," improvisation is emprastised as a kind of parodic authoritarian staging of controlled social encounters modeled on sports or war games:

> I pick the bands and in that sense the Ellington tradition, the selection of the people, is very important. . . . You take one person out and the chemistry is going to be different. . . . You need people who are aggressive, you need people who are going to be docile, you need people with a sense of humor, you need people who are assholes. . . . I basically create a small society and everybody finds their own position in that society. It really becomes like a psycho drama. People are given power and it's very interesting to see which people like to run away from it, who are very docile and just do what they are told, [while] others try very hard to get more control and more power. So it's very much like the political arena in a certain kind of way. (Quoted in Bailey 1992, 77–78)

Alternatively, musicians may link the microsocialities of performance to wider social arenas, as in Misha Mengelberg's portrayal of improvisation, influenced by Situationist and anarchist currents (Adlington 2013), as akin to the everyday lifeworld: "One of the things that inspires me in making any gesture, musically and theoretically, is its relation with daily life in which there is no such thing as an exclusion. One moment I meet you and the next I am washing dishes or playing chess. . . . In certain respects there are parallels between the music and daily life. . . . The sort of improvisation I am interested in is the sort that everyone does in their lives" (quoted in Bailey 1992, 131–32).

Probably the strongest historical example of improvisation as driven by reflexive experimentation with the microsocialities of musical practice is the Scratch Orchestra (SO), founded in 1969 by Cornelius Cardew and others in the wake of Cardew's experiences performing with AMM in the late 1960s. The SO was an experimental music collective of about fifty people with mixed musical skills and experience—students, amateur musicians, avant-garde artists, and others. It embodied the politicized wing of British experimental music in this period and responded to "the demand of a lot of young people who weren't trained musicians to get together to make what we called experimental music" (Cardew, quoted in Taylor 1998, 556). The SO constitution called for a "montage of contemporary practices," including scratch music, popular classics, composition, "improvisation rites," and research projects. Devoted to the democratization of musical expression, the SO mobilized "a large number of enthusiasts pooling their resources (not primarily material resources) and assembling for action (music making, performance, edification)." Tellingly, this experimental period was not sustained. Following two years of growing factionalism, the fluid entity that had been the SO morphed into a "hard-line Maoism [led by Cardew, which] gradually throttled any activity which did not have clear and explicit political objectives and content."[4]

In the remainder of the chapter I want to move beyond these engagements with the first plane microsocialities of musical practice, which represent only the most obvious manifestations of a social aesthetics in improvised music. Through commentaries on two historical cases I intend to show, first, how all four planes of social mediation, articulated in diverse ways, can be mobilized to effect a social aesthetics; second, how experimentation with those planes of social mediation can be the locus—as in the SO—of various kinds of politicization of improvised music (although this is not inevitable); and third, through reflection on an ensemble in which I was myself involved, how problematic it is to invest even the most apparently politically worthwhile experiments in social aesthetics with idealized projections that traduce or misrepresent the nature of the assemblage. Daniel Fischlin and Ajay Heble (2004, 2) argue that improvised music has often been aligned with antihegemonic practices of resistance: there are "identifiable and radical [forms] of improvisational practices in which concepts of alternative community formation, social activism, re-historicization of minority cultures, and critical modes of resistance and dialogue are in evidence." This is unarguable. But one intention of this chapter is to suggest, without contesting these important historical truths, that we might productively be alert to the distinctive nature of these counter-practices, grasp how their orchestration of socialities is immanent in their combined aesthetic and political operations, and permit ourselves through critical appraisal—where appropriate—to acknowledge their fallibility.

Recent seminal research portrays the four planes at work in African American improvised music. In his writings on distinctive genealogies of musical improvisation, George Lewis contrasts the real-time music making of "two towering figures of 1950s American experimental music—Charlie 'Bird' Parker and John Cage," as well as the musical lineages they begat. Lewis (1996, 94) contends that the differences they exhibit are not only musical but concern "areas once thought of as 'extra-musical,' including race and ethnicity, class, and social and political philosophy." On this basis, he charts the commitment in the history of Bird-descended African American improvisation to the way that "sonic symbolism is often constructed with a view toward social instrumentality as well as form" (94). Tracing the goal of social instrumentality back to Bebop's provision of "models of both individual and collective creativity" (95) and its reinvention of African American improvisational musicality as explicitly experimental, Lewis argues that "this radical redefinition was viewed as a direct challenge . . . to the entire social order as it applied to blacks in 1940s apartheid America" (95).

Lewis's argument is expanded onto a vast canvas in his magisterial study of the multiple activities and achievements of the Chicago-based Association for the Advancement of Creative Musicians (AACM), a nonprofit, cooperative musicians' collective founded in Chicago in 1965. The AACM developed a politics that spanned not only musical sounds and performance practices but also, as is evident in the organization itself, invention with regard to institutional form—a "communitarian institution-building" (Lewis 2008, xi) manifest in the evolving infrastructure created to support the AACM's burgeoning artistic and educational endeavors. Lewis points out that "the AACM is part of a long tradition of organizational efforts in which African American musicians took leadership roles, including the early-twentieth-century Clef Club, the short-lived Jazz Composers Guild, the Collective [of] Black Artists, and the Los Angeles-based Union of God's Musicians and Artists Ascension, or Underground Musicians Association" (x). The directions taken by these organizations responded to accelerating urban impoverishment and decay, along with racial segregation in the music and cultural industries. Thus, "The Clef Club's strategy of control of their products had long been pursued by black artists, notably including theater artists and composers Bob Cole, James Weldon Johnson, and J. Rosamond Johnson, who sought to maintain both creative and financial control of their productions in the face of legal chicanery, boycotts, and blacklisting" (88). The AACM, however, "became the most well known and influential of the post-1960 organizations, achieving lasting international significance" (x) in the history of experimental music.

Lewis argues throughout the book that it is only by charting both the AACM's sustained pedagogical and institution-building efforts and the profuse musical experimentation manifest in its members' compositional and improvising activities, as well as—crucially—the synergies between these dimensions, that the scale and ambition of the AACM's interventions can be assessed. He contends emphatically that these efforts can only be understood as interventions in the musical politics of race. Focusing on performances of the Art Ensemble of Chicago, one of the best-known AACM groups, it is clear that compounding the combined sonic, visual, theatrical, and cross-media elements of their performance aesthetic were the particular socialities orchestrated in performance. Paul Steinbeck conveys these dynamics well in his analysis of a performance by the Art Ensemble in 1972, which resonates powerfully with Strathern's conceptualization of sociality outlined earlier:

> At certain moments in Art Ensemble performances, all of the musicians seem to be moving the improvisation in the same direction, and their contributions . . . are easily heard as affirming a processual consensus. At other times the members of the Art Ensemble create interactive frameworks that are multi-directional or "multi-centered," in which the individual musicians temporarily inhabit interactive roles that "function completely independently," as Roscoe Mitchell has stated, or generate musical structures that are oppositional, even unstable. . . . [Indeed,] Art Ensemble performances characteristically pass through multiple divergent and convergent stages before concluding. . . . [A]s the musicians assemble and disassemble interactive frameworks, transforming one texture into another, the rules change: what was a divergent or multi-centered idea in the context of one interactive framework can become a convergent gesture in another interactive framework, and vice versa. (Steinbeck 2008, 401–2)

Ultimately, the "ensemble improvisation is balanced between multiple opposing possibilities" (Steinbeck 2008, 409). Clearly, for the Art Ensemble, the microsocialities of performance play not an incidental but a formative part in the aesthetics—or, better, the social aesthetics—of performance.

What the AACM and Art Ensemble show, then, is how their creative and musical activities were crossed by inventive and politicized engagements in all four planes of social mediation. Regarding the first plane, how the microsocialities of performance were immanent in the social aesthetics of performance. Regarding the fourth plane, how these social aesthetics were enabled, compounded, and complemented by invention in the institutional forms supporting the artistic work—institutional forms that themselves modeled creative social cooperation and the toleration of difference. Regarding the third plane, how the first and fourth planes, in turn, refracted evolving wider social formations of race and class, including the racialized injustices and inequalities faced by African American musicians, that characterized the AACM's environment in and beyond Chicago's South Side. And regarding the second plane, as Lewis eloquently attests, how the AACM affectively mobilized a musically imagined community that not only enrolled its members and supporters in the African American community and, as audiences grew, transnational publics, but that projected social relations across space and time to African heritages. As Lewis summarizes in relation to the Art Ensemble, "The group's blend of sonic, visual, and textual iconography emanated from an overall creative environment—the AACM—that encouraged the assertion of interdisciplinary responsibility for the integration of sonic, visual, and textual materials with intellectual and social history, spirituality, and community accountability." Indeed, the Art Ensemble and AACM "use of body paint . . . is transformative in terms of identity, evocative in terms of spirituality, and promulgative in terms of linkages to African cultural practices" (Lewis 1998, 90). In short, to grasp the magnitude of the AACM's aspirations and achievements is to trace its imaginative contributions across all four planes of social mediation, along with their resonant articulations, as they produce or result in the social aesthetics manifest in, among others, the Art Ensemble's compositional activities and improvised performances.

My second (and final) historical case is that of the Feminist Improvising Group (FIG), an experimental and occasional all-woman performing ensemble founded in London in 1977 in which I played cello and bass guitar. Like the Art Ensemble, FIG was known for its extraordinary and eccentric performance style; along with musical and sonic improvisations, it often entailed the anarchic and uneven use of visual, theatrical, and performance elements that dramatized and parodied aspects of "women's experience" as mothers, girlfriends, daughters, carers, and office workers, with a focus on the subversive or hilarious enactment of mundane activities such as domestic labor, child care, dancing, or dressing up. But the group also parodied and played with the normative roles of jazz and rock groups, particularly the singers' roles as chicks and divas and others' roles as "backing musicians." Performances by FIG therefore reflexively engaged with and remixed—often through hamming it up and slapstick—the socialities both of performance and of women's everyday lives.

As is plain, informing the microsocialities of FIG performances were feminist politics, inasmuch as these politics unified we FIG improvisers as women subject to common gendered experiences of subordination, inequality, and injustice. That is to say, the first plane microsocialities of performance were taken, consciously and experimentally, to refract and be refracted by the third plane: evolving but enduring social relations of gender in the world at large. But the "double ontological status" of the microsocialities of performance as they refracted the wider plane of gendered social relations was more complex, since we FIGgers had been subject to gendered social relations not only as women but also as musicians and improvisers. Indeed, one originating affective drive that fueled FIG came from conversations in which we shared our experiences of performing and playing with bands and improvising ensembles that otherwise comprised all men or mainly men, for we discovered that in these bands and ensembles, in different ways and to variable degrees, we found ourselves in situations implicitly saturated with gender dynamics—tiny instants or sustained passages of interactive sonic domination in which our musical "voice" was rendered somehow inappropriate, or was overwhelmed and could not emerge or be heard, or in which the dynamics of turn-taking seemed to be strenuously competitive or masculinized and to exclude other modes of musical mutuality, relation, or being. These were relatively inchoate, extralinguistic, and embodied experiences for us as individual women musicians, but that these bands and improvising ensembles instantiated gendered musical socialities on occasion was a perception we shared. In this sense, our common experience both paralleled and embodied the gendering of the musical canon and of the processes of evaluation, legitimization, and canonization that over time, performatively, make it up (Citron 1993), just as our experience also embodied how, as Patrick Valiquet (2014, 228) puts it, the making and "marking of musical genre can be just as powerful for what and whom it excludes and delegitimizes as for what and whom it enshrines." It is out of these common experiences of delegitimization and exclusion that the supposition originated—one of several inventive qualities of FIG's founding—that our musical interactions might be different in FIG; that we might evade or transcend these prior, gendered musical socialities or otherwise empractise improvisational socialities differently. And while in some ways this was undoubtedly how we experienced working in FIG, the uncomfortable (antiessentialist) truth is that even when all performers were women, and all were informed by feminist and, often, lesbian feminist politics, the creation of hierarchical, competitive, or exclusionary musical socialities in performance could still occur and could sometimes even be pronounced. Nothing was ideal, then, about the microsocialities of FIG performance. In retrospect, this is quite humorous; at the time, it troubled any complacent essentialism.

The Feminist Improvising Group tended to polarize audiences and critics, as perhaps befits such an insecure and risk-taking entity. And inasmuch as FIG reached out affectively, mobilizing its followers and audiences into a (second-plane) musically imagined community, this tended to be a fuzzy operation under the sign of the feminisms and lesbianisms of the time. The group did not seem so affectively powerful at a "purely musical" level. Indeed, for our critics our musical proficiency was questionable, and we clearly did not know what we were doing: our ambiguous, possibly feigned "incompetencies" and apparent lack of technical virtuosity were felt by such critics to be intolerable to witness. Here, gendered projections, manifest perhaps in gendered listening and audiencing, compounded our sometimes already wobbly experimental practices. In terms of the fourth plane, FIG was typical of the marginal and self-managed organizational forms constructed by many improvising ensembles in the late 1970s and 1980s, when the do-it-yourself ethic of punk and that of the small-scale, "alternative" venue, label, and distribution networks of groups like Henry Cow and the Free Jazz scene, had become models. We scraped a living as freelancers working across a spectrum of activities, producing a cassette of FIG performances and getting by on the modest fees for our often publicly subsidized gigs.

The case of FIG therefore shows, like that of the Art Ensemble of Chicago, how the social aesthetics of performance can be grasped only through an analysis of both the autonomy and the entanglement of the four planes of social mediation. But through FIG I want also to point to the dangers of teleological histories of practice that smooth out differences and conflicts, and that render unevenness even. Of course, I write autoethnographically, with the attendant perils of that subjective project. By analogy with the AACM's response to a racist environment, the founding of FIG responded to the exclusions and denigrations experienced routinely by women classical, jazz, rock, and punk musicians and improvisers. Like that of the Scratch Orchestra, a principle of FIG's membership was to be inclusive of women musicians with regard to level of skill and experience and musical style, although from the start FIG's core consisted of highly experienced performers from improvised music, jazz, avant-garde rock, and performance art: Lindsay Cooper, Maggie Nicols, Irène Schweizer, and Sally Potter. In addition, the majority— but not all—of FIG's members were lesbian. There was an amusing aspect to this situation in that Cathy Williams and I, and a few others, would sometimes find ourselves "the only heterosexual(s)" at the feast—particularly at the lesbian feminist "women's festivals" at which we often performed during the 1980s. Perhaps it was FIG's happy "inversion" of norms of gender and sexuality that engendered the strenuously irreverent humor, risk-taking, and pathos that characterized FIG performances, in which little was planned and ingenious use was made of the performance site, social situation, and any other immediate resources (e.g., props, linguistic challenges) to hand.

But to take this analysis further, and to understand FIG performances, necessitates entering into the politics informing and crossing between our lives and our musical work at the time. The late 1970s and early 1980s were the height of European second-wave feminism's discussion of political lesbianism in Europe and the United Kingdom. This was manifest in issues of the leading socialist-feminist journal *Feminist Review*, as well as at political meetings called by the journal, and several of we British FIGgers participated in these debates.[5] One of the key questions at stake, which fiercely (but productively) divided feminist opinion, was whether, or the extent to which, being lesbian was an involuntary result of genetic programming—one was, in this sense, born rather than made a lesbian—or whether it was (also) a response to a gendered and heterosexist environment. A closely related question therefore was whether being a lesbian was first and foremost an issue of involuntary sexual identity and only as a result an issue of political identity, or whether adopting a lesbian identity should be understood as primarily a result of political conviction, such that any woman might choose to take up a lesbian subject position for political reasons, with the assumption that her sexuality would, as it were, follow suit. These and other, Marxist and socialist political challenges animated some of the women who became members of FIG. Several of us had worked, with different levels of energy and conviction, with left-leaning organizations prior to FIG: Lindsay Cooper and I in Henry Cow; Maggie Nicols and Cathy Williams in other leftist musical and political groups. Indeed, FIG's first performance was at the inaugural "Music for Socialism" festival held at the Almost Free Theatre in London. The performance style of FIG sat astride, and was informed by, this cauldron of unresolved, animated, and conflictual political debates. There was no settlement, little unity, and no foreordained politics, and there were plenty of undiscussed differences and fractures. Palpable tensions arose due to the coexistence of a willed (and, in our circles, fashionable) adoption by some of political lesbianism, along with others' "lifelong" lesbianism, and yet others' socialist feminism unyoked to lesbian identities. These political tensions and conflicts mattered, and they got into FIG performances, which were far from a smooth or consensual rendering of a "queer perspective" emanating from "queer women." To depict this situation as an occasion "for women to foreground their bodies and their sounds for the pleasure of other women" (J. D. Smith 2004, 240–41) is a misinterpretation that essentializes and subsumes FIG's practices under an idealized queer politics. It is to project later categories back onto the group and its improvisations, in the process overlooking what remained heterogeneous, contentious, troubling, and unresolved—and, arguably, most productive—in the experimental and politicized social aesthetics set in motion by FIG.

I began this chapter by suggesting that we find social aesthetics, in different guises, in contemporary art practices. I pointed to several such modalities of the social in recent art and aesthetics—three unhelpfully elided in Bourriaud's relational aesthetics, and another identifiable in socially engaged art. I proposed that Claire Bishop's important rejoinder to Bourriaud—asking: if art is engaged in producing social relations, then "what types of relations are being produced, for whom, and why?"—shows the need to develop conceptual tools to disentangle and identify the distinctive forms of sociality produced by art and musical practices, thereby avoiding their elision and fostering a more acute appreciation of both their singularity and their mutual refractions. To this end, the analytics of four planes of social mediation developed in the main body of the chapter is offered as a conceptual foundation, and I worked it through with reference to improvised music in which the articulation of the four planes is manifest in richly reticulate socialities. Indeed, implicit comparisons were drawn between the varieties of social aesthetics in contemporary art practices and those evident in improvised music. I have argued that close empirical and historical research is necessary to advance this kind of analysis, without which there is little resistance to the idealization of the microsocialities of improvised practice, as they are disembedded from the wider social relations and formations that they transform or "distort" and in which they nest, as well as little resistance to the projection of post hoc interpretations that override historical realities and complexities. In an era in which post-formalist music, art, and interdisciplinary practices are exploding our very understanding of "art," "music," "performance," and "work" (Born 2013b; Born and Barry 2010), it is imperative to advance our categories of analysis with regard to how variously the social enters into the aesthetic so as better to conceptualize the experimental and novel socialities, imagined communities, and social and institutional formations summoned into being by these practices. My hope is that, while I have indicated how this framework can assist in the analysis of improvised music, it may also fold back and provide a measure of rigor for those concerned with theorizing art's multiple social mediations.

Notes

1. On Deleuze's definition of, and distinction between molar (or major) and minor politics, see DeLanda 2008; Patton 2000; Thoburn 2003, chaps. 1–2. For Deleuze, "the minor is in opposition to the molar or major. Minor and major are expressions that characterize not entities, but processes. . . . Essentially, major processes are premised on the formation and defense of a constant or a standard that acts as a norm and a basis of judgment. As such, major relations . . . are relations of identity." In contrast, minor politics involves "the process of deviation or deterritorialization of life . . . against the molar standard." Minor politics is not "a process of facilitating and bolstering identity, or 'becoming-conscious,' but . . . of innovation, of experimentation, and of the complication of life, in which forms of community, techniques of practice, ethical demeanors, styles, knowledges, and cultural forms are composed" (Thoburn 2003, 6–8).

2. As in the introduction to this volume, the term "empractise," meaning a fully embodied and social putting into practice, is intended in part to avoid any Cartesian account in which improvisation is understood as entailing cognitive processes that initiate or supervise the bodily and social processes inherent in it. But it is also intended as an alternative to the term "enactment" introduced by science and technology studies—notably, the work of John Law, where it is endowed with an ontological status linked to the performativity of the world. Hence, "the social sciences have always been embedded in, produced by, and productive of the social. . . . They *participate in, reflect upon*, and *enact* the social" (Law and Urry 2004, 392). Where enactment derives from a social theory focused on notions of "action," then, empractise is practice-centered while carrying no ontological implications.

3. A variant of Small's stance is enunciated by Thomas Turino (2008, 19), who, referencing Victor Turner's concept of *communitas*, states: "For me, good music making or dancing is a realization of ideal—*possible*—human relationships where the identification with others is so direct and so intense that we feel . . . as if our selves had merged. It is the sounds we are making . . . that continually let us know that we have done so or that we are failing to achieve this ideal."

4. Stefan Szczelkun, "Twenty-five Years from Scratch: ICA Sunday 20th November 1994," November 1995, http://www.stefan-szczelkun.org.uk/PHD-SCRATCH2.htm (accessed January 1, 2014).

5. Indicating the lively spectrum of feminist politics being debated in this period, issues of *Feminist Review* ranged between socialist feminist internationalism, as in the first issue's articles on "Women and Revolution in South Yemen" and "Female Sexuality in Fascist Ideology" (1979) and the twelfth issue's articles on "ANC Women's Struggles" and "Documents from the Indian Women's Movement" (1982), and the burgeoning challenges from black feminism, as in the seventeenth issue's theme "Many Voices, One Chant: Black Feminist Perspectives" (1984), as well as a growing focus on sexuality, as in the eleventh issue's theme "Sexuality" (1982) and the thirty-fourth issue's theme "Perverse Politics: Lesbian Issues" (1990).

CHAPTER 2

SCRIPTING SOCIAL INTERACTION

Improvisation, Performance, and Western "Art" Music

Nicholas Cook

There is a long-standing tradition of seeing jazz, particularly free and avant-garde jazz, as the expression of an ideal society. This has gone along with a corresponding tradition of seeing Western "art" music (WAM) in precisely the opposite terms. For example, in a contribution to the *Cambridge Companion to Jazz*, Bruce Johnson (2002, 102) characterizes jazz as the opposite of WAM along a series of dimensions. In line with today's official, institutionalized culture, Johnson says, WAM is "ocularcentric"; centered on the notated text, it is "a spectacle of scopic hegemony, the eye engaging with a 'product.'" Jazz, by contrast, is "distinguished from art-music models in the priority of the ear, in collective improvisational performance" (104). In this way it is "a vehicle for a form of musical socialization, that is peripheral to the tradition of the artist-as-individual, as 'soloist'" (106). The approach is riddled with binaries: the eye is opposed to the ear, compositional product is opposed to improvisational performance, individual is opposed to community. And it does not take much knowledge of the role of jazz within the history of American racial politics to understand why this might be the case. Johnson's binaries map directly onto Ben Sidran's opposition of "literate" and "oral man," where "the peculiarly 'black' approach to rhythm" is linked to "the greater oral approach to time" and the "inherently communal nature of oral improvisation" (Walser 1999, 299). It is also worth observing that ocular-centricity, an ontology based on the musical product, and the individual author together represent the foundational premises of copyright law, which Eric Lewis (2007, 182) has described as "a racist and classist practice" that "attempts to hide its exclusionary nature behind a metaphysics of the musical work which purports to be objective and universal, but in fact is not."

In this context, a positive mythologization of jazz has gone hand in hand with a negative mythologization of WAM. This goes beyond its characterization by commentators from jazz and the skewed representation of music as an element of the capitalist economy within the courts. It is also reflected in the manner in which WAM is invoked, again often in opposition to jazz, within the context of broader cultural commentary. This can be illustrated from the field of urban planning, investigated by Dean Rowan in an article published in *Critical Studies in Improvisation/Études critiques en improvisation*. Rowan quotes Rutherford Platt and Jon Moloney-Merkle's characterization of the uniform, statewide procedures that at one time governed the planning of open space in Illinois as "a classical score from which the individual cities once uniformly played," whereas following the removal of the legal basis for these procedures "the cities' solutions were improvised, albeit not purely spontaneous, deviations" (2004, 16). He also writes that Leonie Sandercock's approaches to planning "vibrantly accord with improvisational methods, employing practices of active listening, alleviation of oppressive hierarchy, and invitation and acceptance of differences"; by comparison, traditional, rational planning "has musical analogs in strict allegiance to the composer's score and obeisance to the hierarchical command of the conductor" (Rowan 2004). The very vocabulary adopted here (vibrant, active, alleviation of oppression, acceptance of difference versus strict allegiance, obeisance, and hierarchical command) testifies to the dense network of ideology within which WAM has become enmeshed.

In "Averroes's Search," Jorge Luis Borges (1964, 150) recounts that the traveler Abulcasim al-Ashari claimed to have been to China but that his enemies, "with that peculiar logic of hatred, swore that he had never set foot in China and that in the temples of that land he had blasphemed the name of Allah." In the same way, WAM is on the one hand condemned for the undesirability of its social content, and on the other for lacking social content altogether. In this chapter I aim to answer both charges, thereby opening up the potential for thinking of WAM in terms of social action (and of social action in terms of WAM). My argument is based on the assumption that music's primary mode of existence lies in the act of performing it, an act that is inherently social. But it goes further than that. I hope to show how the written notations that play so conspicuous a role in WAM function as vehicles for social action and interaction. And I approach this by interrogating the distinction between improvisation and the performance of precomposed scores that, in musicological terms, forms the hub of the various binary oppositions I have invoked. This is an issue I have explored in a previous paper, "Making Music Together, or Improvisation and Its Others."[1] There I set out a series of musical examples beginning with improvisation and ending with performance. This second pass over the terrain can accordingly be brief and will focus on the question of the point at which we can identify a category shift from one to the other. No prizes will be awarded for guessing that no such point will be found.

Improvisation and Performance

At the furthest remove from the performance of precomposed scores is free improvisation, a term that is used in the contexts of both jazz and WAM. There is some variability in the practices referred to by this term, particularly in terms of how far they work within or seek to transcend established styles or idioms, but certain features remain constant. Jared Burrows (2004, 10), whose background as an improvising musician is in jazz, writes that the process of improvisation creates "its own time-dependent meanings— let's call them short-term archetypes—specific to each improvisation," while groups that frequently perform together develop "archetypes" that persist from one improvisation to another. In other words, specific patterns of interaction between performers develop as they play together, both within an individual performance and across repeated performances, and these interactions are as much social as musical. At the opposite end of the aesthetic spectrum from Burrows is Pierre Boulez, the archetypal postwar modernist for whom improvisation was an evasion of the real challenges of creative innovation in music, but his lampooning of the avant-garde improvisations of the 1950s reflects the same features: at first there would be some excitement, he says, "and so everybody just made more activity, more activity, louder, louder, louder. Then they were tired so for two minutes you had calm, calm, calm, calm, calm. And then somebody was waking up so they began again, and then they were tired, sooner this time, and so the rest was longer. You cannot call that improvisation" (quoted in Oliver 1999, 147). Boulez's basic point is that the freer the music is, in the sense of avoiding overt references to established idioms or predefined musical materials, the more it reverts to banal patterns of behavior that are not specifically musical at all. However skewed by his own compositional agenda and the larger aesthetic ideology of postwar modernism, Boulez's claim is one also found in the discourses around jazz. Charlie Mingus is supposed to have told Tim Leary, "You can't improvise on nothin', man. . . . You gotta improvise on somethin'" (quoted in Kernfeld 1995, 11). In improvisation as in other areas of life, freedom is relative.

Classic jazz improvisation based on jazz standards illustrates Mingus's claim. The role of such standards is relatively minimal, in essence comprising a series of chord changes (which, however, can be voiced very flexibly) that define a sectional structure (but not its repetitions, so that the structure remains open); solo improvisation may or may not reference the song melody, and in either case it may also reference other well-known solos, as well as the "ideas, licks, tricks, pet patterns, crips, clichés, and, in the most functional language, things you can do" that make up the fabric of jazz improvisation (Berliner 1994, 102). Although one speaks of, say, the Clifford Brown Quintet "performing" Billy Strayhorn's "Take the 'A' Train," audiences do not come to hear Strayhorn's composition (they are unlikely to know in advance that it will be played). They come rather to hear the solo and collective improvisation that the song structure affords. And this focus is reflected in the difference between a jazz lead sheet and a classical score. As José Bowen (1993, 148) observes, lead sheets attempt to provide an exhaustive list of the typical attributes of the work in performance, a consequence being that a literal performance of the lead sheet, including all of these attributes, "would barely be considered a performance of the tune at all. It would be a *caricature* of the tune." In that sense, lead sheets both underdetermine and overdetermine the performances they afford. They signify them, but in a complex and highly mediated way.

Yet on consideration, the difference between a lead sheet and a classical score may prove elusive. Corelli's original notations of the slow movements from his Violin Sonatas, Op. 5, look equally unlike the performances they signify. In fact, they hardly look like violin music at all: they resemble nothing so much as the Renaissance-style counterpoint exercises used in the eighteenth century to teach basic principles of composition. However, these slow movements have also been transmitted in a multitude of contemporary notations prepared by players and pedagogues, which show how Corelli's skeletal melodies were embellished through violinistic ornamentation that could vary from the restrained to the wildly flamboyant. Terms such as "embellished" and "ornamentation" are misleading, however, because what Corelli wrote sometimes disappears completely behind the new violin part, and although the violone (cello) part is nowadays performed as written, there is evidence that in the eighteenth century it was extemporized, too (Watkin 1996). Under such circumstances, what Corelli wrote and what was played might have little more in common than the chord changes, and the similarity to jazz standards is further enhanced by striking affinities between baroque continuo realization and the voicing practices of jazz pianists. It might, of course, be objected that these supposedly improvised embellishments or alternative versions of Corelli's music may in reality have consisted largely of the performance of precomposed scores, as the multitude of surviving notations might suggest and as is predominantly the case today. But then, the same is sometimes the case of jazz: witness the copyright deposit versions of Louis Armstrong's music from the mid-1920s, produced to comply with the law's ocular-centric conception of the musical object, which are remarkably close to the improvisations Armstrong recorded two or three years later with the Hot Five (Gushee 1998, 297–98). All this fits uneasily with Sidran's distinction between literate and oral man: written and oral transmission are inextricably linked in the performance cultures of both jazz and WAM.

And it does not stop there. Any string quartet by Haydn, Mozart, or Beethoven will suffice to make the point. Here, unlike in the previous instances, the musicians play the notes as written—except that, of course, they *do not* play the notes as written. The notes are represented as fixed pitches with proportionate durations (a quarter-note lasts twice as long as an eighth), with dynamics being indicated only schematically and without any specification of timbral quality. But in performance every one of these is negotiated between the players, both in the course of rehearsal and in the real time of performance. Each player accommodates his or her intonation to the others'; rhythms are nuanced in the service of structural articulation or emotional expression and accommodated within the overall ensemble; dynamic and timbral values are adjusted between the players. In other words, the players do not do some things that are specified in the score and do others that are not. The way in which classical scores, like lead sheets, may overdetermine as well as underdetermine performances becomes particularly clear when composers, such as Beethoven on occasion, include fingering in their piano music. Modern orthodoxy has it that players should seek to understand the musical point that Beethoven is conveying through fingering and then try to express that understanding using whatever fingering best suits them. Just as in the case of jazz lead sheets, then, the relationship between WAM notation and performance is highly mediated, with many decisions being delegated to performers and with at least some of these needing to be negotiated in real time. Playing the notes is nowhere near as straightforward as it sounds.

In saying all of this, I have been trying to make two points. The first and more obvious one is that there is improvisation in WAM and performance of precomposed materials in jazz. The second and less obvious point is that there is no categorical distinction between improvisation and performance; rather, there is a continuum of practices. Of course, a different attitude toward the text informs the performance of Mozart and Strayhorn, as well as the way it is experienced by listeners (who, in the case of the Mozart, are likely to know in advance which quartet will be played and may have come specifically to hear it). Such obvious differences may disguise but do not eliminate the irreducible core of real-time determination that is shared between WAM performance and jazz improvisation, and it is this irreducible core that I see as grounding the social dimension of all music, WAM included. Regarded as a lead sheet, Mozart's score functions as a framework within which the players negotiate specific values in real time, and they do so by ear, through processes of continuous accommodation between self and other. To this extent, playing a Mozart quartet might be described as an act of "collective improvisational performance," to repeat Johnson's (2002, 104) words, and another of his characterizations of jazz becomes even more telling when applied to WAM: it is "an earsite in an epistemology dominated by eyesight." Similarly, Ingrid Monson's (1996, 84) observation that in jazz, "To say that a player 'doesn't listen' . . . is a grave insult," applies with no less force to classical quartet performance. Small wonder then that Richard Cochrane (2000, 140) concludes that "the practice of improvisation in fact exists in all musical performances except those carried out solely by machines"; and when George Lewis (2009, 4) claims that "improvisation's ubiquity becomes the modality through which performance is articulated," he intends this to apply not just to music but to social action in general.

In putting forward these arguments I do not claim that Johnson's distinctions between eye and ear, product and process, or individual and community are illusory. They are real and deeply embedded in musical culture, but they have been drawn in the wrong place. The crucial distinction lies not within the practices of performance, which are aurally mediated and public (because you can hear me as well as I can hear myself), but between the practices of performance and the discourses around music that are predicated on the ontology of eye, product, and individual. I can illustrate this by going back to the string quartet, which I now declare to be the first page of Mozart's String Quartet No. 14 in G major, K. 387. A traditional musicological description (what is often, and tellingly, referred to as a "reading") of the first ten bars might go something like this:

> A two-bar opening phrase moves from the tonic to the supertonic and is balanced by another two-bar phrase that returns through the dominant to the tonic; this pair of matched two-bar phrases leads in turn to a four-bar phrase in which a distinctive motif ascends from the viola through the second violin to the first violin. This culminates in a homophonic but deceptive cadence on the submediant, which is immediately rectified through the addition of a two-bar closing phrase that cadences in the tonic, resulting in an extension of the normative 8-bar sentence to 10 bars.

This musicological language is abstract and depersonalized: reference is made not to people making music together (the description is of "the music," not a particular performance of it) but to instrumental agencies. These are conceived as timeless entities, which is why the whole description is expressed in the present tense. Then there is the "distinctive motif" that ascends through the instruments (the ascent is an ocular image): it is passed from one instrument to another, rather like handing over the baton in a relay race. It is in that sense an object and as such potentially can be owned (the fact that it is distinctive means that it could in principle be copyrighted). And if we ask what this object is made of, the answer will probably be "sound structures"—that is, specific configurations of pitch classes and rhythms—but since they can be usefully specified only in notational terms, this is tantamount to saying that the object is made of text. In any case, the object is something that exists independently of performance, with the performance accordingly being reduced to an optional extra or supplement, rather like reading a poem out loud.

The strange ontology of musical works draws on long traditions of textuality and Platonic idealism, elaborated through Romantic notions of individual creative vision and the correlative concept of art addressed to the experiencing subject. It is also linked to the aesthetic ideology of musical autonomy, according to which music's value lies in its transcending of the social and its access to a higher plane of being. The New Musicology of the 1990s was defined by its opposition to this ideology. Susan McClary (1991), for example, argued that the canonic WAM repertory embodies hegemonic values such as misogyny and racism and does so in a particularly pernicious way because the apparent naturalness and self-evidence of musical meaning disguises its ideological constructedness. Influenced by Adorno, the New Musicologists sought to demonstrate the deep links between music and social meaning, but they did so through textual analysis, aiming to identify and decode social articulations composed into the score. In this way they retained the depersonalizing discourse of traditional musicology even as they redirected it to new ends.

But again, this is not an issue restricted to WAM. Monson (1996, 26) observes, "In an improvisational situation, it is important to remember that there are always musical personalities interacting, not merely instruments or pitches or rhythms." She also complains that the contribution of individuals has been overemphasized at the expense of the group contexts from which improvisation emerges. "The melodic vocabulary of the improvising jazz soloist," she writes, "must always be seen as emerging in a complex dialogue between the soloist and the rhythm section" (Monson 2002, 114). In the same way, Wadada Leo Smith condemns the belief of those he witheringly refers to as "'musical analysts'" that "the solo-line is the creation of a 'soloist,' and that the other improvisers involved are mere accompaniment," adding "this is an invalid evaluation" (Walser 1999, 321). Daniel Fischlin (2009, 4) goes as far as to claim, "The individual does not in this sense really exist, except as a function of the community out of which s/he emerges." And Monson (1996, 80) extends her attack on the persistent misunderstandings of jazz as far as that stronghold of ocular-centricity, the musical text. "At the moment of performance," she says, "jazz improvisation quite simply has nothing in common with a text (or its musical equivalent, the score)." Almost half a century earlier, Alfred Schutz (1964, 169), for whom making music together was a paradigm case of intersubjective communication, made precisely the same comment about WAM. He went on to claim, "There is no difference in principle between the performance of a string quartet and the improvisations at a jam session of accomplished jazz players" (177). I maintain that all of Monson's points apply as much to WAM as they do to jazz.

One implication of this is that the distinction between improvised and performed music cannot be established on empirical grounds—that is, in terms of the analysis of musical material. That, indeed, is the outcome of a recent study by Andreas Lehmann and Reinhard Kopiez (2010). Their subjects were quite consistent in rating how far various musical examples were "spontaneous/improvised" or "coherent/rehearsed," but there was no significant correlation between these ratings and whether the example in question was in fact improvised or precomposed. This fits with Philip Auslander's (2013, 54) argument that "the fact that music is improvised is not accessible or verifiable through the act of listening." He sees improvisation as "a social characteristic of jazz performance rather than an ontological characteristic of the music" (57), an agreement between players and listeners to treat the performance as if it is improvised. An expression of this is the elaborate gestural stage play through which both jazz and rock musicians create the impression of—or perform—spontaneity. (It is telling that this stage play is essentially identical to that through which WAM soloists perform the authenticity of their emotional engagement with the music they are playing.) In short, Auslander sees improvisation as constituted through a form of social contract, and there are a number of other musicological concepts of which the same has been argued. Jeffrey Kallberg (1996, chap. 1) has applied this approach to genre, which, despite huge efforts, researchers in music information retrieval have failed to define satisfactorily in material terms (Craft 2008). I have described work identity as a social construction only weakly supported by material features (Cook 1999, 203); in this case, it is analytic philosophers of music who have wasted their efforts.

In this chapter, however, I pursue the argument in a different direction. In traditional musicological thinking (as in music philosophy), the concept of the score is thoroughly entangled with the Romantic aesthetic ideology to which I have referred. The question I want to address is how we might think about scores if, in contrast to the traditional musicological approach, we approach them as frameworks for social action and interaction.

Western "Art" Music and Social Interaction

When your discipline gets weighed down by sedimented assumptions and ideology, it helps to view your problems from the perspective of other disciplines. At this point, then, I want to inject two perspectives from art theory and material culture. One is Nicolas Bourriaud's (2002) "relational aesthetics." Though now arguably suffering from overexposure, it embodies an insight that sets into relief the overwhelming orientation of traditional musicology and aesthetics toward subjective experience: Bourriaud proposes that one of the functions of art is to construct social relationships among its spectators. While Bourriaud's purpose is to provide a theoretical basis for specific developments in the art of the 1990s, I see this as one of the basic functions of music in general.

The second perspective arises out of the Peter B. Lewis Building in Cleveland, Ohio, which was designed by Frank Gehry for the Weatherhead School of Management and opened in 2002. Gehry views buildings as expressing and fostering social relationships. Because learning is a social activity, writes Kim Cameron (who was dean of the Weatherhead School during this period), the Peter B. Lewis Building "had to foster lots of chance collisions and productive interaction patterns" (Cameron 2003, 90). The same approach characterized the design and construction process. It is well known, as documented by Eric Abrahamson and David H. Freedman (2006, 87–88), that no detailed blueprints were issued to contractors. They were expected to derive the measurements they needed from a scale model of the building. This forced them "to work with the Gehry team in the task of translating the look and feel of the model into a full-scale structure," expressing Gehry's philosophy that "everyone working on the building should keep creating throughout the construction process." A wide range of visual aids was used as means of engaging the many different parties involved in the project. Richard Boland and Fred Collopy (2004, 11), both faculty members at Weatherhead, refer to the many models they saw as the design developed; Gehry's team "work with their hands," they say, "making models of the exterior and interior elements out of paper, metal, plastic, waxed cloth, or whatever material gives them both the form and feeling that they are seeking."

Perhaps most telling are the freehand sketches that Gehry produced at an early stage of the design process (reproduced in Cameron 2003, 91). These calligraphic sketches are so abstract that if you saw them out of context, it would probably not occur to you that they represent a building. But when you see them that way, the spatial and aesthetic characteristics that they embody become aspects of the building. They do not embody significant informational content in the way that, for example, a quantity surveyor might define it: it would be absurd to think of the building being costed on such a basis. Boland and Collopy (2004, 11) explain that the sketches are "meant to be spontaneous and evocative of both form and emotion," while for Cameron (2003, 90) they express "a playful sense of experimentation and right-brain thinking." But the best insight into their function comes from Gehry himself: "You have to dream an idea. . . . Then you have to work it through the staff in my office. You have to work it through the client, all the people and the committee who have things to do with it. . . . There are thousands of people in the end that touch this thing" (quoted in Cameron 2003, 91). The purpose of these sketches, then, is to facilitate collaborative work, setting out a broad visual and affective framework without preempting the innumerable concrete decisions that must be negotiated in the course of the collaboration. In short, they structure the social relationships that are necessary to bring the project to a successful conclusion.

Such an interaction of human and material agents would lend itself to analysis in terms of Bruno Latour's Actor-Network Theory (2005), and this kind of approach would readily transfer to the analysis of graphic scores in music. However, I shall return to Mozart's K. 387, but now in the context of a conference held in the Peter B. Lewis Building shortly after it opened. Entitled "Managing as Designing," the conference was conceived around Gehry (who attended) and his building, and its aim was to develop a new vocabulary for management on the basis of the concepts and practices of design. "Design" was interpreted in a broad sense, and I was invited. My paper was titled, "In Praise of Symbolic Poverty," and it presented conventional musical notation as a means of designing concerted action. I construed K. 387 as a performative script that choreographs a series of varied social engagements: it sets out a broad vision of what is to be achieved but at the same time, through the radical under-determination that characterizes staff notation, delegates local decisions to be made on the ground, in real time. It invokes and relies on individuals' tacit knowledge and creativity, their ability both literally and metaphorically to play things by ear. This is the musical equivalent of what, in the architectural design process, Gehry (2004, 21) refers to as "staying liquid" rather than fixing design decisions at too early a stage, and to my surprise this turned out to be the guiding idea of the whole conference. In the case of music, it represents not only a more positive but also a more realistic alternative to Dean Rowan's conception of the classical score as an exhaustive specification of deliverables mandating fully accountable implementation, in a kind of musical analog to the ISO 9000 family of quality management standards. In short, my claim, as Monson (1996, 186) says of jazz, is that music has "as one of its central functions the *construction* of social context"—an idea that precisely parallels Bourriaud's relational aesthetics.

In talking about the string quartet as a model for social interaction in music, I have chosen the classical genre that perhaps most closely resembles jazz improvisation. Both embody the same relational values: the need to play by ear—to communicate through the public medium of musical sound—means that everyone is open to everyone else, resulting in an ensemble that is egalitarian or, at least, in which hierarchies are dynamic and negotiated. Both genres involve the same give and take that characterizes polite conversation, and it is no accident that the metaphor of conversation was as deeply embedded in eighteenth-century thinking about chamber music as in twentieth-century thinking about jazz. But this is not the only form of sociality that is embedded in classical music. If the metaphor of conversation serves to define classical chamber music, then one of its features is that each player has something to play that makes sense both in its own terms and in relation to what others are playing. This is not only the case of Mozart's string quartets. As a former oboist, I would maintain that it is the case of his symphonies, too—but not of Beethoven's. Seen from the oboists' desk, a change took place in symphonic writing around the beginning of the nineteenth century. From then on, a given textural element might be assigned at one moment to one instrument or set of instruments and at the next moment to another. The overall sound makes sense for the audience, but for the players the individual instrumental parts no longer make the kind of sense that they did in Mozart's symphonies.

The music still makes sense, of course, but it makes sense as heard from the conductor's podium or from the auditorium, not from the oboists' desk or the back row of the violins. And that means that performance becomes the expression of a different structure of social relationships from the chamber music model. The rank-and-file players become not so much participants in a collective social event as skilled workers employed to perform certain predefined services for the benefit of the ticket-buying public. It is at this time that the conductor appears, a silent performer who coordinates and supervises operations, rather in the manner—to continue with the architectural analogy—of a project manager, essentially representing the clients' interests, though with due attention to other stakeholders. One such stakeholder, although normally absent, is the composer, who now becomes not so much a musical dramatist, choreographing real-time interactions between performers, as a sound designer. In short, a fundamentally different management structure is in place compared with that in a Mozart symphony (which normally would have been led, rather than conducted, by the principal violinist). There are new lines of accountability. It is still an insult to say that orchestral musicians do not listen, but it is now most crucially the conductor whom they are not listening to. And this new conception of symphonic performance is retrospectively imposed on eighteenth-century repertory conceived in terms of a quite different form of social organization. The interesting thing is the extent to which this social dimension of the orchestra has been overlooked by the historical performance movement that began in the 1970s as a reaction against the one-size-fits-all consensus of the postwar performance mainstream and by the century's end had become a mainstream of its own. It is not hard to think of period-style orchestras that set great store on the use of authentic instruments and playing techniques— and then perform Mozart symphonies under a conductor.

This story is really too easy to tell. I could now go on to locate the emergence of ocular-centricity and the rest in this transition from chamber music understood as the collaboration of free individuals to the modern orchestra understood as a top-down structure, with management and employees having highly segmented roles and responsibilities, almost in the manner of Ford-style mass production. (The major constraint on such segmentation—the fact that everyone had to play together at the same time and place—disappeared with the introduction of multitrack recording.) And jazz fits into the story as a mode of resistance to the juggernaut of capitalist reification and alienation. But such a narrative of cultural and social decline is grossly oversimplified and illustrates the temptation to make translations between music and society—and back again—in a manner that is far too glib and literal. I shall make the point from two different points of view. The first is that of management studies, which has built up quite an extensive literature on how conductors and orchestras work together. The general assumption has been that the globe-trotting conductor is a prime exemplar of charismatic leadership—the kind of leadership that involves a top-down relationship between leader and followers. However, the management consultant Yaakov Atik (1994) carried out extensive interviews with conductors, players, and orchestral administrators, from which he concluded that all of these parties considered the most effective leadership style to be a transformational one. This involves "an interactive and dynamic perception of the relationship between superior and subordinate" (27), characterized by the delegation of local decision making to individual players. One of Atik's informants, an administrator and former player, spoke of the conductor who will "communicate a point about something and from that point on, leave it up to the abilities that he knows the players have" and added, "That is true leadership" (26).

The point can also be made in musicological terms. To do this, I focus on changing practices in the performance of Webern's music (as described in Day 2000, 178–85). The composer's later music, for example, his Concerto Op. 24 (1934), is highly pointillistic in style. Melodic fragments of just one or two notes pass from instrument to instrument, often with large registral leaps or dynamic disjunctions. It was precisely Webern's later music that was valued by the hard-core modernists associated with the Darmstadt *Ferienkurse* in the 1950s, owing to the perceived objectivity of its compositional engineering, but no performing tradition for this music had at that time come into being. As a result, when Robert Craft made his pioneering recordings of Webern's complete published works, issued by Columbia in

1957, he coached each player individually "until he had learned his part like a cipher" (Stravinsky and Craft 1972, 95). In other words, the music was performed in just the way Rowan supposes, with each note being slotted into place in accordance with the specifications of the score. In terms of the social interaction involved here, a parallel might be drawn with a number of other musical contexts both within and beyond WAM: the opening of the final movement of Tchaikovsky's Sixth Symphony (*Pathétique*), in which alternate notes of the tear-jerking melody are assigned to first and second violins, resulting in a peculiar stereophonic effect (but only if first and second violins are arranged in the old-fashioned way, to the left and right of the stage); change ringing of church bells, where each ringer controls one bell; and such non-Western traditions based on the principle of hocketing as the Indonesian angklung ensemble or central African horn orchestras.

The narrative of decline might seize on such practices as embodying an even clearer version of Ford-style segmentation, the model of an alienated society in which the individual worker has no investment in the overall process of production. But in reality these performance situations are neither socially nor musically dysfunctional. They have merely been misdescribed. Writing in the mid-1970s, by which time his own performances of Webern had become much more continuous and even lyrical, Boulez (1976, 79) was highly critical of the performances of twenty years earlier on the grounds that "the musicians did not seem to understand their roles." As a conductor, he explained the implications of this for rehearsal and performance: "You have to discover how an instrumentalist can play an isolated sound in a way that links it *intelligently* with what has gone before and what follows. You must make him understand a pointillistic phrasing, not just with his intellect but with his physical senses. So long as a player does not realize that when he has a note to play it comes to him from another instrument and passes from him to yet another, . . . he will . . . produce a note that is 'stupid,' divorced from context." As Timothy Day suggests through the judicious juxtaposition of these and other quotations, Boulez was in effect replicating the more general advice offered by the famous modernist conductor Hermann Scherchen (1933, 94) in his *Handbook of Conducting*: "Melodies that are not given out by one soloist throughout, but pass, in subdivision, from one instrument to another, cannot be correctly performed unless each player sings the whole of them as they are played, and contributes his share in accordance with the conception of the whole thus formed."

As it happens, Scherchen had been in the audience six years earlier when the composer Ernst Krenek achieved a musical *succès de scandale* through the premiere of his Second Symphony. According to his biographer John Stewart (1991, 43), Krenek "told the players: 'Now we are going to play a piece which you will not understand one bit. Whoever thinks he has the theme please play very loud.' The players dutifully did so, and the ragged performance had a colossal effect that produced an immediate uproar in the audience." Krenek, in other words, created his musical effect through constructing a social situation in which the players precisely did not listen to or negotiate with one another, resulting in a "vision of terror and catastrophe" that "simply overwhelmed" another audience member, the twenty-year-old Adorno.[2] By contrast, Scherchen's utopian image of an orchestra whose members collectively "sing" the melody of which each plays only a few notes dramatizes the nature and extent of the social interaction involved in orchestral performance. The first and second violinists in the fourth movement of Tchaikovsky's *Pathétique* each "sing" the complete melody, although they play only half of it, and the effort to coordinate individual and social action, matching collective instrumental sound to individually imagined vocalization, arguably results in an effect of concentration, of the forging of social community against the odds, that would be hard to create in any other manner. (Why else would Tchaikovsky have scored it that way?) The hocketing of change ringing, angklung performance, and African horn orchestras can similarly be seen as both fostering and expressing a particular kind of social interdependence and cohesion, and in this way what might too easily be misinterpreted as an extreme form of segmentation or alienation turns out to be more realistically understood as an extreme form of communality. In essence, what we are talking about is distributed cognition. As Burrows (2004, 2) writes, "Cognition may literally be shared among individuals through the mediation of objects, tools, symbols, and signs" (although in Scherchen's case, the mediating element is melody). Tellingly, Burrows introduces the idea of distributed cognition in order to explain the "subtle, web-like interplay" of social and musical relationships that develops in the course of free, collective improvisation—what, in a neat inversion of Jung's terminology, he terms "the collective conscious" (2004).

I conclude from this that the irreducibly social dimension of musical interaction extends all the way from free jazz to modernist orchestral music and that it is only the lingering effect of idealist aesthetic ideologies, on the one hand, and painful racial histories, on the other, that lead us to think otherwise. But I would pursue the argument one step further. I hope I have deconstructed the opposition between jazz and WAM as musical practices. Despite the obvious differences between jazz improvisation and WAM performance, not to mention the equally striking differences between different genres of jazz and WAM, there is a level at which both are socially grounded through mutual listening, real-time interaction, and collectivity. But that does not explain away the image of WAM presented by Johnson and by Rowan. Given WAM's marginalized role in contemporary culture, it is ironic that it remains widely associated with a hegemonic establishment, with institutionalized authority in terms of education and validation, and with bureaucratic documentation. Even if in important ways WAM notations function like Gehry's sketches, the notations look a lot more like the blueprints Gehry did not give to his contractors. The contrast with the highly mythologized culture of free jazz is palpable. But there is a sense in which this might be seen as one of WAM's strengths. We do not live in the utopian community signified by free jazz. We live in an administered world constituted by a hegemonic establishment, institutionalized authority, and bureaucratic documentation. The issue is how we can make this world habitable, how we can personalize and take possession of it in the same way that, in the built environment, individuals "refuse the neat divisions and classifications of the powerful and, in doing so, critique the spatialization of domination" (Cresswell 2006, 47, paraphrasing Michel de Certeau). At a literal level, personal stereo from the Walkman to the iPod has been celebrated as a means of taking possession of the cityscape, but at a deeper and more social level, the most characteristic transformational potential of classical music may lie in its demonstration of how the administered world may be opened up to improvisation, social interaction, and creativity. And seen from such a perspective, music does not just symbolize social actions and relationships: it enacts them. It is not just a metaphor but a metonym.

Second Thoughts

But if that is a conclusion, it is a problematic one for a number of reasons. One is that characterizations of music as the expression of an ideal society tend to be unrealistic and sentimental. Alan Stanbridge (2008, 8) complains about Jacques Attali's "rather idealized claim that free jazz was a prime example of a music that heralded 'the arrival of new social relations' . . . and offered the possibility of the 'emergence of a truly new society.'" (Stanbridge also casts doubt on Attali's basic knowledge of jazz.) A related issue is the extent to which the enactment of social relationships in performance translates into actual relationships between human individuals. I made a distinction between the depersonalized agents of traditional musicological descriptions of Mozart quartets and the social interactions that the music choreographs. But what do these interactions have to do with the actual relationships between the male second violinist and three female members of a student quartet, in which the second violinist was the weakest player but felt that, as a man, he should exercise an authority that was musically inappropriate (Davidson and Goode 2002)? What this shows is that although musicians enact their parts, they do so in the same sense that actors play their roles. While theatrical and cinematic diegesis is based on the difference between the time that is narrated and the time of narration, musical diegesis exists only in real time—but it is still diegesis, and it is as diegesis that it enters the realm of the aesthetic. There is, then, a diegetic gap between the social enactment I have been talking about and the actual social relationships between the players. How easily this gap is jumped is not easy to say. It is the same issue that confronts understanding of the real-world effects of videogames and pornography.

Even if we accept the efficacy of music's directly enacted microsocialities—which represent only the first of Georgina Born's (2010a, 232) four orders of music's social mediation—we still have the issue of how they might be disseminated across society, as Attali's vision implies. According to Gustavo Dudamel, former member and conductor of the Simón Bolívar Youth Orchestra, "An orchestra is a little community, but the perfect community, because you need to listen [to] the other musicians."[3] But what makes the Simón Bolívar Youth Orchestra different from other such ensembles is that it is the apex of an entire system of orchestral education in Venezuela, through which the microsocialities of performance are translated into broader social action. And, of course, if we consider musical participation across all styles and genres rather than merely in relation to WAM, the extent of teenage socialization that is grounded on musical performance adds up to a significant intervention in the wider social order. There is also the issue of how far socialization might be achieved through virtual participation—that is, through watching or listening to music: when I listen to classical chamber music I feel I am hearing the sound of social interaction, and that is what keeps me listening however well I know the music in a score-based, informational sense. In the absence of empirical support, however, the idea that listening can in itself constitute a medium of socialization may amount to no more than wishful thinking.

And then, how can all this be reconciled with the awkward fact that free jazz and classical chamber music—the genres on which I have concentrated, and on which other writers about music and social interaction also concentrate—represent niche practices? It is again Stanbridge (2008, 10) who makes the argument most pointedly: the "more challenging forms of contemporary jazz and improvised music remain resolutely minority tastes," he writes, "which tends to circumscribe rather severely the utopian and far-reaching claims made regarding the development of 'new social relations' or 'the transformation of societies' based primarily on free jazz or the avant-garde." Perhaps, he concludes, the editors of *Critical Studies in Improvisation/Études critiques en improvisation* should acknowledge "not only the positive socio-political potential of improvisatory creative practice, but also its social and political limits" (10). But here the problem may be that, in stressing the socializing power of musical performance, commentators have laid too much emphasis on a few iconic genres in which core values of interaction are elaborated into symbolically resonant representations of ideal societies. After all, real-time processes of entrainment and imitation are widely distributed across the spectrum of the world's music. As Tal-Chen Rabinowitch (2010) explains, entrainment is linked to emotional empathy, "which depends first and foremost on the ability to adjust to someone else's inner pace, to shift from one's own rhythm and be prepared to open up to and synchronize with someone else who is in a different emotional state," while imitation "is able to provide us with an experience that is very close to the first-person experience, enabling us to recognize and internalize the emotional conditions of another." Rabinowitch's experimental study, based on a battery of empathy measures, showed that children who were taking part in a year-long program involving games-based musical participation outperformed a control group who participated in similar games but without the music component.

There is increasing evidence that music has evolved as a means of coordinating social interaction and, in particular, managing situations of social and emotional uncertainty (Cross 2006). If that is the case, it would explain the apparent universality of entrainment as a phenomenon that is equally musical and social. To this extent, as with music and film or music and performance, it is not a matter of music *and* the social, because music is already part of the social (as well as the other way round). And that would imply that there is a level at which the empirical evaluation of music's role in socialization becomes impossible, because—unlike in Rabinowitch's study— there is no possibility of having a control group. The experiment of creating a human society without music has never been attempted.

Notes

1. Since I wrote this paper in 2010, I have developed certain parts of it in *Beyond the Score*: see Cook 2014, esp. chaps. 7–8.

2. I owe this quotation to Matthew Pritchard, who points out that it conflicts with Krenek's account of the incident (in which the words are attributed to the conductor).

3. Verity Sharp, interview with Gustavo Dudamel, *The Culture Show*, BBC Two, June 10, 2008, http://www.bbc.co.uk/cultureshow/videos/2008/06/s5_e2 _dudamel_extra.

CHAPTER 3

FROM THE AMERICAN CIVIL RIGHTS MOVEMENT TO MALI

Reflections on Social Aesthetics and Improvisation

Ingrid Monson

In my view, social aesthetics concerns delineating relationships among aesthetic forms, discourses, positionalities, and social structures. The goal of pondering social aesthetics is not to arrive at an overarching theory encompassing all possible relationships between the aesthetic and the social but, rather, to offer rich interpretations of complexly positioned artistic practices that challenge our taken-for-granted understandings of what music and the social *are*. I begin by mapping out the relationships among these things in my own work and, hence, from within the intellectual trajectory of my training in ethnomusicology and the various interdisciplinary linkages that I have encountered either actively or passively in my many years in academia. The legacy of the literature in ethnomusicology on social aesthetics, it seems to me, is curiously omitted from much of the recent literature.[1] By comparison, the understanding of the social and the aesthetic appearing in the so-called relational aesthetics seems superficial (see Bourriaud 2002).

I have published two books that address in different ways the relationship between the musical and the social: *Freedom Sounds* (2007) and *Saying Something* (1996). In *Freedom Sounds*, I was interested in the impact of macrosocial events on the microsocial world of jazz and especially the effect of large-scale historical events such as the Civil Rights Movement and Black Power Movement on aesthetic debates within jazz. More informally, I describe the book as being about the things everyone fought about in the jazz world: race, politics, black nationalism, integration, civil rights, economics, activism, and aesthetics. To understand the aesthetic debates under way in jazz—particularly the relationship of jazz to various forms of modernism—I argued, it was important to recognize that the agonizing debates over race, black nationalism, color-blindness, and liberal versus radical understandings of social transformation were basically the same as those taking place in the Civil Rights and Black Power movements themselves.

I put forth a three-part theoretical framework to organize my discussion, combining aspects of post-structuralism and practice-theory-oriented anthropological social theory.[2] I suggested that the framework of discourse, practice, and structure might be useful in thinking through the complexities of very polarized debates. I was interested in what people said; what they actually did; and how structural racism, in particular, shaped the possibilities open to various actors in the musical scene. Since these actors took apparently contradictory positions from time to time—at one moment waxing universal about the utopian qualities of the music, and at another, emphasizing the specifically African American need for self-determination—a crucial dimension of my emphasis on practice had to do with understanding that the erection of the essentialist wall between black and white was often situational. That is, it was less a matter of ideology than of pragmatically situated issues of power and respect. The various discourses, including musical ones, that people used to justify their positions in various situations provided a way to get at the very human complexity of the political and musical aspirations of various jazz communities.

The burgeoning Civil Rights Movement called out to jazz by demanding that artists, especially African American artists, do various things to indicate which side they were on—from refusing to play at segregated theaters to playing benefit concerts, participating in demonstrations, and making albums and performances speak to black pride and racial and social justice. The symbolic importance of music as an arena in which the racial hierarchy was inverted—where white musicians struggled to keep up with an African American leadership and African Americans felt compelled and inspired to stay one step ahead of the game—gave improvised music an especially important place in the social and musical discourses of the time. Aesthetic debates over what jazz improvisation was and should be, over which version of aesthetic modernism jazz should embrace, over which sounds were the most political, and over who should play what forms of music and why were politicized in the quest for justice, self-determination, and utopian notions of communal wholeness. African Americans were not the only people transformed by these debates that took place in both the musical and political spheres, as a generation of young liberal and radicalized white Americans also began to question, however incompletely, the politics and aesthetics of whiteness at mid-century.

The crucial issue at the center of the historical analysis in *Freedom Sounds* was the insistence that the aesthetic streams contributing to jazz were far more mobile and hybrid than the sociological and economic statuses of the various demographic groups who played the music. Put another way, the musical language of jazz has been far more pluralistic, democratic, and cosmopolitan than the racially stratified society that produced it. By developing the idea of aesthetic agency, I sought to present a picture of musicians as actors free to draw on a wide variety of aesthetic traditions, whether or not they were historically associated with their home ethnic group. I suggested that musicians at mid-century drew on a palette consisting of five broad aesthetic streams: (1) the aesthetics of African American vernacular music as expressed in jazz, blues, gospel, and rhythm and blues; (2) the aesthetics of American popular song as descended from Tin Pan Alley and musical theater; (3) the aesthetics of modern classical music; (4) the aesthetics of Africa and its diaspora, especially Afro-Cuban music; and (5) the aesthetics of other non-Western music—most notably, in this time period, that of India. Although these aesthetic streams overlap in some respects, there are certain musical resources associated with each one. The African American stream valorized improvisation; intensity of emotional feeling; the rhythmic feels of swing and the shuffle; harmonic progressions from blues, spirituals, and hymns; and timbral complexity. From Tin Pan Alley, musicians learned about song forms, the use of chromatic harmonic in crafting them, and repertory enabling them to cross into the mainstream. From classical music, musicians were inspired by form, orchestration, modern methods of creating sonorities (such as quartal harmony), and the idea of modern art. From the African diaspora came an expanded set of rhythmic feels, such as Afro-Cuban clave rhythms and West African asymmetric time patterns. From other world music, such as Indian music, came ideas of the expanded time frame of improvisation and modal systems beyond those used in the West.

Despite the boundary-shattering musical explorations of various artists, when they left the bandstand they entered a world that insistently put them back into the various social categories they sought to transform. Perhaps the greatest difference between black and white musicians in the 1950s, I argued, was the fact that white musicians had access to structural white privilege, no matter what their individual relationship to the blues and African American aesthetics more broadly, while black musicians experienced structural racial discrimination, no matter what their individual relationship to Western modernism and mainstream culture. Aesthetics alone, in other words, could not achieve social transformation.

In *Saying Something*, I addressed the way interactive improvisational processes operated at both a musical and an interpersonal level and the processes by which they indexed larger social issues, especially race. The direction of analysis accomplished in *Freedom Sounds* was reversed in *Saying Something*: I moved instead from microsocial to macrosocial. In ensembles building emergent musical trajectories through improvisation, I suggested that the relationships among sounds were simultaneously relationships among people. Consequently, inherently social as well as musical bonds were created in improvisational performance. I had in mind acoustic musical performances of musicians performing in the same place and at the same time, something that the vast expansion of digital and electronic capabilities has rendered but a small spectrum of contemporary performance possibilities.[3]

In *Saying Something*, the idea that music and, especially, improvisation create social bonds was hardly new at the time I wrote, as a long-standing conversation in ethnomusicology about the relationship between the social and the musical was well known. I took my point of departure from Steven Feld's article "Sound Structure as Social Structure" (1984), the title itself a paraphrasing of Alan Lomax's "Song Structure and Social Structure" (1962). Feld's article critiqued Lomax's cantometrics project, which attempted to correlate in a rather deterministic fashion sound characteristics with social and cultural traits. Like other discussions of improvisational and participatory music in ethnomusicology, Feld's (1994) analysis of the music of the Kaluli in Papua New Guinea associated the classless egalitarian social structure of Kaluli society with the participatory, multipart organization of the musical aesthetic of Kaluli "lift-up-over-sounding." The ceremonies in which music making took place, which had as their principle objective moving the audience, especially women, to tears, were not in his opinion arenas for the demonstration of power. As Feld wrote, "Soundmaking provides no format for the assertion of power, dominance, or personal excellence at the cost of others. The recognition of skill in composition and performance is clear, and its pragmatic outcome is the weeping of the hosts. Despite all this, competition is not a major agenda in the ceremonies, and the provocation involved is not a manipulation for the sake of power" (393). Although Feld implicitly argued for a correlation between egalitarian social structures and participatory musical making, he recognized the limits of mapping supposedly egalitarian social structures onto sound structures. Men, he noted, appropriated and controlled the most prestigious expressive resources, generated a social focus on themselves and their evocative powers, while the expressive weeping of the women mobilized far less social power. Even in an egalitarian social structure, in other words, Feld recognized the existence of inequalities and unequal distribution of prestige. Nevertheless, the tendency to map participatory musical experiences onto a utopian ideal of a liberatory equality achieved through music remains a persistent discourse surrounding improvisational musics of the African diaspora, jazz, and popular music. It seems to have been my function in the literature to rain on the parade by insisting that, however emotionally satisfying and spiritually transforming improvisational performance can feel, issues of power and prestige persist whether they take the form of leader-side person relationships within a band, aesthetic respect or lack thereof, gender dynamics, racial dynamics, or something else drawing a line of inclusion or exclusion. I might also explain my position by saying that I do not deny that transcendent social and musical connections can be and often are created in performance; nevertheless, a great deal in the life of professional and nonprofessional music making falls short of this ideal. Once the band leaves the stage, the performers and audience members return to the everyday world—perhaps nourished, revitalized, moved, and inspired but pushed by forces larger than themselves back into the various positionalities they occupied before the performance. There are limits, in other words, to the social relations that improvisational musical performance can create.

I find myself much in sympathy with Claire Bishop (2004), who is suspicious of the emancipatory claims made for the collaborative, relational work of art which Nicolas Bourriaud argues should be judged by the social relations that it produces. The open-ended artwork—not framed by or resulting in an object, insisting on the participation of its audience, not existing without the participation of the audience—may offer something revelatory to the art world transcending the "shelter" of art history of the 1960s and its values, but to me it reinscribes something utterly '60s in music: emancipatory claims for artistic practices veiling nagging hierarchies, power plays, and human fallibility, even in the most sincere. Just what frame is required to have everyday experience, such as cooking and eating, turned into relational art, after all? The setting and the audience seem paramount—an art gallery populated by the strata of people who circulate through art galleries—and create the frame of artistic significance for what, were it to take place in a kitchen in Flatbush where neighbors stop by, is simply an everyday activity. The ability to frame such things as art requires a set of positionalities that are anything but innocent of power and prestige.

My career-long suspicion of overly emancipatory claims for improvisation is informed most directly by the gendered walls of inclusion and exclusion that seemed to haunt my experiences as a trumpet player. From my gendered position, for example, I could easily see the hypocrisy of white men claiming to be excluded by black players, for few seemed to see an ethical problem in the exclusion of women. Women somehow deserved exclusion due to our inadequate skill or because having us on the stage with the real (male) musicians somehow undercut the mystique of the entire enterprise. We were seldom status-enhancing, in other words, even if we played well and had good camaraderie with our male colleagues. Although things have improved since those days—with the success of amazing players and composers such as Ingrid Jensen, Matana Roberts, Geri Allen, and Maria Schneider—the complexity of the relationships between participatory musical forms and the quality of social relations produced by them seems to be particularly visible when issues of gender are factored into the rest of the social picture. Sherrie Tucker, of course, is the one who has written the most eloquently about this subject (see esp. Tucker 2000).

My discomfort with uncritical claims for the creation of new social relations through music has led me to take the position that ensemble improvisation is not inherently egalitarian or emancipatory; instead, it offers only the *potential* for such human interaction, necessarily subject to the very human and social shortcomings the various individuals bring into the circle of sound that frames musical experience. Can that circle of sound transform us internally? Of course. Can the internal transformation inspire the self-conscious creation of new forms of social organization? Yes. Can it just be fun? Yes. Can it eliminate global hierarchies, anomie, economic stratification, poverty, racism, and disease? Not by itself. Whatever microsocial claims we make for musical process as modeling the social relations we would like to achieve, in other words, need to be tempered by a larger understanding of power and social hierarchy.

My most recent work in Mali with the balafonist Neba Solo illustrates an improvisational music that has a different relationship to the discourses and values generally assumed in defining aesthetics and social consciousness in improvisational and popular music in the United States and Europe. Although many aspects of modernist aesthetics are alive and well in Mali— the importance of originality and virtuosity and a special place for the artist—there is a far less oppositional stance to society and tradition than has usually be associated with the rebellious stances of figures such as Charles Mingus, Max Roach, and Public Enemy. In most musical styles in Mali, tradition is actively invoked to exhort people to live up to the deeds and values of their ancestors, even if in practice people fall short.

I should qualify this claim by saying that in the past decade there has been noticeable growth in the presence of hip hop, especially in the capital city, Bamako, and that many young rappers have taken on the oppositional stance, attitude, and styles of American hip hop. They nevertheless operate in a popular music scene dominated by the broader aesthetic I am about to describe. In 2002, I began doing ethnographic work on Neba Solo (whose given name is Souleymane Traoré) from Sikasso, Mali's second-largest city. Mr. Traoré is a Senufo *bala* (wooden xylophone) virtuoso who is widely known in Mali as the *balafon* (genius of the bala), but he has a relatively low international profile. He is fabulously virtuosic as an improviser and a composer of complex compositions and arrangements, and his songs' lyrics comment on contemporary social and public health issues, such as vaccination, AIDS, female excision, environmental protection, and political corruption. Traoré views part of his mission as sensitizing people to important ethical and political issues of the day, as well as alerting them about what they can do to keep themselves healthy. *Vaccination*, his song urging people to get their children vaccinated, was written in 1997 to persuade elders that allowing the vaccination of children was important, despite rumors that it caused sterility. Since only 30 percent of Malian youth are literate, the exhortations of musicians are an important arena of public health education.

Neba Solo's composition *Yiri* is both a homage to trees and a call for environmental responsibility. The song recounts the richness of the gifts of trees, from shea butter to medicine and food, and urges people to honor and respect them as living beings and to refrain from burning them in the countryside, which will ultimately cause deforestation and desertification.[4] Traoré's social message is personalized by testifying to all the things that he has received as the result of trees, for the bala itself is made of wood. He and his band members are especially proud that the Senufo use the wood only of trees that have died naturally.

Neba Solo's music is not traditional in the usual sense of the word. Rather, his music represents a professionalization, modernization, and reconfiguration of traditional Senufo bala music. When he was eighteen years old, in 1987, Solo heard Alpha Blondy's reggae recording of *Jersualem* as he walked through the streets of Bamako. He was enchanted by the bass line and was inspired to try building a bala with added bass notes when he returned home. His father and other Senufo were at first skeptical of the changes he wanted to make to the instrument. By Senufo tradition, in order to proceed Traoré had to secure his father's permission. They came to an agreement: he would be allowed a period of time in which to develop his ideas and make a recording. If the results pleased his father, he would give his blessing to his son's musical direction. He added three bass notes to the traditional seventeen keys and experimented with various tunings. First and foremost, he wanted to expand the role of the bass line in his music. His new version of traditional Senufo musical pieces, with an expanded texture and new tuning, earned the approval of both his father and local audiences.[5]

The new style reconfigured the musical ensemble. Traoré used two balas instead of the traditional three. The accompaniment parts were distributed between the two instruments: the treble bala player typically improvises melodies with the right hand while playing accompaniment parts with the left hand; the bass bala player usually improvises bass lines with the left hand and plays accompaniment parts with the right hand. The interplay between the two balas creates a rich contrapuntal texture between interlocking parts. In performance, Neba Solo (on the bass bala) and his brother Siaka Traoré create endlessly rich textures by modulating from one configuration of parts to another. This new contemporary sound for the bala modernized an instrument that had been dismissed by urban dwellers as a primarily village instrument that was not suitable for modern (professionalized urban) music. Indeed, to understand the respect with which Solo is now regarded, one needs to know that when he first came to Sikasso many dismissed him as a player of the *fali gala bugula*, or donkey ribs. When he and his group were scheduled to play on the anniversary of Radio Kene in Sikasso, the station's director, Daouda Mariko, took one look at the balas and bara drums (signs of the village) and asked them to leave the stage. They began to play offstage and won over both the audience and Mariko, who became one of Neba Solo's principal advocates.[6] In this sense, Traoré has become a figure of particular pride for the people of Kenedougou who live in the dozens of small villages surrounding Sikasso.

The moral exhortations in Malian music sometimes surprise my students, many of whom have drawn from Western representations the idea that African music is about lack of restraint and bourgeois inhibitions. The work ethic expressed in Neba Solo's song *Bɛɛ k'i Bemba* (Let's Strive), has strong cross-cultural resonances with the Protestant work ethic but also expresses a kind of patriotism that is consistent with the Malian national motto: One People, One Goal, One Faith (*Un peuple, un but, une foi; Jama kelen, kuntilenna kelen, ŋaniya kelen*). Neba Solo is directing his comments not to individual ethnic groups, such as the Senufo, Fulbe, Maraka, Bamana, or Dogon, but to all of Mali, a place where developing and improving the country is a major preoccupation.

NEBA SOLO, *BƐƐ K'I BEMBA* (LET'S STRIVE)
Se ko ni don ko dugu jɛ le
Bɛɛ k'i jija ka bara kɛ
Kenedugu mɔgɔbaluw
Senekelaw o yo
Bagan maralaw o
Bɛɛ k'i jija ka bara kɛ
Bɛɛ k'i jija

Faso denw minw bɛ jamana kɔnɔ
Faso denw mun bɛ jamana kɔ kan
N'aw ye aw kɔfilɛ faso la
Faso nin bɛ diya
An ka dugu bɛ diya
An ka jamana bɛ diya, o ho

O farafin denw
A y'i wuli o
Anw ka bara
Ni anw ma bara kɛ
Fangantanya tɛna b'anw na
N'anw ma bara kɛ
Gɛlɛya jugu tɛna b'anw na
N'anw ma bara kɛ
Kɔngɔ jugu tɛna b'anw na
Bɛɛk'i bemba ka bemba
Bɛɛk'i bemba ka bemba
Se ko ni don ko dugu jɛ le
Bɛɛ k'i jija ka bara kɛ

| | | |

The time has come for our culture to come to light
Let's all strive in our work

Dignitaries of *kenedugu*
Great farmers
Great herders
Let's all strive in our work
Let's strive

Malians living here
Malians living abroad
If you remember the homeland
It will be a better place
Our country will be a better place
Our country will be a better place

Black people
Stand up
Let's work
If we do not work
Powerlessness will not end
If we do not work
Hard times won't end
If we do not work
Hunger will not end
Let's all strive, let's strive
Let's all strive, let's strive
It is time to show our culture
Let's all strive in our work

In the song *Sababu*, Solo exhorts people to do good by invoking divine cause, or *sababu*. The religious expression in the text—which advises people not to be arrogant, because God can take away what he has given—gives some feeling for the pervasiveness of everyday invocation of God in Mali, a country where 94 percent of the population self-identifies as Muslim. Although Muslim spirituality is directly invoked in this piece, the line between Islamic and traditional spiritual beliefs is often quite blurry.

NEBA SOLO, *SABABU*
Ka n'i wasɔ fangantan lu la
k'i ele ye waritigi ye duɲaɲa
Ala min ye ele ke waritigi ye
O Ala kelen b'i se k'i kɛ fantan ye
I miiri o la, i kana yada, yada

Kana i waso ko mogolu la
k'i ele ye ɲemɔgɔba ye
Ala min ye ele ke ɲemɔgɔba ye
O Ala kelen bɛ se ki kɛ ko mɔgɔ ye
I miiri o la, i kana yada yada

Ka n'i waso denwtan nu la
K'i ele ye dentigi ye duniya na
Ala min ye i ele kɛ dentigi o
O Ala kelen bɛ se k'i ke dentanya ye
I miiri o la, i kana yada yada

  | | |

Do not show off among poor people
about your money in this life
God who made you rich
Can make you poor
Think about that, do not be arrogant

Do not show off
because you are a great leader
God who made you a great leader
Ala can also make you a common person
Think about that, do not be arrogant

Do not boast among those who are childless
because you have children
God who gave you children
Can also make you childless
Think about that, do not be arrogant

Sababu's exhortations to not be arrogant highlights a very important principle of Malian ethics: *mɔgɔya*, or being a good person. A common Bamanankan expression is, "Foyi te mɔgɔya bɔ." Nothing is better than being a good person; even if you do not have money, if you have good relations with other people, you are rich.[7] Western travelers are often surprised by the generosity and hospitality of Malians, despite the crushing poverty and lack of infrastructure in the country. There is relatively little petty street crime toward Western visitors, despite the tremendous disparity in economic status.

Much of Malian music, including the music of *jeliya* (or the music of the griots), reminds people of the fundamental principles of being a good person in Mali, which include greeting people, thanking God, hospitality, respect, and living up to the wisdom of the elders and ancestors. Most songs of political and social critique point out the ways in which people have failed to live up to these traditional principles, which are broadly shared across Mali's multiple ethnic and language groups. A generational split of greater intensity is emerging in the world of Bamako hip hop over the mode of acceptable critique. A standard trope in song lyrics of social critique is to ask for forgiveness before criticizing one's target. Many in the older generations find the mode of critique in hip hop to be too disrespectful—that is, lacking in the principles of mɔgɔya.

The idea of improvisation as contributing to the making of community is certainly a value shared across the cultural divide between Mali and the West. So are ideas of being an artist, originality, and the linking of music through technology to the broader world. The idea of sonic dissonance and avant-garde experimentalism as a sign of social and cultural critique, however, is pretty foreign. Although there are hierarchies of musical style in Mali—with international stars (such as Salif Keita, Oumou Sangare, and Toumani Diabate) at the top, followed by the music of the *jeliw* (griots), urbanized popular music, regional traditional stars, and village musicians— they are marked not so much by musical language as by professionalized performance practices and economics. Being popular is a good thing, not a sign of lack of seriousness in one's art. Bamako elites attend performances of the most famous stars, often in expensive traditional clothing and jewelry, and paying prices that would be prohibitive to most. They hear exhortations to live up to their ancestors, often from singers who circulate through the crowd, singling them out and reciting the history of their families. While there are love songs, and cautionary tales about the trials and tribulations of romantic relationships, there is very little sexual explicitness by American standards. The public primness of much performance is belied by the neverending gossip about the actual humanly fallible personal lives of various performers, but in general the defiance and countercultural assertiveness that seem endemic to Western ideas of social engagement through music seem mostly to be missing. Artists seem to critique from inside a larger sense of tradition rather than in opposition to it.

In thinking about social aesthetics cross-culturally, that is, relationships among aesthetic forms, discourses, positionalities, and social structures, it is helpful to consider issues of power at all levels of analysis. A series of questions lead to some conclusions. Who is included/excluded in the musical circle or, conversely, what are the criteria for entrance? What are the ethical values developed by musical practice and how are they evaluated by larger audiences? Which musical tropes, lyrical themes, and participatory practices index a performance to larger-scale social and political issues? How do social stuctures, geopolitical issues, religion, economics, race, and politics affect the music industries in particular locales? Do Western presumptions about aesthetics, resistance, and music apply in whole or in part? Analyzing social aesthetics cross-culturally requires thinking broadly and noticing overlaps and resonances in geographically distanced musical practices, while cultivating grounded ethnographic and historical research. Such empirical contextualization serves to illuminate compelling differences, raise new interpretive questions, and temper the all-too-human tendency to overgeneralize.

Notes

1. Examples of work on social aesethics in ethnomusicology include Feld 1982, 1988; Meintjes 2003; Monson 1996; Perlman 1998.

2. Literature that was important to shaping my perspective includes Comaroff and Comaroff 1991, 1997; Bourdieu 1977; Foucault 1972; Giddens 1984; Ortner 1996; Sewell 1992.

3. In the Internet age, what interests me is how the computer has become a nonhuman interactant, enabling musical interaction across different times and spaces, as well as an instrument that has moved contemporary popular music in a direction that is more compositional than improvisational. The nature of the social connections and communities forged through such digital mediations, it seems to me, is an open question and one that contemporary researchers are bound to illuminate in the coming years.

4. In Mali, it is not uncommon to see fires alongside the road in the dry season. In some cases, people set fires to chase game from the brush. More problematically, some people set fires for fun.

5. Interview with Neba Solo and Yacouba Traoré, January 12, 2005, Sikasso, Mali.

6. Interview with Neba Solo, February 16, 2006, Sikasso, Mali.

7. Indeed, Charles Bird's textbook on the Bamanankan language includes a discussion of this principle in a teaching text: see Bird and Kante 1977. See also Skinner 2015, for a comprehensive account of the use of *mɔgɔya* among artists in Bamako.

CHAPTER 4

FROM NETWORK BANDS TO UBIQUITOUS COMPUTING

Rich Gold and the Social Aesthetics of Interactivity

George E. Lewis

Since its inception in the early 1970s, the loosely constituted field of inter-active computer music has drawn on artificial intelligence (AI), cybernet-ics, and socio-musical networks of free improvisation in creating models of social aesthetics that include machines as central actors. Interactions with these systems in musical performance produce a kind of virtual sociality that both draws from and challenges traditional notions of human inter-activity and sociality. Efforts to imbue interactive systems with values such as relative autonomy, integral subjectivity, and computer individualism, and with musical uniqueness rather than repeatability, were accompanied by an upsurge of bricolage and homegrown elements that were seen as mani-festing resistance to institutional hegemonies. Musical computers were de-signed to stake out territory, assert both identities and positions, assess and respond to conditions, and maintain relativities of distance—all elements of improvisation, in and out of music.

Among a number of interactive artist-theorists, Simon Penny (2016, 402) has been particularly perceptive in observing that the advent of real-time computational technologies has led to art "objects"—artifacts that "possess behavior, 'make decisions' and 'take actions' based on changes in its context in real time." According to Penny, "This development has led to categori-cally new kinds of cultural practices" (401), for which aesthetic theory has been lacking. Today, according to Penny, these kinds of systems include such "new media" forms as "online interactive worlds, augmented and mixed reality work, locative media and fully physically embodied interactive installation and performance—in single and multiple participant, discrete and distributed modalities" (401).

Recent new media histories (see Chandler and Neumark 2005; Salter 2010) have implicitly challenged the field's conventional wisdom that traces the origins of interactive computer-based art making to the mid-1980s. Around the time that the first voltage-controlled synthesizers were being invented by Donald Buchla and Robert Moog, the young composer Joel Chadabe (1997, 286) was putting together hybrid analog-digital constructions that generated music autonomously by means of pseudo-random processes. By 1977, Chadabe had created one of the earliest computer systems for live musical performance. The heart of Chadabe's CEMS system was a Digital Equipment Corporation PDP-11 "minicomputer," which was able to both input and transform analog data and control analog hardware. Frequently found in academic music departments, minicomputers were relatively portable in that, unlike the mainframe systems of the period, they could be loaded into a van or truck and transported to concert sites.

Chadabe (1997, 291) characterized his devices as the first fruits of a practice of "interactive composition" in which the instruments "made musical decisions, or at least seemed to make musical decisions, as they produced sound and as they responded to a performer. These instruments were interactive in the sense that performer and instrument were mutually influential. The performer was influenced by the music produced by the instrument, and the instrument was influenced by the performer's controls." Roughly coterminous with Chadabe's work, a number of young composers began making interactive computer music using the new eight-bit microcomputers, systems far more portable and less expensive than Chadabe's. Much of the most influential work took place in the San Francisco Bay Area, a center for experimental music since the 1950s. Their music and ideas were developed in itinerant settings among independent researchers, designers, and artists in public performance spaces such as the Blind Lemon in Berkeley and, most crucially, the Center for Contemporary Music at Mills College, which became an important gathering place for new ideas and practices around the emerging interactive directions.

The college already possessed a strong reputation for supporting cutting-edge music. In the 1930s, the Mills Concert Hall featured performances of works by Béla Bartók, Henry Cowell, Igor Stravinsky, and Anton Webern, as well as the American premiere of Alban Berg's *Lyric Suite*. Around the time that Darius Milhaud began his long tenure at Mills in 1940, John Cage was teaching music (in the Department of Dance). Harry Partch lived at Mills for two years, between 1951 and 1953, and among the composers who taught at Mills over the years were Luciano Berio, Lou Harrison, Pauline Oliveros, Morton Subotnick, Iannis Xenakis, Anthony Braxton, Gordon Mumma, David Rosenboom, Frederic Rzewski, Larry Polansky, Maryanne Amacher, Alvin Curran, and Roscoe Mitchell. Former Mills students represent a great diversity of musical directions; among those whose work intersected with experimental music were Subotnick, Maggi Payne, Laetitia Sonami, Paul DeMarinis, Charles Amirkhanian, Leland Smith, Richard Felciano, Miya Masaoka, Steve Reich, Dana Reason, and Frankie Mann.[1]

In 1966, the San Francisco Tape Center, founded in 1961 by Subotnick and Ramon Sender, received a Rockefeller Foundation grant that supported its eventual move to Mills, where in due course it became the Center for Contemporary Music (CCM), with Oliveros as its first director.[2] In 1969, Robert Ashley became a co-director of the CCM, and in 1978, his fellow Sonic Arts Union founder, David Behrman, joined him.

While the Bay Area has continued to produce what, at this writing, amounts to nearly two generations of innovative computer music artists, this chapter focuses on the early flowering of the scene, as represented by the work of the League of Automatic Music Composers and the artists and institutions surrounding it. The earliest version of the League was formed by a group of Mills graduates and graduate student composers, including John Bischoff, Jim Horton, and Rich Gold, and remained active until 1983 (Chadabe 1997, 296). Other active members of the League included Donald Day, Tim Perkis, and Behrman, who became a key early adopter of the KIM-1, which he used along with his own "homemade" electronics to produce one of the first released recordings of interactive computer music, *On the Other Ocean* (Bischoff 1991).[3]

After presenting a sense of the developing social aesthetics of that scene—in particular, its connection with practices of improvisation—I pursue the evidence for my contention that the work of Rich Gold (1950–2003), a co-founder of the League of Automatic Music Composers, bridges the historical lacuna separating practices of interactivity in computer music of the early 1970s from the development of interactive multimedia in the 1980s. Gold's later work in the corporate sector and at the Xerox Palo Alto Research Center (PARC) was influential on new models of gaming and, in particular, the early development of ubiquitous computing, a technology that framed relations among people and interactive systems as microcosms of the social. Both system design and real-time interactions with the results were marked by a utopian politics of interactivity, with an emphasis on establishing non-hierarchical, collaborative, and conversational social spaces that were none-theless indeterminate at the level of structure—aspects of a social aesthetics of free improvisation that dates from the mid-1960s. Through Gold, these technologies continue to exhibit the genetic imprint of the social aesthetics of early Bay Area interactive music practices.

"Let the Network Play"

This early period produced a number of "interactive" or "computer-driven" works and practices, representing a great diversity of approaches to the question of what interactivity (then usually called "interaction") was and how it affected viewers, listeners, and audiences. In many cases, works were designed precisely to stimulate this kind of reflection, to explore communication not only between people and machines, but also between people and other people. The ideals of this creative community also reflected emerging debates and social changes in U.S. society, with particular emphasis on emergent musical phenomena; itinerant rather than institutional activity; social, conversational, convivial, and communitarian ethics; and collective, networked, democratic work, expressed in terms of a lack of hierarchy between human and non-human roles, as well as between humans and other humans.

Chris Salter (2010, 206) recounts the reminiscences of Joel Ryan and David Behrman, who saw the Mills scene as "driven by an anti-authoritarian attitude combined with an experimental atmosphere of tinkering and aesthetic curiosity." Indeed, the developing social aesthetics of this scene embraced bricolage and autodidacticism, reflected in preferences (born of economic necessity, to be sure) for portable, inexpensive, homegrown, and personal systems rather than general-purpose devices, and for an artist-programmer model of techno-musical development rather than institutional separation of roles.

At many public events, artists from around the community would present electronic circuits and software of their own design to audiences and other composers (Chandler and Neumark 2005, 378). In this way, the new technology was also widely viewed as providing possibilities for itinerant social formations that could challenge institutional authority and power. As League members Gold, Horton, and Bischoff (1978, 28) declared, "The advent of not-very-expensive micro-systems can help free the computer musician from the pressure to conform to the mores of highly-structured business and academic institutions."

Salter (2010, 206) identifies the Bay Area scene around Mills College as "the first known use of cheap, portable computing technology for real-time musical performance." League members, among a number of other Bay Area artists, adopted as their computing platform the MOS Technology KIM-1, one of the first single-board microcomputers. The KIM (an acronym for "Keyboard Input Module"), which could be had via mail order for as little as $250, sported an eight-bit microprocessor running at 1 megahertz, an interface and timer chip, an operating system stored in read-only memory (ROM), a hexadecimal LED readout, and anywhere from 1,000 to 4,000 bytes of random-access memory (RAM).

John Bischoff called the League of Automatic Music Composers "the world's first computer network band."[4] From the start, as Bischoff and his colleagues declared, they intended to create computer music that valorized sociality and performativity, concepts that they mapped onto the signifier of the "band":

> Music over the milleniums [sic], traditionally, has involved more than one person, either in its composition, in its production or both. In fact, it seems to be one of the most social of the artforms. While there has been individually produced music as well, computer music, until very recently, because of its nature, could only be individual, solitary music. However, with the introduction of microprocessors at a reasonable cost, composers can now own their own computers, and, operating free from major institutions, true computer bands are possible. While such bands can take many forms, network music seems best suited and the most contemporary. (Bischoff et al. 1978, 24–25)

This model of performance presented a new model of liveness that included computers as part of the matrix while affirming the central place of the human: "To bring into play the full bandwidth of communication there seems to be no substitute, for mammals at least, than [sic] the playing of music live" (28).

Each of the League's computers was running a program created by one of its composers that was able to produce music without outside intervention—an automatic composition (or improvisation) program—as well as taking in data that could affect the behavior of its own system and outputting data that could affect the behavior of the other machines.[5] Jim Horton's description of a performance by Bischoff, Tim Perkis, and himself in 1980 encapsulates the characteristic social aesthetic behind the approach:

The musical system can be thought of as three stations each playing its own "sub"-composition which receives and generates information relevant to the real-time improvisation. No one station has an overall score. The non-hierarchical structure of the network encourages multiplicity of viewpoints and allows separate parts in the system to function in a variety of musical modes. This means that the moment-to-moment form the music takes is the combined result of the overlapping individual activities of the parts with the coordinating influence of the data exchanged between the computers.[6] (Horton 1999)

League performances were exoskeletal; the composers were often seen programming, debugging, and even soldering as the concert proceeded. "Envision a table full of electronic circuits, little boxes, computers, all kinds of wires and so forth," Horton told an interviewer. "A typical concert would be us at this table, continually fooling around with electronics, changing parameters on the programs" (1999).

Particularly transgressive was the League's penchant for simply sitting back and listening as the computers created the music. League performances often cast the computer in the role of independent composer-performer rather than instrumentalist. In 1979, the League set up a biweekly series of concerts at the East Bay Center for the Performing Arts. As Bischoff recalled, "Every other Sunday afternoon we spent a few hours setting up our network of KIMs at the Finnish Hall in Berkeley and let the network play, with tinkering here and there, for an hour or two" (quoted in Chandler and Neumark 2005, 378). Often, the composers would leave the stage and join the audience as the computers played (380).

As Bischoff remembers, "After a while it seemed more fun to perform along with the network, so we began to sit around our large table of gear, adjusting parameters on the fly in an attempt to nudge the music this way or that" (quoted in Chandler and Neumark 2005, 380–81). However, it is important to note that when League members took hands-on improvisative roles with their machines, they did so from a collaborative rather than an instrumental standpoint, negotiating with their machines rather than fully controlling them. "Letting the network play" became a key aspect of its performance practice, and when the humans performed, they became part of the network, as well.

Several possible precursors and probable influences on the League and other artists in this scene can be identified. First, in terms of processes and materials, the work of this scene appears closely related to the open-form music of Christian Wolff, who created compositions for performing musicians in which complex structures emerged from the results of several interacting decision-making processes rather than the chance operations for which Cage was noted. Works such as "For 1, 2, or 3 People" (1964) require the musicians to perform actions according to, among other things, their perceptions of what other musicians are doing, their position in the score, and certain overarching rules. The composer provides an environment in which real-time decision making by performers, and therefore responsibility for the direction of the music, is paramount.[7] The similarity of this human-driven performance process to the processes of networked exchanges of musical data that we see in the work of the early interactive computer musicians is striking. As Bischoff and his colleagues (1978, 28) wrote, "An extension of that idea is to write 'reactive' compositions which can interact with one another as well as with their players."

Second, in the wake of works such as Cage's *Cartridge Music* (1960), work on electrically and electronically modified acoustic sound developed into a practice of "live electronic music" that differentiated itself in terms of approaches to temporality and performativity (and, in many unacknowledged cases, improvisativity) from electronic works whose primary medium of presentation was magnetic tape playback. Composers associated with Cage, such as Behrman and Gordon Mumma, invented hardware to transform human sounds and gestures musically. Mumma's series of "cybersonic" works, beginning with *Medium Size Mograph* (1963), were "hardware compositions," pieces for which the "score" would include a circuit diagram.

Mumma's *Hornpipe* (1967) for horn and electronics appears particularly prescient with respect to what was coming in live computer music:

> The acoustical feedback loop which exists between the French Horn, the resonant pipes, and the loudspeaker, is part of an electronic feedback system which employs amplitude gated frequency translation. As the performance begins the system is balanced. Sound is produced only when something in the acoustic-electronic feedback-loop system is unbalanced. The initial sounds produced by the French Hornist unbalance parts of the system, some of which rebalance themselves and unbalance other parts of the system. The performer's task is to balance and unbalance the right thing at the right time, in the proper sequence. (Mumma 1967)

The conception of performance as task in *Hornpipe* is both dialogic and exploratory. The performer treats the electronics as a quasi-independent co-performer and can glean the inner state of the electronics only by making a sound and ascertaining its effects through listening observation. The music results from three factors: the acceptance and performance of the task of restoring balance, the real-time adjustments in musical strategy by the performer, and the similarly real-time sonic behavior in response to the performer's initiatives.

Following Mikel Dufrenne (1989, 196), the electronics become a quasi-subject, an object not simply and totally constituted by a Kantian perceiving and constituting subject: "But what of a world of the aesthetic object? We may speak of this too—if the aesthetic object is a quasi-subject, that is, if it is capable of expression. In order to express, the aesthetic object must transcend itself toward a signification which is not the explicit signification attached to representations but a more fundamental signification that projects a world." The performance as whole becomes a form of real-time world making, a roughly delineated, reciprocal mediation between the exhibited behavior of human and machine actants.

Third, a number of the early interactive pieces drew on open-form compositional procedures, and a number of these composer-performer-technologists directly identify Cage as a major influence in terms of pioneering "an important form of collaborative music, that is of the simultaneous playing of compositions" (Bischoff et al. 1978, 28). Thus, the composers advance an aesthetic of emergence *avant la lettre*: "Independent simultaneous activities viewed as one single activity always bring to mind the idea that groups can work wonderfully together without the anxiety of control structures that supposedly insure success" (27). What also comes to mind is a notion of productive freedom rooted in anarchy, and in that regard it comes as no surprise that for these composers, "Making music together using ideas and structures developed independently without thought of future collaboration now seems a natural musical process due, in large part, to the work of John Cage," himself an avowed anarchist (27).

At the same time, in contrast to Cage's well-known antipathy to jazz, the League's members express a social aesthetic of voice that would be familiar to any jazz musician: "At this stage in the development of the experimental tradition it is thought well to develop a personal, even idiosyncratic, approach to music. To find such an approach is not always easy" (Bischoff et al. 1978, 28). We can easily compare this to the Afrological trope of "telling your own story" (G. E. Lewis 1996, 118–19). A similar affinity with both Cageian aesthetics and the Afrological arises as the composers declare, "At each stage in the development of the network the music changed unpredictably. It became clear that it was impossible to tell beforehand where the music was going to come from (Bischoff et al. 1978, 28)." Similarly, the saxophonist Steve Lacy observed of his musical practice of improvisation, "You have all your years of preparation and all your sensibilities and your prepared means but it is a leap into the unknown" (quoted in Bailey 1992, 57).

"Listening to the combined result," wrote Bischoff and Chris Brown, a computer musician and professor at Mills College, in 2005, "one hears independent musical processes at work—each station has its distinct musical viewpoint—along with the coordination of those processes through a real-time choreography of data flow" (quoted in Chandler and Neumark 2005, 381). This aesthetic valorization of the melding of individual voice with the unforeseen undoubtedly stems from the machine-improvised nature of the networked music itself. "At times, the computers did indeed seem to have minds of their own," Horton (1999) wrote, "sounding not unlike a group of musicians playing off each other, be it free improvisation or an almost unified consciousness." Indeed, we can read Horton's recollections in terms suggested by sociologist of science Andrew Pickering (2010), as an account of post-humanist dances of human and nonhuman agency: "Sometimes when the system enters a strong interactive mode, its activities may be heard as if there is a unified mentality improvising or composing. Because the semantics of whether we can ascribe intentional acts to nonliving entities seems to be open, we can choose to consider that we have invented a (partially guided) musical artificial intelligence" (Horton 1999). With regard to this aspect of League ideals, I want to take into account Nicolas Bourriaud's (2002, 14) declaration that "the possibility of a *relational* art (an art taking as its theoretical horizon the realm of human interactions and its social context, rather than the assertion of an independent and private symbolic space), points to a radical upheaval of the aesthetic, cultural and political goals introduced by modern art." One of these upheavals has to do with Penny's (1995, 216) observation of "a novel art form in which the key aesthetic element is the 'behavior' of the work in response to the viewer." We do not need to embrace Bourriaud's urban-based origin narrative for the aesthetics of relational art to see that the League's version of interactive computer music making, following Bourriaud, is a kind of work for which quasi-independent behavior is key, where "the substrate is formed by intersubjectivity, and which takes being-together as a central theme, the 'encounter' between beholder and picture, and the collective elaboration of meaning" (Bourriaud 2002, 15).[8]

In the particular form of sociality created by the League's interactive performances, a world is constructed in which the hierarchy of agency of humans over machines is not at all axiomatic.

Bourriaud does not address technological artmaking directly, but a work of relational art, in his view, "may operate like a relational device containing a certain degree of randomness, or a machine provoking and managing individual and group encounters" (30). Relational works propose "moments of sociability" and present "objects producing sociability." Membership in the relational world is centered on this primary criterion: "Does this work permit me to enter into dialogue? Could I exist, and how, in the space it defines?" (109).

Cybernetics and AI discourses were important influences on this generation of computer music artists. Horton's posthumously published diaries, "Unforeseen Music: The Autobiographical Notes of Jim Horton," composed in August 1996, set out a number of elements of an emerging social aesthetics of interactivity that are not only compatible with Bourriaud's ideas but are also strongly inflected by AI and cybernetics discourses. In one diary entry, Horton explicitly cited the cyberneticist Gregory Bateson's ideas as an influence on a performance of 1980:

1. A mind is an aggregate of interacting parts or components.
2. The interaction between parts of mind is triggered by differences [*sic, difference*].
3. Mental processes require collateral energy.
4. In mental processes, the effects of difference are to be regarded as transforms (i.e., coded versions) of events which precede them.
5. Mental processes require [*sic, Mental process requires*] circular (or more complex) chains of determination.
6. The description and classification of these processes of transformation disclose a hierarchy of logical types immanent in the phenomena. (Quoted in Horton 1999)[9]

A remarkable prefiguring of the work of the Bay Area computer musicians appears in the unusual odyssey of the British psychologist and cyberneticist Gordon Pask. After conversations with Norbert Wiener, who was lecturing on cybernetics at Cambridge, the young Pask was moved to demonstrate how a machine could learn. Adapting his electronics expertise to the artistic connections he had developed in the theater, between 1953 and 1957 Pask developed the Musicolour, a unique device that used the sounds of music performance to control theatrical lighting. Signals from a microphone were passed through a set of tuned filters whose output controlled the lights in response to the pitch and beat of the music.

Andrew Pickering's (2010a, 316) account of the Musicolour makes it clear that the device operated according to the tenets of cybernetics: "In analogy to biological neurons, banks of lights would only be activated if the output from the relevant filter exceeded a certain threshold value, and these thresholds varied in time as charges built up on capacitors according to the development of the performance and the prior behavior of the machine."

In an essay about the device, Pask presented his notions of "an aesthetically potent environment":

a. It must offer sufficient variety to provide the potentially controllable variety required by a man (however, it must not swamp him with variety—if it did, the environment would be merely unintelligible).
b. It must contain forms that a man can learn to interpret at various levels of abstraction.
c. It must provide cues or tacitly stated instructions to guide the learning process.
d. It may, in addition, respond to a man, engage him in conversation and adapt its characteristics to the prevailing mode of discourse. (Pickering 2010a, 322)[10]

The relationship between subjectivity and agency was prefigured by Musicolour, which "staged the encounter of two exceedingly complex systems—the human performer and the machine—each having its own endogenous dynamics but nevertheless capable of consequential performative interaction with the other in a dance of agency" (Pickering 2010a, 319). Pickering tells us that "the cybernetic brain was not representational but *performative* . . . and its role in performance was *adaptation*" (6). Thus, again prefiguring the questioning of the human-machine distinction, Pickering writes that "a Musicolour performance undercut any familiar dualist distinction between the human and the nonhuman. The human did not control the performance, nor did the machine. . . . A Musicolour performance was thus a joint product of a human-machine assemblage" (319).

As Pickering notes, in such an assemblage considerations of power inevitably arise, and the Musicolour's ontology was remarkably similar to what we find a decade later with Mumma and Oliveros, as well as the implicit and explicit politics of performance that emerged twenty years later among Bay Area interactive computer musicians: "In contrast to the traditional impulse to dominate aesthetic media, the Musicolour machine thematized cooperation. . . . The Musicolour performer had to find out what constituted a synesthetic relation between sound and light and how to achieve it. We could speak here of a search process and the temporal emergence of desire—another Heideggerian revealing—rather than of a preconceived goal that governs a performance" (Pickering 2010a, 320).

Across the Great Divide: From Network
Bands to Quotidian Computing

In this chapter I extend my interest in pursuing what the first-generation new media theorist Erkki Huhtamo, in the title of a 1999 article, called "an archaeology of interactivity."[11] Huhtamo's archaeology traces the desire for a dialogically real-time human-machine relationship across a period from the cybernetics talk of the 1950s to the then emerging new media discourse of the 1990s. Huhtamo sees this real-time concept as having come to fruition only in the late 1980s—notably, with Jeffrey Shaw's well-known virtual reality piece "The Legible City" (1989–91).[12]

Part of the reason that early and now canonical new media histories appear to be unaware of the earlier history of interactivity discussed in this chapter may be laid at the door of the computer music community itself. As we now see from Horton's diaries, the early experimenters realized privately that their work aimed at projecting new models for the study of meaning and sociality. However, as I remarked in an earlier essay, their public transcripts evinced a certain tardiness in coming to terms with the social implications of their technologies, practices, and aesthetics:

> The field of interactive music quickly recapitulated the stance of the earlier mainframe-based work in tending to see itself as heir to a tradition of vanguard Euroclassical music that, after the explosions of 1968, had once again retreated from contact with popular culture, political concerns and the social world generally. Unprepared to contextualize their issues beyond the frame of pan-European composition, the questions they raised would be left to a later generation of interactivity artists and theorists whose work became subsumed within the field of "new media." (G. E. Lewis 2007, 109; see also Born 1995)

Well after the early network performances with Bischoff and Horton, League co-founder Rich Gold (2008, 27) said, "The Terrain Reader, in all its myriad forms, was my primary computer music work and could easily be called my only real work." The Terrain Reader, which Gold deployed frequently in League performances, composed music algorithmically by modeling a virtual landscape in software and a virtual hiker that freely traversed the terrain. The hiker's activity would be reflected in the sounds coming from the speakers.[13] As Gold whimsically put it, the program had "three notable qualities: it could produce a wide range of sounds; it could fit within my KIM-1; and it had a charming metaphor which made it fun to explain. If I were to describe the music it made today I would say it was *syntho-bebop*, a form approximately fifteen years too early" (27).

In distinction to his Bay Area artist colleagues, and at variance with earlier League critiques of "highly-structured business and academic institutions," Gold joined the corporate world, working for much of the 1980s as director of the Sound and Music Department of the U.S. division of Sega USA, which was still well known for its home gaming devices and for the strong presence of its machines in coin-operated arcades ("In Memory" 2003, 253). By that time, Gold had replaced "syntho-bebop" with a new term, "Algorithmic Symbolism" (AS), which he usually described as a "field"—one for which he was the inventor.

Gold presented various explanations of the intent and subject of the field. In one formulation, published in 2008, algorithmic symbolism became "a form of art where the underlying procedures of generation contain meaning that interplays with the surface meaning. The algorithms matter and need to be presented as part of the art" (Gold 2008, 30). This formulation describes the Terrain Reader rather well and forms the basis for his self-distributed Party Planner program, which was featured in a *Scientific American* article published in 1987. In Bourriaud's terms, the Party Planner is a relational artwork that combined sophisticated programming with humor and whimsy as it sought to advise users as to the best way to foster congenial sociality through counsels on social space (Dewdney 1987, 112–15).

Gold's 1993 description of AS encapsulates a post–Party Planner ideal: "Algorithmic Symbolism uses various computer programs that seem to have a lifelike quality—a charm and humanness—in their ability to make things happen that can only occur in the anti-natural world. That pool ball going uphill, for example, shows a lot of determination on the pool ball's part. These programs would include chaos, fractals, cellular automata, and neural nets" (Gold 1993a, 10). Taking a position at Activision, a competing firm, Gold, with a collaborator, David Crane, produced a highly successful commercial example of this latter version of AS: Little Computer People (LCP), described in one article as "the first fully autonomous, computerized AI game" ("In Memory" 2003, 253). The game, which was released in 1985, ran on new, sixteen-bit microprocessor computing platforms, such as the Atari ST and the Amiga. These machines adopted the now universal WIMP-style (windows, icons, menus, pointer) graphical user interface, which had been popularized earlier in the decade in Apple's Lisa and Macintosh computers, and was itself an outgrowth of a system invented by Alan Kay and his associates at PARC in the early 1970s (see Broneck 2002, 207–9).

The activities of the LCP demonstrated the extent to which algorithmic symbolism was an outgrowth of the social aesthetics of Bay Area microcomputer experimentalism. The screen presented a two-dimensional representation of a house, with dining room, living room, recreation area, kitchen, and other areas visible. The virtual person played the piano, exercised, watched television, and performed other quotidian tasks while completely ignoring the so-called user, who was often relegated to the status of voyeur—hence, the characterization "autonomous."[14]

The user manual strongly encouraged anthropomorphization and subjectivization of the LCP, informing new purchasers of the protocols needed to encourage him to move into his new home:

> The first time you visit your LCP, his house will be empty when it appears on the screen. This is because most LCPs are quite shy and will not readily rush into a new situation. In fact, it may take several minutes before yours actually musters the courage to step inside the new home you're providing for him. On the other hand, LCPs are also quite loyal. Once he's moved in, you can expect him to be home on subsequent occasions.
>
> When an LCP enters a house for the first time, he will usually inspect the new home for anywhere from 5 to 10 minutes. Then he'll leave to retrieve his belongings. Yours will probably return shortly with his suitcase. Most LCPs also bring their dog. (Polley and Nelson 1986, 3)

There were channels for communication with the little man on the hard drive, however, via a set of keyboard commands. Like the Tamagotchi digital pet of the late 1990s, LCPs required care and feeding, including food and water for both the LCP and his dog.[15] In anticipation of emotional computing and the humanoid robots created by Cynthia Breazeal and other researchers at the Massachusetts Institute of Technology,[16] users were also required to monitor and tend to the LCP's "emotional needs" via "mood boosters." To get the user's attention, the LCP would "knock on the glass of your TV or monitor" (Polley and Nelson 1986, 7). Mood boosters included "phone calls" ("unless they are constantly interrupted to the point of irritation"), petting ("he must be sitting in his easy chair in the living room"), playing card games (including Blackjack and Five Card Draw), and leaving a new LP record at the front door for the LCP's listening pleasure (6). The LCPs were fine amateur pianists and were often seen reading the newspaper in front of the fireplace or playing with their computers.

Users could communicate with the LCP via text, including making requests and suggestions and asking questions. "LCPs are especially responsive to good manners," the manual said, "so remember to incorporate words like 'please' and 'thank you' into your requests" (Polley and Nelson 1986, 7). In the end, however, users became aware that "LCPs are basically quite independent" (4), thus bringing into the picture a mode of machine agency that framed the LCP not only as an object invested with agency conceived along Latourian lines but also as a quasi-subject (see Latour 2005).

In the terms suggested by Penny, we can theorize the LCP as an artwork exhibiting behavior. Moreover, following Bourriaud, we can conceive of the LCP as a relational work that proposes and produces dialogue and sociability. Finally, as with the League's computer network performances, we can theorize the LCP's quasi-independent behavior as an improvisative form of machine-human sociality, a social improvisation that constructs a world that challenges the hierarchy of humans over machines.

The interaction becomes improvisation when a third term of freedom enters the picture: when the LCP's analysis of the situation mirrors that of its "user," who is no longer a user of software in the traditional sense. Both the human and the LCP are responding to conditions and actions that cannot be wholly foreseen by either, which obliges a recognition by the human that in the world of the game, both parties to the improvisation become free agents with respect to the position of the other.

Finally, it is important to recognize that this kind of relational artwork pursues an improvisation that could potentially take place over very long time spans—days, weeks, months—thereby undercutting the notion of improvisation as an ephemeral practice bound to the moment. Another way to put it is that the improvisation between the human and the LCP expands the notion of the moment itself, as well as positing a notion of shared temporality along the lines suggested by both the sociological phenomenology of Alfred Schutz and the music-informed Christian theology of Jeremy Begbie (2000, 207; see also Schutz 1964), who maintains, "When I, the improviser, come to terms with and engage with another improviser, I come to terms with the other's temporality." Thus, what is being proposed in this analysis of LCP is not a metaphysics of machine consciousness but a phenomenology of freedom as dialogic interaction.

In 1991, Gold took a position at Xerox PARC and became an integral part of the development of "ubiquitous computing," or ubi-comp, working with a team that included Marc Weiser, a computer scientist who was then chief technologist at PARC and had headed PARC's Computer Science Laboratory. According to an article written by Weiser, Gold, and John Seely Brown (1999), the concept of ubiquitous computing dates back to the founding of the ubi-comp program at the Computer Science Laboratory in 1988.

In Weiser's words (1993, 76), "The idea of ubiquitous computing first arose from contemplating the place of today's computer in actual activities of everyday life." In the article "This Is Not a Pipe," Gold complements Weiser's view by troping the surrealist painter René Magritte's famous painting to present a vision of the computational remediation of everyday objects such as toys, and indeed, a pipe:

> Ubiquitous computing is a new metaphor in which computers are spread invisibly throughout the environment, embedded and hiding as it were, within the objects of our everyday life. Each of these computers can talk with any of the other computers much like chattering animals in a living jungle, sometimes exchanging detailed information, sometimes just noting who's around. The everyday objects themselves become a kind of ruse: a baby doll (or toy block) might look like a familiar remnant of childhood, but It is really only one of a thousand distributed nodes which control the functioning of the whole house. Likewise, the baby doll itself activates its own mechanisms, behaviors, and charms based partly on the comings and goings of its adopted (organic) family, and partly on digital discussions with other objects in the house. (Gold 1993b, 72)

Gold ends the article by invoking a vision of the independent decision making of embedded systems: "This new augmented reality is perhaps a little like the enchanted village in which common objects have magically acquired new abilities, a village where toy blocks really do sing and dance when I turn out the lights" (Gold 1993b, 72).

By the fall of 1993, Gold had distilled this vision into a set of five fundamental characteristics of ubi-comp objects, using as examples computational analogues to lunchboxes and pipes:

> UBI-OBJECTS ARE SENSUOUS AND REACTIVE. They feel, see, hear, and touch the environment and then respond to it in various ways.

UBI-OBJECTS ARE COMMUNICATIVE. They talk a lot among themselves, between themselves and other ubi-objects, and between themselves and us.

UBI-OBJECTS ARE TACITLY AND INVISIBLY EMBEDDED INTO DAILY SOCIAL LIFE.

UBI-OBJECTS ARE ANTI-NATURAL. When an object says "hi" in the morning, it is hard not to say "hi" back.

UBI-OBJECTS ARE EVERYWHERE. (Gold 1993a, 4–6)

Gold concluded that through computational remediation, everyday objects would become "deeply enspirited" (Gold 1993a, 3), an invocation of what I have elsewhere called "technology-mediated animism" (G. E. Lewis 2000, 37).

As Jane McGonigal (2006, 8) notes, "Although Gold never uses the term 'performance' to describe the phenomenon of ubiquitous computing . . . [his] vision for ubiquitous computing is fundamentally a vision of distributed networks of play and performance." Again, we can trace these networks back to the social aesthetics of Bay Area interactive computer music improvisations. As the human-computer interaction theorist Paul Dourish (2004) notes, Weiser cites the anthropologist of technology Lucy Suchman's notion of "situated actions" as a source for the ubiquitous computing idea. Dourish quotes Gregory Abowd's view that "Situated action emphasizes the improvisational aspects of human behavior and deemphasizes a priori plans that the person simply executes. . . . Ubicomp's efforts informed by a situation action also emphasize improvisational behavior and would not require, or anticipate, the user to follow a predefined script" (quoted in Dourish 2004, 20).[17]

The ubi-comp team produced a number of patents for devices that included early versions of palmtop and notepad computers. However, for the most part, these devices were less compelling than Weiser, Gold, and Brown's (1999, 694) prescient conceptual realization that "ubi-comp created a new field of computer science, one that speculated on a physical world richly and invisibly interwoven with sensors, actuators, displays, and computational elements, embedded seamlessly in the everyday objects of our lives and connected through a continuous network." Arguably, both Gold's early work with the League and the creation of LCP presaged this conception of quotidian, deeply embedded human-computer interaction. The presence of computers in everyday life in the West has become, as Tolmie notes, "unremarkable" (quoted in Dourish 2004, 29).[18] In this sense, the advent of ubi-comp objects has also transformed human experience and potential.

Epilogue

As with ubiquitous computing itself, the social aesthetics of the early inter-active computer musicians have now become unremarkably embedded in the fabric of our everyday encounters with computing devices. As a final ex-ample, consider the famous world-building game *The Sims*, whose author, Will Wright, was queried about his experience with LCP:

> MAX STEELE: Will, did you ever play "Little Computer People Research Project" from Activision, and did it influence you at all?
> WILL WRIGHT: Yes, a long time ago. I've since gotten to know several people who were involved with that project, and many of them gave valuable feedback on *The Sims*, especially Rich Gold.[19]

Gold's posthumously published *The Plenitude* (2007) lays out a complex and contradictory vision of the connection among computing, commerce, inter-activity, and everyday life, informed by his leading role in Xerox PARC's ubiquitous computing area and, later, its artist-in-residence program, whose vision pursued strong connections between artists and scientists. When Gold joined PARC, as the interactivity theorist and designer Anne Balsamo re-members, the center's director and chief scientist, John Seely Brown, en-couraged him to "become a corporate provocateur, cultural mediator, and institutional visionary, and to act as a catalyst for creative thinking and prac-tice" (Balsamo 2011, 57). From this point, Gold's work developed into a vec-tor of transmission linking the cybernetics orientation and social aesthetics of the early interactive computer musicians with a later vision of interac-tivity that may one day embrace an understanding of improvisation as a fun-damental aspect of the human condition.

Notes

1. See "A Brief History of the Music Department," http://www.mills.edu/aca demics/undergraduate/mus/history.php (accessed July 3, 2016). See also "Music at Mills: An Illustrious Musical History," http://musicnow.mills.edu/music_at _mills_history.php (accessed July 3, 2016).

2. For the definitive history of the San Francisco Tape Center, see D. W. Bern-stein 2008.

3. The Behrman work is recorded on David Behrman, *On the Other Ocean*, Lovely Music CD 1041, 1976.

4. See the introduction by Bischoff in Horton 1999.

5. For a first-person account of a rehearsal of the League by a nonparticipant, see Roads 1985.

6. According to Bischoff, Horton (1944–98) began working with musical micro-computers as early as 1976 and was "the first composer to postulate the idea of using computer networks to make music," as well as creating the first network music performance with Gold in 1977.

7. Christian Wolff, "For 1, 2, or 3 People," music score, C. F. Peters, New York, 1964.

8. For a discussion and critique of Bourriaud's ideas, see Georgina Born's chapter, "After Relational Aesthetics: Improvised Music, the Social, and (Re)Theorizing the Aesthetic," in this volume.

9. For the original, see Bateson 1979, 92.

10. As we can see, the trope of conversation was central not only to the famous Turing Test, but also to other forays into human-machine relations in AI and the arts.

11. See Huhtamo 1999. For my earlier article on this topic, see G. E. Lewis 2003.

12. See http://www.jeffrey-shaw.net/html_main/show_work.php?record_id=83.

13. For a technical explanation of the program, see Bischoff et al. 1978, 26–27.

14. I remember running into Rich, I think in San Francisco. He told me that he was working on "a little man that lives on your hard drive." "What's he going to do there?" I asked. "Whatever he wants," came the reply.

15. For a personal account of life with a Tamagotchi, see Turkle 2012, 30–34.

16. For a critique of the project of humanoid robotics, see Suchman 2007.

17. Originally in Abowd et al. 2002.

18. Originally in Tolmie et al. 2002.

19. "Will Wright: A Chat about 'The Sims' and 'SimCity,'" CNN.com, January 20, 2000, http://www.cnn.com/chat/transcripts/2000/1/wright/index.html (accessed July 3, 2016). The iPhone application Pocket Guy is also based on LCP.

II · GENRE AND DEFINITION

CHAPTER 5

THE SOCIAL AESTHETICS OF SWING IN THE 1940S

Or the Distribution of the Non-Sensible

David Brackett

Back in the early 1990s, I became aware of several series of recordings produced by the Time Life company that were organized into different categories of popular music and grouped by year. These series included titles
such as "Rhythm and Blues," "Classic Rock," "Easy Listening," and "Country
USA," as well as the series that was the genesis of this chapter, "Your Hit
Parade," with each CD containing twenty-four top hits for the years 1940 to
1958. The wonderful thing about these CDs was what I would call their arbi-
trary quality: little apparent sorting went on in their preparation other than
finding songs that were popular according to *Billboard* magazine's charts
during a given year and that had a relatively low bar when it came to acquir-
ing the rights for reproduction. The Time Life series thus made few obvious
nods to the notion of which recordings might be canonical. "These recordings were popular and could be included here," the collections seemed to
say, and nothing else needed to be added—neither claims of greatness nor
claims of historical significance.

Such collections give rise to differing perceptions of music history than
do those based on an individual artist, a record label, or the greatest hits
of a genre spread out over time, all formats familiar to anyone with even a
modest claim to being a collector of popular music recordings. The focus on
a year anticipates turns in historiography toward "annualism" or "annualization" as a way to construct a history, as opposed to the more common
approach that covers an epoch, the time span enclosing a famous event or
a related group of people, artworks, inventions, and so on.[1] The impact of

these recordings exposed me to a range of recordings to which I would not have otherwise chosen to listen and heightened my appreciation of the importance of circulation in the emergence, persistence, and decline of trends, cycles, and genres. Topoi for lyrics, instruments, tempos, and even specific musical-style features might be shared among a broad array of artists within a short period of time, only to disappear suddenly, indicating a large, and otherwise undocumented, dialogue between musicians operating in the popular sphere. Among the hundreds of tracks in a collection such as *Your Hit Parade, 1940–1958* lay the canonized as well as the trivialized, hidden treasures as well as historical oddities. This chapter is indebted to the latter.

For example, in the volume of *Your Hit Parade* devoted to the year 1947, crooners such as Perry Como and Buddy Clark rubbed shoulders with the African American close harmony quartet the Mills Brothers, and throwbacks to the prewar heyday of the big swing bands coexisted peacefully with a plethora of novelty numbers. It was just such a number that began the 1947 volume, a song titled "Open the Door, Richard!" recorded by Count Basie. My curiosity piqued, I pondered how it could have been that Count Basie, the Ur-canonical jazz pianist and bandleader, had topped the charts in 1947 with a recording that was clearly based in vaudeville, featuring a skit performed in broad African American dialect that evoked nothing so much as minstrelsy. The context provided by the other songs on the 1947 volume of *Your Hit Parade* gave suggestive hints, the CD producing a kind of synchronic snapshot of the popular music field at that moment, a cross-section confirmed and amplified via consultation with *Billboard* and other trade publications of the time. In the wake of considering a broad range of recordings circulating at roughly the same time, the question arose as to how Count Basie's "Open the Door, Richard!" fit into the popular music mainstream of the period. Consultation of earlier volumes of *Your Hit Parade* provided more clues: by thus providing a series of synchronic snapshots, these recordings projected a diachronic transformation of the mainstream, as well.

One thing that became clear to me in the course of listening to these CDs was that, although recordings by swing bands were rare in the 1947 volume, they were plentiful in the years 1940 to 1942, which was not surprising, as I had already been told by countless histories of jazz and popular music that those years represented the height of the "big band era." While no recordings by Count Basie appeared in these earlier volumes, one by his canonical contemporary, Duke Ellington, did, and in general more recordings by African Americans appeared in the volumes representing the early 1940s than in those covering the late 1940s.[2] The particular juxtaposition of these recordings produced a narrative for me in which racial identification, popular music genres, jazz and popular music historiography, and various axes of prestige based on either symbolic or economic capital intertwined and intersected in a tangled web.

Indeed, by reproducing the era's nearly forgotten musical trivialities and accidents, the volumes of *Your Hit Parade* did not so much contradict the verities of popular music and jazz historiography as complicate them. If popular music histories tend to assert that swing bands died after the war, then this seemed to be true, by and large, although a few big bands did manage hits, and swing-influenced music was very much alive and well. After all, one could say that Count Basie's band was big, and it definitely had a hit. Jazz histories were similarly not wrong so much as overly simple in light of the kind of "tasteless" canvassing of public taste performed by *Your Hit Parade* and summaries of popularity charts. These histories may have agreed that the big bands died and were superseded by small combos playing bebop, but they ignored the continued activity of bands led by canonical figures such as Basie and Ellington, as well as the noncanonical white swing bands, such as Stan Kenton's, that persisted and occasionally even flourished.[3] As Scott DeVeaux observed more than twenty years ago, this postwar moment in jazz historiography is marked above all by the emphasis on symbolic capital (i.e., the approval of musicians by other musicians and critics) and the consequent denigration of economic capital (i.e., the approval by the mass public and financial success) and on evaluations of authenticity based on race.[4] Bebop musicians succeeded in creating a type of music that would be evaluated on its artistic merits, not on how it performed in the marketplace. The consecration of jazz artists in subsequent historical texts (and to some extent in previous jazz histories, though they were far and few between) therefore depended on an inversion between artistic merit and commercial success, meaning that many jazz historians were suspicious about the artistic credentials of artists who were too successful.

It is no small wonder then, that Count Basie's "Open the Door, Richard!" would not figure in such histories. The late 1940s and early 1950s tend to be a lacuna in popular music histories anyway, as the mainstream is seen as marking time between the efflorescence of the big band era and the irruption of rock and roll.[5] At issue here would seem to be the relationship of a category of music called "jazz" as it was understood at the time and subsequently (not quite the same things) to that heterogeneous grouping of sounds that produced the mainstream of popular music. If the usual narratives assert that the instrumental and vocal recordings of the big bands were supplanted by crooners singing ballads accompanied by studio orchestras, then, to reiterate a point made earlier, my argument is not that this narrative is incorrect but, rather, that it obscures as much as it elucidates. My first step toward complicating it is to point out that a succession of genres, such as the procession of swing followed by vocal ballads, is rarely a mere succession of genres. It is, instead, a series of musical styles articulated to identifications with music: the musical gestures comprising the various styles and genres arrive already marked by associations of race, place, class, gender, and so on. Thus, genres are embroiled in a play of power and prestige in which social relations and aesthetics intertwine, but in which relations among the social, aesthetics, and genre are rarely homologous or direct.[6] The very terms in which I have been discussing African American artists such as Count Basie and Duke Ellington in relation to the transformation of the popular music mainstream already suggest such an articulation of musical style and identification. The position of their recordings in by now conventional historical narratives points to the interconnections of style, identification, and prestige. This chapter is devoted to tracing the fortunes of jazz and swing from the start of the 1940s, beginning with the instrumental swing number "Tuxedo Junction" (first recorded by the African American bandleader Erskine Hawkins and then covered by the Euro-American bandleader Glenn Miller), to the commercial triumph of "Open the Door, Richard!" By focusing on the institutional, discursive, and social networks out of which these recordings emerged, this tale of two songs will flesh out canonical narratives with a "genealogical" account.[7]

A Dip into the Politics of Aesthetics:
What's Improvisation Got to Do with It?

Most scholarly discussions of improvisation are based on an opposition between composition and improvisation. While unavoidable, the instability of such terms and their relation to one another frequently goes unstated. In practice few types of music are wholly composed (i.e., preplanned) and then reproduced exactly the same way in performance; neither are many types of music completely improvised. Even the limit cases of composed and improvised music raise difficult issues: electronic, taped, and digital composition may have the potential to reproduce pitches, rhythms, timbres, and changes in amplitude precisely from one hearing to another, but they cannot take into account the effect of differences in performance spaces on the listener, changes in the listener's state of mind, or the effect of repeated hearings of the "same" piece. However, even the most "free" improvisation relies on the formal rhetoric of previous free improvisations and other musical conventions internalized by the musicians; pitch, phrasing, and timbral choices are constrained by the limitations of the instrument and the playing habits developed by musicians over years of playing, as well as internalized ideas about how instruments in free improvisations should sound (one need only imagine the impact on a free improvisation of a little *bel canto* lyricism applied to a diatonic or tonal melody with a clear rhythmic pulse to grasp this point).[8] Central to this chapter is how the concept of improvisation is understood in a particular historical situation and how the concept figures into distinctions made between different types of music and their social connotations. Popular music of the type discussed here has played little role in previous studies of musical improvisation, in which the most frequently found objects of study can at times resemble those found in the art and jazz canons, with their inverted relations of symbolic and economic capital.[9]

The concept of improvisation played a crucial role in the circulation of musical identifications during this period through the prior association of improvisation with musical practices and genres that were in turn associated with African Americans.[10] Here, a musical technique, improvisation, forms part of the play of resemblance and difference between musical categories and group identities. Indeed, something approaching a contemporary notion of what sounds and musical practices might be identified as African American began to take shape during the early decades of the twentieth century, spurred on by the growing importance of commercial sound recording and the increasing dominance of what Karl Hagstrom-Miller (2010) has described as a "folklore-based" model of cultural authenticity, which aided and reinforced each other.[11] All of the by now familiar elements were already in place in discourse about African American music in the 1920s, including a "swinging" rhythmic sense, distinctive vocal and instrumental timbres, a particular approach to dissonance and pitch inflection, and, of course, improvisation (and its affective correlate, spontaneity) — practices associated with genres such as blues, jazz, and gospel. I am not asserting a tight, homological fit between these musical practices and African American identity as such; rather, the connotations of these practices reflect a widely shared belief about an association between musical practices and a group of people. Thus, the ways in which concepts such as improvisation and swing were understood at the time played a critical role in how distinctions were made between different types of music and their attendant social connotations.

In another, broader sense, this period in popular music history is about a struggle over the terms in which debates about popularity would be conducted, with the "work concept" (the song as the unit, measured by sheet music sales, radio plugs, and so on) derived from Western art music aesthetics representing one pole and the sound recording, offering the nuances of performance, representing the other.[12] Whereas the song as text emphasizes structure and fixed identity, which could then be reproduced either on a recording or in amateur performances at home, the recording as text inscribes the marks of spontaneity, of individualized, embodied gestures.[13] In this context, improvisation could begin to figure in the construction of musical categories only if recordings were considered the main format for the measurement of popularity.[14] The alignment of the former work concept with institutional power and dominant social groups appears unmistakably in music industry discourse, from evaluations of performances and recordings to which songs and recordings receive the most attention for their apparent popularity. At the same time, an emerging discourse during this period, which tentatively recognizes recordings as texts, created a conflict with the dominant aesthetic, as formerly unacknowledged audiences— including African Americans and whites from the southern states and rural areas—were strongly associated with types of music affiliated with the sonic aesthetic.

This sonic aesthetic, based on the unique qualities of sound associated with particular performers and performances, could circulate beyond a specific performance space only on mechanically reproducible recordings. Sheet music could not begin to communicate subtle timbral differences, let alone the micro-rhythmic nuances responsible for different grooves (easily felt by dancers but elusive for transcribers) or the pitch inflections that spontaneously enliven melodies with otherwise limited pitch content (easily hummed along with by well-trained listeners but not amenable to even-tempered notation). The circulation of this music, associated with "marginal" elements of the population, which had thrived in the 1920s and almost disappeared during the early years of the Depression, began a vigorous comeback with the launching of the swing era in the mid-1930s. The recording's gradual usurpation of pride of place from sheet music as the primary means of musical circulation figured prominently in a debate in the public sphere between competing aesthetics and different concepts of the musical work.

This particular conjuncture of aesthetics and the social adds an interesting wrinkle to a theory of social aesthetics such as that of Jacques Rancière.

His notion of the "distribution of the sensible" connects the unfolding of new aesthetic regimes with the modes of perception through which both social actions and artistic forms may be understood (Rancière 2004). Thus, the very legibility or audibility of a practice or text as "art" is constrained by the dominant mode of perception. Rancière divides the history of Western aesthetics into three artistic regimes, the third of which, the "aesthetic regime of the arts," emerged during the nineteenth century and is characterized by, among other things, "the equality of represented subjects" and "the indifference of style with regard to content" (81). Rancière disputes Walter Benjamin's notion of the democratizing function of mechanical reproduction by asserting that, prior to the appearance of photography, film, sound recording, and other artistic forms characterized by mechanical reproduction, "equality of represented subjects" had already become "the subject matter of art." Therefore, it is due to this prior shift that "the act of recording such a subject matter can be an art" (32; see also Benjamin 1969).

Several difficulties immediately arise when one attempts to analyze popular music circa 1940 through such a theoretical lens. Rancière's analyses remain resolutely on the level of European (and specifically French) high culture. When asked during an interview to respond to the criticism that he ignores "the social dynamic of history or the plurality of literary and artistic practices," Rancière (2004, 58–59) admits that he focuses on a rather homogeneous group of artists but avers that his ideas about the "aesthetic artistic regime" could be expanded to include authors such as Virginia Woolf and James Joyce. Note that his expansion still steadfastly avoids the terrain of mass culture—that is, it includes Woolf and Joyce but not Richard Wright, Raymond Chandler, or Jacqueline Susann. The model proposed by my analysis of 1940s swing, by contrast, implies the simultaneous and competing artistic and aesthetic regimes that had been enshrined in music industry practice since the 1920s with three main categories: popular/mainstream (implying a white, bourgeois audience), race music (implying an African American audience), and old-time/hillbilly music (implying a white, middle- and upper-class audience).[15] It would also require many semiotic moves, analyzing different stages of connotation, to understand how the recordings analyzed here might project an "equality of represented subjects" (81).[16] "Tuxedo Junction" is an instrumental piece (how instrumental music might "represent subjects" is surely a complicated affair), and the "lyrics" of "Open the Door, Richard!" could only ever represent the "common people," although a version of the song focused on the foibles of European aristocracy would certainly be entertaining. And while mechanical reproduction did not necessarily create these musical practices, such practices could not circulate without sound recording (and it could be argued that the practices responded to the possibilities opened up by sound recording). These forms, by not figuring in Rancière's schema, therefore would not be legible or audible—hence, my subtitle: the arrangement of texts and genres within the popular music field at this time could be understood, *pace* Rancière, as the "distribution of the non-sensible."

Despite what may seem to be the foregoing dismissal of Rancière, some aspects of his theory will help guide what follows. The idea of the "legibility" of an artistic practice and its relationship to power and institutional discourses, for example, highlights the way in which notions of copyright, the role of technology, and representation/presentation of popularity were interrelated. The matrix formed by these notions could be understood as the precondition of a popular music genre's audibility.

Two Stops at "Tuxedo Junction"

This narrative of generic/aesthetic, and thus social, transformation begins at the dawn of the 1940s and traces the history of one of the biggest hits of the period, "Tuxedo Junction." The recordings of "Tuxedo Junction" by Erskine Hawkins and Glenn Miller exemplify how differences in approaches to improvisation and other musical elements were often correlated with the social position of the recordings, the fluidity of their circulation, the size of their audience, and their access to various modes of dissemination.

The bandleader and trumpeter Erskine Hawkins co-wrote "Tuxedo Junction" and recorded it with his band in 1939. Hawkins's band was one of the few African American ensembles to be featured regularly on radio broadcasts, an advantage accorded by virtue of a long-running engagement at Manhattan's Savoy Ballroom, which had a wire pickup (i.e., his performances were transmitted regularly by radio). This arrangement gave Hawkins a forum for self-promotion not quite at the level of the most successful white bands, but one that undoubtedly played a role in the unusual popularity of this recording and the type of attention it received.

"Tuxedo Junction" is a medium-tempo, riff-based number derived from a simplified form of "I've Got Rhythm." The stripped down harmony and texture, which looks forward to the "jump blues" and rhythm and blues that would begin to coalesce as genres in the mid-1940s, allow for an abundance of superimposed riffs and bluesy improvisations, and were joined with orchestration touches that both evoked some of the most successful swing bands of the day, such as Miller's, and recalled the timbres associated with the "jungle style" of Duke Ellington's Cotton Club period of the late 1920s. The trumpet and clarinet soloists both get a full thirty-two-bar chorus on which to improvise. These solos reveal an awareness of contemporary "hot" soloing trends and are supported almost continually by bluesy riffs designed to appeal to dancers.[17]

Any attempt to trace the reception of this recording from music industry discourse necessarily runs afoul of an obstacle created by the aforementioned struggle over what would be the dominant mode of conceptualizing popular music: the abstract template of the song, favored by publishers and the long-established songwriters employed by them, or the recorded performance, which captured the specific nuances of singers and instrumentalists and favored those types of music not supported by the most powerful publishers. A song like "Tuxedo Junction" did not emanate from the world of established music publishers. Rather, it was developed out of the performance practice of certain hot swing bands that could assemble a song out of riffs that were part of a common stock of musical figures circulating among (primarily African American) swing musicians.

Credited to Hawkins and to the saxophonists Bill Johnson and Julian Dash, the song (as composed structure) would not have been promoted by the apparatus then dominant in the U.S. music industry, wherein representatives ("song pluggers") from music publishing companies attempted to persuade bandleaders to record and, most important, to play their songs on radio broadcasts. The reliance on non-notable musical elements and the creation of the song outside the circuits of Tin Pan Alley rendered "Tuxedo Junction" in its first incarnation unattractive to song pluggers. The practice of plugging had ramifications in the generation of discourse in the music industry press, which included the representation of a song's popularity. The number of plays on radio broadcasts was tallied every week, and rankings were compiled based on the number of "plugs" a song received. Charts also recorded "best-selling sheet music," and the music industry press focused on these measures of popularity. Radio, and especially network radio, which drew the largest audiences and counted the most in calculations of popularity, was dominated by live performances of songs rather than recordings, and a popular song emanating from one of the major publishers would routinely be performed by many different artists. All of these factors meant that Hawkins's recording of "Tuxedo Junction" would generate little commentary in the music industry press, which would be incapable of perceiving its popularity, or lack thereof.

Jukeboxes, however, were in the middle of a huge boom when Hawkins released "Tuxedo Junction," accounting for more than 50 percent of all recordings sold at the time, according to most estimates.[18] A section appeared in *Billboard* listing recordings that were popular on jukeboxes; this section included a page of comments, titled "What the Records Are Doing for Me," sent in by jukebox operators from around the country reporting on the records that were attracting nickels. The commentary on jukeboxes, however, was in the back of the magazine in the "amusement machines" section, well separated from the music section, implying, perhaps, that music circulating primarily via the jukebox had not earned the right to be called music, as amusing as these recordings might be. (Indeed, the circulation of music in this fashion had a status similar to that of the revenue generated by pinball and vending machines.) Hawkins's recording did receive some attention at the back of the magazine—that is, by the segment of the industry interested in jukebox play—and jukebox operators often found that many of the people who liked Glenn Miller's band, the most popular ensemble of the period, also liked Hawkins's. One jukebox operator reported to *Billboard* in the December 30, 1939, issue, "As for bands, Glenn Miller seems to grow more and more popular along with Erskine Hawkins, the latter going like a house afire in the colored neighborhoods."[19] After a few weeks of attention, Hawkins's recording seemed to sink without a trace in the pages of *Billboard*, only to reappear several weeks later. Although initially mystified, *Billboard* quickly put two and two together: "Erskine Hawkins, who wrote the tune, recorded it some weeks ago and it enjoyed a slight measure of phono [i.e., jukebox] popularity. Glenn Miller then picked the song up and began to feature it on his radio programs, with the result that requests flooded in for him to record it. The Miller version of the number has already created such excitement that his disk is practically certain to be another *In the Mood*. Be prepared for a big thing here."[20] Subsequent issues of *Billboard* noted that Hawkins's recording had experienced a resurgence of interest in jukeboxes after the appearance of Miller's, which became one of Miller's biggest hits, ranking with previous recordings of his, such as "In the Mood" and "Chattanooga Choo-Choo."

It is interesting to speculate on just how, exactly, Miller managed to "pick the song up." Hawkins and Miller shared a pre-Christmas gig at the Savoy Ballroom on December 2, 1939, soon after the release of Hawkins's recording and a mere two weeks before the first recognition of the song's popularity in *Billboard* in the December 16, 1939, issue. It is not wild speculation to imagine that Miller heard the Hawkins band perform it, saw the positive crowd response, and realized that it could be a vehicle for the type of arrangement he had just used for "In the Mood," a massive hit for him.[21]

Miller considerably rearranges the tune in his recording, using a slower tempo and a heavier approach to groove. The most striking difference is formal, however: Miller takes the AABA form of the original and reduces it, after an initial presentation of ideas, to the opening melodic gesture which is continually interrupted. This results in a transformation of the song into one of the most durable mainstream genres of the era: the "novelty" number. The continual interruptions function as a commercial "hook" for the song that is altogether lacking in Hawkins's version and seems tailor-made to fit Adorno's scathing critique, published at almost exactly the same time, of the use of novel effects to create "pseudo-individualization" in popular songs (see Adorno 2002b). Form is significant here because the recording that is the more "standardized" (also an Adorno term) on one level—Hawkins's—is actually more poorly adapted to commodification in Adorno's terms. That is, Hawkins's version features a thirty-two-bar, AABA form, the sine qua non of formal standardization in the popular music of the era, while Miller's form is very irregular. Yet that very irregularity produces the hook gimmick that can then recur a maximum number of times. The formal regularity of Hawkins's version provides a backdrop for the improvised solos, which in turn produces a kind of moment-to-moment variety lacking in the Miller version. Of course, Adorno believed that all jazz improvisations were pre-digested, but this seems to be a rather famous instance of how his assumption of an identical reception context for Western art music and the popular music of the period actually dulls the force of his argument. Adorno never analyzed jazz improvisation in any detail; however, within his overall focus on composition, Adorno believed that the "hook" would reside in the "pseudo-individualized" melody rather than the form. The interruptions of Miller's "Tuxedo Junction" resemble closely those used in "In the Mood" (a hit for Miller several months before the release of "Tuxedo Junction") in which the formal interruption was used in two different ways: first, to cut off the flow of an improvising soloist; and second, to create suspense during the long fadeout at the coda, the device re-created in "Tuxedo Junction." This formal device had thus become a kind of trademark for Miller, not unlike the way a 1959 Cadillac Eldorado might distinguish itself from a 1959 Chevrolet Impala by the size and shape of its tail fins.

Yet on another level, one could argue that soloistic improvisation actually de-standardizes the moment-to-moment experience of the recording. While Miller's formal irregularities must be repeated as closely as possible from one performance to the next, locking the band into endless restagings of their recording, the improvised, thirty-two-bar choruses of Hawkins's recording make literal repetition unlikely, as well as not particularly desirable from either the listening or the performing standpoint.[22] The projection in Miller's version of group interaction, and therefore a sense of spontaneous social interaction often heard in improvising ensembles, is thereby diminished. Sheet music not only had copyright law and a whole apparatus for measuring popularity on its side but the idea of the song, or a through-arranged song that mimicked the unique form of a through-composed piece of art music, was also in line with the aesthetic values enshrined in the Western art music canon and the "work concept." Heavily arranged versions of songs such as Miller's thus benefited in public discussions of musical aesthetics when compared with versions such as Hawkins's, in which sectional form served as a generic frame to facilitate improvisation.

Somewhat contrary to the most entrenched stereotypes about black music, rhythm is not one of the most obvious differentiating factors between the two recordings of "Tuxedo Junction." "Swing" music, after all, swung at least some of the time, even when played by white bands. Yet one of the most general differences lies (conveniently enough from the standpoint of a volume on improvisation) in the role of improvisation. Once again, this is somewhat tautological in that improvisation was already identified with African American musical practices; however, improvisation permeates popular race records of the time in a way that transcends common understandings of it as soloistic melodic invention.

Thus, improvisation is found not only in solo sections but also in the construction of the song itself, where, as in "Tuxedo Junction," songs are blues- or riff-based and therefore created out of "floating" musical tropes that were recombined in an endless variety of ways from song to song. "Composition" thus comes about often through a performative, improvisatory approach. The vocal melody in most race records of the time is therefore freely varied on repetition based on these same blues melodic tropes. Arrangements in race records featuring small groups likewise are improvised, as individual vocal and instrumental parts are made up by the musicians on the spot in an aural/oral process rather than written down. While improvised "solos" are often featured in the songs, I would argue that improvisation plays a more basic role in the construction of the songs themselves than in big band–based swing music, which almost always relies on some sort of written arrangement, as well as on a separation of creative roles among composer, arranger, and performer.

One Door Opens, Another One Closes

While many of the style characteristics that identified the distinctiveness of race music—the category of music with which a band such as Hawkins's would have been associated—would remain separate, by and large, until the 1950s, changes in the status of African American musicians and the growing presence of musical practices associated with African Americans were recognized by the music industry at the time. The following quote from the January 2, 1943, issue of *Billboard* explicitly connects the shift away from a minstrel-based paradigm for African American music to the popularity of swing:

> The biggest break Negro performers received . . . has been the recognition of Negroes as first-rate jazz musicians. The craze for swing music suddenly put the spotlight on Negro musicians as creative artists and did much to live down the typical presentation of Negro entertainers as carefree, banjo-plucking cotton pickers continually grinning and shouting jazzy spirituals. . . . Negro name band leaders have held their own thru [sic] the years because they presented a brand of music whites could not easily duplicate. (Denis 1943, 28)

After the war, however, the picture had changed, but in a way that the usual narrative of the decline of the swing bands only begins to suggest. The decline of the large swing bands did decrease the amount of improvisation found in mainstream recordings, as well as the circulation of musical tropes associated with blackness. Rather than a sound woven into the fabric of popular music, African American-ness became something that could be performed only literally, by the corporeality of black voices on recordings that signaled a revitalization of racialized tropes, including those that resembled nothing so much as the trope of the "carefree, banjo-plucking cotton pickers" in the quote. This revitalization was found, in a more general sense, in a wide proliferation of novelty recordings during this period, most of which invoked the simultaneous desire and disavowal that comes with the process of stereotyping; unlike minstrelsy, novelty recordings thus formed a genre with the advantage of being adaptable to nonwhite others of all denominations. The words of a tune such as "Managua, Nicaragua" exemplify how exotic images of women's sexuality, travelogues, colonial trade, and imperialism all meld together seamlessly to create a novel sense of humor: the second verse begins, "Managua, Nicaragua is a heavenly place / you ask a señorita for a 'leetle' embrace," while the third begins, "Managua, Nicaragua what a wonderful spot / there's coffee and bananas and a temperature [*sic*] hot."

In addition to novelty tunes, medium- to up-tempo swing tunes played by big bands still occasionally put in an appearance, although they tended to reside solely at the Glenn Miller end of the swing spectrum. More important, elements of musical style derived from the big band era still dominated the sound of the mainstream, even when performed by studio orchestras or by sweet bands such as Freddy Martin's and Sammy Kaye's, which often featured novelty numbers. Without the interaction of these bands with the music of contemporary African American artists, however—either as models for recordings or as collaborators—one could argue that the associations of swing with African Americans weakened. This also occurred because African American musical tropes were mutating and becoming associated with other genres, such as rhythm and blues, on the one hand, and bebop, on the other, or even with some of the country music of the late 1940s (such as that recorded by Hank Williams or the Delmore Brothers).

Phillip Ennis (1992, 161–92) writes compellingly about the synchronization of media—records, jukeboxes, radio, all based on the recording as the most important unit of exchange—necessary for the formation of a black popular music field that could achieve visibility within the larger music industry and that eventually would create crossovers (again) beyond the sphere of the novelty record. With the development of forums such as a "race chart" in publications such as *Billboard* for tracking and producing the popularity of recordings among African American consumers, a realm of black popular music separate from the mainstream was reinforced. As if the tentative mainstream introduction of black musical tropes by swing bands and the boogie-woogie craze of the early 1940s constituted an intolerable threat, the riffs, grooves, and blues notes of the early 1940s were figured as an absence in the remaining vestiges of swing that could only appear somewhere else in the popular music field—that is, in another category with its own apparatus for the evaluation of economic capital, such as "race" music or rhythm and blues (the music industry name for race music after 1949). Black musical tropes after the war thus formed a constitutive outside to a mainstream aesthetic in which nonwhite others would now function only as novelties.

This is where the curious tale of "Open the Door, Richard!" comes in. One of the few recordings by an African American artist (or, more accurately, artists) in the years immediately after the war to be heard on network radio, it could also be found in record stores and jukeboxes outside black neighborhoods. A brief account of the song's tangled history provides a great example of a text without an origin.[23] Dusty Fletcher, an African American vaudeville comedian, learned a routine in the 1920s from a comedian named John Mason, who, in turn, had learned it from another black comedian, Bob Russell (who, we presume, learned it from someone else).[24] The routine describes the plight of a man named Richard who is locked out of his apartment in a somewhat inebriated condition. A saxophonist named Jack McVea, who was playing primarily on Central Avenue in Los Angeles, worked with Fletcher when they both toured with Lionel Hampton's band in the early 1940s. When McVea began touring with his own band up and down the West Coast, he featured a version of the skit, to which he added a memorable chorus. McVea recorded it in Los Angeles in September 1946, and the recording quickly became popular up and down the West Coast. As the recording was about to break out into a national hit, the major record companies rushed to put out their own versions, as did independents that specialized in race records. Fletcher's two-sided version came out in early 1947, and the race was on.

In a portent of things to come, even the first discussion of the song in *Billboard* put the versatile potential of the title to good use: a headline reading "Open the Door, Richard, and Let All the Lawyers in" (1947, 18) referred to a dispute raging between McVea and Fletcher, while the brief review of the disc in the same issue instructed jukebox operators to "Open the door to the jukes and slip these platters onto the changers."[25] Soon the floodgates opened, and radio listeners were treated to versions by (among others) the Three Flames, the Pied Pipers, the Charioteers, Louis Jordan, Bill Samuels and the Cats 'n Jammer Three, Tosh (One-String Willie) and His Jivesters, Walter Brown and Tiny Grimes, the Merry Macs, Big Sid Catlett, the Hot Lips Page Orchestra, and Hank Penny, as well as the recording by Count Basie.[26]

A riot of different versions flooded the market, with Basie scoring the biggest hit—the biggest of his career, in fact. Unlike the example of "Tuxedo Junction" and countless other instances of "crossover" recordings, "Open the Door, Richard!" is an example of a recording by a black artist that was covered largely by other black artists (of the fourteen recordings listed earlier, at least ten are by African Americans). Deemed a "novelty" by music industry publications, and undoubtedly received as such by white bourgeois listeners, the song displayed a remarkable ability to adapt to a wide range of situations. In addition to becoming a punchline for comics of all stripes, a common greeting for door knockers everywhere, and a torment for anyone unfortunate enough to have been named Richard in the preceding years, the song was recorded by hillbilly artists and calypso artists and in Yiddish, Spanish, Swedish, French, and Hungarian. There is even an anecdote with local flavor for residents of Montreal: fans of the local hockey team, the Canadiens, serenaded their star, "Rocket" Richard by shouting the refrain. Moreover, the many recordings of "Richard" appeared to fit in effortlessly with a newfound abundance of novelty recordings that, as I have mentioned, relied on stereotypical others for their punchlines.

In the African American community, however, another debate erupted. Was "Richard" an embarrassing reminder of minstrelsy, an evocation of "Uncle Tom"–like behavior? This view, probably the first to come to mind to someone contemplating the song today, was held by many in the African American community seeking to gain respectability and distance from a history of degrading caricatures. To some younger, more radicalized black listeners, however, "Richard" became a call to arms: "In 1947 students from Georgia colleges marched to the state capital demanding the resignation of segregationist governor Herman Talmadge, carrying banners reading 'Open the Door Herman'" (R. J. Smith 2004, 83). The *Los Angeles Sentinel*, the city's black newspaper, ran an editorial entitled "Open the Door Richard," which called for "political representation at City Hall" and an end to discriminatory housing practices (83).

Figures 5.1 and 5.2 display both the shift in the relationship between race music and mainstream popular music from 1940 to 1947 and how race music recordings that "crossed over" to the mainstream charts were required by 1947 to cite the conventions of the novelty number. Figure 5.2 also shows the growing distance between the mainstream and race music, spurred in part by the decline of big bands, a forum that had enabled African Americans to participate (albeit semi-invisibly) in the realm of instrumental music, and the need for crossover tunes to create novelty effects. The new mainstream styles, relied, on the one hand, on the centrality of a single vocalist, a development that was less hospitable to African Americans because it tended to reveal the social identity of the vocalist, who could project an "adult" persona endowed with subjectivity, an option that was rarely available to African Americans during this period. On the other hand, the rise in novelty recordings either used the stereotypes of nonwhite others as the subject of the lyrics, thereby discouraging African American participation and identification, or revived minstrel practices. African American–associated musical practices, including improvisation in performance and song creation, drained out of the mainstream and into the semiautonomous realm of what in 1949 was renamed rhythm and blues, a category that grew in commercial

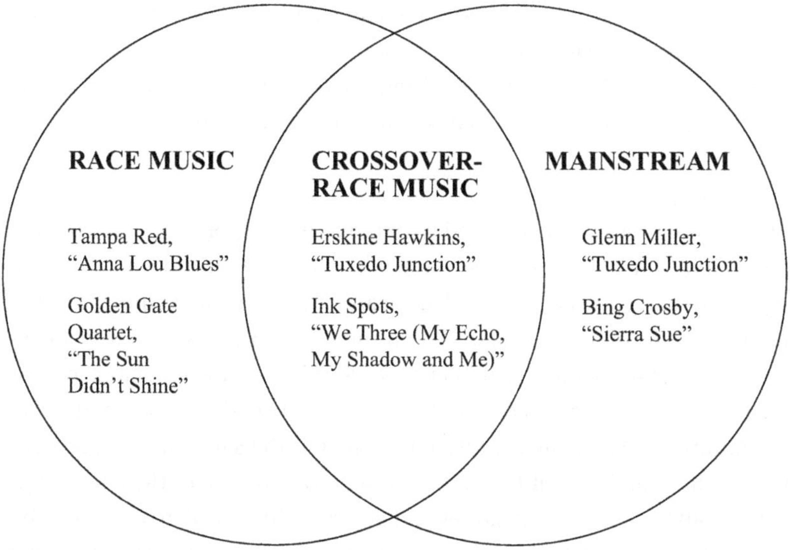

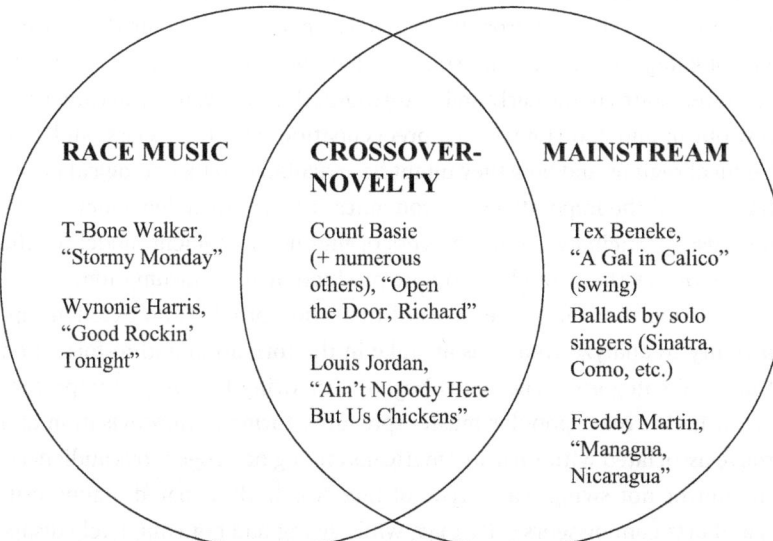

RACE MUSIC

Tampa Red,
"Anna Lou Blues"

Golden Gate
Quartet,
"The Sun
Didn't Shine"

CROSSOVER-
RACE MUSIC

Erskine Hawkins,
"Tuxedo Junction"

Ink Spots,
"We Three (My Echo,
My Shadow and Me)"

MAINSTREAM

Glenn Miller,
"Tuxedo Junction"

Bing Crosby,
"Sierra Sue"

Fig. 5.1 The Popular Music Field, circa 1940.

RACE MUSIC

T-Bone Walker,
"Stormy Monday"

Wynonie Harris,
"Good Rockin'
Tonight"

CROSSOVER-
NOVELTY

Count Basie
(+ numerous
others), "Open
the Door, Richard"

Louis Jordan,
"Ain't Nobody Here
But Us Chickens"

MAINSTREAM

Tex Beneke,
"A Gal in Calico"
(swing)

Ballads by solo
singers (Sinatra,
Como, etc.)

Freddy Martin,
"Managua,
Nicaragua"

Fig. 5.2 The Popular Music Field, circa 1947.

importance after 1945. The focus on solo singers did pay dividends for a small number of African American singers, however, as vocalists such as Nat "King" Cole and Billy Eckstine gave improbable voice to expressions of true love that previously had not had access to a large audience.[27]

This chapter has been concerned with the large categories used by the U.S. music industry and how these categories map certain aspects of musical style onto categories of group identification. Such a study runs the risk of reification, both of music and of identifications. A focus on musical categories and genres would seem on its face to reinforce the emphasis in Western philosophical thought on the idea of identity over difference, the priority of notions of resemblance, representation, and the same over the recognition of the singularity of the event and the evanescence of the phantasm.[28] Yet by looking at these categories and genres as historical artifacts, one becomes acutely aware of how such groupings of musical events can function only through the effects of domination in which the difference of both musical styles and individual subjects is deemphasized in favor of similarity. The similarities that are broadly accepted as pertinent become the conventions of categories as they are consolidated and accepted by the public. In the United States in the early and mid-twentieth century, musical categories grew out of and contributed to a preoccupation with race, class, and geographical regions and how they might be articulated to technological developments and the imperatives of economics. Thus, knowledge about people and music participated in the process of finding an efficient model for the music industry that would coordinate production and consumption.

The period that forms the focus of this study provides an excellent opportunity to analyze what was at stake in the formation and re-formation of musical categories. The 1940s began with swing forming an important part of mainstream popular music, spreading forms of improvisation and groove associated with African Americans among heterogeneous audiences. Whether or not swing was a type of jazz was hotly debated among critics and jazz connoisseurs.[29] By 1947, while swing had not completely disappeared from the mainstream, what remained deemphasized improvisatory practices and had lost much of its association with African Americans. As far as the debate over the meaning of jazz went, big band–based swing was no longer a factor. Instead, within the realm of mainstream popular music, African American-ness appeared as a stereotype grouped with stereotypes of assorted others, while jazz and soloistic improvisation were exiled temporarily to a newly established, semiautonomous field of black popular music, as the "outside" of mainstream popular music acquired greater cohesion due to the increased stability of country and rhythm and blues.

Such an examination of terms such as "jazz" and "swing" and their relationship to race music/rhythm and blues and mainstream popular music has the potential to reorganize our sense of jazz history, which since the 1950s has favored evolutionary models, excluded music that was overtly commercial, and ascribed greater authenticity (and more value) to music made by African Americans. Close attention to a broad range of music that was circulating at the time can also reorganize our sense of popular music history, which tends to look at music from 1940 to 1955 for how it anticipates rock and roll, but in which the complex interactions among style, category, and identity that occurred at the time are often overlooked. Finally, a focus on a broad range of music, canonical or not, that approaches an analysis of the synchronic complicates our notions of the role played by the shifting allegiances between identifications and categories, in which, rather than confirming a sense of their stability, we gain a renewed appreciation of their fluidity and contingency. Insofar as the categories of the popular music industry attempt to reify the relationship between the social and the aesthetic into a hierarchy that speaks to beliefs about the proper place of different types of music, the story told here is also about the transformation of social aesthetics in the music that dominated the public sphere of the 1940s in the United States.

Notes

1. For more on annualization, see North 2001.

2. Although in a similar series, *Hit Parade* (produced by the Dynamic recording company), dating back to 1938, Basie's "Jumpin' at the Woodside" was included in the 1938 volume. The number of these compilations has been proliferating at an alarming rate, as any search of iTunes will readily confirm.

3. This particular usage of "tasteless" is derived from Brooks 1982.

4. The classic theoretical formulation about the relationship between economic and symbolic capital is in Bourdieu 1993; see also DeVeaux 1991. On the exclusion of popular figures such as Louis Jordan, see Ake 2002. On the exclusions of gender performed by the conventional framing of jazz historiography, see S. Tucker 2000.

5. Although for a recent attempt to address this lacuna, see Zak 2001. For broader histories that do not give this era short shrift, see Ennis 1992, Wald 2009.

6. For the most sophisticated model of the different ways in which music and

identification may interrelate (and one which considers homology as a possibility), see Born and Hesmondhalgh 2000, secs. 4–5. I expand on Born's model in the context of a discussion of genre in popular music in "Popular Music Genres" (2014) and in my introduction to *Categorizing Sound: Genre and Twentieth-Century Popular Music* (2016). For a previous formulation of the relationship between genre and identification, see Brackett 2005.

7. The reference to a "genealogical account" invokes the work of Michel Foucault, specifically his essay "Nietzsche, Genealogy, History" (1977a). The purpose of this invocation is not to contrast simply a "presentist" view of history—a role that might be filled by the "canonical narratives" referred to earlier in which a cause-and-effect teleology leads from a point of origin to the present to confirm contemporary beliefs about a subject—with a "historicist" approach that reconstitutes the historical horizon in which events and texts emerge. Rather, such a genealogical approach seeks both to analyze the conditions that make it possible for an event to occur and, at the same time, not to occlude the current events to which an interest in the past is responding, what Foucault called elsewhere a "history of the present" (Foucault 1979).

8. Again, a concept of Bourdieu's—this time, that of "habitus"—is helpful for understanding how improvisation can be experienced as free yet at the same time be constrained and made possible by previously internalized practices that thus become a set of naturalized responses. See Bourdieu 1977, 52–65.

9. For examples, see Nettl and Russell 1998, Solis and Nettl 2009.

10. For contemporary music criticism promulgating two contrasting views of this subject, see Freedman 1940, 7, 20; Kolodin 1941, 78–82. Both of these articles are reprinted in Brackett 2009.

11. Ronald Radano (2003) has examined the emergence of a particular notion of African American music that relies on the trope of "hot rhythm."

12. For more on the work concept in Western art music, see Goehr 1992.

13. A body of scholarly literature exists arguing that the emphasis on the recording as the referential text for a work of popular music after rock and roll displaces the emphasis on print textuality favored by the aesthetics of Western art music and pre-rock Western popular music. For examples, see Gracyk 1996, Zak 2001. While Albin Zak (2010) extends the dichotomy of song as printed artifact versus song as recorded/sonic experience back to the late 1940s, the discussion here suggests that this opposition is central to understanding the formation of the popular music field in the era of mechanical reproduction, with discourse about this opposition appearing as early as the 1920s.

14. A reader (particularly one interested in improvisation) may well wonder about the role of performances, yet the way in which performances were factored into the computation of popularity during this period consisted solely of noting the number of times *which* song was played, not *who* played it or *how* it was played. Tabulations of the number of times a song was played on the radio were counted in the category of "song plugs," a measurement used by music publishers to gauge the success of their attempts to popularize their product.

15. The homologies assumed by these categories functioned partly as an imaginary ideal; the relation of production and consumption to identification were considerably more complex.

16. By an "equality of represented subjects" (Rancière 2004, 81), Rancière means that authors and painters of the Romantic era could focus just as easily on those of lower social status as on the aristocracy. Music only arises in the elaboration of his theory during a discussion of modernism, in which "the language of twelve sounds" is used as an example of how "each individual art would thus assert the pure potential of art by exploring the capabilities of its specific medium," and on the role of nostalgia in the aesthetic regime of the arts, in which he adduces "Mendelssohn replaying the *St. Matthew Passion*" as an example (Rancière 2004, 25–26). Once again, it is difficult to see how these observations might apply to examples drawn from commercial art, thus again banishing such art to the realm of the non-sensible. Part of my argument, and thus my interest in Rancière, is precisely to analyze how different genres of popular music might present or re-present subjects. Popular music genres tend to be associated with one type of subject at a time and thus would still have a difficult time "representing" an "equality of subjects."

17. Indeed, the debate about whether swing music was primarily for dancing or listening was more significant than we might now currently imagine. Ballroom owners disliked the fact that many in attendance clustered around the bandstand for particular ensembles, standing still and listening rather than dancing. Hawkins's recording of "Tuxedo Junction" could be understood as trying to keep both groups of fans involved: listeners, more attuned to the nuances of improvisation, and dancers, engaged by the repetition of swinging riffs. For more of an argument about the role of non-dancing listeners in the swing era, see Wald 2009, 123–25. Lewis Erenberg (1998, 58–62) also describes the tension between "jitterbugs" and swing fans (and musicians) who preferred to listen attentively.

18. On the popularity of jukeboxes, see Rasmussen 2010.

19. "What the Records Are Doing for Me," *Billboard* (December 30, 1939): 150.

20. "Record Buying Guide," *Billboard* (February 24, 1940): 72.

21. See "Miller, Hawkins, Cooper Score at Savoy Xmas Eve," *Chicago Defender* (December 30, 1939): 17.

22. Although, interestingly enough, even in this era musicians were occasionally forced to memorize solos that they had improvised in the studio to avoid disappointing audiences that had come to a performance expecting to hear a recording re-created as exactly as possible. To be sure, this was more often the case with bands such as Miller's, in which solos were often only four or eight measures long, as opposed to the thirty-two-bar choruses to be found in the recordings of the "hottest" ensembles of the day (Wald 2009, 127).

23. The following draws heavily on R. J. Smith 2004.

24. A video of a 1945 performance of Fletcher performing this skit can be viewed at http://archive.org/details/open_the_door_richard (accessed February 26, 2013).

25. This legal dispute reflects the uncertain status of non-notatable elements with respect to copyright law and refers back to questions around the legibility of different sorts of musical texts with respect to the music industry. The sound of a recording and the *way* in which a song was performed were not protected in the same way that the notated melodic-harmonic matrix of a song was.

26. The most exhaustive accounting of different versions is at http://www .jerryosborne.com/8-1-11.htm, http://www.jerryosborne.com/8-8-11.htm.

27. On Eckstine, see DeVeaux 1997. On African American crooners, see Stephens 2008.

28. The formulation here is guided by that of Foucault 1977b.

29. On this debate among jazz critics, see Gendron 2002, 121–42; Gennari 2006, 61–115.

CHAPTER 6

WHAT IS "GREAT BLACK MUSIC"?

The Social Aesthetics of the AACM in Paris

Eric Lewis

In the summer of 1969, members of the Association for the Advancement of Creative Musicians (AACM) recorded a number of albums in Paris. Many of the musicians had recently made Paris their home, including Roscoe Mitchell, Lester Bowie, Malachi Favors, and Joseph Jarman (known collectively as the Art Ensemble of Chicago, or AEC) and the ensemble of Leo Smith, Anthony Braxton, and Leroy Jenkins.[1] The recordings, and their associated performances, were subjected to intense critical scrutiny by both the French press and American and English critics. The many albums issued during this period (a large number on the French label Actuel) are often thought to represent an artistic high-water mark for the music variously called "the new thing," "avant-garde jazz," or, as we shall examine, "Great Black Music." It was certainly viewed by critics as being of great social, political, and aesthetic interest. George Lewis devotes a chapter in his magisterial *A Power Stronger than Itself* (2008) to the AACM in Paris, discussing with characteristic detail and subtlety a wide range of issues related to this period of the association's history and evolution. Building on Lewis's account, I want to explore the aesthetic ramifications of these AACM members' varied artistic activities—from the music they performed, the albums they recorded, and the interviews and press conferences they gave to the critical reception they received and their responses to it—and argue that they *consciously* engaged in what I will call repeated acts of "aesthetic thickening." These acts discharged both aesthetic and social functions and can therefore be fruitfully seen as the articulation of a particular kind of social aesthetics that is deeply rooted in aspects of a more general African diasporic aesthetic and the constellation of political and social issues focusing on identity that many see as an important function of such art.[2] More specifically, these aesthetic and social functions are not distinct but require each other for their effect.

Much of the attention the music of the AACM in Paris received centered on a basic question: what "sort" of music were they creating and what is its relationship to jazz, on the one hand, and European art music, on the other? As we shall see, the members of the AACM were acutely aware of the importance of such genre/ontological judgments. Far from being passive recipients of categories, genres, meanings, and goals foisted on their art and actions by others, the AACM in Paris turned on its head the potential ghettoizing of genre categories and used them to widen the aesthetic and social interest of their art.[3] They accomplished this by destabilizing any single genre perspective from which to critique their art and (therefore) argued that their art was best seen as multi-generic and thus aesthetically thick. As will be discussed more fully later, since membership in a genre partially determines what properties are potentially of aesthetic interest, multi-generic works are aesthetically richer than they might otherwise have been.

I begin by describing two particular recorded performances: "Silence" (1974), by Smith, Braxton, and Jenkins, and the album *Message to Our Folks* (1969), by the AEC. These performances play with and problematize assorted musical genre categories.[4] I then relate this genre play to theorizing on the antiessentialist impulse found in much black art and the hypothesis of multiple authentic artistic identities that is seen to follow from this. After relating this to aspects of genre theory, I argue that the AACM in Paris, aware of the roles and functions of genres and their associated critical discourses, consciously manipulated these categories and expectations against a backdrop of criticism of their art that drew on both modernist and nascent postmodernist theory. I tie this together by sketching a theory of aesthetic thickness and argue that this is what the AACM in Paris were undertaking and show how this thickening discharges both traditional aesthetic and social/political functions. Finally, I discuss the expression "Great Black Music" as coined by members of the AEC, concluding that it takes on the function of a meta-genre, signifying on the notion of genre itself—an act that is simultaneously a social and an aesthetic critique of how genres function and the politics of genre ownership.

"Silence," by Wadada Leo Smith, is a very sparse musical work, with long periods of silence punctuated by usually brief interjections of small percussion, reeds, trumpet, violin, harmonica, flute, or accordion.[5] A skeletal structure is discernible (see table 6.1). The sections that contain sounds, viewed as single temporal blocks, become more closely spaced as the piece progresses. There is also an increase in the number of instruments that play simultaneously and the length of time that they do so, although the pitch density is never very great. There is always much "space" in the music and little in the way of musical syntax as traditionally conceived. It is unclear whether the "environmental" sounds such as footsteps and chair creaks are intentional or residue from a less than perfect recording environment. There is the regular use of extended techniques, although at no times are these foregrounded per se (the playing is controlled throughout and does not draw attention to its techniques). The instrumentation also avoids coding as jazz. The violin is often played in non-standard ways; the percussion lacks the characteristic tones and effects of a trap set; there is a preponderance of small percussion instruments; the trumpet is played with highly inflected timbre decentering its sound from the jazz world; and a series of reed instruments are all played with no sonic gestures toward the jazz idiom. Certainly, this piece is worlds away from the dynamics, pitch density, rhythmic sense, and melodic and harmonic language of what at the time was commonly called "free jazz." It does not sound like how that species of new jazz associated with African American political movements of the time was often characterized, lacking, most obviously, the propulsive beat, loud dynamics, and pitch density.

The AEC recorded its album *Message to Our Folks* around the same time in Paris. The album opens with the piece "Old Time Religion" (itself a traditional), which here is not a spiritual so much as a sermon. Over a repeating four-note arco bass riff Joseph Jarman recites a sermon in what sounds like an archaic style, with vocal responses from the other band members. Soon, long horn tones start to interfere with the spoken sermon, along with a tambourine. The call and response continues, with multiple "amens" that resolve into the melodically sung line, "Give me that old time religion." The vocals throughout are spoken with odd timbres that suggest post-production engineering. The piece rises in intensity with a series of "woops" and half-valve trumpet blasts. Then the horns play the emergent melodic line in unison, and the piece dissolves into a series of soft call-and-response lines, ending with a single long tone.

Taken in isolation, and with no contextual information, it would be very

TABLE 6.1 Structural Outline, "Silence," Wadada Leo Smith

0:00–0:12	Rough violin bowing near bridge
0:39–1:08	Long alto horn (?) tone, mezzo-piano
1:12–1:14	Brief percussion hits, wood then metal with sustained overtones
1:31–1:35	Muted trumpet note
2:07–2:15	Violin note vibrato, mezzo-piano
2:18–2:31	Very soft chair squeaks? Intentional? Environmental?
3:02	Single short clarinet (?) note, with perhaps ghost images before and after, a result of recording process?
3:34	Very faint vocalization?
3:51	Footsteps?
4:04–4:21	Triangle hit > wood block hits > hand muted cymbal? > single tenor horn with white noise
5:59–6:09	Baritone horn notes piano, with overblowing > single soft percussion hit?
6:18–6:20	Chair noises, very soft?
6:32–6:40	Violin notes, bow percussive taps
6:54–7:02	Forte trumpet riff, held note > dense cluster (more ghost tones)
7:07–7:25	Ascending wood flute / recorder riff with simultaneous small percussion taps (first time more than one instrument playing)
7:30–7:33	Brief, soft wood percussion taps
7:45–7:57	Bells *with* scraped cymbal?
7:57–8:15	Harmonica melodic section
8:25–8:37	Low register trumpet glissandos > chimes with single wood flute / recorder tone
8:45	Chair squeak?
8:50–9:45	Accordion notes > high muted trumpet > valve flutter on sax with single short note > violin note with horn tongue flutter then with forte trumpet riff and tenor horn? Upper harmonics / lower growl
9:49–10:21	Assorted percussion playing together > wood flute?
10:30–11:55	Plucked violin with cymbal > cymbals with human voice whistle > soprano sax > harmonica with trumpet and wood flute? > percussion hit (sense of structure here)
12:07–12:47	Cymbals and gongs, wood block, with bass clarinet tone?
12:52–13:42	Percussion with recorder wood flute > accordion
13:44–14:43	Assorted percussion decreasing tone density to end

Note: > = successive sonic acts. The question marks indicate my lack of confidence in my description of the instrument being played. Also, many sounds are discernible during this recording that may be "incidental" but that may still be intended as part of the listening experience. These details are not particularly important here.

hard to place this piece with respect to genre, time, or place. "What is it?" is the question I often get when I play this piece for listeners without supplying any prior information about it. Its reference to, and embeddedness within, African American sacred music is clear, but little else is. It is followed by "Dexterity," a bebop standard written by Charlie Parker. Here the AEC seems to call into question one of the founding rules of the AACM, which is to promote original, or creative, music.[6] While the founding members of the AACM held a range of opinions about both the desirability and interpretation of a prohibition on the performance of standards, this was, I believe, the first time an AACM ensemble had recorded a standard. While the performance is full of small idiosyncrasies, it is played fairly straight, with Malachi Favors's walking bass line serving as a backdrop for a series of solos. While there are vocal interventions, the musicians are clearly sticking rather close to the piece as scored, and the overall structure of their performance places it recognizably within the jazz idiom.

Next is "Rock Out," with Favors moving to fretless electric bass and someone playing brief electric guitar riffs, all over a busy percussion track. The piece is highly repetitive, with little rhythmic variation and no harmonic movement (indeed, for quite a while, apart from the repeating bass riff, no real harmonic or melodic material is present at all). At one point, a horn enters playing a rhythm-and-blues-style solo, with, however, little interest or real commitment; it is more satire than substance. The piece then moves to a brief bridge, after which the horn engages in more forceful honking, evoking the tradition of Texas tenors. The piece lies somewhere between parody and merely boring, as if the AEC are saying that rock music has black musical forms as its source but has denuded them of any musical interest. A brief guitar-driven section follows, with playing that would not be out of context in a punk piece; it, in turn, resolves into a series of distorted tones accompanied by car horns, cymbal crashes, and vocal exclamations. At this point the piece ends (is rock just noise?).

The final piece on the album, "A Brain for the Seine," takes up the whole B side. It is far more abstract; small instruments abound; and the ensemble makes much use of space and silence. This piece occupies a sonic space similar to that of "Silence." There are spoken interludes that ask, "Can I please have a drink of water?" as if one is begging an aloof French waiter or, perhaps, a jail guard.[7] The piece sits squarely within the precise tradition of experimentalism that the members of the AEC and other first-generation AACM members developed. It sounds like the audio track of a performance-art piece, which in many senses it is (given the highly performative nature of live AEC concerts). It lacks any rhythmic propulsion, although it occasionally has an implied beat. Sections include accordion, seeming to evoke French street musicians, while other sections, with piano and reeds, may remind one of modernist European art music before morphing into sonically sui generis ensemble playing. Carefully constructed trumpet and saxophone lines often emerge out of near-silence, with a focus on tone color and timbres produced by the use of extended techniques. There is a great variety of percussion accompaniment (the AEC was known to travel with more than two thousand instruments in total), from bells to assorted idiophones, gongs, horns, and cymbals, which collectively were to suggest to critics both the jungle and the city, along with many imaginary soundscapes. Near the end of the piece a brief melodic line is played in unison, resolving into a series of cymbal taps.

"Silence" (and the performances of the Smith-Braxton-Jenkins trio more generally) and the music of the AEC as exemplified by the pieces on *Message to Our Folks* confused both French critics and those from the English-speaking world precisely because of how the variety of their sonic gestures impeded obvious pigeonholing of their music into one genre category or another and so problematized discussion of their art from any single given critical perspective. It is worth delving into this "confusion" in some detail to flesh out the aesthetic strategies employed by the AACM in Paris related to this genre instability. As Stuart Hall (1992, 26) writes, "By definition, black popular culture is a contradictory space. It is a sight [sic] of strategic contestation. But it can never be simplified or explained in terms of the simple binary oppositions that are still habitually used to map it out." It is a commonplace of postcolonial studies to note and theorize about the (apparently) contradictory elements of African diasporic culture and, in particular, to note the careful negotiations and manipulations of these contradictions undertaken by black artists. Such contradictions are demonstrated not to be "mistakes"—elements that need to be exorcized to create a consistent artistic discourse and practice—but are shown to be the building blocks of creative artistic practices. Hall goes on to say, "In its expressivity its musicality, its orality, in its rich, deep and varied attention to speech, in its inflections towards the vernacular and the local, in its rich production of counternarratives, and above all, in its metaphorical use of the musical vocabulary, black popular culture has enabled the surfacing, inside the mixed and contradictory modes even of some mainstream popular culture, of elements of a discourse that is different—other forms of life, other traditions of representation" (27). Such hybridity,[8] with its element of the contradictory, is itself theorized to be grounded in the affirmation of multiple identities by many black artists, itself seen as a product of colonialism, and to operate as a critique of essentialist racial discourse. A clear statement of this linkage is made by bell hooks:

> Employing a critique of essentialism allows African-Americans to acknowledge the way in which class mobility has altered collective black experience so that racism does not necessarily have the same impact on our lives. Such a critique allows us to affirm multiple black identities, varied black experience. It also challenges colonial imperialist paradigms of black identity which represent blackness one-dimensionally in ways that reinforce and sustain white supremacy. This discourse created the idea of the "primitive" and promoted the notion of an "authentic" experience, seeing as "natural" those expressions of black life which conformed to a pre-existing pattern or stereotype. . . . Contemporary African-American resistance struggle must be rooted in a process of decolonization that continually opposes re-inscribing notions of "authentic" black identity. . . . When black folks critique essentialism, we are empowered to recognize multiple experiences of black identity that are the lived conditions which make diverse cultural productions possible. When this diversity is ignored, it is easy to see black folks as falling into two categories: nationalist or assimilationist, black-identified or white-identified. Coming to terms with the impact of postmodernism for black experience, particularly as it changes our sense of identity, means that we must and can rearticulate the basis for collective bonding. (hooks 1990, 28–29)

In a telling autobiographical passage from a different essay, hooks (1989, 11) tells us, "It was listening to black musicians like Duke Ellington, Louis Armstrong, and later John Coltrane that impressed upon our consciousness a sense of versatility—they played all kinds of music, had multiple voices." While the hybridity of African diasporic art practices, their playful use of contradictions, and their multivocality and denial of single authentic identities is now well established, it is rarely recognized that the enactment of these artistic strategies is itself employed as an aesthetic gambit—that the aesthetic theory that emerges out of these strategies both serves to critique racial and artistic essentialism and uses these contradictions to thicken the aesthetic value of such works. What results are not works fractured from the perspective of an aesthetics bent on revealing aesthetic value but works whose aesthetic worth can be viewed from multiple aesthetic vantage points, from assorted critical positions, and employing varied aesthetic discourses.

What I hope to do is demonstrate that the sort of critique of essentialism that hooks discusses is *consciously* undertaken by the AACM in Paris and that it is an *aesthetic* strategy that enacts this critique—a most intimate entwining of the social and the aesthetic. This can be seen as a way to cash out George Lewis's (2008, 240) claim, concerning the criticism the AACM in Paris received, that "the [black] nationalist strait-jacket that the music of the AACM Paris contingent was being shoehorned into often served to limit the ways in which their music might be perceived and contextualized. . . . These and other reductivist accounts of their work were strongly resisted by AACM musicians working in Paris."

The primary terrain on which contrasting critiques, both laudatory and negative, of the AACM in Paris were constructed, and to which the AACM responded (both while in Paris and in earlier and later statements), is that of the genre designations appropriate for discussing their music. Criticism was not so much directed at individual performances and musical works as it concerned the AACM's musical practices writ large. *What* kind of music was the AACM producing, *why* was the AACM producing it, and (therefore) what critical stance is best suited to come to an understanding of it, were the questions asked, and the site of much controversy. Genre theory can help us both understand what was (and continues to be) at stake and make sense of the AACM members' responses to the reception of their music, for they understood perfectly the role genre determinations play both at the level of general theory and in the precise manner that genre terms were employed by their critics, offering a critique of them. As hooks (1990, 28) says, "Such a critique allows us to affirm multiple black identities, varied black experience. It also challenges colonial imperialist paradigms of black identity which represent blackness one-dimensionally in ways that reinforce and sustain white supremacy."

Genre theorists, particularly those who have focused on music, have stressed the role that musical genres play in the mediation of social identities and investigated the porous (synchronic) and malleable (diachronic) nature of genre boundaries. For example, David Brackett (2005, 75) states, "The notion of genre speaks to transitory divisions in the musical field that correspond in discontinuous and complex ways to a temporally defined social space. . . . Musical genres participate in the circulation of social connotations that pass between musicians, fans, critics, music-industry magnates and employees. That these connotations, these 'meanings' are accepted as 'real' speaks to the phantasmatic nature of identity, that ever-shifting sense of self that finds confirmation and reinforcement in quotidian social practices and in a range of discursive formations, both institutional and shadowy." How the "logic of genres" affects aesthetics is nicely summarized by Georgina Born (1993b, 215), who writes, "Indeed the wider cultural character of popular music, as of non-Western music, forces a reconsideration of the concept of the aesthetic itself—if, by aesthetic, we understand the ways that music-as-culture produces both meaning and pleasure. The point is that, in these cultures, since meaning inheres in the social, visual, discursive and technological mediations of music as well as in the musical sound, we may consider the aesthetic as subsuming these mediations. From this perspective, then, the social, the visual, the discursive and so on are all constitutive of the aesthetic." The aesthetic properties of music are partially a function of the meanings attributed to music, and musical meaning is both partially constituted and constrained by genre.[9] Here we can begin to see the complex intertwining of the social and the aesthetic at the site of genre, since genres are as much about identities (and they are, after all, themselves a kind of identity, a category of being) as they are about aesthetics. Perhaps better yet, no real separation of the two can be made. The AACM in effect combine the antiessentialism of hooks and the social aesthetics of Born in a demonstration that they are in effect two sides of the same coin. The methods for effecting the critique of essentialism are themselves aesthetic gambits, and the music that mediates such critiques is aesthetically richer for undertaking such a critique.

In an influential article concerning the role of art category/genre judgments in the formation of aesthetic judgments, Kendall Walton (1970) explores the manner in which what category we take an art object to be an example of establishes fields of aesthetic value and disvalue. Walton argues that the category into which we place an art object generates three kinds of properties that such an object may or may not manifest, which he calls standard, variable, and contra-standard. While he does not descend to the level of genres within a traditional art form (his account operates at the level of art forms themselves, painting, sculpture, and so on), his account strongly suggests the appropriateness of so doing. He concludes, "What aesthetic properties a work seems to have, what aesthetic effect it has on us, how it strikes us aesthetically often depends (in part) on which of its features are standard, which variable, and which contra-standard for us" (343). Walton goes on to argue that works that can be considered members of more than one art kind, or more than one genre, may well have distinct, even contradictory aesthetic properties attributed to them.[10] In a passage that, as we shall see, can usefully explain some of the response to the AACM in Paris, Walton, considering the aesthetically relevant property "shocking," claims, "Shock then arises from features that are not just rare or unique, but ones that are contra-standard relative to categories in which objects possessing them are perceived. . . . What is important is not the rarity of a feature, but its connection with the classification of the work" (354). In this sense, the aesthetic properties that the works have are relative to the genre of which we take the work to be a member.[11] Here we can see the importance of Jacques Derrida's (1980, 59) notion of "participation without belonging" with respect to a genre, for the tendency to naturalize and view as objective the aesthetic properties, and thus meanings, we find in artworks is actually to a great extent a product of our genre judgments, as both Derrida and Roland Barthes have argued. Again, Born succinctly draws a moral from this:

> But the point is that the relation of these extramusical connotations to music-as-signifier is cultural, historical, established by convention and in social practice. Yet they are experienced as "inherent in" or "immanent to" the music by a process of *projection* of the connotations *into* the musical sound object. It is this process of projection that achieves what Barthes calls the "naturalising" effect: the connotations appear to be natural and universal where they are cultural and historical. It is, then, the forms of talk, text and theory around music—the metaphors and rhetoric explaining and constructing it, whether propounded by composer, theorist or critic—that constitute its inherent discursive intertextuality, and that may liable to analysis as ideological. (Born 1993b, 222)

As we shall see, the AACM in Paris *consciously* fought against such naturalizing readings of its music on ideological grounds; its members attempted to widen the field of connotative projections into their music to avoid the situation in which the acceptance of certain connotations led them to ossify into essentialisms; in effect, to avoid a connotation becoming a denotation, in Derridian terms.

In a passage that he chose not to explore further, Walton recognized the aesthetic value, in and of itself, of the various, perhaps even contradictory, aesthetic properties a work might manifest due to the multiple genres in which it might plausibly be taken to "participate": "Works may be fascinating precisely because of shifts between equally permissible ways of perceiving them. And the enormous richness of some works is due in part to the variety of permissible, and worthwhile, ways of perceiving them" (Walton 1970, 362). If we ignore his prescriptive talk of "permissibility," what we have here is the recognition that what I call aesthetic denseness is itself an aesthetic value; that works located in multiple social fields of art consumption, creation, and criticism, and that thus participate in multiple genres, may well be aesthetically richer for this. What is at stake in the genre debates surrounding the music of the AACM in Paris is not "just" the meaning found in the music, the role such music may play in an antiessentialist social agenda, the place of the association's art in large art-related discourses and therefore history, but also good, "old-fashioned" issues surrounding aesthetic value, or how "fascinating" the AACM's music may be. As Joseph Jarman sarcastically (as we shall see) yet truthfully states, "Yes we hope you enjoy our music."[12]

I now want to consider some of the writing of the members of the AACM in Paris and the criticism their music received to demonstrate how they engaged in collective acts of aesthetic thickening and to demonstrate that these acts discharged both aesthetic and social/political functions. In his dense book *notes (8 pieces)*, Wadada Leo Smith stresses the importance of autonomy in improvisation, which he sees as (among other things) freeing the "sound rhythm" elements from the limitations of reactive improvisation and from traditional elements of meter, tempo, and rhythm. Autonomy is one of the key concepts that the AACM members in Paris use both to respond to their critics and to describe their own music. This makes sense, since they are combating both genre judgments about their music made by others and related assumptions about what sort of music black so-called jazz musicians could, or should, produce. To be autonomous is in this context to be able to take control of these issues oneself. This stress on autonomy in improvisation suggests an emphasis on the autonomy of individuals more generally, something African Americans (among others) historically have been denied. More precisely, the expression of assorted identities, displayed via varied musical constructions, is a robust assertion of both personal and collective autonomy. It is the refusal to be typecast or essentialized.

By employing a variety of small instruments, each given equal footing; refusing to employ a strong rhythmic pulse; and employing long stretches of silence, Smith and the other AACM members in Paris were rejecting standard white constructions of black identity, particularly essentialist constructions of black music. The autonomy the music itself manifests is a product of Smith's and his fellow improvisers' autonomy in deciding what to play (and, crucially, when not to play), and, in particular, their conscious decision not to delimit their choices by genre expectations, themselves created by assumptions concerning what they, as black musicians, should sonically produce and how their productions should be categorized.[13] Smith himself seems to view his music this way: "I, a black man, a creative improviser, strive, through my improvisations and as an improviser to pay homage to the black, the blackness of my people, and that these creations themselves are for all, and the natural laws that are prevailing under these creations are relative as they are interpreted or perceived by beings of other peoples" (W. L. Smith 1973).[14] He also writes, "Critics have applied narrow concepts to this improvisational music so that they could easily write about and define it and dictate what is the essence of black music-creative music. The percussion, brasses, strings and any other beaten, plucked or wind blown instruments in improvisational music are equal—they are all equal in the creation of music" (1973). Smith sees his music as part of a tradition of black music that has been (mis)constructed by critics. In other words, while he does view his music as speaking to issues of black identity, he is not limited by what many see as the characteristics music must have to be coded as black. He wishes to be able to construct his own history and future for his music—to express his personal autonomy via the creation of autonomous music. His music *is* to be considered part of the history of black music; the construction of a historical narrative of such music is at the forefront of what he is trying to accomplish. These thoughts are not mere conjecture but were made explicit by Smith himself with respect to "Silence" during an interview on the New York radio station WCKR-FM on the occasion of the thirtieth anniversary of the AACM:

> Well, we wanted to look at music that would give us a chance *to express exactly who we were.* And once you make that particular commitment, you have to find out how you're going to do this. So we decided that we would write for instruments, and write for ensembles. *We didn't have to accept the history that was given to us before, and we didn't even have to expect some kind of present history or future history.* We were able to contemplate the real essence of creative music. We were able to come in with projects, for example, like "Silence" is a piece that has silence in it, and it came after John Cage's "Silence," but the philosophical connection of silence in this case was to materialize music within the space, and whatever was heard in the environment, whereas in the Cage piece there was absolutely no music in the space, and the gestures were the moments of the environment, you see. So creating a piece that seemed that it would look like and feel like a piece that came out of Cage's tradition, in fact, we didn't have that problem, because as I say, *we are not bound by what came in the past or*

this particular ensemble's history—you know, like a classical ensemble has a history that's specifically European. We didn't have to worry about that.[15]

Smith has consistently made claims such as this, and they form the core of *notes (8 pieces)*, which explains some of the philosophy behind his compositional methods and contains more general thoughts about what has come to be called "creative music." Smith begins with a "warning to black people" to take control of their own history (including the history of their musical practices) and to offer their own critiques of their music. This, he claims, is tantamount to becoming "self-conscious" (W. L. Smith 1973, 1).[16] At the level of musical production, this is an argument for prioritizing improvising, "giving [improvisers] a part in the creation of the music" (13). Crucially, Smith builds this desire for autonomy into his music itself: "The concept that I employ in my music is to consider each performer as a complete unit with each having his or her own center from which each performs independently of any other, and with this respect of autonomy the independent center of the improvisation is continuously changing depending upon the force created by individual centers at any instance [*sic*] from any of the units. . . . In other words, each element is autonomous in its relationship in the improvisation" (22). He goes on to state that his compositional methods are created "in such a way as to preserve the autonomy of each improviser within a group, each group within the orchestra, and each improviser within the unit-total" (23).

Smith's music is an expression of who he is, a self-construction of his identity (and the identities of his fellow improvisers). He rejects a view of "Silence" as just "Cage on the cheap" while denying that he was bound by others' construction of black music's history or similar constructions of European art music. By freeing himself from a history that historically has denied black artists autonomy, that has created a history and identity forcibly for such artists, Smith's music—the silence Smith employs—speaks. It speaks of a new identity; it tells a new history. Silence as employed by Cage was perhaps a "mere" formal musicological element. Silence as employed by society against blacks (and others) was, and still is, a powerful tool of oppression. Silence as employed by Smith is both a musical "tool" serving to undermine a false construction of black music (as being necessarily rhythm-bound and pulse-driven) and a highly creative use of the tools of oppression to express musical and personal autonomy. When viewed against a backdrop of *both* Western experimental music and African diasporic music and the political issues that Smith foregrounds in his discussion of the piece, "Silence" becomes aesthetically thicker than it would be if one were to examine it from any single genre perspective. It is not just that both perspectives are "appropriate" but that the piece actually puts them in dialogue with each other, inviting you to compare your views about each, their differences and similarities, their distinct yet overlapping histories, and what follows from taking them to be mutually exclusive, how this might reveal perhaps often hidden prejudices.[17]

Smith is explicit in his goal of constructing a historical narrative for the ensemble's music by referencing both Cage and the tradition(s) of black music. Thus, "Silence" is aesthetically thickened via genre multiplication, a multiplication that both problematizes our genre assumptions about black music and suggests a political agenda related to autonomy and freedom, both social and musical.

We can see how autonomy in "Silence" operates on assorted planes. The individual performers are given autonomy to choose what and when to play. Silences in particular are hallmarks of this autonomy, since their length, placement, and frequency in the piece direct one's attention toward these performers' decisions not to play. The resultant music, lacking many obvious hallmarks of traditional musical structure and mimetic content, can easily be heard to aspire to the oft-cited goals of autonomous music and to invite the associated acousmatic listening. Yet the emphasis on autonomy also refers to the politics of autonomy and its closely associated concept, freedom, and "Silence" can be viewed as performing—that is, instancing—what a more egalitarian social reality in which all are free to assert their autonomy would be. By using silence—a tool of oppression—to assert autonomy, Smith, Braxton, and Jenkins turn the oppressors' means of oppressing back on itself. Autonomy is performed as much as it is injected into the music. Here what are at one obvious level aesthetic choices (to employ silence, to allow performers great autonomy in their sonic choices, to avoid melodic and harmonic development) discharge social functions and critiques (the assertion of alternative histories of black music and a rebuttal to essentialist readings of such music), and these social functions themselves determine the aesthetic choices that are made. This is a perfectly integrated social aesthetics, and if it has elements of a musical-social homologism that some find simplistic, I hope to have demonstrated that with the AACM this operates at a high level of sophistication and is well theorized.

This brand of social aesthetics is consistent with assorted "founding" documents of the AACM and comments by its original members. Consider the following statement by two of the founding members Muhal Richard Abrams and John Shenoy Jackson (1973, 72): "The AACM intends to show how the disadvantaged and the disenfranchised can come together and determine their own strategies for political and economic freedom, thereby determining their own destinies." This passage echoes their claim that the primary concerns of the AACM are "survival, accountability and achievement." The collective responsibility they have in mind concerns the community of black artists and the wider community these artists represent and partially constitute: "In the area of accountability, Black artists should be held responsible to their brothers and sisters, who, in turn, should demand excellence and give their support to Black endeavors" (73). The notions of accountability and self-determination in these passages, which clearly have a primary social/political meaning, are, as we have seen, enacted or modeled musically by the AACM by holding each improviser responsible for his own sonic contributions, by allowing the music to perform its own history, and by creating, in effect, autonomous music.

These themes are picked up in the following passage:

The AACM is attempting to precipitate activity geared towards finding a solution to the basic contradictions which face Black people in all facets of human structures, particularly cultural and economic. There is an incessant demand in Black communities to solve the disparity *between participation and nonparticipation* in the social process. Our concerts and workshops in the schools and in the community are an effort to expose our Black brothers and sisters to creative artists contemporary to their time and present to them a factual account of their glorious past as an undergirding for facing the future. Demonstrating the creation and production of art will enhance the cultural and spiritual posture of a people and it is our firm belief that artistic appreciation will so enhance cultural and spiritual growth that the individual's participation in the social process will be highly accelerated. It is the contention of the AACM that it is not the potential which Black people have which will determine what they do but, rather, how they feel about themselves.

Finally, the AACM intends to show how the disadvantaged and the disenfranchised can come together and determine their own strategies for political freedom and economic freedom, thereby determining their own destinies. This will not only create a new day for Black artists but for all Third World inhabitants; a new day of not only participation but also of control. (74)

Here participation in social processes that might bring about the better-ment of their community is explicitly tied to participation in the creation of art. Artistic growth is almost presented as a *prerequisite* for social growth or change, and self-determination, as a social/political goal, is both practiced and modeled artistically. The AACM, and other likeminded cooperatives of black artist-activists, intends both its music/art and its organizational struc-tures to model a more participatory egalitarian culture. Statements such as these by members of the AACM can easily serve to ground Jacques Ran-cière's observation that "it is not a misunderstanding of the existing state of affairs that nurtures the submission of the oppressed, but a lack of con-fidence in their own capacity to transform it" (quoted in Bishop 2006, 83). The AACM's practices and art serve to instill this transformative capacity in the association's community.

Let us turn our attention to the critical reception of the AACM in Paris, and other comments by AACM members about their own work, to both flesh out the points made earlier and demonstrate the precise manner in which genre judgments were implicated in critiques of the group's music. As dem-onstrated, the AACM in Paris used its relationship to genres to assert its agency against the danger, which Brackett rightly noted, that particular genre judgments fix too rigidly the meaning attributed to the music and the appropriate aesthetic to apply to it. For this reason, the members of the AACM in Paris steadfastly refused to talk about their music from any single genre perspective, and they constantly problematized attempts at genre pigeonholing by employing a variety of tactics, from straightforward asser-tions of the multi-generic nature of their music through the employment of contradictory utterances about their art and the use of multi-generic pas-tiche in their performances. Many of these tactics and tropes would soon become characteristic of postmodern art discourse, and the French critics were quick to pick up on the postmodern nature of the AACM in Paris's art.

Genre-destabilizing gestures by the AACM have a long history. Consider, for example, the following poems from the liner notes to Joseph Jarman's album *Song For* (1967) and the albums *Reese and the Smooth Ones* and *Mes-sage to Our Folks*, recorded in Paris in 1969 by the AEC:

SONG FOR is made of sound and silences from
Musical
Instruments, controlled by seven men; it's
Music that lasts 13½ minutes, it's for itself,
For love, for hate & for the God within

Us

ALL — it has no "meaning" outside of itself,
The MUSIC.

Then the following "ironic" poem is added:

Yes, we read and write music
And sleep, eat food, have visions, etc. . . .
"just like everyone else." Yes we are humans.
No, we do not think the whole world is full of evil
Only ¾ of it. Yes, some of us have wives and children. No, we do not
    work
Enough. Yes we hope
You enjoy our music.

The first poem appears to be a statement asserting that *Song For* is a work of absolute music, "having no meaning outside of itself." Yet even this claim, in keeping with a major strand of modernist art-music theorizing, is immediately problematized by the claim that the music is for love, hate, and the God within us — a direct renunciation of the claim that it has no external meaning that, in fact, grounds the music in traditional strong emotions and religion, akin to claims often made about so-called primitive music when it is held in contradistinction to Western art music and its oft-theorized purely self-referential character. The second "ironic" poem reads like a series of responses to an imaginary interviewer (and picks up on a theme explored by the composition "Is Jazz Dead?" found on *Congliptious*, by the Roscoe Mitchell Art Ensemble, which is a parody of an interview of Lester Bowie by a jazz critic). Here Jarman is responding to a critic who questions the musical credentials of the AEC ("Yes we do read and write music") and even their very humanity. There is the suggestion of a question about whether he thinks anyone could actually enjoy their music, and a question about his political/ethical take on humanity, itself answered ironically. His responses foreground the AEC members' roles as traditional music makers (they read and write music), what they have in common with all humans (as if this could actually ever be in question), and their desire, almost universal among all artists, that their work be received well, that it be enjoyed. Taken together, these two poems suggest that the AEC members were situating themselves squarely (if not exclusively) within a tradition of Western art-music production and tacitly denying that their music should be read through some sort of narrow, perhaps political/racial lens.

Yet the ironic claim concerning the evil found in the world is picked up in other poems by Jarman in the liner notes of the Actuel albums the AEC recorded in Paris in 1969:

(excerpt)
REVOLT / DO NOT INCITE TO RIOT—INCITE TO / REVOLUTION
Quietly-calmly (to the point) universal energy black yea
he said / LOVE / Observe-poison is what the west would give
us. This message to Our Folks-Seek (love what you are) These songs then
  to offer you your Truth of having what you are GREAT BLACK MUSIC
  your light, sound & being TOGETHER we free together.

And

(excerpt)
INTENSIFY THE STRUGGLE, SEIZE THE TIME . . .
we joined the mau-mau to cut honkie throats, kill their children and
  claim the
soil—it was a love movement seeking peace.

This poem squarely situates the AEC's art practices in the radical black politics of the time—or, perhaps, a (white) reception of these politics. Again, ironies abound. While the message does seem to endorse the need for radical political change and to enjoin blacks to "seize the time," it also plays into the worse (racist) fears of whites by claiming to "enjoy" the murder of white children and to view such actions as part of "a love movement." Of course, the ironic nature of this last claim may reflect as much on white fears and expectations of the nature of black radical politics as it endorses the need for and legitimacy of violent political action. Either way, such statements are a far cry from the "music for music's sake" claims found earlier; thus, these poems taken together led to confusion on the part of critics, many of whom missed the intended message: that the music of the AACM could, and sometimes did, speak to political issues, but that this was not the only lens through which it should be viewed. The music was intended also to stand on its own—to be effective examples of pure or absolute music, to yield "traditional" musical enjoyment. Indeed, as we saw, its autonomous nature, its internal musical structure, is (one) way that it discharges its social/political function. While certain historical discourses about art music would find a fusion of these positions difficult, the AACM do not endorse the agenda of either the absolute music camp or the music as politics (music with propositional content) camp.

The multi-generic, mixed-message nature of the performances by the AACM in Paris was not missed by the French critics of the time. The author of the program notes for the first AEC performance in Paris, at the Theatre Lucernaire on June 12, 1969, states:

> It sounds like Xenakis. . . . Wait, there's Stockhausen, with a beat to boot— here a pop progression, there we're a bit bored—Klangfarbenmelodie— etc. etc. The AACM does everything. Coming into the Lucernaire, watch out for how they're picking your pockets; you'll be beaten, robbed, then abused, and sent back totally naked and crying for your mother. But certainly not back home. . . . If you knew how to listen to the AACM of Chicago, you would become, all at once, a subversive terrorist. You'll see how intoxicating it is to kidnap Boulez, to kill Berio, or to beat up Xenakis. (Quoted in and translated by G. E. Lewis 2008, 223)

While it is perhaps appropriate to assume the author of this passage is manifesting a humorous tone, he does merge both high-art European methods and composers closely identified with absolute music and the radical—in fact, violent—tropes associated with black political radicalism and its associated music's assumed adversarial stance toward European art music. George Lewis confirms both the syncretic nature of the music and the fact that the French both noted and responded to it:

> Quick changes of mood were the rule, ranging from the reverent to the ludic. A quiet, sustained, "spiritual" offered by one musician might be rudely interrupted by an ah-ooh-gah horn or a field holler from another. A New Orleans–style brass fanfare would quickly be dunked in a roiling sea of tuned metal trash cans. An ironically demented fake-bebop theme could be cut up into a series of miniatures, punctuated by long silences and derisively terminated by a Marx Brothers raspberry. This was deformation of mastery, indeed. No sound was excluded and no tradition was sacrosanct, and French audiences and the jazz press quickly fell in love with the ruptures and surprises. (G. E. Lewis 2008, 226)

Lewis draws the conclusion that the practices of the AACM in Paris bore the hallmarks of postmodern artistic expression and seemed to be received that way by the French: "[Such descriptions by French critics] seem to support the notion that the work of the Art Ensemble of Chicago, where visual collage and historical montage combine, could exemplify Derrida's observation that collage/montage is the quintessential postmodern form of expression" (2008, 223).

Such use of collage and montage was recognized by the French press as contributing to the aesthetic of the music of the AACM. The AEC was said to "incorporate everything of value, classical, European, Hindu, African, seemingly without any prohibition against any kind of process of working with sound" (cited by G. E. Lewis 2008, 228). The AEC was not bound to any particular genre or culturally grounded methods of sound/music production, and while this was clearly viewed by many French critics as both new and liberating, it equally destabilized the aesthetic ground from which to critique the music.[18] As Lewis (2008, 234) comments, "Rather than trying to fit in with an existing scene with defined borders of aesthetics, method and practice, AACM musicians in Paris made no attempt to contextualize their work solely within the jazz art world. Rather, they took work wherever they could, and regularly moved outside the frame of jazz, collaborating with a wide range of artists." The aesthetic thickening that the AACM created via its members' refusal to present music tethered to one genre or another also revealed itself via the choice of "scenes" in which they participated and not just the sounds they produced. These "trans-generic" explorations were seen by French critics as fitting squarely within the still-being-developed critical discourse of postmodernism. As Lewis (236) states, "Moreover, in contrast to much post-1990's American scholarship, French critiques of the 1970s positioned free jazz as a postmodernist, rather than a modernist phenomenon," He goes on to quote from Francis Marmande, who in 1971 talked about "ruptures" this music created, seeing in it "a certain lexical world that is constantly called upon ('collages,' 'mixtures,' 'borrowing' . . .) scrupulous inventories of 'quotations' or 'references' from which programs for free music records or concerts are woven" (236). Here, characteristic tropes of postmodernism—intertextuality, collage, quotation—are used to characterize the music and its aesthetic power.

As we have seen, a key terrain on which the AACM in Paris fought for control over the appropriate interpretive context for discussing its art was its relation to black politics and broader issues of black identity and, in particular, the tendency among French critics to, on the one hand, make the linkage between radical black politics and the music of the AEC in particular, but on the other hand, to go on and assume that this political content revealed the primary or privileged position from which to access the AACM's music. The postmodern tendencies the French were so quick to pick up on were often viewed as instrumentally serving the radical black political agenda, which those critics also assumed was "behind" the music. They treated "radical black music" as a genre term, and when they placed the AACM in it, they tended to avoid considering alternative aesthetics. Again, the members of the AACM in Paris did not deny the presence of political aspects to their practices; they just denied particular interpretations of what the political content might be (the refusal to be essentialized with respect to a particular political message) and more global attempts to essentialize their music as being purely or primarily a means of mediating political messages—that is, that it was "just" political music.[19]

Smith articulates these points nicely. The radical black political agenda French critics found in the music was not just a product of the sort of statements AACM members made in interviews and liner notes (as discussed earlier). It was *heard* via the AACM's disassembly (hence, the relation to postmodernism) and "attack" on Western art-music conventions and the high-energy, often dissonant playing characteristic of (some of) the music of the AACM. These are forms of sonic homologism: an attack on white European musical conventions is heard as an attack on colonial power and racism, while high-energy dissonant music is heard as a violent struggle against such oppressive musical rules. As Smith says, "They thought we were going after the Western tradition. . . . We challenged that tradition, but it wasn't our only investigation" (quoted in G. E. Lewis 2008, 242). Lewis goes on to quote Smith as saying: "From my recollection of interviews and interactions with people who were in the media system there, their questions were always limited to just the black issues, and what the music meant in those terms. Even though we would go into these areas of exploration, other ideas, they would always try to refocus it. Their idea was designed to present not just an artist, but a black artist in their society" (G. E. Lewis 2008, 242). As Smith says, "We were looking at music in a much broader way than a lot of other people in the music community at that time" (quoted in G. E. Lewis 2008, 244).

A narrow political reading of the music of the AACM in Paris served as a genre category from which to judge its music. The AACM members did, of course, contribute to the plausibility of such an interpretation. There certainly was a political element to the music, but how that element was best characterized, the fixity of the political stance it took, the relative importance of it to the musicians' aesthetic vision, and, crucially the degree to which they intended their politics to carve out an exclusive position from which to consider their music were all contested by the members of the AACM. Their music was multi-generic and *intended* to be judged through a variety of lens.

Against this backdrop, it is perhaps not surprising that the very day after the AEC played a Black Panther benefit in Paris, an event that naturally contributed to the radical political reading of their music, Jarman told the audience at another concert, "The critics have called it avant-garde, they've called it the New Thing . . . but we have only one name for it: 'Great Black Music'" (quoted in G. E. Lewis 2008, 241). This term, "Great Black Music," which was to become a motto of the AEC and, to a lesser degree, the AACM, is offered by Jarman as a genre to describe the music of the AEC of its/his own choosing. As such, it evinces a sophisticated understanding of the issues at play surrounding the reception of the music of the AACM and can be seen, as I now show, as a perfect genre name, given the assorted commitments of the AACM toward the social and the aesthetic.

The term "Great Black Music" has been received uncritically by many people as squarely grounding the music of the AACM not just in black politics but also in (so-called) radical black politics, as if merely mentioning blackness is to take a politically radical stance.[20] As we have seen, the AACM's members did occasionally position themselves and their music in sympathy with radical black political causes (although they never seem to have advocated a narrow reading of black nationalism per se), but "Great Black Music," while suggesting such a political alignment, also denies an exclusively narrow reading of the music to the exclusion of other critical stances from which to discuss their art. The expression contains three words: "Great," an evaluative term that is deeply and obviously grounded in tradi- tional aesthetic discourse; "Black," a racial category; and "Music," an art- kind term that logically functions in many ways like a genre or meta-genre. The expression is itself a concatenation of aesthetics, politics, and genres and is best read, I claim, as a genre designation intended to include many preexisting genre terms and the critical discourses with which they align themselves, without prioritizing any of them and thereby taking a particular theoretical stance toward genres and their aesthetic function.

The breadth with which Smith claims the AACM was approaching music is intended to be foregrounded in the expression Great Black Music, and it includes, of course, musical traditions that code as European and white. Great Black Music, in a sense, is an anti-genre genre designation that is in- tended to deny any particular narrow perspective from which to categorize, and thus judge, the music while simultaneously seeming to do just that. It is like the "trope of all tropes," which Henry Lewis Gates Jr. calls the sig- nifying trope, or an example of Derrida's claim that there cannot be a text that exists outside a genre. Each of the genres this expression implies (jazz, new thing, experimental music, rhythm and blues, blues, African music, and so on) is, at times, an appropriate perspective from which to consider the

AACM's music and the different histories in which each perspective grounds the music. The distinct, if overlapping, aesthetics with which each perspective is in sympathy; the distinct properties of the music that bear aesthetic weight; and the distinct political and social narratives and functions each music is seen as discharging collectively serve to thicken the music of the AACM aesthetically. This thickening is a result of the multiple aesthetic perspectives one should take when considering the music of the AACM — that is, what the AACM is arguing for and (so) is what the term "Great Black Music" is intended to suggest. Yes, the music of the AACM is critiquing race relations *and* making universalist comments about music and culture *and* contributing to ongoing debates about art music *and* commenting on the received history of jazz *and* exploring aspects of black identity. It simply is not doing just one of these or any of these at the expense of the others. It is political music, and it is music for its own sake. The expression "Great Black Music" can now be seen as an exemplary instance of a double-voiced text: on its surface, it seems to endorse an essentialist reading of race and cultural artifacts closely identified with race, but its very point, on further analysis, is to warn one to avoid essentialist readings of black music (and thus of blackness in general). The essence of blackness is, in effect, to lack an essence, to resist essentialist constructions, and to enact blackness artistically is to repel essentialism.

Notes

1. While in Paris, Don Moye, who was already based there, joined the AEC. There were also musicians from abroad who had gravitated to Paris and engaged in collaborations with the extended jazz community there.

2. One sense in which this can be seen as a form of social aesthetics is the degree to which the aesthetic thickening requires more than just the production of certain sounds to take place. It is the combination of the AACM members' assorted activities related to their music — from the sounds they played to the album titles they chose and the interviews they gave — that brings about this thickening. This account therefore is at odds with what is sometimes called "sonicism" as advocated by philosophers of music such as Julian Dodd (2007), and, in a related sense, Roger Scruton (1997).

3. Cf. Brackett 2005, 77: "The spectral protest of musicians hover before me, complaining that an emphasis on genre, and hence (to some extent) on structure, robs them of agency. . . . Moreover, when one posits a momentary relationship between a musical field of genres and different positions in social space, one is confronted with the instability of social identities, which, like genres, are subject to constant redefinition and which also become meaningful within a field of relationships at a particular moment." I argue that the AACM in Paris used genres

and their characteristic instability to *assert its agency*. In this sense, the AACM was a predecessor to Living Color, as described by Will Straw (1991, 384; emphasis added): "What these logics invite, however, is a reading of the politics of popular music that locates the crucial site of these politics neither in the transgressive or oppositional quality of musical practices and their consumption, nor uniformly within the modes of operation of the international music industries. The important processes . . . are those through which particular social differences (most notably those of gender and race) are articulated within the building of audiences around particular coalitions of musical form. These processes are not inevitably positive or disruptive of existing social divisions, *nor are they shaped to any significant extent by solitary, willful acts of realignment. (Attempts to transform them into the bases of artistic strategy have generally failed, one notable recent exception being that of the group Living Colour)*." For a useful, if at times obscure, account of the function of genres in "creating worlds" and determining actions, see Frow 2006.

4. Anthony Braxton, Leroy Jenkins, and Leo Smith, *Silence*, Freedom Records 278.128, 1974; Art Ensemble of Chicago, *Message to Our Folks*, BYG Records 529.328, Actuel 28, 1969. All listening was done with original vinyl, while timings were generated from digital copies.

5. This piece is usually said to have been recorded in Paris on July 18, 1969, as indicated by the record jacket. In private correspondence, Wadada Leo Smith informs me that it was in fact recorded in Chicago just before Anthony Braxton left for Paris in the early summer of 1969.

6. On the vexing question of defining "original" and "creative" music for the AACM at the birth of the organization, see G. E. Lewis 2008, 98–103.

7. One may well think that the use of the voice and actually spoken sentences distances this piece from "Silence" insofar as this piece makes use of mimetic material and semantics in a way that the purely abstract "Silence" does not.

8. Hall (1992, 27) himself goes on to make the linkage with hybridity.

9. It is commonplace to state that genres establish criteria of both truth and meaning.

10. See Walton (1970, 347–48) for his discussion of what he calls "Guernicas" versus "Guernica." Walton's account can be profitably read alongside Jacques Derrida's "The Law of Genre" (1980), written ten years later. A story for another day would be to locate where these two very different thinkers part company. Their disagreements focus, I think, on the unfortunate fact that Walton in the end wants to graft a theory of true versus false aesthetic judgments on his theory of art categories (a notion that is anathema to Derrida), and while he is sensitive to the changing nature of our genre judgments, he perhaps assumes that it is easier to tease out what these are than is actually the case. In effect he recognizes the importance of considering sociological "facts" but takes such facts to be neater than they often are. For an account of how the "sociological facts" may as often confuse as clarify our genre judgments, see Born 1993b.

11. I use the language of genre membership not as a commitment to a particular ontology of genres (that, say, they are types of which individual works are tokens)

but simply to foreground their classificatory aspect. Others, such as Flew, prefer to talk of works "performing" genres, but this notion also comes with heavy theoretical baggage.

12. Quoted in liner notes for Joseph Jarman, *Song For*, Delmark Records Ds-410, 1967, by J. B. Figi, which are dated June 4, 1967.

13. In this sense, Smith's sense of autonomy in music is crucially different from that commonly employed in modernist art-music discourse, where musical autonomy is not linked to the autonomy of the composers' intentions but is somehow free-floating, wholly internal to the music itself. Smith is concerned most fundamentally with *performed* autonomy.

14. Excerpts from *notes (8 pieces)*, including these passages, are available at http://music.calarts.edu/~wls/pages/philos.html.

15. Interview with Wadada Leo Smith and George Lewis, WCKR-FM, New York, September 12, 1995, http://www.jazzhouse.org/library/?read=panken18.

16. The original is not paginated. The page numbers cited here are my creation.

17. That genre assumptions about black music may rest on prejudices follows directly from the history of race-driven music categories and, in particular, the characteristics of a "pure" form of jazz as being associated with various flavors of primitivism.

18. Similar claims were made by other AACM in Paris members, as found in an interview conducted by Daniel Caux in October 1969. Leo Smith claims that his goal is to employ "all forms of music . . . everything and anything is valuable," while Jarman adds, "We play the blues, we play jazz, rock, Spanish music, gypsy, African, classical music, contemporary European music, vodum. . . . Everything that you'll want . . . because finally, it's music that we play: we create sounds, period" (quoted in Caux 1969).

19. Again, French critics seemed to pick up on the fact that the political and the aesthetic are not at odds with each other in the music of the AACM. In a classic and groundbreaking study, Phillipe Carles and Jean-Louis Comolli state that "with free jazz, one is witness to a real political positioning of the music, through the convergence of directly militant concerns, and their influence, also direct, on the very conception of the music and on its aesthetic explorations" (Carles and Comolli 1971, 71, quoted in and translated by G. E. Lewis 2008, 236). While one may object to aspects of Carles and Comilli's precise account of the relation of "militant" political concerns to the AACM, they seem spot on in recognizing that political concerns, when they surface, need not come at the expense of aesthetics but may help give it form.

20. Recall that the genre "race records" was not abolished by *Billboard* magazine until 1949. It was replaced with "rhythm and blues" until within a month of Jarman's creation of the term "Great Black Music," when the genre became "soul." In a certain sense, "Great Black Music" functioned to broaden the already widely accepted genre term "soul"; however, "soul" was imposed from the outside, by the white record industry, and no longer transparently admitted, for better or for worse, the racial connotations of the genre.

CHAPTER 7

KENNETH GOLDSMITH AND UNCREATIVE IMPROVISATION

Darren Wershler

To be unoriginal with the *minimum* of alteration is
sometimes more distinguished than to be original with
the *maximum* of alteration.
—T. S. Eliot (minimally altered)

Is there such a thing as *un*creative improvisation? If so, how would it operate in the second decade of the twenty-first century, when creativity and improvisation are as likely—or more likely—to be invoked in the business world than in the context of contemporary art? The "uncreative" and "conceptual" practice of Kenneth Goldsmith, with all of its attendant impurities, provides one possible model.[1]

Much of Goldsmith's oeuvre, which involves labor-intensive acts of textual appropriation on a large scale, bears a counterintuitive relationship to the sorts of extemporaneous production that characterize improvisation. However, Goldsmith's fifteen-year stint as a DJ for the free-form New Jersey radio station WFMU (from mid-1995 to mid-2010) offers some possibilities for a reconsideration of how improvisation works in a contemporary context. Goldsmith's show, which went under a variety of monikers, including "Unpopular Music with Kenny G," "Anal Magic with Kenny G," "The Kenny G show with Kenny G," "Kenny G's Hour of Pain," and "Intelligent Design with Kenny G," managed to bridge the gap between improvisation and constraint without resolving the difference in one direction or the other.

In *The Philosophy of Improvisation*, Gary Peters (2009, 52) argues that "free-improvisation is more about power than it is about freedom." As he pushes and pulls against self-imposed limitations, what Goldsmith's uncreative improvisations embody is the struggle between control and autonomy — in other words, what Michel Foucault (1982, 780) dubbed "power relations." Further, Goldsmith's uncreative improvisation provides an important contrast to the ways in which the discourse of contemporary business uses terms such as "improvisation," "innovation," and "creativity." For corporate gurus such as Richard Florida, these terms are always productive — that is, they are a means to make something efficient and commodifiable. Goldsmith, however, is a much more complex beast. Like Andy Warhol and Jeff Koons, Goldsmith knows the techniques of the business world well and cheerfully incorporates them into his repertoire. At the same time, his work gestures back toward decades of difficult, uncomfortable, constrained art and, ultimately, to the freedom that allows for it. However, Goldsmith's astonishing popularity indicates that he clearly and obviously profits from his work and does not occupy anything like the oppositional positions of the historical left. In sum, Goldsmith's uncreative improvisation is characterized by its *impurity*.

As Craig Dworkin (2007, 34) has noted elsewhere, Goldsmith's ongoing personal project, which he has successively dubbed "nutritionless writing," "uncreative writing," and "conceptual writing," falls squarely into a century-old tradition of technologized, high-volume appropriation. Goldsmith's methodology proceeds by identifying a neglected (because mundane, or, in Goldsmith's terms, "boring") repository of cultural discourse, such as an average edition of the *New York Times*, or the artist and album names from his extensive LP collection (*6799*),[2] or all of the traffic reports on a New York radio station that appear at ten-minute intervals over a twenty-four-hour period (*Traffic*). He then transcribes the contents of that repository meticulously, sorts and reconfigures the resulting digital manuscript as a book, and attaches his name to it. In this context, even Goldsmith's curation of the decade-old Ubuweb, the world's largest digital archive of avant-garde sound recordings, concrete poetry, video, outsider art, and related critical materials, is perhaps his most significant work and arguably part of the practice of uncreative improvisation. (Damon Krukowski [2008] explicitly compares Ubuweb's ongoing operation to Goldsmith's DJ practice at WFMU.) Although such projects have been common in the art world for decades, they are relatively rare in what Charles Bernstein (1986, 246) famously refers to as "official verse culture."

The concept of improvisation does not appear very often in Goldsmith's critical writing or in the discourse of contemporary conceptual writing in general. In Goldsmith and Craig Dworkin's 593-page *Against Expression*

(2011), the term appears only twice and never in the editorial sections of the book.[3] In *Uncreative Writing* (2011b), Goldsmith's major statement of poetics to date, it appears three times (and I address two of them). The first is a comparison of Ezra Pound's and Walter Benjamin's methods of literary appropriation: "Pound's is a more intuitive and improvisatory method of weaving textual fragments into a unified whole. Often-times it takes a great deal of Pound's intervening—finessing, massaging, and editing those found words—to make them all fit together just so. Benjamin's approach is more preordained: the machine that makes the work is set up in advance, and it's just a matter of filling up those categories with the right words, in the order in which they're found, for the work to be successful" (Goldsmith 2011b, loc. 2014).

The Benjamin text that Goldsmith has in mind is *Passagen-Werk* (translated as *The Arcades Project* [Benjamin 1999]), an enormous, cross-referenced shuffle text that had no fixed form until its posthumous publication as a volume with a fixed spine. Goldsmith (2011b, loc. 2008) asserts that "it's impossible to determine Benjamin's exact methodology" for authorship of this work, as he left no set of instructions to follow. Goldsmith also cites Susan Buck-Morss's observation that although *Passagen-Werk* has no necessary narrative structure, it does in fact have a conceptual structure, presenting confusion without collapsing into a confused presentation (loc. 2008). Goldsmith's decision to base the structure of *Capital*, his major work-in-progress, on *Passagen-Werk* suggests that while it may be impossible to follow the letter of Benjamin's methodology, improvising in his spirit may be an option. Marjorie Perloff's paper (and subsequent book) "Unoriginal Genius: Walter Benjamin's Arcades as Paradigm for the New Poetics" provides critical support for this position, arguing that *Passagen-Werk* is "paradigmatic for our own poetics," with Goldsmith as its exemplar (Perloff 2008, 251). Just as the flaneur improvises a path through the rigid confusion of urban space, Benjamin and Goldsmith demonstrate that it is possible to repeat something to make a difference.

What form would this sort of practice take? In *Uncreative Writing*, Goldsmith (2011b, loc. 2284) invokes Sol LeWitt's notion of art based on the recipe: "Like shopping for ingredients and cooking a meal, he says that all the decisions for making an artwork should be made beforehand and that the actual execution of the work is merely a matter of duty, an action that shouldn't require too much thought, improvisation, or even genuine feeling." One name for this approach (which Goldsmith implies cannot expunge improvisation entirely) is "scored improvisation," a term that appears in some of Goldsmith's early music criticism and provides his longest statement on improvisation to date (Goldsmith 1999, 180). In "Near the Edge and Off the Page" (1999), what interests Goldsmith is the practice of commingling/composed scores and improvised works. The exemplars of this approach, Goldsmith argues, are Pierre Boulez and John Cage, but he also provides a laundry list of other musicians who blur these boundaries, including John Zorn, Mauricio Kagel, Butch Morris, Iancu Dumitrescu, and Takehisa Kosugi. The transgressions are bidirectional; Goldsmith happily reports, for example, that some of the guitarist Jim O'Rourke's work with Kosugi on John Cage scores "would certainly have upset Cage." For Goldsmith, the result of these experiments is "win-win," producing "flexible and spontaneous" structures that hold composition and improvisation in tension without resolving that tension in one direction or another (180).

But is this improvisation, really? Theorist practitioners have argued that the distinction between scored composition and improvisation is blurrier than we commonly imagine. In the essay "Towards an Ethics of Improvisation," the composer Cornelius Cardew (whom Goldsmith has long hosted in pirated form on Ubuweb), implies that it is. He writes that "scores like those of LaMonte Young (for example 'Draw a straight line and follow it') could in their inflexibility take you outside yourself, stretch you to an extent that could not occur spontaneously" (Cardew 1971, xviii). Conversely, as Marcus Boon (2010, 228), a DJ, university professor, and Goldsmith colleague and collaborator, points out, many improvisers are not all that free in their approach: "Faced with a field of total, open possibility, many improvisers repeat a certain set of gestures that are 'free' but as predictable as the idiomatic forms they seek to move away from. In other words, they copy themselves, or they copy a way of relating to other musicians. This is not necessarily bad, since it can result in new idioms, protocols, forms of beauty and pleasure (what Simon Reynolds identifies as the pleasure of 'cheesiness'). Or not: there are no guarantees." Just as structure can lead to unprecedented occurrences, "total openness" in practice often means a reliance on "common sense," "gut feelings," or some other set of unexamined and clichéd forms.

There is also a philosophical justification for considering Goldsmith's work within the realm of improvisation. Peters argues for a consideration of improvisation that is quite distinct from discourses that invoke the creativity and innovation of the performer:

Instead of situating freedom in a future yet to be attained, the discussion follows Immanuel Kant in tracing the origin of freedom to the prior play of the cognitive faculties, a sense common to all (*sensus communis*) and one that the artwork helps us remember. This strategy is crucial because it allows for a rethinking of freedom in terms of memory rather than hope while also introducing into the past a freedom that, once remembered, must be preserved in the artwork. In other words, the prioritization of the past is able to be conceived in conservationist rather than conservative terms: the conservation of freedom understood as the infinite opening of the artwork. (Peters 2009, 2)

Here freedom is a state that exists not because of but prior to the creation of the structured work, which calls forth memories of that freedom in the minds of the audience. To support his position, Peters also cites Keith Johnstone's *Impro*, which uses the same allusion: "The improvisor has to be like a man walking backwards. He sees where he has been, but he pays no attention to the future. His story can take him anywhere, but he must still 'balance' it, and give it shape, by remembering incidents that have been shelved and reincorporating them" (Johnstone 1979, 116). Once again, the spirit of Walter Benjamin has been invoked; for Peters, the improviser is like Benjamin's Angel of History, blown ceaselessly backward into the future while watching history accumulate in his wake.

Likewise, Goldsmith continually researches the archive of avant-garde practice for performative recipes to pair with texts he has plucked from some forgotten corner of the wreckage of history. As Boon (2010, 140–41) points out, Goldsmith's interventions are minor, because limiting himself to making small changes allows him to maintain his claim to be conceptual, uncreative, and scripted. For Goldsmith, the act of carefully selecting and preparing something for a procedure (however idiosyncratic) is a means to remember that the "givens" of history could have been, and can still be, otherwise.

One outcome that we might reasonably expect from such a model of improvisation is the death and subsequent disappearance of the modernist author as genius, whose acts of bricolage and appropriation succeed precisely because of a refined sensibility. However, this is one place where Goldsmith differs from the more radical improvisers that inspired him. John Cage, for example, eschews the notion of taste along with his attempts to break free of the sovereign subject position:

What I have never appreciated in improvisation is the return to memory or to taste: the return of things that have been learned or to which one has become accustomed—sometimes consciously, deliberately, sometimes insidiously. Phrases thought to be original are only articulations heard a long time ago. In improvisation, when you think you are following your own direction, most of the time you are following someone else's line. At the most, that is not what bothers me so much as the desire for uniqueness that appears in the act of improvising. Once you realize the number of obstacles and of more or less deliberate references that the improviser is struggling with, you can only smile at the claim to originality. (Kostelanetz 1988, 229)

By way of contrast, here is Goldsmith (2011b, loc. 2508): "Sorting and filtering—moving information—has become a site of cultural capital. Filtering is taste. And good taste rules the day." In the same volume, Goldsmith's references to the taste of his heroes Benjamin and Warhol both merit the adjective "exquisite" (locs. 2009, 2508). Where Cage wants to purge taste, Goldsmith hangs on to it, tightly. Regardless of whatever else he is doing, Goldsmith is almost always building his reputation as an artist in the process.

In this as in many other respects, Goldsmith is a residual modernist. As Deleuze and Guattari (1987, 6) described, although most modern methods for creating openness and multiplicity succeed in one aspect, a unity of totalization often reaffirms itself at a different level—in this case, the reification of the author as iconoclastic but tasteful genius. (Krukowski [2008] refers to this as Goldsmith's "Stein-like self-admiration.") In "My Career in Poetry," Goldsmith explains the logic behind the "famous suit[s]" (Goldsmith 2011a, 8) he wore for his readings at the White House for President Barack Obama and the First Lady. Although "John Stewart speculated that it was improvised at the last minute, quipping that the afternoon before I went onstage I glanced at the wall and asked, 'Hey, does that wallpaper come off?'" both the paisley suit that Goldsmith wore for the evening performance and the pastel suit that he wore during the day were "designed by the avant-garde designer Thom Browne under his Brooks Brothers' owned Black Fleece label" (2011a, 6). Call it sartorial scored improvisation, if you like. In any event, it epitomizes Goldsmith's signature ability to make careful planning evoke spontaneity—and increase the value of his personal brand at the same time.

This seems like an appropriate spot to suggest that the "creative" business theory of Richard Florida and the "uncreative" work of Kenneth Goldsmith are reflections of each other. They are strikingly similar but ultimately opposed attempts to address the same basic situation: the cultural economy of late capital. As BAVO (Gideon Boie and Matthias Pauwels) argue, the sort of instrumentalized creativity that has been part of U.S. business since the 1950s is a major component of contemporary business: "When creativity is affirmed as an autonomous value that needs to be nurtured and maintained, it stands in a direct instrumental relation to the current regime. The acquisition of poetic freedom by creative agents is achieved through the agent's voluntary acceptance of the inscription of creativity in the economic process, where it gets put into service as something that cannot be established by capital alone" (BAVO 2007, 163). In a networked milieu, as business claims creativity for itself, turning its factories into playgrounds, art makes a corresponding detour into the boring and the uncreative, turning its playgrounds into factories. Creativity is the imaginary surplus that contemporary business uses to remain "business as usual," wallpapering over the traumas of barely contained global fiscal meltdowns and looming climate change.

As texts such as Florida's bestselling *The Rise of the Creative Class* (2012) and Hal Niedzviecki's *Hello, I'm Special* (2004) demonstrate, the invocation of creativity is deeply imbricated into contemporary neoliberal ideology and ontology: "the creative ethos pervades everything from our workplace culture to our values and communities, reshaping the way we see ourselves as economic and social actors and molds the core of our very identities" (Florida 2012, loc. 525). For Florida, creativity is the new normal, a paradoxical regime of individuality, self-expression, and openness to difference (2012, loc. 486) that somehow includes "heretofore excluded groups of eccentrics and nonconformists" (loc. 438). This cheerfully contradictory contention corresponds closely with Slavoj Žižek's description of today's predominant mental state as a sense of not being fully in the clutches of the dominant power structure. Everywhere we see opportunities for play and creativity (Žižek 1997, 77), although such moments are precisely when we are most fully in ideology's grasp (Žižek 1989, 49). As Alan Liu (2004, 375) points out, the link that the Romantics once forged between creativity and critique is now badly broken, "no matter how functional creativity may be at the lower levels of ideology."

The signature characteristic of the neoliberal formulation of improvisation and creativity is that it is always *useful* (Florida 2012, loc. 424 passim). In Florida's writing, creativity is important because it is the machine that synthesizes nebulously defined "knowledge" and "information" into a thoroughly instrumentalized "innovation," which can be anything (and the range here is breathtaking in its narrowness) from "a new technological artifact or a new business model or method" (loc. 736). In "Struggling with the Creative Class," Jamie Peck provides the following incisive critique:

Rather than "civilizing" urban economic development by "bringing in culture," creativity strategies do the opposite: they commodify the arts and cultural resources, even social tolerance itself, suturing them as putative economic assets to evolving regimes of urban competition. They enlist to this redoubled competitive effort some of the few remaining pools of untapped resources; they enroll previously-marginalized actors for this effort, enabling the formation of new governance structures and local political channels; they constitute new objects of governance and new stakes in interurban competition; and they enable the script of urban competivity [sic] to be performed—quite literally—in novel and often eye-catching ways. (Peck 2005, 763)

Florida (2012, loc. 859), for example, is ready and willing to put even poets, musicians, and artists to work in his caring sweatshops, willfully forgetting that creativity ever bore a strong relation to waste, excess, profligacy, and expenditure.

As Thomas Frank's *The Conquest of Cool* (1997) carefully and convincingly documents, the entry of creativity into the discourse of business is not a recent phenomenon; it spread into the larger business community through the advertising agencies of Madison Avenue between 1946 and 1966 (the *Mad Men* moment), preceding the appearance of the 1960s counterculture. By 1969, when the highly influential exhibition "Live in Your Head: When Attitudes Become Form: Works–Concepts–Processes–Situations–Information" was staged by Harald Szeemann at the Bern Kunsthalle (March 22–April 27, 1969) and the Institute of Contemporary Arts in London (September 28–October 27, 1969), John Murphy could confidently write the following on behalf of the show's patron, the Philip Morris tobacco company:

We at Philip Morris feel it is appropriate that we participate in bringing these works to the attention of the public, for there is a key element in this "new art" which has its counterpart in the business world. That element is innovation—without which it would be impossible for progress to be made in any segment of society. Just as the artist endeavors to improve his interpretation and conceptions through innovation, the commercial entity strives to improve its end product or service through experimentation with new methods and materials. Our constant search for a new and better way in which to perform and produce is akin to the questionings of the artists whose works are represented here. (Murphy 1999, 126)

The ease with which the discourse of business absorbed the art world's notions of creativity explains in part why "When Attitudes Become Form" became so central to contemporary practice, Catherine Spencer writes in her review of the 2013 re-creation of the show: "As well as introducing the ideas of process art and the concept exhibition, 'When Attitudes Become Form' ushered in a new era of overt corporate art sponsorship. You don't need to look much further for an object lesson of money and power uniting to write histories, and select archives for preservation."[4]

During the same period that business began to appropriate the discourses of conceptual art and improvisation to describe its own modes of creativity, European and North American neo-avant-garde art movements (especially Fluxus, pop, and figures such as Jackson Mac Low and John Cage) were making a reciprocal shift into a variety of investigations of the boring and the mundane, including the discourse and methods of business itself. Goldsmith's forays in this tradition are worth considering for several reasons. Just as Warhol incorporated practices from his early days of advertising display and window dressing into his later career and Jeff Koons worked on Wall Street as a commodities broker, Goldsmith, since the late 1990s, has drawn on the discourses and techniques of business—particularly information technology and advertising (although this is seldom, if ever, commented on by his critics).

During the dotcom boom at the turn of the millennium, Goldsmith was working as a creative director for an early New York Internet design firm called Methodfive Inc. Methodfive was an archetypal dotcom success story: founded in 1996 by a twenty-three-year-old University of Pennsylvania dropout named Adeo Ressi, who had already sold a previous Internet startup, the Greenwich Village firm boasted customers such as the New York Times Company and Fox Networks. In January 2000, one month before it was sold to Xceed Inc. for $75 million in cash and stock, Methodfive employed seventy-five to eighty people.[5] One of the few surviving online artifacts relating to Goldsmith from this period is an entry from the online newsletter *Courtney Pulitzer's Cyber Scene*, dated Monday, April 21, 1997. In it, Pulitzer recaps Goldsmith's talk "Ramping Up without Dumbing Down: Lessons Learned from Methodfive's Own Site Redesign," delivered on the same date at the After-5 Web Forum at the offices of NickandPaul in the Chelsea Market. As the following excerpt demonstrates, Goldsmith (who in a business context usually identified himself as "Ken" to immediately distinguish by mode of address on the phone his business contacts from art-world people, who knew him as "Kenneth," and friends who called him "Kenny," and thus shift into the proper persona)[6] was adept at the business argot of the moment:

As the client, ensure that you understand the components and ramifications of what's outlined in the spec before submitting it to the designers or to others involved in your Web initiative, such as the content producers or programmers. All involved parties, especially the designers, should then follow this document to the letter. Using an extranet to post thoughts, comments and feedback regarding the site's development and for designers to post their work helps with communication and meeting expectations. Allow your designers to be experimental and innovative during the first stages of design to get creative juices flowing. Then assign a "cranky monkey" who helps the designers integrate their imaginative and inventive designs into a site that's practical, functional and buildable. While keeping in mind the new technologies that will be able to repackage and distribute information in a new and innovative way, be aware of who your audience is and their level of technology. Analysis on who your user is and what the level of technology they'll be using to access your site is also important. Designing for a lower-end browser and keeping plug-ins to a bare minimum to ensure that the site can be accessed by the greatest amount of people possible is one way to ensure your users are accessing your site with ease.[7]

At the same that he was working for Methodfive, Goldsmith was coding the first pages for Ubuweb, which had launched six months earlier in 1997. In a recent e-mail, he remarked that the Methodfive talk "is the UbuWeb charter statement."[8] Hewing to Methodfive's principles so closely is, in part, what has kept this ancient site in good operating condition for more than a decade with minimal alterations to the underlying code.

Second, Goldsmith (2011b, 258) works explicitly with the categories that the business world's championing of improvisatory creativity exclude (e.g., the uncreative and the boring) to reveal the current bankruptcy of the popular usage of terms such as "creative" and "spontaneous." He alludes indirectly to Florida's arguments, writing, "Having worked in advertising for many years as a 'creative director,' I can tell you that, despite what cultural pundits might say, creativity—as it's been defined by our culture with its endless parade of formulaic novels, memoirs and films—is the thing to flee from, not only as a member of the 'creative class,' but also as a member of the 'artistic class.'" Intriguingly, both Florida and Goldsmith cite Warhol as a major inspiration for their conceptual moves (see Florida 2012; Goldsmith 2011b).[9] However, there are not two perspectives here but a perspective and what eludes it: Goldsmith's work shows, as if in relief, the gaps in the edifice of Florida's approach.

Like Goldsmith, Peter Stallybrass (2007, 1584) has suggested that digital media, and database technology in particular, offer a way out of the regime of originality, creativity, and proprietary authorship. He argues that originality "produces as its inevitable double the specter of plagiarism, a specter rooted in the fear that we might have more to learn from others than from ourselves." As an alternative to the Romantic legacy of waiting around for inspiration to strike, Stallybrass offers instead a program of organizing, annotating, and imitating that is strikingly similar to the self-written job description that Goldsmith provides in "Being Boring," a major statement of his poetics: "I've transformed from a writer into an information manager, adept at the skills of replicating, organizing, mirroring, archiving, hoarding, storing, reprinting, bootlegging, plundering, and transferring."[10] Such an approach is what Charles Bernstein (1986, 164) has dubbed a "strategy of tactics." In opposition to strategy proper, which manifests all of the assurances of the powerful, a strategy of tactics would be a way to combine the hodgepodge of poetic techniques so that they form "a complementarity of critiques," which is then projected onto the social in the manner of negative dialectics, as a transgression against tradition. Goldsmith's notion of scored improvisation is part of a strategy of tactics—neither one thing nor the other but a compromise formation that holds the two approaches in an unresolved tension. This approach is driven by the ethic of impurity that Goldsmith professes to adore. And, as Boon asks rhetorically in the unedited transcript of his interview with Goldsmith for *Bomb*, "Your radio practice also kind of flaunts that impurity, right?"[11]

Uncreative improvisation is most evident in the least discussed aspect of Goldsmith's practice: his three-hour DJ shifts for the free-form radio station WFMU (90.1 FM in the Hudson Valley, Lower Catskills, western New Jersey, and eastern Pennsylvania and 91.1 FM in Jersey City; see also http://wfmu .org). Originally the radio station of Upsala College in East Orange, New Jersey, WFMU is often credited with coining the term "free-form" (Post 1993, 108) and is the longest-operating station of its type in the United States. The content on virtually every radio station in existence—music, commercials, and public service announcements—is dictated by a playlist created and maintained by the station's program director. Steve Post (1993, 107) asserts that "playlists have nearly always been standard operating procedure at almost all radio stations." Free-form stations such as WFMU, which grant total autonomy to their disc jockeys provided that they adhere to Federal Communications Commission (FCC) regulations, such as the need for station identification and restrictions on foul language,[12] are the exception to this rule (WFMU is almost entirely listener-supported, which frees its programming from the need to make a profit or the demands of advertisers). As a result, as Jaime Wolf described in an article for the New York Times Magazine from 1999, which briefly mentions a younger Goldsmith under his nom de radio "Kenny G," the DJs of WFMU have long been arbiters of taste in American music.

What a DJ actually does is synthesize tradition and innovation in a manner that is similar to the notion of scripted improvisation. Siva Vaidhyanathan (2001, 125, 219) surveys the work of a range of cultural theorists (including Gena Dagel Caponi, Brenda Dixon Gottschild, Paul Gilroy, Gerhard Kubik, and Stephen Tracy), all of whom contribute to a tracing of the DJ's logic back through the practices of delta blues musicians to West African aesthetics. Vaidhyanathan distils his survey down to a neat little bouillon cube of theorization: a DJ's practice, he writes, demonstrates simultaneous "individual 'stylization' and mastery of a canon."

It has become a commonplace to invoke the DJ as the paradigmatic creative figure in contemporary culture. Paul Miller (2004, 57; a.k.a. DJ Spooky That Subliminal Kid) claims that "DJ-ing is writing, writing is DJ-ing." Nicolas Bourriaud and Lev Manovich go a step further. For Bourriaud (2005, 47), "The remixer has become more important than the instrumentalist"; likewise, for Manovich (2001, 134–35), the practice of the selection and combination of preexisting elements from the archive is the wellspring of new cultural forms. What remains uninterrogated in this formulation is a deeply modernist investment in the worth of the new. Manovich, for example, sees novelty, creativity, and even "true art" as the inherently valuable results of the DJ's inspired manipulations. It would be more accurate, and more theoretically useful, to conceive of DJs not as the "new" creators, but as the embodiment of an impure aesthetic of uncreative improvisation.

Goldsmith's work as a DJ occasionally has been commented on but has not been explored in any detail, although Christian Bök (2002, 69) argues that it is Goldsmith's print practice that emulates his radio work and not the reverse. The fact that Goldsmith was broadcasting recordings of reportage on the explosion of the space shuttle Challenger, the assassination of

John F. Kennedy, and the attacks of September 11, 2001, before they were transcribed for his book *Seven American Deaths and Disasters* supports such a claim.[13] The reciprocal is also true: Goldsmith notes in an e-mail interview with Ben Baumes (2005), "I'm always plundering and poaching my own writings for my own show." Such activities, whether the provenance of information managers and laptop DJs rather than creative directors and freestyle jazz musicians, are about *working* rather than *thinking*. Running a free-form radio show in the manner that Goldsmith did is arguably more rather than less work for the DJ than usual. Goldsmith added additional, unnecessary constraints to the various chores involved in programming a radio show, revealing the impression of a spontaneous creative DJ as a romantic fantasy. On occasion, such constraints have been literal as well as figurative, as in Goldsmith's three-hour-long on-air performance on September 24, 2003, with the WFMU DJ and multimedia collage artist Vicki Bennett (a.k.a. People Like Us). During the performance, the two DJs were literally bound to each other and gagged in the control room. Every fifteen minutes a rope was loosened, and the two occasionally broke free to change the programming, only to be captured and rebound by guards in the booth.[14] Mic breaks consisted largely of the sounds of the ongoing struggle.

What is noteworthy is that, given almost total freedom, Goldsmith's attention to the formal qualities of radio itself is the source of the disruptive quality of his on-air work. In the Baumes interview, Goldsmith says, "I'm interested in pulling back the curtain on radio, making visible what is always hidden. When I first started on WFMU, [the station manager] Ken Freedman requested that I speak more like a person and less like a DJ, 'Put a few ums and uhs into your mic breaks.' It was an eye-opener for me" (Baumes 2005). The hours and hours of digitized online playlists and audio streams from Goldsmith's radio show indicate that the lesson went deep. There are entire hours in which Goldsmith's broadcasts consisted of nothing but farts (September 16, 2010), screams (July 29, 2010), laughter (July 15, 2010), and silence (July 1, 2010, July 22, 2010).[15] All imply the too bodily existence of the disc jockey, suddenly present to the extent that he overrides any ostensible "content" for his show. At one point, Goldsmith had dubbed his on-air practice as "annoyism"; Jason Kaufman (2007, 81) argues that a central aim of annoyism is not simply to air "bad" art but "to call into question the very standards by which we make such judgements."

The name of Goldsmith's website, Ubu.com, points directly to the theoretical and aesthetic context for Goldsmith's approach: the writing of Alfred Jarry (1996), particularly the parts concerning his crass, loud, barbaric antihero Père Ubu (of the play *Ubu Roi* and its sequels), and the imaginary science of 'pataphysics (*The Exploits and Opinions of Dr. Faustroll, Pataphysician,* and various short essays). Conceived as a fin de siècle schoolboy's response to the bewildering explosion of scientific discourses into the popular, Jarry's 'pataphysics is a principle of functional equivalence, in which any given theory is treated as being as valid as any other. In Jarry's (1996, 21) deliberately obtuse definition, 'pataphysics "symbolically attributes the properties of objects, described by their virtuality, to the lineaments." As Bök (2002, 32) summarizes it, 'pataphysics deliberately prioritizes the superficialities of the imaginary over the substance of the thing. Whereas science produces facts to arrive at generalities, 'pataphysics concerns "the laws governing exceptions" (Jarry 1996, 30–31). Not so much a form of parody as a kind of parallax, 'pataphysics frequently involves minimal or no alterations to its object, relying instead on its ability to create a subtle shift in the perspective in its audience. According to Bök, 'pataphysics operates in three modalities: *anomalos* ("the repressed part of the rule which ensures that the rule does not work," usually manifesting itself as a sort of excessive surprise [Bök 2002, 38]); *clinamen* (a minimal swerve akin to the *détournment* [43]); and *syzygy* ("the neglected part of a pair which ensures that such a pair is neither united nor parted for more than an instant" [41]). All of these modalities are relevant to Goldsmith's work as a DJ, so I am going to talk briefly about each of them in turn.

To the extent that there is anything unusual about how Goldsmith presented particular tracks on his show, it could be described in terms of the *anomalos*: a difference in the degree to which free-form DJs are willing to examine the limits of their alleged freedom. Even among the iconoclastic, taste-making DJs on WFMU, Goldsmith was an anomaly. Ken Freedman told Ben Baumes (2005) that "before [Goldsmith] came along, I felt that FMU had explored all there was to explore in terms of experimental approaches to radio." On a station where DJs are ostensibly permitted to do anything during their shows, though, Goldsmith had the distinction of being suspended on several occasions for violating rules that were not so much nonexistent as unspoken. One infraction involved rebroadcasting material from other stations, but the majority of Goldsmith's suspensions involved obscene content. In his comments on the back of a bootleg CD titled *64 Minutes of Anal Magic,* Goldsmith wrote, "I've been suspended many times on WFMU for playing the kind of music included on this disc. In fact, just a few months ago, I was thrown off the air for 3 weeks for playing track #9, 'Sexual Pleasures Film Documentary Series Reel #2,' which is the soundtrack to a stag film from the 1950s. . . . In selecting the cuts, I've stayed away from standard erotica or straight porn. Instead, I've opted for cuts that are more psychological, more musical, more racist, more twisted."[16] The best known of Goldsmith's suspensions occurred after his show on Wednesday, December 15, 2004,[17] for, in Freedman's words, breaking station policy (not FCC policy) against "descriptions or depictions of sexual or excretory matter, anatomy or behavior from 5 A.M. to 11 P.M." Freedman had asked Goldsmith to change the show's name from "Anal Magic" due to this policy; during the show on December 15, "Goldsmith solicited new names from listeners. . . . Though Goldsmith refused to read many of the suggested titles on the air due to their content, the show still contained numerous references to sexual and excretory anatomy and behavior, prompting the suspension. The thread on the WFMU message board regarding this incident has also been removed."[18] Freedman was also quite clear, though, that this act of censorship was in the interest of protecting the station's license during a period of overweening FCC scrutiny, saying, "I disagree with the FCC's approach, with its guidelines, and with its enforcement. . . . I really respect Kenny G and his show, but this is something I have to do to protect the station in the face of the FCC's ongoing crackdown."[19]

Clinamen was the Roman philosopher Lucretius's term for the Greek philosopher Epicurus's postulate that a borderline-imperceptible, minimal swerve in the motion of atoms makes it possible for an event to occur in the universe. An artist executes a clinamen by making a minimal swerve in relation to the works of their precursors or some other cultural object (Bloom 1973, 14). Works based on the principle of clinamen often begin as identical copies of such objects and depart from resemblance by such subtle degrees that their audiences are stunned to realize that at some point they have entered what Jarry (1996, 30–31) described as a universe "that perhaps one *should* envision—in place of the traditional one." The spiral that always appears on the belly of Père Ubu was the symbol that Jarry used to represent the clinamen. In the universe next door to this one, it might be the groove on a long-playing record.

To return to the opening sentence I stole from Eliot and repurposed, unoriginal improvisation is all about the clinamen. Boon (2010, 140–41), a longtime friend and collaborator of Goldsmith's, writes the following: "Goldsmith's most successful works as a writer/artist/poet are those in which any embellishments of the original material are minor. . . . Goldsmith reveals the deception while carefully concealing his own originality, which consists in small but essential decisions as to format, scale, name, and medium.

When the composer Morton Feldman told Karlheinz Stockhausen that his secret lay in never manipulating the sounds, Stockhausen shrewdly replied, 'Not even a little bit?'" So for a radio DJ, what sort of minimal intervention constitutes a clinamen? Subtle variations, such as temporal shifts, are a good place to start. On his first show after the inauguration of President Obama (November 15, 2008), for example, Goldsmith played Parliament's "Chocolate City"—a five-minute-and-thirty-seven-second track from 1975 that imagines the possibility of a black president—for a solid three hours.[20] On other occasions, he has used software to extend the length of spoken recordings while leaving individual words audible, as in the case of a show where he extended the hour-long finale of *Friends* to the full three hours of his time slot (June 12, 2004).[21] Goldsmith's most extreme versions of the practice of temporal shifting involved digitally condensing his playlists to radical degrees, playing 180 songs in three hours on October 20, 2004, and 360 songs in three hours on October 27, 2004.[22]

Another of Goldsmith's ongoing practices as a DJ, "kenny g sings theory," offers another point for thinking through the structure of the clinamen.[23] In each of these pieces, Goldsmith pairs a digital karaoke audio file with the work of a particular cultural theorist and sings the theoretical text as the lyrics. In karaoke, as in conventional DJing, competence is a mixture of fidelity to traditional form and improvisation, which always departs slightly from tradition. Unlike DJing, however, in karaoke the emphasis falls on the affective force of the performance, which has more to do with a ritual affirmation of belonging to the community of singer-listeners in the karaoke space, a process that inevitably involves attempts to expand that community, than it does with musical competence—hence, the form of the spiral. Goldsmith's on-air karaoke raises a number of questions, not only because of the ambiguity of his affect and the attenuated feedback from the remote radio audience, but also because the potential object of fidelity for his performance is double: is it about the music or the theory? As incongruous as they may seem, there is often an associative logic to Goldsmith's theory-karaoke pieces. For example, "Kenneth Goldsmith Sings Jean Baudrillard" pairs the Disneyland section of Baudrillard's *America*, which concerns the structure of the simulacra, with the theme from Claude Lelouch's *Vivre pour Vivre* (1967), a film that is deeply concerned with themes of self-deception and the substitution of a series of phantasmatic objects of desire.

Johan Fornäs (1994) observes that karaoke exemplifies one of the commonplaces of post-structural theory and cultural studies: "Theoreticians like Wolfgang Iser, Stanley Fish, Julia Kristeva, Roland Barthes, Paul Ricoeur or Stuart Hall have long maintained that all cultural texts leave openings for the individual and collective creation of meaning." By taking theorists literally and plugging their descriptions of the creation of cultural meaning into the epitome of cultural objects that permit such a process, Goldsmith finds a way to be faithful *and* depart from orthodoxy simultaneously. The seriousness of the theory is undercut precisely because Goldsmith follows its spirit rather than its letter, betraying it while repeating it verbatim.

A syzygy is a temporary conjunction or yoking together of entities that otherwise occupy different spaces and trajectories. The 'pataphysical version might include Goldsmith pretending to be another DJ on his own station. Two such pieces are exemplary: "Poem for Ken Freedman" (station manager of WFMU) and "Poem for Irwin Chusid" (the DJ whose show preceded Goldsmith's time slot and the author of *Songs in the Key of Z: The Curious Universe of Outsider Music*). On at least three separate occasions, Goldsmith transcribed every detail of Freedman's and Chusid's mic breaks—their on-air patter from between recordings, down to the ums and ahs—and recited them verbatim as his own mic breaks. The effect was heightened because Goldsmith's voice and Chusid's are very similar. In a rare interview about his work as a DJ, Goldsmith notes that in another case he and Chusid switched time slots and simply pretended that each was the other (Baumes 2005).

When Goldsmith is involved, "pretending to be the other DJ" is already complex, because his on-air persona has always been not "Kenneth Goldsmith" but "kenny g" (all lower case). The potential for confusion with Kenneth Gorelick, the saxophonist also known as Kenny G (capital K and capital G), is immediately obvious. In a Google search for "Kenny G" (at least, *my* Google search for Kenny G; search engines are no longer agnostic about who uses them)—the top eleven results all refer to Gorelick. But the twelfth still points to "kenny g's homepage" at WFMU.org; the eighth, to "kenny g's homepage"; and the thirteenth, to his playlists and archives.[24] What has happened since 1995 as a result of this confusion has a certain wince-producing predictability: fans who believe they have found the secret Gorelick home page inundate Goldsmith's WFMU e-mail address with fan mail, and lowercase kenny g reads the messages on the air.[25]

In the summer of 2007, at a church in Amherst, Massachusetts, Goldsmith began a reading as he often does—with a selection of the Kenny G letters. After the reading, he was approached by a young man in the audience who extended his hand and said, "Kenny G. May I introduce myself? I'm Jon

Zorn" (without the h). To be precise, this was Jonathan Zorn the composer, sound artist, and performer from Middletown, Connecticut, not John Zorn, the composer, sound artist, and performer from New York.[26] The result of this meeting (not unlike the Comte de Lautréamont's chance encounter of an umbrella and a sewing machine on an operating table [Lautréamont 1994, 193]) was an album called *Kenny G Meets John Zorn*, on which the h-less Jon Zorn developed an interactive digital music system to accompany the lowercase kenny g's reading of letters addressed to the uppercase Kenny G. What manifests itself in this project is the possibility of subverting the grip that the fantasies of celebrity culture hold for us by overidentifying with them, revealing the absurdities and inconsistencies of those fantasies in the process.

As Bernstein's notion of a strategy of tactics suggests through the invocation of negative dialectics, the question that uncreative improvisation raises is this: can we fix the problems created by the discourse of corporate creativity by adding uncreativity to the mix? This is also the precise moment that Goldsmith's larger ethos of impurity and uncreativity encounters its own limit. The irony is dialectical. If Goldsmith at one point escaped from Florida's creative class of highly paid new media ad executives into the realms of poetry, art, and the academy, his success in being uncreative has propelled him straight back into what Florida (2012, 858) calls the "Super-Creative Core" of contemporary culture, limiting his ongoing efficacy in staging the very problem that his work foregrounds. Goldsmith recognizes that there are few spaces in "hypercapitalism" that allow for the appearance of the valueless and that others who experimented with boredom and uncreativity found either mixed or too much success.[27] But there is a very real risk that the fate of uncreativity may be, in Alan Liu's (2004, 375) terms, to "simply be lumped together with 'cool' by the dominant corporate, media, and other institutions of society as part of the undifferentiated bread and circuses of contemporary 'entertainment.'" Žižek (2008, 155–56) has commented repeatedly on the ability of capitalism to undermine "all particular lifeworlds, cultures, and traditions" and enlist them to its cause, so why not uncreativity, as well? It is all too possible to imagine the advent of the first "uncreative director" of corporate advertising, if such a person has not already appeared.

A decade ago, Goldsmith wrote, "When I reach 40, I hope to have cleansed myself of all creativity."[28] The ambiguity around whether Goldsmith's acclaim as an uncreative DJ or uncreative writer is due to succeeding or failing in this aspiration is beside the point, as Gayatri Chakravorty Spivak pointed out more than thirty years ago:

> We are the disc jockeys of an advanced technocracy. The discs are not "records" of the old-fashioned kind, but productions of the most recent technology. The trends in taste and the economic factors that govern them are also products of the most complex interrelations among myriad factors such as foreign relations, the world market, the conduct of advertisement supported by and supporting the first two items, and so on. To speak of the mode of production and constitution of the radio station complicates matters further. Within this intricately determined and multiform situation, the disc jockey and his audience think, indeed are made to think, that they are free to play. This illusion of freedom allows us to protect the brutal ironies of technocracy by suggesting either that the system nourishes the humanist's freedom of spirit, or that "technology," that vague evil, is something the humanist must transform by inculcating humanistic "values," or by drawing generalized philosophical analogies from the latest spatio-temporal discoveries of the magical realms of "pure science." (Spivak 1979, 209)

What matters is how a system that presents us with such a false choice marginalizes us all. Goldsmith's (2011a) recent turn toward institutional critique suggests that he is attempting to take the political form that his work implies and actually fill it with politics. Having the history of institutional critique already at hand as an example of what does and does not work, he asks: "So what happens when the institutional critique is so easily absorbed by the institution, that it moves from a 'critique of institutions to an institution of critique?' We've seen this already in the art world where performative acts of institutional critique are regularly commissioned by the institutions themselves" (2011a). Goldsmith speculates that it might be possible to proceed by "at once fondly caressing these institutions, while at the same time driving a stake into their backs. To imagine it in any other way would be insulting" (2011a). With no way around the "conceptual, political, and institutional complexities of parapoetic practice," the only way to proceed is to point out the deadlock between creativity and work rather than try to resolve it (2011a). The next question is whether the throngs of newly professionalized "uncreative writers" and DJs can use such practices to shift culture away from this impasse.

Notes

Epigraph: T. S. Eliot, "Poetry in the Eighteenth Century," in *The Pelican Guide to English Literature 4: From Dryden to Johnson*, ed. Boris Ford (Harmondsworth, UK: Penguin, 1957), 272.

1. Kenneth Goldsmith, "Paragraphs on Conceptual Writing," Electronic Poetry Center (State University of New York [SUNY], Buffalo), http://epc.buffalo.edu /authors/goldsmith/conceptual_paragraphs.html. Accessed March 13, 2010; Kenneth Goldsmith, "Uncreativity as a Creative Practice," Electronic Poetry Center (SUNY Buffalo), http://epc.buffalo.edu/authors/goldsmith/uncreativity .html. Accessed March 13, 2010.

2. This number is the title of a publication (Kenneth Goldsmith, *6799*. New York: zingmagazine, 2000. Also available at http://epc.buffalo.edu/authors/gold smith/works/6799.pdf. Accessed August 26, 2016). At the time it was also the number of albums in the author's collection.

3. See Shigeru Matsui, "Pure Poems," in Dworkin and Goldsmith 2011, 397; Wiener Gruppe [Vienna Group], "Ideas for a 'Record Album/Functional' Acoustic Cabaret," in Dworkin and Goldsmith 2011, 571.

4. Catherine Spencer, "When Attitudes Become Form: Bern 1969/Venice 2013," blog post, Ca' Corner Della Regina, Venice, September 2, 2013, http://www.thisis tomorrow.info/viewArticle.aspx?artId=1999. Accessed March 13, 2010.

5. See David Leonhardt, "When Button-Down Meets Buttonless," *New York Times*, January 26, 2000, http://www.nytimes.com/2000/01/26/jobs/when -button-down-meets-buttonless.html. Accessed March 13, 2010; "Metro Business: Web Design Firm Sold," *New York Times*, February 15, 2000, http://www .nytimes.com/2000/02/15/nyregion/metro-business-web-design-firm-sold.html. Accessed March 13, 2010.

6. See the dedication in Pashenkov 2002. In the acknowledgments, Pashenkov (2002, 5) refers to his former boss, "Ken Goldsmith at Methodfive."

7. Courtney Pulitzer, "Methodfive after 5 Forum," *Cyber Scene*, April 21, 1997, http://www.thecyberscene.com/1997/04/methodfive-after-5-forum.html. Accessed March 13, 2010.

8. Kenneth Goldsmith, "Re: [Conceptual-Writing] Blast from the Past: Kenny's Prose as a Business Guy," e-mail to the Conceptual Writing list in response to Darren Wershler, December 24, 2013, http://groups.yahoo.com/neo/groups/concep tual-writing/info (restricted). Accessed March 13, 2010.

9. See also Goldsmith's edited collection of interviews with Warhol (Goldsmith 2004) and his comments throughout Bluttal 2006.

10. Kenneth Goldsmith, "Being Boring," Electronic Poetry Center (SUNY Buffalo), 2004, http://epc.buffalo.edu/authors/goldsmith/goldsmith_boring.html. Accessed March 13, 2010.

11. Kenneth Goldsmith, "Unedited Transcript: Kenneth Goldsmith," interview by Marcus Boon, *Bomb* 117, 2011, http://bombsite.com/issues/117/articles/6071.

12. Kathleen O'Malley, "Definition of Freeform," WFMU.org, 2006, http:// wfmu.org/freeform.html. Accessed March 13, 2010.

13. These recordings are still audible at Kenneth Goldsmith, "Playlists and Archives for Kenny G's Hour of Pain," WFMU.org, n.d., http://www.wfmu.org/play lists/KG. Accessed March 13, 2010.

14. Brian Turner, "WFMU DJs Bound and Gagged," WFMU.org, n.d., http:// www.wfmu.org/~kennyg/plu.html. Accessed March 13, 2010.

15. Goldsmith, "Playlists and Archives for Kenny G's Hour of Pain."

16. Kenneth Goldsmith, liner notes from *64 Minutes of Anal Magic*, bootleg CD, n.p., n.d., http://cdtrrracks.com (inactive). Accessed March 13, 2010.

17. See Goldsmith, "Playlists and Archives for Kenny G's Hour of Pain," http:// www.wfmu.org/playlists/shows/13585. Accessed March 13, 2010. No audio archive of the show is available.

18. See http://ahab.com/venom/up_the_ass_with_the_fcc.html (inactive). Accessed March 13, 2010.

19. Christopher Zinsli, "Indecency Fears Prompt DJ Suspension: WFMU's Kenny G Put on Seven-Week Hiatus for Station Policy Infractions," Hudsonreporter.com, January 8, 2005, http://www.hudsonreporter.com/view/full_story/2402486 /article-Indecency-fears-prompt-DJ-suspension-WFMU-s-Kenny-G-put-on-seven -week-hiatus-for-station-policy-infractions?mobile_view=false. Accessed March 13, 2010.

20. See Goldsmith, "Playlists and Archives for Kenny G's Hour of Pain," http:// wfmu.org/playlists/KG2008. Accessed March 13, 2010.

21. See Goldsmith, "Playlists and Archives for Kenny G's Hour of Pain," https:// wfmu.org/playlists/shows/11266. Accessed March 13, 2010.

22. See Goldsmith, "Playlists and Archives for Kenny G's Hour of Pain," https:// wfmu.org/playlists/shows/12931; https://wfmu.org/playlists/shows/12999. Accessed March 13, 2010.

23. "Kenneth Goldsmith, audio recordings, n.d., Center for Programs in Contemporary Writing at the University of Pennsylvania, http://writing.upenn.edu /pennsound/x/Goldsmith.html. Accessed March 13, 2010.

24. Google search for "Kenny G" on December 29, 2013.

25. Kenneth Goldsmith, "From *the Kenny G Letters*," Electronic Poetry Center (SUNY Buffalo), 1999, http://epc.buffalo.edu/ezines/deluxe/three/kennyg.html. Accessed March 13, 2010; Kenneth Goldsmith, "A Selection of the Kenny G Letters," Brooklyn Rail, 2006, http://brooklynrail.org/2006/3/poetry/a-selection -of-the-kenny-g-letters. Accessed March 13, 2010.

26. See UbuWeb: Sound, Kenneth Goldsmith and Jonathan Zorn. http://www .ubu.com/sound/kg-jz.html. Accessed March 13, 2010.

27. Goldsmith, "Uncreativity as a Creative Practice."

28. Goldsmith, "Uncreativity as a Creative Practice."

III · SOCIALITY AND IDENTITY

CHAPTER 8

STRAYHORN'S QUEER ARRANGEMENTS

Lisa Barg

In mid-January 1956, Billy Strayhorn flew to Los Angeles from New York to begin a collaborative recording project with the pop singer Rosemary Clooney. Although Clooney was an experienced band singer, having recorded with Harry James and Benny Goodman, her stardom was most closely associated in the pop imagination with a string of hits she cut in the early 1950s for Columbia Records—most notably, the Mitch Miller ethnic novelty songs "Come On-a My House" and "Mambo Italiano"—as well as for her featured role alongside Bing Crosby and Danny Kaye in Paramount's Technicolor blockbuster *White Christmas*.[1] The collaboration with Clooney would be the first of its kind for both Strayhorn and the Ellington Orchestra: not only did it mark Duke Ellington's first collaboration with a singer for a full-length LP, but for the first time in his seventeen-year relationship with Ellington, Strayhorn was offered creative autonomy on a major recording project, one that (also among the first) daringly paired a star white female pop singer with an African American jazz orchestra. Even with a band as prestigious as the Ellington outfit, this pairing must have raised a few red flags for executives at Columbia—or, at least, it would seem so, to judge by the evidence of the cover art for the resulting LP, *Blue Rose*. Images of Ellington and Clooney appear on the cover in a split visual space that juxtaposes, collage-like, a large filmic image of Ellington with a much smaller photographic image of Clooney. In the background, placed directly under the title "Blue Rose: Rosemary Clooney and Duke Ellington and His Orchestra," a grainy smoke-filled, black-and-white image of Ellington's face appears as if being projected onto a movie screen. He smiles gently, his eyes cast downward toward a brightly colored, pasted-on photographic head shot of Clooney floating in the foreground; she, in turn, innocently gazes out-

Fig. 8.1 *Blue Rose* (1956), LP Cover.

ward toward an unseen camera, seemingly unaware of the celluloid Elling-ton looming behind her. This stylized separation of Ellington and Clooney in the visual field delineates, however satirically, racial and sexual boundaries through a technologically mediated, safe distance.

Yet the design of the LP cover, with its contrast of Clooney's "in-color" head against the "black-and-white" Ellington, also referenced the real-life "virtual" conditions involved in recording the LP—just one of a set of the unusual conditions surrounding Strayhorn and Clooney's working relation-ship. At the time, Clooney was pregnant with her second child and was suf-fering from extreme nausea and vomiting, a situation that precluded her from traveling from Los Angeles to New York to record the session.[2] On top of this challenge, the two collaborators had to work under a very tight dead-line. As the story goes, the producer Irving Townsend initially pitched the idea for *Blue Rose* to Ellington and Strayhorn on January 12 during the opening night of the Ellington Orchestra's engagement at Café Society Uptown. At the end of their initial discussion, "Strayhorn, Townsend, and Ellington had agreed on a basic approach to the album: whatever Clooney and Strayhorn wanted to do" (Hajdu 1996, 148). However, "whatever [they] wanted to do" was set to begin on January 23—and in New York, not Los Angeles. Townsend overcame this obstacle by making use of the then relatively novel (at least for jazz) technology of multitrack recording; Strayhorn would fly to New York to direct the session for the instrumental tracks, then travel to Los Angeles to record the vocal overdubbing with Clooney. Originally, Ellington and Strayhorn wanted to title the LP *Inter-Continental* to highlight the bicoastal recording process, but that concept was nixed by Columbia in favor of the more pop-friendly title *Blue Rose*.

With Townsend's plan in place, Strayhorn, armed with records, manuscript paper, and pen, arrived at Clooney's home on Roxbury Drive, in Beverly Hills, where he stayed for more than a week in her older child's bedroom doing double duty as caregiver and musical collaborator (often simultaneously). Clooney's husband, the director, actor, and singer José Ferrer, was abroad working on a film project. In David Hajdu's biography of Strayhorn, Clooney recalled the ensuing mix of musical, personal, and domestic intimacy:

> He made me breakfast in bed. We didn't know each other at all before that, and we became incredibly close immediately. I was having a very difficult pregnancy. I was really suffering and he got me through it. I'd say, "Oh God, I'm going to throw up again," and he would say, "Okay, now. It's okay," and he would take care of me. He said "Don't get up, honey," and he'd make me crackers and milk. I felt a bit better one day, and he baked me an apple pie. He cared about that baby. He cared about the fact that I couldn't afford to get tired, and he watched out for me. I would just stay in bed and talk about things. Most of the time, we didn't even talk much about music. We did work on the music, it was like I was working with my best friend. I wanted to do my best for him, and I would do anything he wanted. . . . I was never associated with a man who was so completely unthreatening and uncontrolling *and* so completely in charge. (Hajdu 1996, 147, 149)[3]

While Clooney's memory conveys her genuine affection and respect for Strayhorn, it is difficult to ignore the troubling histories of race, gender, sexuality, and power that haunt her story of Strayhorn as trusted domestic caregiver. That this tale of a white woman served by a caring and "unthreatening" black man takes place in a Hollywood mansion only underscores the close proximity of Clooney's narrative to the racialized and sexualized legacies of the subservient black domestic worker in popular culture (see, e.g., Bogle 2001; DuCille 1997, 10–32; Guerrero 1993). In this context, the way Clooney narrates her memory of Strayhorn's actions as domestic care-giver, coupled with her characterization of Strayhorn's non-normative masculinity, hails Strayhorn's black queer body according to the scripts of historical white affection for gendered asexualized black service.[4]

Yet as a description of her working relationship with her collaborator, particularly as it marks socio-musical practices and effects of empathy, support, and nurturing, Clooney's memory aligns strongly with a broadly held perception of Strayhorn as collaborator—one pervades the retrospective comments of many other singers (and instrumentalists) with whom he worked. Lena Horne, Strayhorn's lifelong friend and self-described "soulmate," remembered him as a "perfect mixture of man and woman," "very strong," and "at the same time very sensitive and gentle" (Hajdu 1996, 96). When Horne first met Strayhorn, he was "sent" by Ellington to "keep her company": "Duke could be very possessive with women . . . so he arranged for Billy to be my chaperone. He assumed that Billy was safe, which I guess he was in the way that Duke saw me, which was as a sex object" (94–95). Horne credited her work with Strayhorn around this time as a formative experience in her musical training, helping her to discover her own voice: "Billy rehearsed me. He stretched me vocally. Very subtly. . . . He knew what songs were right for me. He knew my personality better than I did . . . and he wrote arrangements that had my feeling in the music" (94–95).

I want to highlight the gendered and racialized terrain of these remembrances not only for the paths of musical meaning to which it directs us, but also for how they might align with what the film scholar Matthew Tinkcom (2002) has called in a rather different, but not unrelated, context the "queer labor" of gay male artists working behind the scenes in the U.S. film industry. In Tinkcom's work, this group includes auteur directors, songwriters, arrangers, art directors, and choreographers. Clooney's and Horne's descriptions of Strayhorn's practices as a collaborator are a case in point insofar as they resonate with the title phrase of Tinkcom's book, *Working Like a Homosexual* (2002). Tinkcom borrows this phrase from an observation made by Lela Simone, a rehearsal pianist and vocal coach who worked with Vincente Minnelli and the legendary Arthur Freed Unit at Metro-Goldwyn-Mayer (MGM) in the 1940s–1950s. Recalling Minnelli's working persona in an interview in 1990, Simone explained, "Vincente was not a man who was a dictator. He tried to do it in a soft and nice way. He worked in let's say . . . I don't know whether you will understand what I say . . . he worked like a homosexual" (quoted in Tinkcom 2002, 38).[5] Tinkcom argues that Simone's statement "encourages us to theorize the possibility of a capitalist enterprise accommodating marginalized sex/gender subjects because their labor could enhance a product's appeal through its differentiated style" (36–37).

Working behind the scenes in the Ellington organization, Strayhorn similarly cultivated a "differentiated style," but under conditions of creative anonymity irreducibly bound to his identity as a black queer subject. As a musician friend quoted in Hajdu's (1996, 79) biography put it, "Billy could have pursued a career on his own—he had the talent . . . but he'd have had to be less than honest about his sexual orientation. Or he could work behind the scenes for Duke and be open about being gay." While previous critics—most notably, Hajdu (1999, 189–96)—have claimed a generalized gay sensibility for Strayhorn, little attention has been given to historicizing this sensibility by considering it in relation to the particular social and material conditions under which Strayhorn worked. This article explores the "queer position" under which Strayhorn labored in relation to his collaboration with singers and to his aesthetic practices as a vocal arranger. My intention here is not to reify Strayhorn as an exceptional black gay subject in the world of mid-century jazz (or, accordingly, to reproduce an undifferentiated homo-hetero binary) but to describe and analyze specific instances of queer affiliation, affect, and identifications surrounding Strayhorn's work as an arranger and ask how such instances mark, enact, or embody a sociality of arranging. Strayhorn's vocal arranging oeuvre is extensive and varied, stretching from his hip, swinging charts for Ivie Anderson in the late 1930s and early 1940s to lush, ethereal backings for Ella Fitzgerald in the late 1950s. I focus closely on two recordings from this body of work that provide useful snapshots of contrasting working conditions and historical moments. Specifically, I first consider the collaboration between Strayhorn and Clooney on the LP *Blue Rose* and then trace a range of queer historical and aesthetic paths surrounding Strayhorn's celebrated arrangement of the pop tune "Flamingo" in 1940.

As a prelude, however, I want to consider briefly how my focus on arranging in jazz addresses the broad theme of this volume: social aesthetics and improvisation. Questions abound. What socialities are involved in the aesthetic practices of arranging? Does arranging facilitate or dictate sonic dialogue and interaction? How do vectors of identity such as race, gender, and sexuality shape the relationships between the arranger and the musicians with whom she works, and how might such relationships come to bear on the final musical assemblage? While I am not going to explicitly theorize these questions (much less provide definitive answers), I want to make a few preliminary observations. First, the category of arranging in jazz raises some of the same issues as that of improvisation insofar as it troubles normative distinctions between composing and arranging and their hierarchical aesthetic and legal status with respect to authorship and ownership. Yet as discursively constructed categories, notions of composition, arranging, and improvisation are grounded in historically and culturally contingent roles and practices; here I would argue that when it is talked about at all by jazz scholars and critics, arranging (and the image of the arranger) in jazz often appears as the "scripted" other in relation to improvisation. This was not always the case. Just to give one rather obscure example, in his influential article analyzing the effect of the American Federation of Musicians' recording ban on the development of bebop in 1942, Scott DeVeaux (1988) notes the threat that arrangers for "jazz oriented swing bands" posed to music publishers because of the interdependence of arranging practices and improvisation. DeVeaux (135) quotes one publisher's complaint: "Who can count on them for just one straight melody chorus to plant the refrain with those who might want to buy the song, if they could only tell what the tune was like—what with their way of going haywire after the first eight bars?" This leads me to my second point: the interdependence of arranging and improvisation in the practices of arranging in "jazz oriented swing bands." Here arrangers craft variegated sonic contexts (backings, formal design) that frame and facilitate improvising voices and in some cases may be said to crucially shape the conditions or scripts through which improvisatory performance takes place. With the Ellington Orchestra, this process was famously instigated through narrative acts, or "telling stories." A favorite metaphor of jazz musicians, "telling stories" explicitly attaches to instrumental music what Samuel A. Floyd (1991) has called a "semantic value," whereby individual musicians deploy communicative modes that give expression to and critically comment on a range of attitudes, feelings, and cultural values.[6] Part painter, part dramatist, Ellington blended, juxtaposed, and stitched together the collaborative "sound identities" and contributions of his soloists.[7]

Whether through narrative or other texts or contexts, arranging involves weaving together or "composing" in time and space the formal dimensions of a song or musical material and specific bodies, voices, or sonic personalities, itself a process that fundamentally depends on collaboration and interaction, although one typically worked out prior to the moment of performance or recording.[8] We would do better here to follow Eileen Southern's prescient use of the label "composer-arranger." As Jeffrey Magee has argued, this hyphenated, hybridizing category not only usefully indexes the dynamic creative continuum in jazz among the practices of composing, arranging, and improvisation; it also eschews the value-laden (and juridically enforced) distinctions between composition and arranging (Southern 1997, 392, quoted in Magee 1999, 62–63).[9] One could, of course, point to any number of compositional and improvisational practices that similarly blur the lines between composition and arranging, such as graphic scores or structured improvisations/conductions, both of which often function very similarly to arrangements. A third and critical point to make about my approach to linking the social and aesthetic in arranging: arrangers and arrangements in jazz function in the background, behind the scenes (whether on or off the bandstand), and I am interested especially in how these two senses of arranging—the social and the aesthetic—emerge in the sociality of arranging.

Grievin'

After Strayhorn arrived at Clooney's home, the two collaborators set to work selecting their songs for the LP and, when time and health permitted, rehearsing the arrangements at the piano, which, presumably, Strayhorn had worked out with the singer over that same week (Hajdu 1999, 147). In addition to haunting versions of Ellington classics such as "Sophisticated Lady" and "I Got It Bad (And That Ain't Good)" and a newly composed Ellington original, the eponymous "Blue Rose" (an instrumental with vocals), the LP included two original Strayhorn songs from 1939, "Grievin'" and "I'm Checkin' Out, Goom-Bye," along with one Strayhorn instrumental, significantly a full-band arrangement (of film noir–like proportions) of his great ballad for the alto saxophonist Johnny Hodges, "Passion Flower." As Clooney explained it, "Having 'Passion Flower' on there was sort of a wink, an inside thing to those in the know that this was basically Billy's record" (149).[10]

The tracks for *Blue Rose* were cut in four sessions. The instrumental tracks were recorded in New York on January 23 and 27, and the vocal overdubs were recorded in Los Angeles on February 8 and 11. Of the new arrangements of Strayhorn's two songs, Clooney's version of the blues-based ballad "Grievin'" stands out. Notably, the manuscript for the vocal arrangement—the first and only recording of the song with Strayhorn's lyric—bears a dedication under the title, "For Rosemary Clooney," and Strayhorn made extensive alternations to the 1939 instrumental arrangement that included a newly composed introduction.[11] Strayhorn's new introduction immediately announces the ballad's orchestrally lush stylistic updating in relation to the expressive and formal lexicon of the blues. Harry Carney (baritone sax) states the A-strain of the melody in a slow swing tempo backed by a dissonant-charged, dark plunger mute "wha-wha" chordal texture that unfolds over a truncated blues chorus. A particularly interesting feature of the melody is how Strayhorn maps the conventional two-bar symmetrical phrase structure onto a series of rhythmic displacements, which begin on the upbeat to the first full bar with a three-note pattern (two eighths followed by a dotted-half note), rising upward from C-sharp to D to F. In measures 1–4, the pattern expands melodically with pendular leaps covering a ninth from F to G before descending downward through the tonic triad via an eighth-note triplet figure that leads to A-flat on the downbeat at measure 4. The triplet figure reverses in measure 5 (B-flat to C to D), landing on F, where the melody lingers for the final two measures over an E-flat minor/major seventh (functioning as the dominant), before cadencing in B-flat with the "grieving'" figure, a bluesy half-note pendular leap.

With her signature warm and sensuous yet light sound, Clooney delivers the lyric in a stylish and rhythmically subtle yet straightforward manner, backed for the first two vocal choruses (AA) by riff figures that respond in rhythmic unison (example 8.1).

These riff figures are derived from rhythmic and melodic features described earlier (e.g., repeating triplet pattern, pendular contour, blue notes) and appear throughout the arrangement in various guises (example 8.2). By far the most dramatic incarnation occurs in the third vocal chorus after the bridge: the texture thickens, with reeds and brass playing the riff figure in unison behind Clooney as she pleads, "Every day, every night, how I pray that you'll treat me right." The emotional tension spills into the next bar as the riff figures give way to a trombone trio playing a half-note chromatic step for Clooney's climactic ultimatum: "You will regret and you'll cry some, If I die from grievin'," a moment that itself suddenly morphs into an expressive, improvisatory rupture in the form of a particularly memorable (and perfectly timed) wailing, coloratura trumpet solo by Cat Anderson. While truly astounding, the full force of Anderson's blowing on this chorus depends, nevertheless, on the sonic backing that frames—or, more accurately, propels—him.

Directly after Clooney intones the grievin' figure at the cadence, the full band lurches upward in unison through a syncopated, chromatically inflected two-bar climb, a kind of sonic launching pad for Anderson. As the

Ex. 8.1 Strayhorn, "Grievin'," mm. 9–16.

trumpet part takes off, the reeds and brass choir continue in the upper register, but now in an extravagant call-and-response pattern punctuated by a chromatically rising and rousing full-throated rhythmic ostinato based on a variation of the riff figure (a tied-quarter-note triplet ostinato that we first hear sung in the B-section of the melody). With Anderson's trumpet climbing further into the stratosphere for the final jaw-dropping measures of his solo, the backing instrumental choir intones fragments from the first half of the melody.

The collective dramatic force of Anderson's chorus is so startling that we might conclude that it actually overwhelms Clooney, as if stealing her emotional spotlight through an affect of improvisatory combustion. But such an interpretation would be possible only if we ignore the larger expressive and musical arch of the arrangement. Here Anderson's solo functions theatrically, amplifying—quite literally—the feeling that Clooney authorizes in the lyric of the preceding climatic vocal chorus. This blues-saturated emotional

Ex. 8.2 Strayhorn, "Grievin'," mm. 27–34.

transference might also be heard as a kind of phallic excess beyond the racialized and gendered proprieties of Clooney's vocal persona. Formally, Strayhorn weaves Anderson's solo chorus into a quasi-through-composed architecture that unfolds the latter part of the arrangement and leads the modulation, moving the song as if through sheer propulsion, from B-flat to D-flat.[12]

Taken as a whole, the foregoing discussion of form, style, and sonic affect in Strayhorn's vocal arrangement for "Grievin'" suggests how the practices of composers/arrangers, singers, and players collaboratively refashion from within the formal and affective layers of a song. Strayhorn conceived the process of arranging as a kind of co-text: "You really need to write something you think fits his sound and is *your* sound, too—a combination of what you do and what he does" (quoted in Dance 1970, 30). Strayhorn's notion of sonic fit implies that tailoring an arrangement around the technical abilities and stylistic persona of a singer (or soloist) creates a comfortable space for a performer to discover or imagine "her space" within the music—in other words, a fit that facilitates rather than dictates and thus helps to facilitate effective improvisations. From this perspective, it is possible to hear Strayhorn's elaborate, blues-tinged arrangement as enabling a sonic space for Clooney to fashion a new vocal persona, one that she understood as helping her to break free from the limiting racial and sexual codes of the 1950s novelty song (an argument that can, of course, also be extended to most, if not all, of the other arrangements on the LP). Indeed, in her autobiography *Girl Singer*, Clooney (1999, 154) associated the experience of collaborating on *Blue Rose* with artistic self-discovery and empowerment. Her comments on the subject arose in the context of recalling a memorable evening she spent with Billie Holiday just a few months after the Strayhorn-Ellington session: "Billie said it wasn't work to do a song she could feel—the only kind of song she would do—and I felt 'Blue Rose' and all the songs on that album in a way I could never feel 'Come On[-a my House].' I wasn't in a position to change my material, and had I been, I might not have had the confidence to do it. Now I did."[13]

In terms of vocal persona, Clooney's sound on *Blue Rose* aligns with the hipper, jazz-influenced mainstream white big band singers of the day such as Peggy Lee and Frank Sinatra. Yet as I noted earlier, Clooney had already cut few sides in the early 1950s (including a Columbia disc with Frank Sinatra) in which we can also hear this stylistic orientation (and in fact some critical assessments of these sides compared Clooney to Ella Fitzgerald).[14] Beyond these larger stylistic references and associations, however, I am interested in what it meant for Clooney to "do a song she could feel" in relation to the specific working conditions and set of constraints surrounding her collaboration with Strayhorn. The sociality of the arranging process on *Blue Rose* required forms of intimacy improvised within both domestic/private and public/professional spaces and across lines of gender, race, and class. How, then, might we connect such forms of improvised intimacy to the collaborators' personal engagement with the affective registers of specific song arrangements?

To return again to the example of the blues ballad "Grievin'," for Clooney the choice of this song may have been guided by her ability to "feel" the song (a choice itself guided by Strayhorn's sense that the song would fit her well). The lyric "I" expresses pain of a lover dealing with an unfaithful and callous partner, a theme that animates another song on the LP, Strayhorn's poignant, slow-tempo, dissonant-tinged arrangement of Ellington's "I Got It Bad (And That Ain't Good)." Although generic with respect to the thematic conventions of pop/jazz ballads (and blues), both songs would have had a particular personal resonance for Clooney and thus could have provided a vehicle for her to address difficult personal feelings surrounding her life circumstances. During this period, Clooney (1999, 131) struggled to maintain the heteronormative image of, in her words, "the perfect Fifties Wife" in the face of her husband's flagrant philandering (which began shortly after their honeymoon) and intimidating temper tantrums—all while she paid the bills and worked tirelessly to support their rapidly growing family.[15] Her pregnancy during the Blue Rose collaboration led to the second of five children born between 1955 and 1960 (all of whom she was left to support after she and Ferrer first split up in 1961).[16]

As noted earlier, Blue Rose also signaled a new direction in Strayhorn's career with respect to his partnership with Ellington. Handing Strayhorn the creative reins for the project amounted to a kind of peace offering from Ellington following several years of estrangement between the composing partners. Strayhorn's decision to separate from Ellington was precipitated by frustration over his uncredited creative labor and "accumulations of grievances, from copyright issues to artistic conflicts," a situation Clooney seems to have been aware of, given her comment about the inclusion of "Passion Flower" as a covert tactic to mark Strayhorn's largely uncredited public authorship (van de Leur 2002, 115; see also Hajdu 1996, 113–14). In fact, just a few days before Strayhorn met Ellington and Townsend at Café Society Uptown to discuss the project, he went to the club with a small group of friends to celebrate his homecoming to New York after a liberating extended trip to Paris. While in Paris, Strayhorn visited his former longtime partner, the pianist Aaron Bridgers, and spent many evenings at the vibrant, gay-friendly jazz bar the Mars Club, where Bridgers worked as the staff pianist and where Strayhorn was treated as a celebrity by the city's expatriate gay cabaret subculture. Returning home to New York from Paris meant leaving behind the transforming cultural energy, communal support, and warm admiration he found in the City of Lights for professional uncertainty and reckoning. Strayhorn's difficult feelings about his return can be gleaned from Hajdu's (1996,

145) account of his homecoming party at Café Society Uptown. With a group of friends, including his soon-to-be boyfriend Francis Goldberg, Strayhorn "bought a few rounds in salute to Bridgers, and charmed the group with droll descriptions of the Mars Club."[17] At one point, he noticed a bill plastered on the wall advertising the upcoming Ellington engagement of January 12. As narrated by a musician friend, Strayhorn responded sardonically, "'Well, I'll *have* to come to see Duke Ellington—and hear all those Billy Strayhorn songs,' after which he looked around the tiny little club . . . puffed on a cigarette and quipped 'If there's room for them'" (145).

In recounting these stories, I do not mean to suggest that we can unproblematically impute (auto)biographical meaning into the music or claim a reified homology between the social and musical. Nor am I simply pointing to the generalized affective power of songs to sonically embody or project personal feelings and fantasies—although I do believe that is always a potential function of songs. What I am arguing is that such specific everyday life circumstances and contexts acted as a constellation of social "texts" (among others) that framed their collaboration and, as such, played a role, however ineffable, in the selection of songs and in shaping the arranging process, specifically along paths of cross-gender projection and identification. Sometimes these paths emerged through creative directorial advice given during the vocal overdubbing.[18] When Clooney was recording Strayhorn's other original number, a charmingly "retro" arrangement of the up-tempo swinger "I'm Checkin' Out, Goom-Bye," she recalled Strayhorn's direction for realizing the lyrics, with its lighthearted yet pointed message to a deceptive lover, this way: "He told me not to do it angry. He said, 'Just because you're leaving the other person, it doesn't mean you're angry. You're in charge. You're leaving, because you're the strong one. You might even come back. Who knows?'" (Hajdu 1996, 148).[19] But what does this gendered improvisatory field of intimacy and identification have to do with the larger set of queer issues that I raised at the outset? It is to this question that we now turn.

Flamingo(s)

The musical transformation of "Grievin'" from its original 1939 instrumental incarnation to Clooney's 1956 vocal version is not only a story of formal and stylistic change. It also indexes to some extent the evolution of Strayhorn and Ellington's working relationship. While Strayhorn wrote the tune, it is Ellington who is credited for the larger part of the 1939 arrangement, an effective but largely conventional swing-band arrangement. As Walter van de Leur (2002, 32) points out in his groundbreaking book on Strayhorn's music, during Strayhorn's first two years with the organization his creative partnership with Ellington tended toward a division of musical labor in which Ellington worked out the instrumental sections and Strayhorn worked out the vocal sections. However, this situation changed rapidly. In 1941, Strayhorn co-composed and arranged many of the songs for the celebrated black Popular Front "revusical" *Jump for Joy*. And by 1942, he was responsible for all of the vocal arranging and was supervising a roster of singers that included Ivie Anderson (who had been with the orchestra since the early 1930s), Herb Jeffries, Kay Davis, Marie Ellington, and Joya Sherrill (Hajdu 1996, 97).[20]

To the extent that Strayhorn's work during this period revolved around creating arrangements to showcase singers for the legendary Blanton-Webster band, his work as a vocal arranger—and that of the singers with whom he collaborated—were viewed largely as "commercial work," a devalued category under which the contributions of women in jazz (especially singers) historically have been marginalized (see, e.g., Pellegrinelli 2008, 31–47).[21] At once central to the orchestra's commercial appeal yet operating at the margins, Strayhorn negotiated a similar but in no way identical gendered field of power as that which structured the position of many of the singers with whom he collaborated.

Notably, Strayhorn's vocal arrangements during this period were rarely recorded, and only a few made it into the Ellington book. One that did stick, and in a big way, was Strayhorn's 1940 arrangement of the Ted Grouya–Edmund Anderson pop song "Flamingo" for the baritone crooner Herb Jeffries.[22] "Flamingo" was a hit for Ellington in 1941 and a career-making song for Jeffries, who in an oft-cited remark proclaimed, "That's the bird that brought me. Most people come to this planet by stork; I came by Flamingo, and Duke Ellington delivered me."[23] Strayhorn recalled, "I think what really clinched the vocal chores for me was when Herb Jeffries came with the band [in 1939]. He was singing in a high tenor range, and I asked him whether he liked singing up there. He said he didn't, so I wrote some things for him that pulled his voice down to the natural baritone he became after 'Flamingo'" (quoted in Tucker 1993, 500). As in the case of his collaboration with Clooney, these comments convey the ways in which Strayhorn's arrangement for Jeffries facilitated a space for him to refashion a vocal persona, one he understood as more natural, conveying a more authentic self. "That's the kind of thing he did with the singers in the band," Jeffries remembered. "He'd work very, very closely with you, and he sensed what your strengths were. Then he picked songs and did arrangements to bring out the best in you" (Hajdu 1996, 97). As with Clooney, Jeffries's comments index a social aesthetics for arranging in which the scripts of musical and personal identification work in tandem. Strayhorn's collaborations with Lena Horne, which I discussed briefly at the outset, can also be considered in this light. Strayhorn coached, accompanied, and arranged for her, "applying," in Hajdu's words, "his gift for musical empathy to the artist he loved so" (96).

Of all the vocalists on the Ellington roster in the early 1940s, Strayhorn felt a special affinity for Jeffries who, like Strayhorn, was an avowed Francophile. The two friends enjoyed conversing in French, particularly in public spaces in which such displays of sophistication could speak back to and trouble U.S. racist culture and stereotypes, "There was a tremendous amount of discrimination," Jeffries said, "and you could show a certain amount of sophistication by the mere fact that you could speak a language that the next white person couldn't. Strayhorn and I both felt this showed you weren't that lowly person, that Amos 'n' Andy character that everybody thought you were" (Hajdu 1996, 73-74).[24]

The registral placement and reorientation of Jeffries's voice in Strayhorn's arrangement of "Flamingo" also performs "a certain amount of sophistication," one that can be fully grasped only by hearing how Jeffries's voice interacts and fits in with the musical context that surrounds it—that is, by considering the aesthetics of the arrangement as a whole. As van de Leur (2002, 38-43) brilliantly describes in his analysis of "Flamingo," Strayhorn's arrangement extends considerably and transforms the original pop song through the addition of new material in the form of elaborate introductory, transitional, and modulatory sections).[25] These additions and revisions exemplify Strayhorn's innovative approach to pop tune arrangements in which "carefully worked out introductions, transitions, and codas" are used as "structuring elements to secure the internal logic of an orchestration" (67). Indeed, my discussion of Strayhorn's arrangement of "Grievin'" pointed to these types of "structuring elements" but also emphasized the role of affect and style—both of which are crucial elements at play in Strayhorn's arrangement of "Flamingo." The introduction for "Flamingo" is a case in point (example 8.3). Strayhorn's newly composed introduction supplies a sonic modernist orchestral gloss on the essential generic topos of the song: Latin-tinged, tropical exotica in the "dreamy" romantic mode. A solo trombone intones the "flamingo" call, a three-note figure encompassing an octave leap upward and minor third down, echoed languidly by the trumpet.

Ex. 8.3 Strayhorn, "Flamingo" (1941), Introduction, mm. 1–8.

In the next few bars, a chromatically moving theatrical "curtain-rising" passage is answered by a jarringly dissonant, swift series of parallel moving saxophone chords. These chords outline notes that are sounded in the closing gesture that directly follows, a repeated, tonally ambiguous low register brass chord (Fmi over D or dominant tritone substitution). As van de

Leur (2002, 38) observes, the closing dissonant passages and the "flamingo" call heard in the initial bars serve an expository function: the intervallic design and rhythmic profile of the "flamingo" call form "one of the arrangement's unifiers" while the complex dissonance foreshadows the "tonally ambiguity Strayhorn explores in the arrangement."

Along with Strayhorn's sophisticated harmonic palette, his penchant for creating intricate introductory, bridging, and modulatory design in arrangements has typically been read as a sign of his French-accented modernist classicism. "The rich modern harmonies of the introduction," writes Mark Tucker, "betray the taste of someone who admitted a fondness for Ravel and Debussy."[26] Along similar lines, van de Leur (2002, 42; see also Hajdu 1996, 86–87) credits the song's arrangement specifically with bringing a new classicism to the Ellington sound, one that departed radically from the conventions of vocal arranging of the time. As he writes, the "liquidity of its casura-less arrangement, its structuring elements, the sophisticated modulations and integrated introductory, transitory and closing sections . . . make 'Flamingo' unique in the jazz writing of its time." Van de Leur's insights echo Ellington himself, who proclaimed the arrangement "a turning point in vocal background orchestration, a renaissance in elaborate ornamentation for the accompaniment of singers" (quoted in Nicholson 1999, 226).

I would like to extend these comments about Strayhorn's signature classicism in a queer direction, first along a path suggested by Tinkcom's model of "queer style enhancements." As mentioned earlier, Tinkcom (2002, 36–37) argues that the opulent and glamorous camp stylizations of Arthur Freed Unit production numbers for the classic MGM film musicals (what he calls "camp encodings") constituted an "extra-added labor" on the film's narrative texts that indexed the "emerging presence of queer metropolitan subcultures in shaping mass taste and aesthetic sensibilities." In doing so, Tinkcom rethinks the visual and sonic stylistic markers of camp—artifice, excess, and performance—from the perspective of production. Camp thus functions for Tinkcom as both a form of queer labor *and* as affect/style, a coupling of social and aesthetic modes that shows "how queer subjectivity emerges within the dynamics of capitalist cultural production for audiences that extend well beyond queer male subcultures" (36–37). Insofar as Strayhorn's creative labor as a vocal arranger was in fact the arena in which he would most explicitly have been required to negotiate his ideas and sensibility with the popular song as commodity, Tinkcom's theory has special pertinence. However, questions arise in applying Tinkcom's model of the Arthur Freed Unit's camp sensibility to the differently located affective world of Strayhorn's "style enhancements" in an arrangement such as "Flamingo." Put another way, are the lavish camp stylizations (or "encodings") created by a privileged group of gay white male artists working for big-budget Hollywood musicals a relevant point of comparison for hearing—queerly or otherwise—Strayhorn's African American jazz-based classicism? Yes and no. Certainly there was a considerable amount of traffic (and cultural resonance) between New York–based entertainment (e.g., Broadway and Harlem revues) and Hollywood staff composers and arrangers, but this traffic gravitated toward de facto white-only routes.[27]

Nevertheless, an argument can be made for a camp hearing—or, perhaps, a queerly signifyin' one—of Strayhorn's sophisticated, elaborate orchestral gloss on the popular song's clichéd romantic tropical tropes. In the A-strain of the vocal chorus, this comes through the lilting melody, the beguine-like beat in the staccato brass accompaniment, and the modal sound created by major-minor mixture. Also notable here is the affect of Strayhorn's stylized orchestral additions, such as the opening "flamingo" trombone call passage with its dramatically held half-diminished seventh sax chord on the downbeat and exaggerated trumpet echo, and an almost over-the-top moment of word painting that occurs in the opening bars of the bridge—also in the form of an echo that references the melodic contour of the opening echo. As Jeffries croons through an octave leap the first two words of the line, "The wind (sings a song to you as you go)," the saxophone section sounds an undulating "wind" motive that sweeps rapidly upward, lingers for a half-measure, then languidly drops back down (see example 8.4). Another stylized highlight comes through the ethereal, erotic, yet restrained affect of Jeffries's vocalizing during the arrangement's most formally breathtaking addition: an elaborate thirty-bar transition section that moves through a series of complex modulations derived from the source song's material (van de Leur 2002, 39). This part of the arrangement, which does not appear in Strayhorn's written arrangement, arose spontaneously during the recording session when Strayhorn directed the singer to improvise: "Do that 'Oh, oh' in there, and do that modulation down through it" (39). Even Lawrence Brown's trombone solo receives a sensuous vocal embroidery as Jeffries interjects the "flamingo" call in the middle of his chorus, as if whispering in the ear of the listener.

Taken together, the song's sophisticated harmonic design, complex architecture, programmatic simulations, dreamy "Oh, oh" vocal stylizations, and exotic signifiers would seem to resonate with some of the sonic idioms of camp—minus the strings—showcased in Arthur Freed Unit/MGM produc-

Ex. 8.4 Strayhorn, "Flamingo" (1941), Bridge, mm. 17–24.

tion numbers, as well as the ways in which such stylistic discourse served the demands of the Hollywood fantasy industry.[28] Yet a theory of camp from the perspective of production such as Tinkcom's always depends on the potentially problematic claim of ironic intent and, as Lloyd Whitesell has recently argued, "Stylistic extravagance does not need to be ironic to count as queer."[29] I want to put aside the question of camp affect for the moment to pursue a different story of queer affiliation between film musical production number and Strayhorn's arrangement of "Flamingo," one that places the arrangement on the stage of a minor Hollywood studio.

This story begins on January 3, 1941, the day the Ellington Orchestra kicked off a West Coast tour with a seven-week gig at the Casa Mañana ballroom. Thus also began Strayhorn's extended encounter with white and black Hollywood from 1941 to 1942. "He got into the whole exotic trip of the West Coast," Jeffries remembered. "It was a kind of mecca to us—all the glamour. . . . Strayhorn bought into all that" (quoted in Hajdu 1996, 93; see also Bogle 2005, 213–24, 246–50). Adding a crucial personal depth to his Hollywood adventure was the close companionship of Lena Horne, who herself was famously "discovered" during this period by the arranger Roger Edens. In fact, according to Horne, Strayhorn encountered Edens at Horne's home in 1942 around the time that Horne was cast in her first big starring role in the Vincente Minnelli/Arthur Freed Unit black-cast musical *Cabin in the Sky* (which is also significant for featuring the Ellington Orchestra).[30] While the artistic culmination of Strayhorn's "glamour" year came earlier, in the summer of 1941, through his work on *Jump for Joy*, sometime during the last two months of that year Strayhorn's arrangement of "Flamingo" was given filmic realization as one of five Ellington "soundies" produced by the Hollywood company RCM, which was then managed primarily by the songwriter Sam Coslow (of Cotton Club fame).

A short-lived phenomenon of the early 1940s, soundies were three-minute low-budget performance films made for coin-operated automated viewing machines—or "visual jukeboxes"—primarily under the trade name Panorams. Film production companies such as RCM marketed soundies in reels that contained eight different film segments, which together formed a *Soundies Miniature Revue*. Customers paid ten cents per soundie but had no choice as to which of the eight possible segments—or part of the revue—they would see. Like jukeboxes, Panorams operated in entertainment spaces such as bars and amusement parlors and could be found in the lobbies of upscale hotels and theaters.[31]

Klaus Stratemann's (1992, 180–85) detailed commentary on the Ellington soundies, all of which were directed by Josef Berne, categorizes "Flamingo" as the "exotic dance number" in *Soundies Miniature Revue No. 1049* (seventh position), sandwiched between two patriotic numbers (the reel also featured Ellington's "Bli-Blip" from *Jump for Joy*, with Marie Bryant and Paul White). The "exotic dancing" is delivered by Janet Collins and Talley Beatty in two quasi-narrative dance sequences set in a generic Afro-Caribbean "tropical" mise-en-scène. This secondary footage is intercut with Jeffries and the Ellington Orchestra performing "Flamingo" on a studio-constructed "nightclub" stage. Stratemann, along with virtually every other source on this soundie, identifies Collins and Beatty as "two members from Katherine Dunham's famous black dance troupe" (180–85).[32] Although Janet Collins, who a decade later would become the first African American prima ballerina to be hired into the corps of the New York Metropolitan Opera ballet, probably was not dancing for Dunham at the time the soundie was filmed, she had performed in her company for a brief period that year. Talley Beatty, however, was a principal dancer with Dunham and one of a number of gay male members of her troupe, which included Dunham's frequent on-stage partner Archie Savage, who was also associated with the queer interracial social circle around Carl Van Vechten (Manning 2004, 157).

According to the dance historian Susan Manning (2004, 157; by way of George Chauncey), the Dunham Dance Company was a center for gay life in Harlem during the 1940s and 1950s. Gordon Heath, a black gay actor, for example, characterized Dunham's productions as "the highest prancing camp in the business." Manning argues that Dunham's particular amalgam of techniques from classical ballet and modern dance with Black Atlantic vernacular and Africanist dance forms "presented legibly queer images for gay spectators" (157). She develops her argument with reference to the type of images and movements featured in Dunham's early 1940s breakthrough program *Tropics and Le Jazz "Hot,"* which premiered at the Windsor Theater in New York to critical and popular acclaim. The middle section of the work, "Tropics" (subtitled "Shore Excursions" and set in Martinique), featured Dunham dancing in her celebrated "Woman with Cigar" role. One critic described the scenario this way: "[Dunham] meets dockhand and flirts with him and his companions" (quoted in Manning 2004, 145).[33] The dockhand in question was danced by Archie Savage. Through their association with Dunham's troupe during this period and through, as I describe later, the influence of Dunham's work (as shown in aspects of dance technique, the scenario, and costuming), Beatty's and Collins's work in the soundie's dance sequences links up to this queerly inflected choreographic discourse of stylistic and stylized fusion.[34] On this point, my reading of the soundie as a scene of collaboration brings together bodies, sounds, and movements that make legible a historical network of black gay cultural production and artists' affiliation.[35]

Yet a queer reading of the dance sequences is perhaps most convincingly secured through its placement in and interaction with Strayhorn's arrangement. Indeed, the larger visual, choreographic, and sonic assemblage in the soundie, as well as details of editing work, actually heighten the arrangement's registers of stylistic extravagance and classicisms discussed earlier. For example, in the second vocal chorus we see a series of striking close-ups of Jeffries and Ellington, initiated through a frontal close-up of Jeffries as he croons the "flamingo" call. The camera then cuts quickly to a close-up of Ellington: he smiles, eyes sparkling, gazing admiringly at Jeffries. Our gaze replaces Ellington's as the camera cuts back to Jeffries for the line, "For it's you I rely on, and a love that is true"; the dramatic visual frontality of this image coupled with Jeffries's suave crooning and handsome, urbane visage, gives a special charge to this part of the arrangement, amplifying the aura of sophistication and exotic-romantic fantasy.

At the bridge, the camera crosscuts from its close-up on Jeffries to Collins. She is clad in an ornate, ruffle-laden Caribbean dress and bandana and is balancing a large tray of fruit with one hand. On the plain white backdrop behind her we see a somewhat menacing shadow of a giant flamingo. In sync with Jeffries's octave leap on the words "the wind," Collins arches her back and sweeps her arm melodramatically over her head, heightening the already theatrical affect of the wind motive. The camera pulls back to reveal a tiny and bare patch of "beach" on which we see Beatty dressed as a native "sailor" or dockhand replete with head wrap, a striped shirt with a pattern of circular cut-outs, and loosely cropped white pants. In the dance sequence that ensues, the longer and more substantial of the two, Collins and Beatty perform an erotic barefoot pas de deux. The first part of the sequence lasts from the bridge through the intricate "Oh, Oh" modulatory/ transition section: in it they dance slowly around each other, with undulating, swaying hip movements and other choreographic gestures associated with Afro-Caribbean and African American vernacular and theater dance. At one point, Collins lifts the billowy, sheer white "picnic" cloth off the ground and wraps it seductively around her body as she writhes and undulates around in a kind of brief Salome-esque veil dance.

For the trombone solo, the choreography shifts stylistic gears, and the two dancers present an extended ballet sequence. Beatty executes a series of

Fig. 8.2 Still from "Flamingo," 1941, Ellington gazes at Jeffries.

Fig. 8.3 Still from "Flamingo," 1941, Jeffries, frontal close-up.

Fig. 8.4 Still from "Flamingo," 1941, Collins & Beatty pas de deux.

Fig. 8.5 Still from "Flamingo," 1941, Collins & Beatty pas de deux.

quick turns (chaînés) around Collins punctuated by delicate jumps (sissone) and leg extensions, while Collins continues her undulating hip movements. The two dancers then perform variation-like exchanges of turns, jumps, and leg extensions such as attitude and arabesque. As the trombone solo moves toward the cadence, Collins and Beatty slowly drop to their knees, arching their torsos back to the ground in to an extreme limbo position. This ends the sequence, and the camera crosscuts back to the performance just as Johnny Hodges stands to take his solo.

Conclusion: Blue Rose (Again)

The director's choice to showcase Hodges's solo visually in the "Flamingo" soundie is of particular significance to my project for several reasons. First, it points to a crucial difference between mainstream Hollywood arranging practices and those of African American swing bands: the centrality of solo improvisation. Second, along with Strayhorn's songs, the string of ballads he wrote for Hodges throughout his career stand out as his most intimate, intense, and certainly most sensuous lyrical statements. The close collaborative relationship between Hodges and Strayhorn was established almost immediately after Ellington hired Strayhorn in 1939. That spring he composed the gorgeous ballads "Day Dream" and "Passion Flower," as well as "A Flower Is a Lovesome Thing." Interestingly, Strayhorn and Hodges left the Ellington organization for roughly the period in the early 1950s; *Blue Rose* would mark the return of both artists to the Ellington fold, announced with stylized abandon in Strayhorn's dramatic, noir-tinged new arrangement of "Passion Flower" (followed some seven months later by the extraordinary recording of "Ballad for Very Sad and Very Tired Lotus Eaters"). The queer affective registers I have explored with respect to "Flamingo" have something in common with Strayhorn's ballads for Hodges, which similarly bear titles and call forth sounds that evoke the sensate world (and pleasures therein) of exotic objects and the utopian spaces of dreams and fantasy.[36]

In this context, I would like to close by considering again the title of the Strayhorn-Ellington-Clooney LP *Blue Rose*. I would argue that it also radiates toward this queer affective register, although in a way that—like Strayhorn's "differentiated style" itself—accommodates the intended commercial appeal of the title, with its play on Rose(mary), "blues," and associations of the blue rose flower with ideas of feminine elegance and mystery.[37] But as a desired or sought-after yet unattainable natural object, the blue rose also holds an intriguing symbolic history as a figure for fantasy and the impossible.[38] Here it bears pointing out a symptomatic tension between the absenting of Strayhorn from the LP's cover image, and thus from the public face of the collaborative project, and his sonic presence behind this (the) scene(s). My reading of Strayhorn's arranging for Clooney (and for Jeffries) suggests ways in which such a simultaneous absenting and presence can be productively linked to his "queer position" in the Ellington Orchestra and to his arranging practices. Strayhorn's sexual identity required that he work behind the scenes, a space from which his voice facilitated spaces and created contexts for other voices to be heard, to discover new vocal personas and new ways of sounding and being. As I have shown, these contexts and spaces merged the personal and musical across scripts of race, gender, and sexuality. To be sure, a critical element in the art of arranging revolves around cultivating skills of musical sensitivity and empathy in collaborative music making. Yet for Strayhorn, as with any number of gay male artists working behind the scenes, this talent for sonic empathy in collaborative efforts was profoundly shaped by and through his dissident sexual identity.

Notes

An earlier version of this article appeared as Lisa Barg, "Working Behind the Scenes: Gender, Sexuality and Collaboration in the Vocal Arrangements of Billy Strayhorn," *Women and Music* 18 (2014): 24–47.

1. Clooney also starred in another Paramount musical, the Western parody *Red Garters* (1954), with Guy Mitchell and Jack Carson. For a recent discussion of Mitch Miller's critical role in popular music during the 1950s, see Zak 2010, 43–75.

2. Both Irving Townsend and David Hajdu state that Clooney was pregnant with her fourth child; however, her fourth child, Monsita Ferrer, was born in 1958, nearly two years after *Blue Rose* was released. Her second child, Maria Ferrer, was born in 1956: see Hajdu 1996, 147; Irving Townsend, liner notes to Rosemary Clooney and Duke Ellington and His Orchestra, *Blue Rose*, compact disc, Sony B00000JBDV, 1999.

3. As a parting memento of their time together and to thank him for his caregiving, Clooney presented Strayhorn with a Cartier watch with the ironic inscription "To Svengali" (Hajdu 1996, 149).

4. I am using the word "non-normative" here to signal how dominant perceptions of Strayhorn's black masculinity align with what Roderick Ferguson calls the racialized logic of "nonheteronormativity"—that is, the tangle of pathologizing histories and discourses of difference ascribed to African American cultural formations broadly and, more particularly, to internal variations of black queer

masculinity within these discourses/histories. See R. A. Ferguson 2004, 13; see also Harper 1996; Somerville 2000.

5. In her autobiography, Lena Horne characterized the lyricist and producer Arthur Freed and arranger Roger Edens (whom she credits with "discovering" her in 1942) as "men of a certain sensitivity. . . . As long as I worked with them I was treated with great decency and respect" (Horne and Schickel 1986, 135).

6. Extending the work of Floyd, who situates "telling stories" within African American cultural memory and practice, George Lewis (1996, 91–122) identfies "telling stories" as a key component of "Afrologicial" improvisation.

7. For Ellington's statements on the importance of "telling stories," see, e.g., Ellington 1972, 97. For a recent discussion of the "literary imperitive" in Ellington's narrative imagination see Edwards 2004, 326–56.

8. This model shows interesting parallels with the productive interdependence of scripts and improvisation in theater rehearsals and productions as explored by Zoë Svendsen in her contribution to this volume. For a discussion of the practrices and sociality of (mostly) small group jazz arranging, see Berliner 1994.

9. As Magee (1999, 62–63) further notes, Southern's discussion also extends the category of "composer" to include the solo improviser.

10. And, indeed, only insiders would know that "Grievin'" and "I'm Checkin' Out, Goom-Bye" came from Strayhorn's pen, as these two songs are credited only to Ellington on the original release, a perception emphasized in Townsend, liner notes. (Townsend identifies the songs as Ellington originals.)

11. The manuscript is housed in the Duke Ellington Collections, Archives Center, National Museum of American History, Smithsonian Institution, Washington, DC.

12. Cootie Williams's trumpet solo in the original 1939 recordings does not modulate.

13. Following the birth of her daughter Maria in the summer of 1956, Clooney officially registered Billie Holiday as Maria's godmother. Interestingly, Clooney (1999, 153) refers to the song "Blue Rose" in her autobiography as "a new number Billy [Strayhorn] wrote especially for me."

14. See, e.g., Will Friedwald's (1996, 415) discussion of Clooney during this period in which he argues that Clooney's greatest affinity is with "the great male icons of the jazz-and-pop mainstream: Sinatra, Bennett and, most of all Crosby."

15. "I wanted to be married, to have babies. Mrs. José Ferrer wanted to sit by his side and listen to him talk, even though Rosemary Clooney was paying the bills" (Clooney 1999, 131).

16. Clooney (1999, 186) offered the following account by a reporter of the divorce court drama: "Weeping uncontrollably on the witness stand, singer Rosemary Clooney, thirty-three, today accused her husband, actor José Ferrer, forty-nine, who fathered her five children, of 'having affairs with other women since the beginning our marriage' and 'violent acts of temper.'"

17. Hajdu (1996, 145) quotes here an unidentified "black gay musician familiar with the Paris scene" who likened Strayhorn at the Mars Club in Paris to "a miniature, black Noel Coward."

18. The mediating role of multitrack technology in Strayhorn and Clooney's collaboration in the recording studio is also at issue but is beyond the scope of the present study. For an account of the recording studio as a intermundane space of "deadness" in which human, nonhuman, and other entities collaborate, see Stanyek and Piekut 2010, 14–38.

19. In her autobiography, Clooney (1999, 153) also recalls how Strayhorn helped her overcome extreme nerves around the overdubbing sessions in Los Angeles: " 'I want you to imagine you're living in New York and you've got a really hot date and you're ready to go,' Billy said to me through his big square glasses. 'You're a beautiful woman, looking into the mirror and combing your hair, and there's Duke Ellington and there's no band. The radio is playing the record, and you just sing along with the orchestra, and we overhear it." See also a similar account in Hajdu 1996, 148.

20. While Strayhorn and Kay Davis were good friends, he wrote little for her due to her role as Ellington's vocalese specialist.

21. It is also worth mentioning here that, as van de Leur (2002, 63) reminds us, in taking on work that Ellington neither had time for nor interest in, Strayorn's creative labor made it possible for Ellington "to realize his goals"—namely, ones that we now identify with the extraordinary pieces he composed for (and with) the legendary Blanton-Webster band of this era.

22. According to Hajdu (1996, 86), the tune was "discovered by Ellington's friend, Edmund Anderson, a businessman, who added the lyrics." Jeffries, however, claimed the song was given to him by the composer Grouya himself, a little-known figure then working in the music publishing division of MGM, in hope that it would get a hearing from Ellington. As he narrates it, Jeffries put the song on his dressing-room table, where Strayhorn later discovered it and, within earshot of Ellington, began playing the song at the piano. Ellington liked what he heard and instructed, "Whatever you're playing, make a chart of it." Jeffries also claimed that Grouya contacted him after "Flamingo" was charting to complain that his words had been altered, thus suggesting he had a hand in writing the lyrics: Herb Jeffries, " 'Bronze Buckaroo' Is Still Singing at Age 82," interview by Don Freeman, *San Diego Union-Tribune*, December 13, 1993; see also Nicholson 1999, 226.

23. "Herb Jeffries," August 15, 2002, www.herbjeffries.com. The Ellington Orchestra recorded "Flamingo" on December 28, 1940, at Victor Studios in Chicago, a date that marked the end of a grueling year of cross-country travel, playing mostly one-nighters.

24. Along with that of his white gay American counterparts, Strayhorn's Francophilia functioned as a sign of queer affiliation. In remembering his attraction to Strayhorn, for example, Aaron Bridgers explained, "We had the same favorite musicians, especially Tatum and Teddy Wilson. And we both loved the French classical composers. I had always had a love for all things French, and I discovered that Billy did too" (Hajdu 1996, 66). In a different but not unrelated context, the black gay poet, novelist, and literary critic Melvin Dixon (2000, 84–109) recalled

of his Francophile-oriented college education in the early 1970s, "Most men who studied French were gay; so there was a connection there, and my best friends were Francophiles, and I guess, it was a way to establish one's sophistication and sissyhood and all that." On queer Francophilia and Euro-modernist composers, see Hubbs 2004.

25. The following discussion of "Flamingo" is indebted to van de Leur's (2002) insights. As he specifies, the new material adds nearly a third to the model.

26. Mark Tucker, "Duke Ellington 1940–42," liner notes to *The Blanton-Webster Band*, RCA Bluebird, 1986.

27. On this point, while Tinkcom (2002) does clearly acknowledge white racial privilege in his analysis of the camp aesthetics of MGM, Vincente Minnelli, and the Arthur Freed Unit, he does not fully explore how this racialized environment might figure into his analyses of camp, gender, and sexuality. For a historically nuanced discussion of racism in the Arthur Freed Unit, see the account of the arranger Phil Moore's struggles at MGM during this period in Bogle (2005, 224–32). For an excellent history of the practices and cultural meanings associated with the symphonic jazz arranging tradition, see Howland 2009.

28. A particularly resonant example from the classic MGM film musical archive here would be Leo Arnaud and Connie Salinger's arrangement for Tony Martin's crooning of Nacio Herb Brown's "You Stepped Out of Dream," the "dream number" choreographed by Busby Berkeley in the hit backstage musical *Ziegfield Girl* (1941), with the starring triumvirate Lana Turner, Judy Garland, and Hedy Lamar. The film was released in April, just as "Flamingo" was charting.

29. Lloyd Whitesell, "Musical Glamour and Queer Aesthetics at MGM," working paper, n.d. As an alternative to camp, Whitesell develops a theory of glamor as a distinctly queer aesthetic mode through a focus on the Freed Unit arrangers Roger Edens and Conrad Salinger and outlines a valuable typology for analyzing representations of glamor based on "the blending of four qualities: 1) sensuousness, 2) sophistication, 3) elevation, and 4) restraint." I am grateful to Professor Whitesell for sharing this work with me.

30. This meeting is implied in the following quote in Horne's autobiography: "Strayhorn was often in California and we were very, very close. Roger Edens frequently dropped over in the evenings usually with a couple of people from M-G-M music department" (Horne and Schickel 1986, 157). For critical accounts of Ellington's role in *Cabin in the Sky*, see, e.g., Gabbard 1996, Knight 2002.

31. The initials stand for its three founders: James Roosevelt, Sam Coslow, and Gordon Mills. The screen in the Panoram machine measured twenty-two by twenty-five inches and was placed at eye level encased in seven-foot-high, art deco-style walnut cabinets. (The speakers, which used RCA sound reproduction technology, were placed below the ground-glass screen, and the movies themselves were back-projected off two mirrors.) Daniel Egen (2010, 348) has estimated that at the "height of popularity, there were approximately 4,500 Panorams operating commercially."

32. The set for "Flamingo" was also used in several of the other Ellington

soundies—for example, "Hot Chocolate (Cottontail)." Moreover, Collins and Beatty appeared in two other soundies that featured black theater dance numbers taken from (or based on) contemporaneous Dunham productions. See also Willard 1999, 405–6.

33. Manning (2004, 157–58) specifically argues here for a reading of Dunham's "Woman with Cigar" in terms of queer eroticism.

34. It is highly unlikely that Dunham had a direct hand in the choreography. While she was on the West Coast during this time, having just finished a cross-country tour of *Cabin in the Sky* (in fact, Ellington is reported to have attended a performance of the Los Angeles run in November), the fees that would have been incurred for both the Ellington Orchestra and Dunham were almost certainly beyond the limited budgets of soundie productions, and in any case, the sequences themselves were not substantial enough to require her participation or presence. The choreography may have come out of a nightclub act that Collins and Beatty toured during the early 1940s (they billed themsevles as "Rea and Rico DeGard" to pass as Latino). Also in evidence here is the influence of Lester Horton's technique on Collins's dancing (she trained in modern dance with Horton). I am grateful to Susan Manning (private communication, July 11, 2011) for sharing this and other insights with me.

35. Indeed, just after the war, Strayhorn and Beatty would meet again at the black gay salon gatherings held in the home of Dorcas and Frank Neal; these encounters led to several postwar collaborations (including Beatty's staring role as Carribee Joe in the Ellington-Strayhorn *A Drum Is a Woman*, broadcast on CBS in 1959).

36. The historical affiliations of these qualities with a gay sensibility were not lost on Strayhorn's posthumous critics, who, however, explicitly construed this sensibility in homophobic terms as a kind of dangerous, perverse feminized excess vis-à-vis Ellington. I examine these issues in more detail in Barg 2013.

37. The title may also have evoked associations with another blue flower pop song from the period, "Blue Gardenia," which was the title song for Fritz Lang's 1953 film noir (arranged by Nelson Riddle and sung in the film by Nat King Cole). The song was also recorded by Dinah Washington in 1956 for her critically acclaimed LP *The Swingin' Miss "D"* (arranged by Quincy Jones).

38. To give one mid-century example, in Tennesse Williams's *The Glass Menagerie* (which debuted on stage in 1944 and was made into an MGM film in 1950), the blue rose symbolizes the various forms of "difference" embodied in the misfit character Laura Wingfield; they include her retreat into a fantasy world of small glass animals and popular songs; her disability; and her extreme fragility, shyness, and inability to conform to heteropatriarichal social expectations.

CHAPTER 9

WHAT'S LOVE GOT TO DO WITH IT?

Creating Art, Creating Community, Creating a Better World

Tracey Nicholls

What's love got to do with social aesthetics? With improvisation? And with otherness? One way to think about aesthetics in relation to the social world is through consideration of the extent to which one's membership in community—that is, one's social identity—shapes one's approach to art making and art appreciation. Conversely, we might consider how one's relationship to art shapes one's social identity. These kinds of questions are shaping the emergent discourses in relational aesthetics, founded and labeled by the French art critic Nicolas Bourriaud, and social aesthetics, exemplified by the French sociologist Pierre Bourdieu's (1984) critical rebuttal of Kantian aesthetics on the grounds that "taste" is not a universal trait that identifies a single standard of artistic merit but is instead indexed to one's class position. Similar ways of looking at oneself and at others are also examined in bell hooks's *Art on My Mind: Visual Politics* (1995a), a book that is not typically considered part of these discourses, despite its treatment of these questions from a perspective that is fundamentally compatible with the concerns of social aesthetics.

Art on My Mind, hooks's approach to art making and art appreciation, is worth investigating in any discussion of aesthetics that implicates issues of identity and otherness, in part because of the slippage between the identity hooks claims for herself and the identity attributed to her by others. In the book's first chapter, hooks identifies herself both as a member of a working-class African American community and as an artist and art critic who is deeply committed to the project of expanding the art world to include the voices and perspectives of marginalized others. But the fierce commitment to art that permeates the book is not widely acknowledged as "the public face" of bell hooks. The reviewer Brian Wallis (1995) notes in his assessment of *Art on My Mind* that hooks is not widely acknowledged as an art critic, even though she has woven aesthetic judgments and considerations into much of her writing.[1] Because she is typically taken to be commenting on sociopolitical matters of race, decolonization, and liberation, her attention to aesthetics is overlooked, and as a result, an identity she wishes to claim for herself disappears. This eliding of her self-image—be it accidental slippage or deliberate erasure—makes hooks an interestingly subaltern voice on matters of art and culture and figures prominently in the questions of domination and decolonization that I raise later in this chapter.

On my way to those questions, and by way of explaining why I think hooks is being seriously misrepresented by those who cast her as someone whose social philosophy has nothing to say about aesthetics, I want to explore the view of art making and art appreciation that she develops in *Art on My Mind* and draw connections to the "ethic of love" that she develops in other writings. The view of art making that emerges from this book is, in many respects, a valorization of improvisatory practices. It is, to be sure, a mostly implicit valorization, as she devotes little attention to the art form most closely associated with improvisation: music. No doubt, this lack of attention to music and the other performing arts is the result of her concern in *Art on My Mind* with the plastic arts, in particular—as the subtitle unambiguously telegraphs—the visual arts. Certainly, hooks does analyze the social significance of African American music making in other works. Notably, in *Talking Back: Thinking Feminist, Thinking Black*, hooks (1989, 11) attributes to "black musicians like Duke Ellington, Louis Armstrong, and later John Coltrane" the imparted awareness that it is possible to speak with multiple voices. They "impressed upon our consciousness a sense of versatility," she observes, "[through playing] all kinds of music." But even in *Art on My Mind*, with all of its focus on arts not normally enumerated in discussions of improvising, there is an insistence on perspectives and practices that I argue are consistent with the theorization of improvisation as a social practice. The convergence between her notion of art as a populist concern and improvisation as a site of theorizing social relations lies in attitudes of openness toward contingent inspiration and in the possibilities of political resistance that both reveal.

Everyday Art Making, Popular Empowerment, and Improvisation

As a way into her discussion of the visual politics of art, hooks recalls that what drew her to painting in her youth was its formal properties, the abstract independence from social concerns that warrants the claim that "art has no race or gender" (hooks 1995a, xi). This is admittedly an odd way to start a book on "the place of art in black life, connections between the social construction of black identity, the impact of race and class, and the presence in black life of an inarticulate but ever-present visual aesthetic governing our relationship to images, to the process of image-making" (57). Her claim about the artwork's independence, in this context, can, I think, only be motivated by a desire to open up our ideas about who can be a producer of art. Understanding social aesthetics as a concept that occupies the space in which the aesthetic and the political overlap, I argue in this section that hooks's attention to the beauty of everyday objects and crafts—her "aesthetics of the ordinary"—is a basic component of her project of making space within aesthetic discourse for the artistic practices and preferences of people who are not legitimized within an institutional theory of art and art making.

Thinking about art and its place—or lack of place—in black communities, however, hooks (1995a, 3–4) speculates that the problem runs much deeper than under-representation of black artists in galleries. "Most black folks," she contends, "do not believe that the presence of art in our lives is essential to our collective well-being" (3). This attitude has historical roots, she claims, "with respect to black political life, in black liberation struggles— whether early protests against white supremacy and racism during slavery and Reconstruction, during the civil rights movement, or during the more recent black power movements—the production of art and the creation of a politics of the visual that would not only affirm artists but also see the development of an aesthetics of viewing as central to claiming subjectivity have been consistently devalued" (3).[2] Although she grew up passionately interested in art, this attitude was considered odd by many of her family members, she recalls. It was, therefore, an amazing experience for her when she visited the museums and galleries of Paris and found so much African art in them. "It occurred to me then," she writes, "that if one could make a people lose touch with their capacity to create, lose sight of their will and their power to make art, then the work of subjugation, of colonization, is complete" (xv).

It is worth noting here that the problem hooks is identifying is fairly medium-specific, at least insofar as what she is implicitly excluding; the in-difference to art that she attributes to African American communities is an indifference to visual arts, not music. As I think will become clearer in the discussion that follows, she is particularly concerned with visual arts, and not music, because of the role representations of African Americans play in the development of self-image—a point true of people generally, of course, but it is the decolonization of African Americans that motivates hooks's analysis. She does not make an explicit distinction between visual art and music as different types of art forms, but I think we might see both her con-cern with representation and her relative silence on the topic of music (in this book, at least) as implicitly committing her to a taxonomy that sorts visual arts as representational and musical arts as expressive. Alternatively, this inattention to music may flow from a practical consideration concern-ing suppression of art forms: it is harder to stop a colonized people from singing than it is to stop them from painting; to paint requires materials to which economically deprived people may not have access, and to paint pro-duces objects that may be destroyed.[3] To restore the sense that visual art really matters, "For more black folks to identify with art," hooks (1995a, 4) writes, "we must shift conventional ways of thinking about the function of art. There must be a revolution in the way we see, the way we look [to] stimulate collective awareness that the creation and public sharing of art is essential to any practice of freedom."

This collective awareness, which she thinks can be stimulated by pro-moting art making within the community—notably, through a strong and wide-reaching commitment to art programs in public schools—should aim to elicit popular participation, to instill the idea that, theoretically, anyone can be a maker of art. In part, this awareness can be nurtured through atten-tion to the aesthetic values and practices that are still, or already, present in everyday life. This is the compelling point of *Art on My Mind*: hooks wants to highlight the extent to which African American communities have con-sistently maintained aesthetic visions, values, and practices, even as mem-bers of these communities might be tempted to dismiss "capital-A art" as an activity meaningless to and disconnected from their lives. It is in Afri-can American communities, hooks (1995a, 19) argues, that we see "a con-cern with the soul . . . that black people have consistently highlighted and shared with mainstream white culture. The aesthetic vision of 'soul music' was precisely one in which a need to care for the soul was foregrounded." Concern with the soul, which she sees as being "situated within the context of everyday life," is a common element she identifies in the work of many of the particular artists she writes about in *Art on My Mind* (20, 24, 49). We see her touching on issues in social aesthetics, for instance, when she writes about the work of installation and photography artist Felix Gonzalez-Torres, whose work stresses "the moment of experience, of human interaction,"—that is, sociality, relationality—and insists that "elegance and ecstasy are to be found in daily life, in our habits of being, in the ways we regard one another and the world around us" (49).[4] hooks describes Gonzalez-Torres's work as one might describe improvised musical performances; it "welcomes our presence, our participation . . . , [which] is made more manifest by the spaces left vacant in the work that leave room for us" (50).

She links the work and the vision of these professional artists—Gonzalez-Torres, Alison Saar, Jean-Michel Basquiat, among others—to the aesthetic lessons she learned as a child in rural Kentucky: the extent to which simplicity and utility could reveal aesthetic qualities of otherwise overlooked objects. She remembers her community as having had "a shared belief in the idea that beautiful things . . . were necessary for the spirit. The more downtrodden and unfortunate the circumstances, the more 'beauty' was needed to uplift, to offer a vision of hope, to transform" (hooks 1995a, 120). This recognition of a need for beauty in one's life ranged across classes, and the need could be filled in diverse ways. For her parents and many of the other adults she knew as a child, the need for beauty was satisfied in "objects that could be considered luxurious, that were expensive and difficult to own," but there were also people like her grandparents who opposed materialism and sought beauty "in a world that was not subject to monetary exchange" (120). Quoting Alice Walker's reminiscence of her mother's flower garden in her essay "In Search of Our Mothers' Gardens," hooks describes this non-materialistic everyday attention to aesthetics that she learned most comprehensively from her grandmother as "a legacy of respect . . . for all that illuminates and cherishes life" (120; 2009, 121).

This quiet, respectful, everyday aesthetic is one that hooks associates explicitly with a democratization of art, achieved through popular participation. Democratization, to the extent that it exists, has been accomplished through art media to which ordinary people have access, such as photography. This medium is significant, hooks tells us, because "the history of black liberation movements in the United States could be characterized as a struggle over images as much as it has also been a struggle for rights, for equal access. . . . Cameras gave to black folks, irrespective of class, a means by which we could participate fully in the production of images. Hence it is essential that any theoretical discussion of the relationship of black life to the visual, to art making, make photography central. Access and mass appeal have historically made photography a powerful location for the construction of an oppositional black aesthetic" (hooks 1995a, 57). "Had the camera been there when slavery ended," she writes—by which she means, of course, had it been *available to* African Americans[5]—"it could have provided images that would have helped folks searching for lost kin and loved ones. . . . Half a century later . . . black folks . . . became passionately obsessed with the camera . . . because it offered a way to contain memories, to overcome loss, to keep history" (60). Because it gave ordinary black people a way to preserve the histories of their families and communities, and because it gave them a way to resist and oppose the racist misrepresentations of them that circulated in the white-dominated world outside their segregated communities, the "camera became in black life a political instrument," says hooks (60). The resulting walls of family photos that were on display in all of the houses of hooks's childhood "were essential to the process of decolonization," she asserts. "To enter black homes in my childhood was to enter a world that valued the visual, that asserted our collective will to participate in a noninstitutionalized curatorial process" (61).

Popular participation in the production of art offered the opportunity for more than political resistance, however important that may have been. The accepted practice of building one's own house democratized architecture and encouraged improvisatory strategies such as contingent expansion in response to immediate needs rather than preplanning. Another process both artistic and practical that allows us to read improvisation onto it is the quilt making at which hooks's grandmother excelled and through which she articulated her own vernacular aesthetic. Women who exercise their creativity by sewing these necessary household items draw inspiration for their artistic production out of materials that are contingently there—for instance, reusing scraps of fabric from old clothes to make "crazy quilts" (hooks 2009, 158). hooks acknowledges Cynthia Redick's thesis that these "folk art" objects originated as a late-nineteenth-century fad among privileged white "ladies of leisure" but argues instead that crazy quilts more likely developed out of the creativity of black slave women who, from time to time, were permitted to keep the fabric scraps that otherwise would have been discarded after they finished making more conventionally designed quilts for their so-called owners (158).[6] Now one might perhaps think that house making and quilt making ought not to be considered arts; that they are, if anything, crafts. But hooks is arguing deliberately for an expansive notion of the artistic. These two activities count for her, because they accommodate a link between aesthetic attention to everyday objects and popular empowerment. "The spirit of self-reliance and self-determination that was aroused and is aroused by quiltmaking, by this fusion of the practical with the artistic, stirs the imagination in ways that almost always lead to emotional awareness and emotional growth," hooks (167) argues, and "that spirit of self-reliance often creates the social context that made survival possible."

Although hooks does not address improvisation in any great detail in *Art on My Mind*, her discussions of salvage art, folk arts, and popular art practices do suggest fruitful links between popular empowerment and improvisation. Her actual mention of improvised art making appears only in her analysis of Basquiat's graffiti-inspired paintings. One of the aspects of his project hooks (1995a, 42) wants to valorize is his celebration of the creativity and innovation of black jazz musicians: "the avant-garde dimensions of the music that affirm fusion, mixing, improvisation."[7] Beyond this fairly tangential observation, however, hooks offers some tantalizing hints as to how her aesthetic views incorporate or cohere with improvisatory attitudes toward art making. Her view of the artistic process, for instance, is that "even moments of premeditation are disrupted by the unexpected" (26). And her claim that "the very nature of artistic practice is rooted in a philosophy of risk" is, in my view, an improvisatory way of understanding art making (83). Further, when she says that "to truly champion artistic freedom we must be committed to creating and sustaining an aesthetic culture where diverse artistic practices, standpoints, identities, and locations are nurtured, find support, affirmation, and regard," hooks, without explicitly recognizing it as such, is calling for an improvisatory culture (139).

I want to make clear here that I am not intending to essentialize African American identity through attribution of an "inherent" style of art making. Neither hooks's identification of an African American aesthetic nor the improvisatory orientation I am drawing out of her view is dependent on the notion of a particular essence.[8] Instead, both are best seen as a response to colonization. Improvisation historically has functioned as a resistance to power of the kind that hooks endorses, one that attends to contingency, empowers its participants, and responds to the community within which it is performed. It has the capacity to manifest an inclusive aesthetic vision consistent with the ethic of love and the political philosophy of liberation that hooks is ultimately committed to as postcolonization social goals. The call for diversity, inclusivity, and participation that we see in politically resistant improvised music supports a link between the aesthetic value judgments we make and those that are typically labeled "ethical" or "political" and draws on postcolonial/anticolonial assertions of the prima facie value of every voice. hooks seems to be echoing the work of improvisation theorists—I have in mind here, in particular, Ingrid Monson's *Saying Something* (1996)—when she tells us, "Art constitutes one of the rare locations where acts of transcendence can take place and have a wide-ranging transformative impact" (hooks 1995a, 8).

Inclusive Aesthetics and an Ethic of Love

For hooks (1995a, 138), the relation between an aesthetic that includes and transforms and a politics that liberates is necessary and inextricable. "In a democratic society," she contends, "art should be the location where everyone can witness the joy, pleasure and power that emerges when there is freedom of expression." "Art [is] the practice of freedom" and, in its capacity for representation, is "a means by which the self is constructed and made visible" (144, 163).

She sees representation as the function through which art is revealed as political, but, as I noted earlier in my discussion of her attention to the artistic status of crafts, she is deliberately defining the concept of art as broadly as possible. Representation as politics is not a limiting of artistic possibilities as in, for instance, Soviet realism; instead, it is a wide-ranging appreciation of the connections between objects and the communities in which they take on their meaning. So, for instance, her grandmother's quilts were representational, not in the sense that they were what hooks (2000, 15) calls "story quilts," but because her grandmother could and did pull them out to recount tales of family history, pointing to a piece of cotton in a quilt and recalling its first life as a dress hooks's mother had once worn. This *is* social aesthetics in its attention to the way who we are and how we live influences the kind of art we make. And that is the point hooks (1995a, 57) insists on in her analysis of visual politics: "All colonized and subjugated people who, by way of resistance, create an oppositional subculture within the framework of domination recognize that the field of representation . . . is a site of ongoing struggle." The problem of representation that hooks (1992, 1) identifies as particularly pressing for African American communities is the prevalence of images that reinscribe white supremacy and internalized racism, a problem that is particularly acute in mass media. "For black people," notes hooks, "the pain of learning that we cannot control our images, how we see ourselves [and] how we are seen [by others] is so intense that it rends us. . . . Often it leaves us ravaged by repressed rage, feeling weary, dispirited, and sometimes just plain old brokenhearted" (3–4). This, too, is social aesthetics, how the kind of art we live with influences who we are. And if hooks's contention that African American communities do not care—or do not care enough—about visual art is correct, perhaps we have here a partial explanation: people on constant guard against racist imagery may be easily worn down by visual politics and can, as a result, be discouraged from producing (or sharing) images of their own. The confluence of racist representations in the media and an oppositional subculture can lead to a lively contestation—an image war, if you like—or it can lead to a passive withdrawal. The path hooks endorses is, of course, contestation. Art matters, for her, because it offers a sense of agency (hooks 2009, 132).

Liberation and healing can happen, though, only if image making is taken up as a central political project in which communities examine "both the kind of images we produce and the way we critically write and talk about images" (hooks 1992, 4). But, hooks (1995a, 32) cautions, "Willingness to critically engage art by black folks in all its profundity is still very difficult in a culture of domination where people do not learn to look beneath the surface." The starting point she suggests for cultural liberation is the aesthetic education she received, an introduction to aesthetics that "is more than a philosophy or theory of art and beauty; it is a way of inhabiting space, a particular location, a way of looking and becoming" (hooks 2009, 122). By this, she means to underscore the enduring point she makes across many of her books about culture and community (see hooks 1992, 1995a, 2000, 2009): aesthetic appreciation ought to be understood as part of our daily lives, something we learn through experience of, and with, the people and places we love. A connection to art and beauty in our lives is a crucial human need, hooks says, and it is fulfilled in the same way that all other human needs are: in community with others. It is these particular locations and ways of looking that are rooted in the everyday she foregrounds in the critical discussions of particular artists that are interspersed among the theoretical essays of *Art on My Mind* (hooks 1995a). In Basquiat's work, she celebrates what she sees as decolonizing impulses that mark African American art making, explaining that "a dual critique is occurring [in his work]. First, the critique of Western imperialism, and, then, the critique of the way in which imperialism makes itself heard, the way it is reproduced in culture and art. This image is ugly and grotesque. That is exactly how it should be. For what Basquiat unmasks is the ugliness of those traditions. He takes the Eurocentric valuation of the great and beautiful and demands that we acknowledge the brutal reality it masks" (hooks 1995a, 38).

The analysis of Basquiat draws our attention to the ugliness of art and the art world, whereas much of hooks's "cultural" writing stresses the other side of the coin, the "aesthetics of the everyday" that I sketched in the previous section. The connection, as I see it, lies in her observation, quoted earlier in her recollection of discovering African art in Paris museums, that separating people from the artistic traditions of their communities is a tactic of colonization and marginalization (hooks 1995a, xv). Basquiat's attention to the ugly highlights the alienation that results from this tactic, and hooks's attention to relearning an appreciation for beauty and creativity through everyday engagement with the people and places one loves highlights the empowering solution of developing solidarity through aesthetics. There is also, she thinks, a decolonizing function in the work of Gonzalez-Torres that is similar to the one she identifies in Basquiat. Gonzalez-Torres speaks to her of the need to reject philosophical notions that perpetuate oppression—specifically, the distinction between a public sphere and a private one that feminist theory takes up as the condition of possibility for domestic abuse, between the collective and the individual[9]—so that we can "open ourselves to the possibility of communion and community" (53). Art criticism that attends to location—of the artist, of the audience—enables "a . . . critical culture where we can discuss the issue of blackness in ways that confront not only the legacy of subjugation but also radical traditions of resistance, as well as the newly invented self, the decolonized subject" (93).

Even "learning to see and appreciate the presence of beauty is an act of resistance in a culture of domination that recognizes the production of a pervasive feeling of lack, both material and spiritual, as a useful colonizing strategy," says hooks (1995a, 124). But charging that the progressive left has been too preoccupied with material needs and benchmarks, she also observes, "Without love, our efforts to liberate ourselves and our world community from oppression and exploitation are doomed" (hooks 1994, 243). While resistance to politically oppressive structures such as colonization is important, developing an appreciation for both beauty and love serves to remind us that we must attend to the spiritual aspect of human life and human communities. The art to which hooks wants to draw our attention is not just concerned with philosophical critiques of material deprivation. At its most potent, art draws us into a mind-set in which we come to respect and value all of our fellow human beings, through our experience of valuing those whose creative abilities move us.

She attributes the inspiration for her ethic of love to Martin Luther King Jr.—whose commitment to nonviolence, solidarity, and the notion of "beloved community" is drawn from his Christian belief in love for all human beings as fellow children of God—and cites his belief that we find the highest good through love, that it is love "that unlocks the door to the meaning of ultimate reality" (hooks 1994, 244). "It is in choosing love," she argues, "and beginning with love as the ethical foundation for politics, that we are best positioned to transform society in ways that enhance the collective good [and in c]hoosing love we also choose to live in community. . . . The moment we choose to love, we begin to move against domination, against oppression," she continues; "the moment we choose to love we begin to move towards freedom, to act in ways that liberate ourselves and others. That action is the testimony of love as the practice of freedom" (247–48, 250). hooks does not endorse the explicit commitment to Christianity that drives King's theorizing of love and the ideal he speaks of as "the beloved community," but she does share his robust view of what love is. In his Nobel Peace Prize acceptance speech, King explains that his call for "an all-embracing . . . love" is not the "oft misunderstood and misinterpreted concept so readily dismissed by the Nietzsches of the world as a weak and cowardly force, . . . not . . . some sentimental and weak response which is little more than emotional bosh." By way of explaining what he means by love, King quotes the British historian Arnold Toynbee: "Love is the ultimate force that makes for the saving choice of life and good against the damning choice of death and evil." King asserts, and hooks agrees, that "love is the key to the solution of the problems of the world."[10]

hooks (1995b, 263) does not take up King's call for love and for a "beloved community" uncritically, however. In another move that we might want to see as reminiscent of improvisatory strategies, she takes up his concept and revises it to meet the needs of a different context. She notes that his vision of "a *beloved community* [is one in which] race would be transcended, forgotten, where no one would see skin color." This, says hooks (263), is what makes King's ideal "a flawed vision. The flaw, however, was not the imagining of a *beloved community*; it was the insistence that such a community could exist only if we erased and forgot racial difference." A disregard of difference, expressed in King's dream of a world in which his children would be judged by their character rather than their skin color,[11] makes much more sense in the context of a movement to integrate white and black America than it does today, in a more multicultural world where the fissures and divisions among communities are visible to all—not just those who are marginalized as a result of their "difference." Today, the doctrine of racial colorblindness is the target of harsh criticism by hooks, who insists on both an aesthetic and a politics in which the other is not homogenized. She charges, "The notion that differences of skin color, class background, and cultural heritage must be erased for justice and equality to prevail is a brand of popular false consciousness that helps keep racist thinking and action intact" (265).[12] In her view, "*Beloved community* is not formed by the eradication of difference but by its affirmation, by each of us claiming the identities and cultural legacies that shape who we are and how we live in the world" (265).

Even as hooks recognizes the color-blindness of King's vision of community as flawed, however, she fails to identify the blind spot in her own thinking: her idealization of community. This, too, represents a point of convergence between her theorizing of the aesthetic and the political and the theorizing we find in improvisation studies. Indeed, one might go as far as to argue that the problem in both cases is a failure to theorize community at all; instead, it is just uncritically accepted as an affirmative and nurturing condition of possibility for social change.[13] Untheorized belief that "community," and our immersion in it, is a panacea fails to acknowledge the experiences some people have had—in musical ensembles, in religious congregations—of their membership in community as repressive of creativity and hostile to independent thought or self-expression. This need to critically theorize the possibilities and limitations of community is, I think, all the more pressing, all the more important for improvisation studies and relational aesthetics scholars to attend to, precisely because there are compelling responses available to counter this criticism.

We who think of community as a crucial factor in human flourishing do ourselves no favors by ignoring or dodging such criticisms. Instead, I think we should face this ambiguous capacity of community head-on, in much the same way that the western Canadian political philosopher Roger Epp does in *We Are All Treaty People: Prairie Essays* (2008). Epp's project is to articulate a political philosophy that has at its heart the values and social experiences of rural farmers and residents of small-town farming communities. This, he argues, is a necessary opposition to mainstream political theory, which begins with, and from, urban centers. He writes about having grown up in small towns—the kinds of communities most often thought of as the paradigm of stultifying repression—and frankly acknowledges that the members of these communities can limit one's opportunities for personal and economic growth and for self-expression through, for instance, prejudice and assumptions drawn from community gossip about one's family. However, he also insists on the generative possibilities of the deeply personal knowledge small-town residents have of one another, a knowledge that strikes those of us from urban environments as invasive and limiting. Epp wants us to take notice of the subtle and ongoing ways that intimate knowledge of one another can function as support and encouragement and ways that the judgments small-town residents make of one another can inspire commitments to personal and social transformation.[14] In addition, this knowledge base gives us access to our own histories and insight into the range of interpretations that others may place on those histories. Communities, in other words, can grind us down, but they also ground us. We need not be naïve to see them as valuable.

In a similar vein, hooks (1995b, 264) insists, "We cannot surrender that longing [for *beloved community*]—if we do we will never see an end to racism." Returning to the importance of the everyday, and emphasizing the individual engagement that is sometimes used to distinguish ethics from politics, she argues that we can see the plausibility and the potential of King's "beloved community" in "the small circles of love we have managed to form in our individual lives" (264). Our own lives can "represent a concrete realistic reminder that *beloved community* is not a dream," that it can be achieved through strategies of antiracist education and critical consciousness raising (264). "Our devout commitment to building diverse communities is central," hooks tells us, "like all *beloved communities* we affirm our differences. It is this generous spirit of affirmation that gives us the courage to challenge one another, to work through misunderstandings, especially those that have to do with race and racism. In a *beloved community* solidarity and trust are grounded in profound commitment to a shared vision. Those of us who are always anti-racist long for a world in which everyone can form a *beloved community* where borders can be crossed and cultural hybridity celebrated" (272).

Reading (into/onto) the Marginalized Other

Having laid out the framework that situates hooks's commitment to an aesthetics of the everyday and an ethics of love, I want now to return to the question of how she is represented by commentators on her work. This is a question that I think has a much wider relevance than simply how we see hooks; it is, I would argue, a valuable illustration of how otherness has been treated in mainstream attention to both aesthetics and politics. Distortions of hooks's work, and therefore her identity, are interestingly similar to misrepresentations of Frantz Fanon's theorizing of decolonization and John Coltrane's "free jazz" experiments. What I want to interrogate in this section is the extent to which these falsifications are a function of a systematic devaluing of political-philosophical and aesthetic contributions by people of color. How are they silenced or deflected? And what is it that their contributions threaten?

I spoke at the outset of this chapter of Wallis's observation that hooks usually is not recognized as a legitimate voice in the art world, despite her sustained attention to art making and the aesthetic contexts in which representations of dominant and marginalized cultural objects are situated, and notwithstanding her own declared sense of herself as an artist and art critic. Where hooks's contributions to aesthetic discourses have been ignored, her contributions to social and political philosophy have been quite blatantly misrepresented. In making these observations, I have in mind responses to hooks I have encountered in casual conversations with friends and in teaching her work in classrooms that are predominantly populated by privileged white students. hooks is perceived by some of her readers as angry, anti-male, anti-white, and inexplicably, unjustifiably aggressive in her demands for change. Lest one think that this is a defect unique to the circles in which I travel, hooks's own essays recount ways her work has been twisted by interlocutors. She discusses, for example, an interview that she gave to *Esquire* magazine on the topic of how attitudes toward sex supposedly distinguish the militant "old feminist" of the 1970s from the cooler, more overtly sexual "new feminist" of the 1990s (hooks 1994, 73–81).[15] hooks contends that her views were blatantly misstated and edited to make her sound as if she was conforming to the stereotype of the oversexed black woman, even as the interviewer also shaded her comments about the feminist movement of the 1970s to reinforce the popular view of it as man-hating. "It has always served the interest of the patriarchal status quo for men to represent the feminist woman as antisex and antimale," she notes, and it has always been acceptable to appropriate the words of black women to add the appearance of racial inclusivity to mainstream discourse, even as the contributions of black women to racial and sexual equality movements are ignored (75, 78).

Regardless of whether her words are being ignored or being twisted, the common theme of these re-presentations of bell hooks is their failure to acknowledge the humanism that consistently permeates her work. She speaks and writes inclusively of African American culture in ways that affirm the value of both the middle-class aspirations of her parents and siblings and the working-class values of her grandparents, but—despite the charges of careless readers—she does not engage in bitterness, special pleading, or race baiting. She writes from a racial perspective she realizes she needs to defend against racist devaluations and a gender perspective she defends against sexist devaluations, but neither defense is mounted at the expense of those who are not African American or not women. The obvious goal of her defenses is to assert the humanity of the marginalized group, its belonging in the "beloved community." In this, her work and responses to it are eerily similar to Fanon's position in discourses on decolonization and postcolonial reorganization. In the opening chapter of his major work, *The Wretched of the Earth*, Fanon (1963, 30–33, 42–43, 73–74) analyzes the violence he claims is inherent in colonial relations. This analysis reveals the ways in which the violence settler governments impose on native populations produces a circuit that channels that violence through native communities and internalizes it, such that members of these communities attack one another rather than those who rule the colonies. There is "no possible coming to terms," Fanon (48) declares. "[Colonization] is violence in its natural state, and it will only yield when confronted with greater violence." The point of this analysis is to argue for the liberation from enslavement and exploitation of all human beings and "to set afoot a new man" who will live in a new, decolonized world (255). This, too, is a strong and persistent humanism, but all too frequently the Fanon who appears in academic discussions of colonialism is a ruthless, simplistic advocate of bloody violence, despite the obvious connection of this analysis of violence to the larger context of his assertion of the moral value of all human beings.[16] In both cases—hooks and Fanon—a positive program of human liberation is disregarded, and largely tangential or highly contextual comments are foregrounded, with the result that the very arguments these thinkers are putting forth are inverted. In this way, their critiques of status quo politics can be dismissed as radical and dangerous nonsense.

It may seem odd to include Coltrane in this group and to thereby suggest that African American musical practices are disregarded. But reflect for a moment on the popular misrepresentation of Coltrane's "free jazz" musical experimentations and consider whether there is a similarity to the devaluing through distortion that is imposed on hooks and Fanon. Most notable, in this regard, is the critical attention given to his collaboration with Eric Dolphy in the early 1960s, described by *Down Beat*'s editor John Tynan as "a horrifying demonstration of what appears to be a growing anti-jazz trend" (quoted in DeMicheal 1998, 110). Of Tynan and the critics who subsequently jumped on the "anti-jazz" bandwagon, Coltrane remarked, "They made it appear that we didn't even know the first thing about music—the first thing. And there we were really trying to push things off" (quoted in Kofsky 1970, 242).

Speaking of the contemporary art world, but making a point that I think applies to the entire history of African American arts and music in the twentieth century (and quite possibly to that of earlier eras), hooks (1995a, 58) observes, "Commodification of blackness creates a market context wherein conventional, even stereotypical, modes of representing blackness may receive the greatest reward [and] images that would subvert the status quo are harder to produce."[17] This is a perennial problem in the jazz world: conventional representations of black jazz musicians constrained and mystified the efforts of many who sought to expand and explore the boundaries of the genre, Coltrane among them. The limitations of standard set lengths and the commercialization of nightclubs focused on profits derived from their "two drink minimum" were such a straightjacket for Coltrane that his later years were characterized by a reluctance to perform in clubs and a search for alternative venues, such as community centers (Kofsky 1970, 418–20). Perhaps the most toxic stereotype facing jazz musicians, though, is the primitivization of genius that explains the artists' talents as if they are intuitive conduits of a "spirit of music" rather than acknowledging them as skilled and, in many cases, highly trained creators.[18]

So what *is* achieved through these blatant acts of revisionism? One of the things that hooks, Fanon, and Coltrane have in common is their opposition to mainstream thought, and as hooks has noted, challenges to (including subversion of) the status quo are always at risk of being suppressed in favor of more orthodox views. "The fierce willingness to repudiate domination in a holistic manner is the starting point for progressive cultural revolution," hooks (1994, 6) tells us. In a number of her essays, hooks makes a crucial distinction between revolution, a complete transformation of a system, and reform movements that make local adjustments that may ameliorate burdens that fall on some people but leave the overall framework of "the system" largely unchanged (see, e.g., hooks 1994, 73–81, 2008, 36–40). So my answer to the question of what their contributions threaten is, simply: the status quo. And what revisionism achieves in these cases is a discrediting of these voices, these claims to represent a point of view that society must take seriously if we are to progress. In discrediting voices such as hooks, Fanon, and Coltrane, the dominant culture can attempt to remain as it is.

Conclusion: What's Art Got to Do with Decolonization?

Of course, the dominant culture's dream that it can maintain itself unchanged is just that: a dream. Visions of how things might be are available to revolutionaries, as well. hooks (1995a, 123) tells us that "rather than surrendering our passion for the beautiful . . . we need to envision ways those passions can be fulfilled that do not reinforce the structures of domination we seek to change." We need to make of art "a place where boundaries can be transgressed, where visionary insights can be revealed within the context of the everyday, the familiar, the mundane" (138). Or, to put the point in language more consistent with the discourse of social aesthetics, we need to improvise a diverse and multicultural world—united by love (political solidarity), not an imposed, coercive homogenization—*through* an aesthetic of otherness. This is where the insights of social aesthetics can help us: drawing attention to the ways our art shapes us and the ways we shape our art requires us to consider closely who *we* are—the differences that distinguish us from each other *and* the common projects that can bring us together. It requires us to cross borders, to share ideas and strategies for change, and to build a world that has input from, and space for, us all. In hooks's view, "To claim border crossing, the mixing of high and low, cultural hybridity, as the deepest expression of a desired cultural practice within multicultural democracy means that we *must* dare to envision ways such freedom of movement can be experienced by everyone" (hooks 1994, 5; emphasis added). And "to live in anti-racist society we must collectively renew our commitment to a democratic vision of racial justice and equality. Pursuing that vision [means] we create a culture where *beloved community* [characterized by solidarity and meaningful coalition] flourishes and is sustained" (hooks 1995b, 271). For that, we most desperately need "an aesthetic sensibility that is redemptive," that sustains us even as it transforms us (hooks 1995a, 121).

Notes

1. Wallis (1995) identifies hooks's *Yearning: Race, Gender, and Cultural Politics* (1990) as the more theoretical "companion volume" to this examination of aesthetic representation and judgment. However, aesthetic concerns also mark hooks's *Black Looks: Race and Representation* (1992) and *Outlaw Culture: Resisting Representations* (1994), as well as the much more recent *Belonging: A Culture of Place* (2009).

2. There is perhaps a partial explanation for this phenomenon that we can find in writing that hooks has done elsewhere. In an essay on psychological effects of racism titled "Healing Our Wounds: Liberatory Mental Health Care," she implies that failure to empower communities at the grassroots level may be particularly pronounced in African American communities due to the influence of

"racial uplift" strategies such as W.E.B. Du Bois's notion of "the talented tenth" (hooks 1995b, 133–45). "Passionately devoted to the political goal of racial uplift, [nineteenth-century and early twentieth-century black critical thinkers] highlighted the achievement of exceptional individuals [and] did not talk about the psychological casualties" (133). This suggests that the subjectivity of successful elites may historically have been celebrated to the exclusion of the majority of members of the communities that produced these "exceptional individuals."

3. I am grateful to Eric Lewis for this point.

4. The coherence of this language with the discourse of relational aesthetics suggests hooks as a precursor to that discourse. However, it is important to see that hooks continues to use the language of traditional aesthetics—"elegance," for instance—and does not distance herself from the aesthetic to take note of the social and political aspects of art, as some contend the more postmodern strands of relational aesthetics do.

5. Because the camera was there, of course, busy producing Matthew Brady's iconic photographs of Civil War soldiers. It was simply—as a novel technology deployed by elite segments of the dominant class to provide solemn mementos of their history—unavailable to serve African American projects of family reunification.

6. Although hooks discusses quilt making as a solitary pursuit, focusing on her grandmother's single-handed production of household necessities through which she developed her artistic talent, there is also current research that stresses the collective production by African American women of quilts. This is yet another link to improvisatory practices.

7. She notes that "he felt a strong sense of affinity with jazz artists in the shared will to push against the boundaries of conventional (white) artistic tastes" and his celebration of this affinity made it possible for him to imagine himself as part of a thriving black artistic community (hooks 1995a, 42).

8. Of the debate about essence and identity, hooks (1995a, 11) observes, "When the ground is shaking under one's feet, fundamentalist identity politics can offer a sense of stability. The tragedy is that it deflects attention from those forms of struggle that might have a more constructive, transformative impact," like decolonization.

9. The "public sphere-private sphere" distinction has been criticized as oppressive (or, at least, potentially oppressive) from a feminist perspective on the grounds that women and children are vulnerable to abuse by husbands and fathers in a system that conceives of families as "private" and under the exclusive, undisputed control of the male head of household. See, e.g., Engels 1972, MacKinnon 1983, Okin 1999. This view of the family as a private domain in which the man is the undisputed sovereign effectively removes the other members of the household from the types of protection that the state might claim to offer to citizens in the public sphere—for example, protection from coercion by a stronger or more powerful fellow citizen. The "sovereignty" accorded to men through deployment of this distinction is analogous to the status given to the leader of a

nation-state in the jurisprudential theory of John Austin's "command theory" of law (Austin 1996) and the political theory of Thomas Hobbes (2007) and Max Weber (1946). In all of these accounts, the leader stands in for and assumes the power to dictate the will of the collective, which supersedes the will of the individual, thereby producing the classical philosophical tension between the citizen/individual and society.

10. Martin Luther King Jr., "The Quest for Peace and Justice," Nobel lecture, University of Oslo, Norway, December 11, 1964, http://nobelprize.org/nobel_prizes /peace/laureates/1964/king-lecture.html.

11. Martin Luther King Jr., "I Have a Dream," Lincoln Memorial, Washington, DC, August 28, 1963, www.afn.org/~dks/history/dream.

12. Her point here—that the claim of a human community that is "beyond color" or post-racial actually perpetuates the very phenomenon it presents itself as having transcended (for instance, by marking as deviant all those who are not similarly willing to drop allegiance to racial identity)—is remarkably similar to Pierre Bourdieu's rebuttal of Kantian aesthetics. Kant claims that "taste," the judgment of beautiful and sublime objects made in a position of "disinterested interest," is universal, a thesis Bourdieu rebuts through the presentation of empirical data on a variety of aesthetic judgments indexed to the class identities of the judgers. Kant's assertion that taste is universal acts to delegitimize as judgers those who do not make "the right" judgments and, as Bourdieu (1984) shows, cultural acceptance of a universal notion of taste results in a retreat from judgment by groups already socially marginalized.

13. I am grateful to Georgina Born for raising this point in response to my presentation of an earlier version of this chapter at the Improvisation and Social Aesthetics conference held at McGill University, March 2010.

14. The kind of intimate knowledge of a person that Epp (2008) has in mind is the small community's knowledge of one's family members that one may not have oneself: their memories of the musical ability shown by a never known uncle who died in a long-ago war or their awareness of the alcoholism that caused a grandparent's inexplicable behavior. The community's transmission to an individual of these observations can be inspiring or cautionary and can help one form conceptions of life's possibilities that would be much less available to one raised in the studied anonymity of more urban areas.

15. Bizarrely, this interviewer talked to her as someone who could describe anthropologically the "old feminist" movement (in which she participated) and simultaneously as someone who embodied the attitudes of the sexually free "new feminist."

16. For more detailed discussions of how Fanon's analysis of violence is misread, see Carastathis 2010, Gratton 2010, Nicholls 2010.

17. In an interview on hip hop, hooks discusses the phenomenon of gangsta rap as "upscale primitivism" marketed to white kids and notes that rap artists are simultaneously pushed by two contradictory forces: the demand that they present themselves as killers, pimps, "playahs," and conspicuous consumers of luxury

products (champagne, cars, jewelry) and the demand that they conform to popular notions of what it means to be a good role model: see bell hooks, "bell hooks on Video: Cultural Criticism and Transformation," Racialicious blog, 2007, www .racialicious.com/2007/06/19/bell-hooks-on-hip-hop. hooks glosses this irresolvable tension as a demand we make of rap artists that they be more moral than any other artists. Note, in the context of her comment about the need to conform to conventional stereotypes in order to succeed, that similar analyses of the narrowing of hip hop—which began as radical grassroots resistance to the corporatization, gentrification, and destruction of public spaces of urban communities—to gangsta rap are offered in Byron Hurt, dir., *Hip Hop: Beyond Beats and Rhymes*, God Bless the Child Productions, 2006; Rose 1994.

18. This view of the jazz musician as unthinking conduit of music, primitive and therefore capable of channeling emotionally powerful music without being able to analyze musical genius (the role of the jazz critic, of course), is pervasive in jazz histories. See the histories traced by Kofsky (1970)—notably, the critic's contempt and disrespect for the musicians—in the first chapters of this book; by Jones (1963), particularly in the chapters dealing with the emergence of the blues from the Deep South; by Heble (2000), especially in his analysis of Theodor Adorno's cultural framework; and by Porter (2002).

CHAPTER 10

IMPROVISATION IN NEW WAVE CINEMA

Beneath the Myth, the Social

Marion Froger, Translated by Will Straw

In the introduction to his study *Godard au travail* (Godard at Work), Alain Bergala (2006) draws our attention to the myth of improvisation that took shape in the 1960s around the filmmaking of Jean-Luc Godard. Godard maintained this myth through postures designed to enhance his image as a creator. He loved to speak of his constant improvisation, whether it involved dialogue that he would dream up the night before shooting and suggest to actors on the set—using earphones—or happened at the level of mise-en-scène itself, as when he waited until bodies and scenery were in front of him before deciding how the actors and the camera would move. This posture resonated with the idea he had forged of his creative practice. As Bergala (2006, 154) makes clear, "Godard proclaimed a cinema of the *found* against a cinema based on the execution of a programmed script."[1]

This conception of improvisation cannot help but resonate with that embraced by jazz musicians of the 1950s, as described by Howard Saul Becker (1963). The musicians Becker studied divided themselves into two groups: on the one hand, there were those players who belonged to dance bands and devoted themselves to pleasing audiences drawn to familiar melodies and rhythms; on the other hand, there were the improvisers or "true" musicians, recognized by their peers but unable to live off their art because the "straights"—the customers at the "joints"—had no taste for that kind of playing. In cinema, the appearance of the Nouvelle Vague (New Wave), with its new shooting methods, its liberated stories that no longer followed strictly linear narratives, and its editing techniques that broke with those of classical continuity, generated the same line of division—between the "improvisers," led by Godard, and the others, who belonged to a profession and entertainment industry from which they made their living. The emergence of this line, which divided the filmmaking community over the question of improvisation, is what interests us here.

It is important that the link we want to establish, between cinema and jazz, not be misunderstood; our intention is not to somehow compare the various "arts of improvisation" or to collapse one community into another, for example, the French film world of the early 1960s into the American jazz scene of the 1950s. Rather, we want to try to understand the processes of community formation that played themselves out around the question of improvisation. If we treat each of these as a medium, in fact, we see that jazz and cinema cannot share the same relationship to improvisation, for one key reason: while musical improvisation takes shape within performance, the direction of a film involves making a finished product that cannot claim to offer viewers the live experience of an improvisation. In technical terms, improvisation is the act by which one simultaneously composes and executes a musical piece at one and the same time or simultaneously composes and utters dialogue. This happens either because circumstances require that it happen or because it is presumed it will produce a superior effect, unless it is, simply, the rule of the creative game that one has adopted. Such a definition of improvisation emphasizes the simultaneity of the time of invention, execution, and audience reception. However, this simultaneity is not possible in the case of cinema, where the time of projection is always deferred relative to that of shooting and editing. To be sure, the cinema can record performances that may be improvised—those of actors who invent their lines and of the filmmakers who follow these actors and react the best they can to what is happening.[2] However, setting aside the fact that these circumstances are extremely rare, at least in the case of fiction film, improvisation in what is filmed, or in the act of filming itself, is very difficult to detect in the viewing of a film. In the first place, there is no single, unique form of representation that would signal its character as improvisation at the moment in which it takes place, through its difference from a written text or prior performance with which the public would be familiar. And even when one has filmed improvised action, the arrangement of images and sounds in the act of editing—which uses and mixes various kinds of visual and sound recording as needed—effaces the sense of a performance taking place in front of the camera in favor of the after-the-fact construction of a story's spatiotemporal continuity. Moreover, a scene may occasionally appear improvised even if it has been meticulously prepared in advance. In other words, the status of improvisatory elements is obscured by the mediatic apparatus that strives for transparency. One is never sure whether there has been improvisation (we know it only through the more or less reliable testimony of the director or crew). Improvisation, we might say, is that ethereal and elusive *something* in the image in which one wants to believe. Depending on the case, it is capable of eliciting admiration, repulsion, and even indignation. It is precisely these affective responses of viewers to improvisation, which have little to do with the actual presence of improvisation in cinema, that will concern us here.

In the early 1960s, improvisation invaded films and the discourses about them. Directors embraced or rejected it. In the films of Godard and his cohort, critics looked for traces of the influence of Jean Rouch, a master of improvisation (in front of the camera and behind it) who was seen as the "guru" of the Nouvelle Vague (cf. Gauthier 2002, 70–75). In discourses on cinema, improvisation took on a level of importance that was not justified by the actual practices of the young filmmakers of the movement. In fact, improvisation was rarely practiced, but it nevertheless crystallized many of the breaks with which the movement was credited: a break with traditional methods of shooting and a rupture with the consensual, literary realism that the former masters of French cinema used to bring the "truth of life" into their films. One of the most common explanations of this phenomenon was aesthetic in character: improvisation was seen as bound up with the emergence of cinema verité, which shattered the boundaries betweeen fiction and documentary and which inspired the directors of the New Wave. Cinema verité had been introduced by Jean Rouch in his film *Moi un noir* (1958). It involved filming documentary images—which required improvisation on the part of the cameraman, who had to adapt to an event as it was unfolding—and then "fictionalizing" them through editing and commentary. The resulting contrast with those fiction films characterized by polished writing, acting, and shooting was sufficiently engaging that it set in place a "style" for makers of fiction films that evoked the in-the-moment and improvised character of documentary filming.

This style was generated by methods of working that were highly unusual in the film world. They involved the use of amateur actors and of exterior shooting, sometimes with hidden cameras. The temporalities of invention and execution were often collapsed into the moment of filming itself. The new generation of filmmakers set out to make its name on the basis of this distinctiveness. It must be noted, however, that these methods were practiced in only a very few films and that the "style" that resulted was limited—in the case of Godard, in particular—by an editing practice that left nothing to chance. The resulting films were closer to the model of a carefully constructed artifact than to that of a performance.

One of the key ideas of the critic and theorist André Bazin, to the effect that cinema was the art of revealing the real, served to enhance the appeal of improvisation. In his account, the cinematic image bears an ontological relationship to the event—by definition unique—that unfolds before the camera. Beyond sets and acting, what the camera captures, quite definitively, is the improvisation of life itself; the cinema conserves the form of change of something that happens only once. Out of these claims about the essence of cinema, the filmmakers of the Nouvelle Vague derived the imperative to break with false studio sets, showy acting, and finely chiselled dialogue.[3] This led to the idea of leaving room for improvisation while shooting, an idea in line with the notion of cinema capturing the improvisation of life itself. However, improvisation would have to remain invisible so it would not break what film theorists have called the "effect of the real" of the cinematic image.[4] This effect of the real is the lot of any shot in film, since it is produced by visual and sonic analogies that obscure the medium and point directly to things heard and seen out of camera range. This effect of the real reinforces the reality effect produced by a fictional universe. While it does not completely fool the viewer, it nevertheless gives the impression that a film's characters really exist. To notice improvisation would undermine this effect, since it would draw our attention to the real performances, those of the acteurs and the filmmakers, and thus *rupture the analogic illusion by forcing the viewer to notice the ways in which the analogy has been fabricated.* Arguably, this explains the commercial failure of François Truffaut's second film, *Tirez sur le pianiste* (1960), which was characterized by improvisation much more than was his first film, *Les 400 coups* (1959), which was an unexpected success.[5] The impression of spontaneity and freshness that ensured the success of *400 coups* owed nothing to a practice of improvisation—which was limited to two or three asides by Jean-Pierre Léaud—or to the perception of improvisation.[6] When improvisation is noticed, it interrupts our immersion in the world of the film; the film is then seen to be "sloppy" and judged a failure, and audiences react negatively, as was the case with *Tirez sur le pianiste.* This is what Godard understood so well. Conveying the impression that he improvised was part of a larger strategy designed to undermine the narrative and logical conventions of verisimilutude, transparency, and naturalism (which Truffaut had no intention of abandoning, and which his audience had not asked him to give up), even if, in reality, Godard scarcely improvised at all.

If improvisation—rare in any case—did not have the desired effect when used, why was it so important for those active in the field of cinema in the 1960s? What was it that, crystalized within improvisation, proved so interesting both to the cinema's young rebels and to established professionals? The first thing that might be said here is that "improvisation," before becoming a *technical* issue (involving the practice of filmmaking itself) or an ontological one (having to do with the very definition of cinematic art[7]) emerged as an issue on the social terrain of work itself. To improvise is to act without preparation, either because one already possesses the necessary skills to do so or, on the contrary, because one's incompetence requires that one improvise. In the 1960s, the question of improvisation was posed in these terms as much as in relation to the cinema as an art form. Indeed, it was as a result of the confusion between these two perspectives that *l'affaire* of Jean Aurel and Roger Vadim unfolded. The controversy received a great deal of attention in the press, partly because of the involvement of Brigitte Bardot and partly because of what might be called its "tribal" character. The Nouvelle Vague had torn itself apart in public in response to the accusation of slander launched by Vadim against Truffaut, who had attacked Vadim in an inflammatory article published on December 22, 1960, in the weekly magazine *France Observateur*. Truffaut wrote that Vadim had maneuvered to take the place of Jean Aurel, the contractual screenwriter and nominal director of *La bride sur le cou* (*Please, Not Now!* in the United States), a film starring Bardot. The actress, who also produced the film, was alarmed by Aurel's lack of preparation—this was his first film—and turned for help to Vadim, who moved from simple technical consultant on the film to becoming its director mere days after his arrival on the set. Truffaut then came to the defense of Aurel, who felt he had been pushed aside and accused Vadim of disloyalty. Why did Truffaut defend Aurel? He did so in part because he saw Aurel as a young filmmaker much like himself. Truffaut's intervention, which won the highly publicized support of Godard before and during the trial,[8] amounted to declaring something along the lines that he and Godard, too, had been beginners; they, too, had had supervisors and "technical consultants" (with the difference being that, unlike Vadim, they respected their work); and they, too, had delilberately chosen not to script everything in advance and looked for ideas that would guide their directing in the act of filming itself. This "improvisation," which was really no such thing, was part of their profession. As filmmakers, they had the right to choose their methods of working, and no producer could break a (moral) contract on the grounds that they made use of such methods.

Nevertheless, Truffaut lost at trial as the court recognized Aurel's lack of preparation, which caused delays and resulted in retakes, and his low level of involvement in the writing of the script and direction once Vadim arrived on the set.[9] It is worth noting that the film's technicians supported Vadim against Aurel in a letter published in *Le Figaro* on January 14, 1961. It should also be pointed out that, in French cinema at the time, the culture of labor was *ouvrière* ("workerish") and artisanal, marked by a level of care for work well done and respect for the director but limited by some distrust of the innovations of intellectuals who seemed to overstep the boundaries of their roles.

This episode allows us to highlight what, in the discourse of both sides concerning improvisation, touches on the social value of "work." Here, the issue of improvisation itself changes character. Let us return to Godard's posturing in this context and consider the ways in which posing as an improviser might be seen as a denial of the social value of work. In the 1950s, the French cinema was a world dominated by artisans, whose enshrined values were work well done, technical perfectionism, and mastery acquired through experience. In contrast, the filmmakers of the Nouvelle Vague came from the world of criticism, in which they had made their names fighting for the recognition of cinema as an art form. As a result, they sought to impose a different sense of the value of work in the cinematic field: one that set the artist against the artisan. Following this logic, we might see young rebels as bringing an artistic sense of work into a milieu that would not acknowledge it. There were, in fact, artists working in the world of film, many of them already recognized as such at the beginning of the 1960s. However, they were *master* figures and included, in particular, Henri-Georges Clouzot, whose name would be invoked during the Aurel-Vadim trial.[10] Like the directors of the Nouvelle Vague, Clouzot challenged the professional culture of the filmmaking world while he was making *L'Enfer* (1964), a film he was forced to abandon afer several months of tests and weeks of filming, even though his status as a "genius director" had given him an unlimited budget and absolute freedom on the project.[11] Clouzot was not an improviser, however; he was something like its very opposite: an "experimenter." The greatest obstacle to the completion of his films was that they were overprepared.

However, Godard's improvisatory poses are not simply those of a newcomer seeking to transform a cinema dominated by a culture of artisanal work and to impose himself as an artist or intellectual.[12] His poses were received differently in the film world of the period. They were seen, in moral terms, as proof of off-handedness, flippancy, confirmation that Godard was content to make "little films" on the fly, as it were, such as *Bande à part, Une femme est une femme*, and *Made in USA*, which annoyed half of the critics and delighted the other half. In the case of *Une femme est une femme*, Godard's improvisation was interpreted in two ways, each of which expressed the affinities (or lack thereof) felt toward him. Michel Capdenac (1961) wrote in *Lettres françaises* about a "cinema which clearly does not take itself seriously and which, with its flippant tone of never-ending improvisation, will say anything at all, no matter how perfectly futile, like a hawker who invents, in proclaiming them, the bountiful qualities of his merchandise, but with such brashness, brilliance, talent and, for once, a kind of secret tenderness."

By not taking himself so seriously, Godard showed "tenderness," modesty, and generosity, according to his most enthusiastic supporters. They focused on the sociability that they saw as one of his key virtues. Conversely, his improvisation would be read by others as proof that he did not take his audience seriously, that he had no qualms about leaving them feeling excluded and humiliated: "The prince of little tricks, Godard piles up the corny jokes to kill time, like a clock ticking off the minutes. . . . The result is a film that, most of the time, seems to have been conceived solely to amuse its director while it was being made: we, the audience, *feel embarassed, left out*" (our emphasis).[13]

These polarized responses recall an imaginary scene of interaction that the work of Erving Goffman may help us to interpret. Goffman (1967, 6) has shown how, in direct interaction, each person follows a line of behavior designed to avoid losing face and to ensure that the other not lose it, either. He describes those lapses or lulls in which an unease between the partners develops—when one of them is embarrassed or feeling left out, as in the second of the reviews just quoted—and has recourse to a "reportory of face-saving practices" that aim to neutralize this embarrassment to stop the interaction—this minimal sociability—from floundering (14). Inasmuch as the viewing of a film may be seen as an indirect form of interaction, the improvisatory gestures of Godard may be seen as provocations in this sense. In *Interaction Ritual* (1967), Goffman draws our attention to the threat of offense that runs through every interaction, noting that a significant part of every interaction is devoted to ignoring or warding off that which is offensive by cutting it short, disarming it, or offering a riposte. The price to be paid when the offense is too strong is a breakdown of the relationship. Goffman insists on the fact that the percepton of an offense presupposes a public witness possessing norms and values of which both the offended person and the person committing the offense are aware. It is very much in relation to the values of this "public" that the defense or condemnation of Godard organizes itself, being concerned fundamentally and precisely with the respect to be shown toward a filmmaker on the basis of how much he is judged to show the same respect toward others. The first of the reviewers quoted earlier uses the occasion to express his complicity with Godard and avoid the rupture that so much flippancy on Godard's part might have engendered; the second denounces what is insulting in Godard's indifference toward others (i.e., toward those viewers whom he ignores to have his own fun) (Goffman 1959, 47). An imaginary scene takes place in which a film replaces the Goffmanian face-work of a partner, leaving the viewer feeling either at ease or wronged, like an accomplice or a victim. However, this viewer, now represented by the author of a published review, endorses his chosen posture, for all his readers, and from this flows a moral tone that either offers a protest in the name of a general civility or supports the filmmaker, justifying his behavior in the name of a new sociability that arrives in a roundabout way but nonetheless founds a new communality. In the latter case, Godard's "flippant tone" and "never-ending improvisation," to borrow Capdenac's words, are in the service of that "secret tenderness" that animates new partners and players ready to demonstrate their solidarity and complicity on the social scene.

Why did the impression of improvisation—left or perceived—carry such importance? Perhaps it is because, at the time, it was bound up with the signs of respect people showed one another in their various social activities. Let us return to Clouzot, a master whose genius was said to express itself in his hard work. On November 4, 1960, *Le Canard Enchaîné* noted about *La vérité* (1960): "a scenario whose architecture is a model of ingenuity and precision, a staging that leaves nothing to chance, performances directed with a master's hand, . . . consummate understanding of story, [a] constant concern for perfection, [and] a solid grasp of the audience's tastes."

For the journalist, this valorization of work went hand in hand with a denunciation of the "skewed, unreasonable, worthless youth" represented so well by Bardot's character, but the article included an ironic reference, typical of the newspaper's satirical tone, to the laborious character of "the director's efforts." We see here, in fact, evidence of a certain ambivalence toward the value of work of a sort misisng from another review, published in the conservative *Carrefour*: "Working like an ox, leaving nothing to chance,

Clouzot not only demonstrates a rare sense of professional responsibility but shows, as well, that he is modest."[14]

Through one's work, then, one signals to the others the respect one has for them and reassures them of one's sociability. Moral accents of this kind are not rare in the debate surrounding improvisation. Critics of the period who denounced improvisation in the Nouvelle Vague were looking for evidence of work, which they took as proof of morality. Work is the fruit of labor and an essential part of the respect one owes to the person who has performed it; conversely, the person who has produced the work shows respect for the others by giving to them the best that she can produce. The quality of work is one of the major signs through which respect is expressed, and, through it work enters into the circuit of the gift, in which the merit of everyone is recognized in the fruits of their work. Indeed, critics of the time interpreted films as, in effect, gifts offered to audiences. Worthless films could signify only the contempt in which their authors held the audiences for which the films were destined. While improvisation was ultimately nothing more than a working method that produced superior works, the partisans of the Nouvelle Vague were obliged to struggle against the impression of disrespect provoked by Godard's up-front flippancy. Associated with carelessness, improvisation was, in fact, a synonym for imposture, the equivalent of an insult for those at whom it was directed and, ultimately, toward the larger community interpellated by a film. It should be remembered that, at the beginning of the 1960s, improvisation was not simply a Godardian posture but a collective rallying cry. Ultimately, at the time of the Truffaut-Vadim affair, the foot soldiers of the Nouvelle Vague might well have said, "We are all 'improvisers.'"

Improvisation was a declarative act: for auteurs, to be seen to improvise or not was part of their *enunciative strategies*, reinforced by punchy pronouncements. For film viewers, improvisation, above and beyond the impression made by any particular stylistic gesture, carried a moral sense that called on their social rather than their aesthetic sensitivities. In a sense, their social sensitivity expressed itself in the perception of improvisation.

What impulse was contained within the call to improvise? More than anything else, for the young rebels of *Cahiers du Cinéma*, this call was a means of acceding to the role of director. These rebels had not been formally trained in school, had not served apprenticeships—and so, in a sense, they improvised their status as filmmakers and did so collectively, most notably through the making of shorts such as *Le coup du berger* (Jacques Rivette, dir., 1956). Improvisation revealed the collective to itself. By improvising themselves as filmmakers, they were obliged to function as a tribe, in a network outside professional circuits. Improvisation, then, through its liberating function, was the founding act of their "community." The first films of the Nouvelle Vague were marked by solidarity, expressed through brief appearances by directors in one another's films, through the borrowing of actors, through references by one film to another (as Godard did on so many occasions in *Une femme est une femme*). One after another, their films made reference to this founding act and maintained a semiotics of solidarity and liberty (e.g., through the transgression of aesthetic and dramatic rules) that guaranteed, for those who recognized it, a sense of community.

Creative improvisation also belongs to an ideal of successful social interaction. Cinema, after all, involves a collective mode of production that produces a sense of collectivity through interaction. The creative dimension of improvisation appears to guarantee the formation of an ideal community; it points in the direction of utopia. Within it, a model of sociality crystallizes that sets aside rivalry among egos and builds on promises of relationality. One must be able to improvise together to belong to a group that is taking shape outside the usual rules of the field. In 1961, Agnes Varda (1994) had Godard and Anna Karina shoot a silent film to be included as a film within her film *Cléo de 5 à 7*. She describes the shoot as symbolizing, for her, "*La Nouvelle Vague* as we experienced it, with imagination in charge and friendship in action."

"This dynamic of deviance," to borrow a term from Becker (1963, 192), is of the same order as that produced by traditional communities. It, too, will end up establishing rules and generating exclusions: "We see that people who engage in acts conventionally thought deviant are not motivated by mysterious, unknowable forces. They do what they do for much the same reasons that justify more ordinary activities."

Very quickly, these people came to defend themselves against the frivolous and incompetent imitators who usurped those signs of lightness, spontaneity, and complicity among filmmakers, technicians, and performers that characterized the "true family" of the Nouvelle Vague. In *La Nouvelle Vague*, Antoine de Baecque repeats Claude Chabrol's comments describing his "distrust towards the crowd of anonymous first-time filmmakers" getting ready to make their first films. Chabrol was even more outspoken on the subject in *L'Express*: "Let us be under no illusions. There is an underside to the current success of the Nouvelle Vague: the fact that certain people, who are incredible charlatans, will be able to direct films" (quoted in de Baecque 2009, 72). In private, Truffaut also deplored the fact that certain films had been branded Nouvelle Vague, films that "quickly gathered together all those things considered reproachable in young filmmakers, their amateurism, their banality, their incomprehensible and eccentric characters" (quoted in de Baecque 2009, 102). In a long interview in the October 22, 1961, issue of *Nouvel Observateur*, however, he expanded on the moral rather than aesthetic problem that lay behind this rejection, emphasizing the refined moral values of "his" tribe: "The deliberate lightness of these films often comes across, sometimes wrongly and sometimes with good reason, as frivolity. Confusion arises because the qualities of this new cinema—its grace, lightness, modesty, elegance and speed—go hand-in-hand with its faults—its frivolity, obliviousness and naiveté" (quoted in de Baecque 2009, 103).

Why did these improvisers bother the professionals of cinema to such an extent? What contextual knowledge is needed to help us understand the opposition between two political models of the "communal?"[15] In 1958, the communist unions in the film world mobilized against a reform of government policies that would have brought stronger political control over film. In their eyes, the new agreement—meant to bring the film industry in line with the rules of the European common market—threatened the tradition of quality in French cinema that had been rooted in a sense of craft, which was seen as opposed to the industrial standardization characteristic of Hollywood cinema. There were also worries about employment in the field, with France falling behind a German industry now swollen with American money invested in the film sector. There was no place for questions about improvisation, which found themselves edged out in the opposition between an industrial, capitalist rationalization of filmmaking labour and an artisanal practice. The artisans of cinema had no desire to sacrifice their self-respect, rooted in a sense of craft, to the dictates of an industry suspected of wanting to make films the way one makes canned food.[16] When the first films of the Nouvelle Vague were released, the professional milieu, along with a significant faction of the communist-leaning critics, did not support them. The fact that the directors had become filmmakers by staking claims to improvisation was seen as irritating by those writing in the columns of union newspapers. Laurent Marie (2005, 146) explains, "Through a series of editorials and articles whose main targets were the methods and amateurism of these new filmmakers, the editors, including several of the old guard (Max Douy, Jean Dréville) of the union newspaper *Technicien du spectacle*, accused the young filmmakers of undermining the professional rules then in effect. Many people felt threatened by these first-time filmmakers [who had] no respect for common practices." Admittedly, Truffaut had fired the first shot in his articles, regularly going after screenwriters and directors, as well as the producers who hired them, and all those who lay claim to the French quality that gave them distinction. Nevertheless, the improvisation embraced by the directors of the Nouvelle Vague had to do with something more profound than their simple corporatist self-interest. The young rebels (Godard, Truffaut, Chabrol, Rivette, Rohmer, Malle) who demonstrated their contempt for simple technique had found the means to make films in part through family money, through personal relationships, or by working within closed communities. In this respect, improvisation was on the front lines of a class conflict. The professional unions set two social models against each other: on the one hand, that of a social advancement that necessitated connections with bourgeois circles and built its members' reputation in opposition to the values of professionalism to produce a community of amateurs and newcomers; and on the other hand, a *society of craftspeople* in which it was necessary to pay one's dues to get ahead and be recognized by the collectivity. In the latter model, it was the profession that gave individuals a social value based on their competence. In this case, it was craft that was to be defended and craft that was felt to be under attack by improvisers who used exterior locations, stripped-down crews, and amateur actors.

We can see here how improvisation, from the perspective of those opposing it, was perceived as a lack of (or an attack on) the respect to which people felt they were entitled. This question of respect would emerge regularly during a period of social unrest marked by heightened tensions among different groups, classes, and generations. To improvise was also a sin of youth that could be pardoned more or less easily depending on the context. Those who had fought in the Second World War worried about a younger generation, seduced by materialism, that seemed to be on the rise in the early 1960s. Indeed, some of the older generation accused young people of being immoral and uncivil "monsters" (Fournier 1958). This worrisome youth was the focus of two hotly debated and compared films of the late 1950s, *Les tricheurs*, directed by Marcel Carné (the most respected craftsman in French cinema), and *Les cousins*, the second film by the young prodigy Chabrol. The denunciation in both films of the incivility of selfish, disrespectful youth masked a deeper anxiety about the social, and thus about the future of a society that judged social relationships on the basis of a respect whose meaning was precisely what the heroes of these films seemed to have lost.

The upheaval in morals engendered by modernity fed this alarm. Traditional civility, which reassured members of a group of their common desire to live together, no longer existed; the modes of socialization surrounding new dances and new appetites for consumption frightened the elderly, as in the scene from *Adieu Philippine* in which a friend of the young heroine's father refuses to dance a cha-cha-cha with her, saying, "You are a marvellous teacher, but I prefer more tender dances, and I consider these brutal dances the perfect expression of the heartlessness at the heart of today's youth." It was nevertheless people like him who sent the youth of this period to Algeria, from which they returned with horrific memories, and it was precisely to "save" her friend from such a departure that the young woman attempted to seduce the older man. However, *Adieu Philippine*, filmed in 1960, was not released until 1962. By then, the war was over, even if its shadow hung over the future of several of the film's characters. And the inconsequential love story was ultimately reassuring, as was the profile of the main characters, modest workers with sensible leisure activities who were far from the characters of *Les tricheurs* or *Les cousins*. Youth rediscovered the qualities of freshness and spontaneity that made it possible to find value in the improvisation offered up without fanfare by the filmmaker, a young person who improvised to escape the codes and conventions for representing youth on the screen:

> The truth of character. For the first time in French cinema, here is a young man, he might be from public housing, or a Renault plant, or a boy's gang. He isn't an actor. In real life, he works in a bank. He came to cinema by accident. He doesn't speak dialogue written to please. *He says what he wants to say, he improvises as in cinéma-vérité.* He speaks with his own words, in his own tone. If Mr. Delon played this role, with dialogue by Michel Audiard in a film by Henri Verneuil, we'd find it delicious. In this case, because it's real and truthful, people protest. However, it's the truth that's making them cry out. Or, rather, it's crying out the truth. (Collet 1963)

In order for spontaneity to have a positive value, however, it is necessary that it appear in a context in which the older codes of interaction have become heavy and unworkable. As long as these codes are still in force, spontaneity is perceived as a false mode of interaction, a threat. In Goffman's terms, it is a source of unease. The valorization of spontaneity as a means of reviving the social bond presumes that this bond is threatened by encrusted conventions. In 1962, at the moment of *Adieu Philippine*'s release, these conventions were doubly exhausted—both sociologically and dramaturgically.

The recognition of improvisation, then, produced a greater sense of truth—or, conversely, of falsity, as when improvisation in one film rendered false the scenes of interaction written and filmed for another—in the films of Jacques Rozier. However, a threshold had been crossed. One soon passed from the impression of spontaneity to the sharing of intimacy, at that moment in which the truth of interaction threatened to become a psychodrama unfolding in front of the camera, at that point at which one asked actors to invest, in their performance, feelings, and emotions that they really felt at the moment of shooting. This is what Jean Rouch had asked of his actors in *La pyramide humaine* (1961). Those actors were, in fact, adolescents in their first year of high school in Abidjan. Rouch laid out for them the initial situation: a new student, white and just arrived from the homeland, sets out to break down the barriers between whites and blacks. These barriers, according to Rouch, were real for the students, and the film allowed them to effectively overcome them. He claimed that the emotional relationships that produced this result, and that one sees develop in the film, really transpired and that his role was essentially that of exploiting the situation to dramatic ends, relying mostly on scenes that were improvised.

From the viewer's perspective, this kind of improvisation places one in a relationship of intimacy one is not always ready to occupy or that one has not really desired. Viewers do not leave their social sensitivities in the cloakroom when they enter the viewing room. Film viewers are not voyeurs looking to see what they are forbidden to see. They are watching a spectacle legitimized by the conventions of theater (or cinema), of which the most important is this: that what confronts them is the intimacy of the characters, not that of the actors. When actors bare themselves, the viewer is surprised, even embarassed. Goffman reminds us that the spectacle of intimacy unfolds only within the frame of a very specific kind of theatrical experience: that of a theater in which actors and spectators play at being intimate without really being so. In real life, we are called on to manage the modesty of others, to protect their intimacy. In theater or cinema, tact is not required when we are dealing with characters. What happens when the character is the actor laying herself or himself bare, when she or he is no longer acting but living the situation as a person—when the performed interaction becomes, on the contrary, an instrument by which the performer reveals her or his intimate being? Writing about *La pyramide humaine*, Georges Sadoul suggests:

> The truth—and [Rouch] tells us this—is that the game imagined for the
> film became reality. Love and rivalry were born in the course of the film,

leading on occasion to little dramas. . . . We would have prefered to see these episodes of truth rather than those others which sometimes smell of fiction . . . [but] if we can imagine super electronic cameras using thermoplastic film that made it technically possible to record romantic or social conflicts unknown to their protagonists, we can be sure that the very honest Jean Rouch would prevent himself from pushing his quest quite that far. To show human intimacy on the screen is, in fact, obscene—not in a pornographic but in an etymological sense. The intimacy of the heart cannot be staged, shown naked in public.[17]

Since Rouch's time, however, it is not only that filmmakers no longer prevent themselves from pushing their quest quite so far—even though they deny this—and not only that viewers may or may not be duped (as when they perceive real relational games as scripted interaction) but that these viewers, without the filmmaker's complicity, may see something hidden from everyone else (from filmmakers and actors) when they suspect, beneath the performance and outside its control, an independent interaction revealed in an improvisation that the viewers believe they have detected. Suddenly, the intimate relationship among actors, or between actors and crew, becomes clear to the viewer, who then "loses" the characters. If the viewer is embarassed, Goffman tells us, it is because he or she is pulled between two postures: on the one hand, that of a viewer who has paid to applaud a spectacle, and on the other, that of an observer who is present, much to his or her surprise, at a real interaction between people. The ordinary viewer "sympathetically and vicariously participates in the unreal world generated by the dramatic interplay of the scripted characters. He gives himself over. He is raised (or lowered) to the cultural level of the playwright's characters and themes, appreciating allusions for which he doesn't quite have the background, marital adjustments for which he doesn't quite have the stomach, varieties of lifestyle for which he is not quite ready, and repartee that gives to speaking a role he could not quite accept for it were he to find such finery in the real world" (Goffman 1986, 130). The onlooker is confronted with a scene of real interaction—people who are very much interacting under the guise of producing a performance. Two outcomes are possible: either the onlooker, excluded from an interaction that is taking place between actors and no longer between characters, feels out of place, even embarassed for having been an unexpected witness, or bound to the actors in a real or imaginary way, the onlooker's sharing of intimacy may reinforce a sentiment of complicity with them. In the latter case, the onlooker will share with these actors—or take pleasure in the belief that he or she is sharing—an emotional experience that strengthens the sense of communal belonging. With reference to the important role played by the perception of improvisation in the critical texts defending the Nouvelle Vague, we can now understand those texts as expressing a sense of closeness to those who belonged to this movement. To detect improvisation in the performance of an actor or in the approach of a director is also to attain an intimacy with this person—an intimacy that the game of roles and masks, in theater as in life, usually hides and blocks. It is to live, with that person, a moment of intimacy that is able to feed our imaginary attachment to them.

My analysis of the debates over improvisation that accompanied the rise of the Nouvelle Vague has shown the close ties between that movement and the social dynamics of their era. The social sensitivities of the French in the early 1960s were, at least in part, bound up with those particular artistic and aesthetic orientations that characterized the Nouvelle Vague. The social experience of the French was characterized by systems of values that were inherited, defended, or rejected by conventions and customs that regulated relationships and constrained them, by methods of work that enforced or complicated collaboration, and by frameworks of experience that protected reticence and modesty. For film audiences entering into the imaginary scene of interaction among spectators, actors, and directors, the ambivalences of a desire for intimacy were maintained, determined by the level of proximity people felt or wanted to feel with one another. The question of improvisation enables us to go to the heart of those social dynamics—of inclusion and exclusion, defiance and trust, promise and frustration, openness and vulnerability—that were engendered by the uneasy attention of people toward one another, toward those with whom they had to deal in the performance of everyday life.

Notes

I thank Lucie Szechter for her invaluable assistance, which was made possible by a research grant from the Fonds de Recherche du Québec sur la Société et la Culture.

1. In Bergala's book, we find the note that Godard sent to his American producer, Joseph A. Levin, to justify the lack of shot breakdowns in a scene from his scenario for *Le mépris*: "This sequence will last about 20–30 minutes. It is difficult for me to recount exactly and chronologically what will happen" (quoted in Bergala 2006, 149). However, the structure of the scene, both dramatically and aesthetically, was thought out in precise terms; bits of dialogue were written;

and, most important, the characters' states of mind were identified. It was up to Godard to find the space and rhythm with which he would orchestrate the exchange of looks and bodily relatonships that translated this to film.

2. Raoul Coutard, the Nouvelle Vague cameraman hired by Georges de Beauregard for *À bout de souffle* (1959), often told the story of how Godard would treat filming as a kind of *reportage*, with cameras on the shoulder and natural light, which presumed if not an element of improvisation, at least a sense of professional risk, since it required that he give up such guarantees of photographic quality as the tripod, which minimized the camera's incidental movements and directional errors, as well as the ability to control light through the use of lamps. The reception of these films would comment more on this "amateurishness" than on their improvisatory qualities.

3. For Jean Douchet (1998, 255), all of the ruptures enacted by the Nouvelle Vague were rooted in a concern for truthfulness aimed at preserving the improvised character of life itself: "What interested the Nouvelle Vague was no longer the story contained in the script, but, on the basis of this script, the encounter between a unique story and the truth of life itself. The true story told by a film rose out of this duel between fiction and reporting. Editing, as a result, was subservient to the unpredictable and the random. It was no longer about organizing shots in a pre-established, determined sequence, but about organizing the breaks, gaps and ruptures in sound and image which were provoked by an event and which intruded, in a surprising and even disruptive fashion, into camera range."

4. "The effect of the real designates the fact that, on the basis of a sufficiently strong reality effect, the viewer arrives at a judgement as to the existence of the representational figures and assigns them a referent in the real" (Aumont and Marie 2007, 65). The idea is that the reality effect, which may be obtained through the use of those conventions acceptable to realistic representation, will be reinforced by an effect of the real carried by the analogic character of the image.

5. *Tirez sur le pianiste* (1960) was Truffaut's biggest failure. It was photographed by Coutard and influenced by Godard's techniques, which, in turn, were inspired by Rouch's methods of filming.

6. In 1959, Truffaut stated in the magazine *Arts*, "Where the seasoned director shoots fifteen takes, we shoot two or three. This stimulates the actors, who have to take the plunge. . . . I believe strongly in chance and in the strokes of luck that happen during filming. Things move on a set. Filming outside shakes things up even more. And that allows us to be on the lookout for these kinds of accidents. *Parfois d'improviser*" (quoted in de Baecque 2009, 82).

7. Cf. André Bazin (1967, 14–15): "Viewed in this perspective, the cinema is objectivity in time. The film is no longer content to preserve the object, enshrouded as it were in an instant, as the bodies of insects are preserved intact, out of the distant past, in amber. The film delivers baroque art from its convulsive catalepsy. Now, for the first time, the image of things is likewise the image of their duration, change mummified as it were."

8. "Twenty-seven filmmakers, including Jean Cocteau, Claude Chabrol, Jean

Delannoy, Julien Duvivier, George Franju, Jean-Luc Godard, Alex Joffe, Pierre Kast, Jean-Pierre Melville, Louis Malle, Alain Resnais, Jacques Tati and François Truffaut have just signed a joint protest following the replacement of Jean Aurel by Roger Vadim. . . . In their protest, the 27 directors declare that Roger Vadim's attitude toward Jean Aurel went against the spirit of collegial brotherhood. They argue that one cannot replace the director of a film already underway without his consent, and that no argument invoking force majeure can replace the consent of the ousted director" ("De nombreux réalisateurs prennent Parti dans l'affaire Aurel-Vadim," notice in *Le monde*, January 14–15, 1961). The trial took place in 1962. Several of the filmakers who signed the petition were called on to testify, including Jean-Luc Godard.

9. As noted in the report of the public hearing of March 27, 1962, "Given that [Jean Aurel] has only himself to blame if the sequences directed by the co-directors were not entirely faithful to his original scenario, since, at the moment that the camera began filming he had only produced a third of the shot breakdowns and had not yet found the conclusion to his story; given that, faced with work scarcely begun, and under pressure as a result of the financial demands inherent in the making of any film, Roger Vadim and Claude Brûlé were obliged to devise the various sequences of a film whose author had not, in contravention of standard practice and in violation of his obligations, completed the shot breakdowns before filming, said circumstances explaining why Vadim, called upon to oversee the project, had to play a more important role and recreate the unfinished scenario." The tribunal of the Grande Instance du Département de la Seine recognized Vadim's good faith and found Truffaut guilty of defamation.

10. The press commented on one detail of the hearing involving Bardot's deposition in the trial: while she offered, as proof of Aurel's incompetence, the fact that he had forced her to redo some of the scenes shot on the first day, Truffaut felt compelled to reply that "Clouzot also made Mademoiselle Bardot do retakes of scenes already shot for *La vérité*." Lifting her blond hair, which was held by a black headband, Bardot furiously answered, "I don't accept the comparison. When Mr. Clouzot reshot scenes, those scenes were already good, and this great director had prepared his shot breakdowns many weeks ahead of time" (*Le Berry Républicain*, January 30, 1962).

11. On this subject, see Serge Bromberg and Ruxandra Medrea, dir: *L'enfer d'Henri George Clouzot*, documentary, 2009.

12. This is the analysis offered by Esquenazi (2004) in *Godard et la société française des années 1960*.

13. "Un Godard audacieux prisonnier d'un Godard collégien," *L'Express*, September 14, 1961, Cinémathèque Française, on-site press clippings database. http://www.cinematheque.fr/bibliotheque.html. Italics added for emphasis.

14. *Carrefour*, November 9, 1960.

15. Max Weber (1978, 40) defines "communal" relationships in terms of the subjective sense of belonging.

16. It is interesting to note at this point that filmmaking professionals refused

to invoke improvisation to justify the basic creative dimensions of their work. in his study of "dance" musicians, Becker noted that those musicians who considered themselves craftsmen refused improvisation—which would have seen them barred from their professional milieu—but nevertheless sought to distinguish themselves from the simple sheet readers of dance orchestras. Their sense of craft allowed them to maintain their self-respect while giving them a sense of social inclusion that jazz improvisation would have made impossible.

17. Georges Sadoul, "La chronique de George Sadoul," *Lettres françaises*, April 27, 1961, Cinémathèque Française, on-site press clippings database. http://www.cinematheque.fr/bibliotheque.html.

IV • PERFORMANCE

CHAPTER 11

SOCIAL AESTHETICS AND TRANSCULTURAL IMPROVISATION

Wayde Compton and the
Performance of Black Time

Winfried Siemerling

The presence and coexistence of deconstructive and antiessentialist impulses, exemplified by postmodern artistic practices, within contestatory strategies of reconstructed identity formation is a recurrent issue in postcolonial and critical race theory. I am interested here in the improvisational crossroads where different transcultural and migrant resources meet. Transposed into new contexts and often fragmented, how can sounds and signs fitted to the original circumstances of their making yield a new, socially mediated and historically rooted aesthetics elsewhere? After a brief introductory consideration of the contingencies that come with the displacement of diasporic sounds facilitated by recording technologies, I look at the work of Wayde Compton, a black British Columbian artist who makes context-specific use of musical improvisation and hip hop as a model for textual production and turntablism-mediated performance. In works such as *49th Parallel Psalm* (1999) and *Performance Bond* (2004), Compton relies on hip hop turning into transformative textual "lit hop" to articulate historical conditions, border crossings, and possible futures of black British Columbian diasporic subjectivity and performance.[1] But how does he achieve this effect by means of compositional techniques that in many cases seem to disperse cultural specificity? The very processes of sampling and postmodern citation that drive Compton's artistic practice, after all, have also been accused of betraying historical depth and the social relatedness of signs that undergo substantial transformation in improvisational performance and redeployment.

Improvisation, Sound Writing Technologies, and the Displacements of Diasporic Sound

Improvisation often proves to be an effective practice in the contact zones of diasporic and transnational cultures. Transcultural improvisation can adapt and appropriate existing archives, materials, and techniques and combine them through inventive sampling to produce new effects and solutions in a present defined by local circumstance. While such "dis-location" of erstwhile differently used ingredients is arguably the hallmark of invention generally, the increasing recirculation of entire entities and sequences of artistically or otherwise produced artifacts has also been considered a defining feature of postmodern intertextual and often parodic rearticulation of earlier materials (see, e.g., Hutcheon 1988). Employing a term from audiovisual culture in this respect, the cultural theorist and curator Nicolas Bourriaud (2005) speaks of "postproduction"—the manipulation of previously recorded material—as an increasingly relevant form of artistic practice.[2]

But to what extent do disc jockeying and other intertextually resourced forms of performance and improvisation convey or "eradicate" the earlier contexts of their presumably "raw" materials in this process of "dis-location" and recontextualization? Do they leave the social dimension connected to these contexts entirely behind? Do they elide, re-cognize, sublate, assimilate, or otherwise mediate them? And how does this question relate to the status of "the social" not only of the resources, but of the performance itself?[3] With reference to George Lewis's distinction between Afrological and Eurological perspectives on improvisation,[4] for instance, the musician and theorist Jesse Stewart (2010, 339) calls for more scholarship that brings into view "the culturally specific aspects of Afrological engagements with postmodernism." Stewart posits an "Afro-postmodernism" that "denotes the kind of fragmentation, plurality, and intertextuality normally associated with postmodernism, but locates these processes with the cultural matrix of the African diaspora wherein they often function in unique ways" (340). In particular, he suggests, they operate here "as strategies of identity formation that remember and honor the cultural past, while at the same time working to construct visions of a better future" (340–41). Stewart's reflections are particularly interesting here since they are made specifically with reference to DJing and turntablism and thus concern intertextual or intersonic practices of mixing and transforming mechanically transcribed "written sound" that often migrates across cultures and locations.

The availability of mechanical sound transcription with Edison's invention of the phonograph in 1877 contributed to the later dissemination and migration of blues, jazz, and, eventually, hip hop sounds. This development intensified dramatically, first with new transmission technologies from electromagnetic radiotelegraphy to television, and eventually again with digitization and its attendant possibilities of dissemination. In the words of Georgina Born (2005, 25), "If music notation and recording were the means by which musical ideas, and then sounds, became spatially mobile— released, or alienated, from both place and co-presence—then digital media have accelerated those processes." Mechanical sound writing thus opened the way for a secondary orality that was increasingly freed not only from limits of time and space, but also from communities based on face-to-face contact, a necessary local condition of oral cultures that distinguished them from print cultures (see Anderson 1983). The media following Edison's invention facilitated what Paul Gilroy (1993, 8) calls "translocal solidarities" that rely on mediated nodes of exchange or appropriation of past-produced resources and thus unsettle the time flows and circulation patterns of "traditional" rooted cultures. The channels of conveyance and circulation signified by the agrarian metaphors of "root" and "culture" are opened to the chance of trades in other traditions.

These openings, however, can seem a mixed blessing. George Lipsitz (1994, 4) suggests that, "like other forms of contemporary mass communication, popular music simultaneously undermines and reinforces our sense of place. Music that originally emerged from concrete historical experiences in places with clearly identifiable geographic boundaries now circulates as an interchangeable commodity marketed to consumers all over the globe." Yet while "consumption" may connote a certain passivity and absence of agency, it can also suggest a highly strategic and active practice of everyday life. This is also the case in certain styles and practices of musical consumption. Gilroy (1993, 105) thus argues that through performance in "black diaspora styles . . . the basic units of commercial consumption in which music is fast frozen and sold have been systematically subverted by the practice of racial politics." As he points out, such consumption as performance turns object into event. With reference to Michel de Certeau, Gilroy calls for "an enhanced understanding of 'consumption' that can illuminate its inner workings and the relationships between rootedness and displacement, locality and dissemination that lend them vitality in this countercultural setting"

(105). Indeed, for de Certeau (1988, xii–xiii) consumption channels agency "through its *ways of using* the products imposed by the dominant economic order." Of course, Bourriaud (2005, 13) highlights "a scrambling of boundaries between consumption and production" that is typical for postmodernism and notes that, "in our daily lives, the gap that separates production and consumption narrows each day" (33). But what interests de Certeau more specifically are "the tactics of consumption, the ingenious ways in which the weak make use of the strong" (de Certeau 1988, xvii, quoted in Gilroy 1993, 103).

Gilroy sees such tactics of consumption at work in the "montage" strategies that musical innovators such as Kool DJ Herc (a.k.a. Clive Campbell) operated by cutting and mixing available record tracks to produce what became hip hop. Such montage, however, and the transcultural and transnational migrations of hip hop and its commercialization, draw attention also to the relationships between what Gilroy (1993, 105) calls "rootedness and displacement, locality and dissemination." Commercialization is certainly part and parcel of a nonetheless socially and historically specific aesthetics of hip hop. As the sociologist Herman Gray puts it:

> Hip Hop is a commercial form fashioned from a specific confluence of social, cultural, and historical articulations that brought together different subjects, traditions, and narratives, recombining them so that they spoke to the specific local circumstances out of which they were fashioned. At the same time, as a popular commercial form, Hip Hop travels widely—across different social, geographic, media, and discursive spaces—adapting as it is adapted, recombining as it is itself recombined, to speak to local and specific conditions at the same time as it continues to signal identification and belonging to a global imagined community. (Gray 2003, 205)

Hip Hop in the Boondocks?

Wayde Compton is a black writer from Vancouver who often performs his poetry together with turntablists or improvising musicians and has done much to unearth the black British Columbian archive.[5] His use of hip hop as literary metaphor and performance practice to channel black British Columbian voices is a case in point. Compton has emphasized hip hop as one of the factors intervening in his usage of forms of black englishes: "For black writers in North America, these conditions constitute a new relationship to the old and treasured orality of our collective memory. While writers like

Langston Hughes and Amiri Baraka looked to blues and jazz as their sources for memory and form in both poetry and prose (blues and jazz were received as much live as they were from recordings), black writers today have hip hop as their musical concomitant, their living extension of orality" (Compton 2003b). Compton is aware that hip hop, like any form and medium, comes with its own historical and cultural weight and logic. The relationship "between rootedness and displacement" evoked by Gilroy and Gray is one of Compton's concerns when he reflects on the mediated nature of this orality in hip hop, and the mediation of place that determines some of the meanings of consuming, and performing, hip hop in British Columbia: "Ironically, it is a type of music that is never quite completely live, but is plugged into a vast media machine that extends into every home and every ear individually more than communally. In the small culturally isolated black communities of western Canada, this individualization is exacerbated" (Compton 2003b). In *Performance Bond*, he thus speaks of "hip hop / in the boondocks, / the relief package / drop zone. I echo New York back / like a code cracker. / Reality hacker" (Compton 2004, 108). Yet he will also claim (via Chuck D), "Hip Hop is black Canada's CNN [sic]. / Talk stops for no border cop" (102).

While Compton reflects critically on the mediated, transcultural, and potentially colonizing effects of hip hop "in the boondocks," he effectively consumes and practices hip hop in de Certeau's sense and in keeping with the claims to the style's adaptability to local circumstance. Compton employs hip hop as literary structural metaphor and practiced improvisational form. The result is a border-crossing and intermedial social and historical aesthetics that adapts a number of historical and symbolic "tracks" to make them answer to the needs of a black British Columbian here and now.

History as Present: Legba's Technological Tidalectics

Compton's remixing of borders and histories for local consumption is coded under the sign of Legba, the Voodoo trickster at the crossroads who controls traffic between humanity and the *loa* who preside here indeed over numerous other crossroads. Compton's text crosses the borders not only between the written and the spoken (black) word, music, and various other modes of conveyance, but also between the present and the past. Consider the opening poem of *49th Parallel Psalm*:

conductor, conductor,
this is over

ture. I sure
foot halfstep
to drums splayed for you. does rum

conduct electricity? drop a dram
on the ground to be grounded,
to be landed,
so we can dig the sound
of the switches and the channels.
Shango flows into the amp.
the tubes warm up.
the filaments erupt.

go fourth and multiply,
go north and fly
to each cardinal point,
and us just
the forth generation from slavery. (Compton 1999, 12)

The book opens under the sign of the "MC," here the first in a "cast" that
is introduced in the first section and that includes, among others, Sam, the
Voodoo loa of Baron Samedi; J. D., the initials of James Douglas, the first
governor of British Columbia; and, at the end, DJ, the disc jockey as modern-
day *griot*, Papa Labas or Legba at the crossroads.

The opening doubled invocation of a "conductor" replays and mixes musical and electronic references with historical tracks that point here to the
legacies of slavery, black disenfranchisement, and diaspora. The "conductor" as Underground Railroad guide across borders and to freedom of oppression takes on multiple references and overtones, first in musical terms as
a kind of orchestral DJ, and then in electronic terms as a channeling device.

These doublings of the first line are replayed and complicated by the line
break, with its remix of the word "overture." In terms of doubled content,
the break signals historical pastness (e.g., of the Underground Railroad and
the following history of black British Columbia) *together with*, or as a form
of, a new beginning, as "over" becomes "overture": musical and historical
opening, but also "overture" as "proposal," a meaning that also links the past
of "over" to future possibilities.

The line break links also with some of Compton's acknowledged inspira-
tions—for instance, Black Mountain–influenced Vancouver TISH poetics[6]
along with Edward Kamau Brathwaite's poetic trilogy *The Arrivants* (see

Compton 2003a, 492–97) and his concept of "tidalectis," with its emphasis on repetition. In the introduction to his anthology *Bluesprint,* Compton describes the larger emphasis on repetition in tidalectics as

> an Africanist model for thinking about history. . . . In contrast to Hegel's *dialectics* . . . *tidalectics* describes a way of seeing history as a palimpsest, where generations overlap generations, and eras wash over eras like a tide on a stretch of beach. . . . Repetition, whether in the form of ancestor worship or the poem-histories of the *griot,* informs black ontologies more than does the Europeanist drive for perpetual innovation, with its concomitant disavowals of the past. In a European framework, the past is something to be gotten over, something to be improved upon; in tidalectics, we do not *improve upon* the past, but are ourselves *versions* of the past. (Compton 2001, 17)

Commenting again on Brathwaite's tidalectics in a discussion of the connection between poetry and hip hop turntablism, Compton applies similar ideas of repetition and variation to small-scale decisions of utterance and rearticulation in black and electronic orality (here especially through remixing): "I think he means that each person, each beat, each stage of culture is a version of the last one, and is not a progressive disjuncture. If this is the case, then the orality of temporally and spatially removed Africa can also be this new electronic orality. The idea is not to break, or even to preserve, but to repeat; and to celebrate repetition, knowing that you will mis-duplicate—and that the mis-duplications are the closest achievable thing to an actual you" (Compton 2003b). This sense of connection and repetition also plays out, on a smaller scale, in the sound repetitions and connections that modulate meanings and overlays as "MC" continues its remixing of historical tracks, personal identity, electronic circuitry, and Voodoo mythologies. From the narrator's *dance* we come to *drums,* associated with the Voodoo loa Shango, and then—guided again by the sound pattern—to a *dram* of *rum,* often associated with Baron Samedi, the loa of death but also of sex and resurrection (and the subject of the following poem). The poem first inquires about rum as a "conductor" in its various senses (material, spiritual, historical), then recommends a small sacrifice of it—or feeding of the loa—"to be grounded / to be landed" as immigrant in this enabling tidalectic mixing of Voodoo mythology, black history, and electronics. This circuitry continues as Shango, the loa associated with thunder and hence the African resistance to enslavement, as well as with drums and music, dance and art, is amplified by the old-school heat-radiating conducting technology of tubes and filaments. The remix, here, is clearly part of a historical and social aesthetics, replaying and mis-duplicating in the next lines Noah's post-deluge command "go forth and multiply"—also urban slang for "get lost"—as the misspelling doubled double "go fourth and multiply" to signify finally the direct connection ("go north . . . and us / just the forth generation from slavery") between the speaker's here and now with slavery-fleeing earlier generations of the black diaspora moving north into Canada.

At the Border of History and the Present:
Legba's Turntables, James Douglas, and the DJ

The enabling figure of Legba is omnipresent in Compton's improvisational tidalectics. As Voodoo trickster at the crossroads, he is here also the gate-keeper at the border. He appears later in "MC" and then again in two poems connected as inverted doubles by their titles, "JD" and "DJ." The first title evokes James Douglas, the mixed-race first governor of British Columbia, who invited a founding group of blacks from San Francisco to cross the bor-der into his province in 1858. The inversion of his initials as the title of a poem a few pages later, "DJ," relates him to the manipulator of tracks and hip hop. The time-crossing remix of the two signals, or what Compton calls "the temporal conflation of past, present and future (synchronic narrative)" that he associates with Voodoo syncretism (Compton 2003a, 484), channels again a historical and social aesthetics through tidalectic Voodoo poetics and electronic media. Compton's James Douglas, apostrophized as "our own quadroon Moses," is a Legba at the crossroads:

> you held the keys
> like a lesser Legba—laughing, shuffling passports,
> passing
> in your black and white
> archival stance. (Compton 1999, 18)

Chains of alliteration and assonance tidalectically replay and remix here again sounds that lead from a "lesser Legba" to "laughing" and "shuffling" (and thus, card playing and chance), and from "passports" to James Doug-las's own "passing" and mixed race. This "black and white" is then remixed as the signifier of print and of the vagaries of historiography and the writ-ten archive.

The later, doubling poem "DJ" calls on "Papa Labas / [to] open the doors /

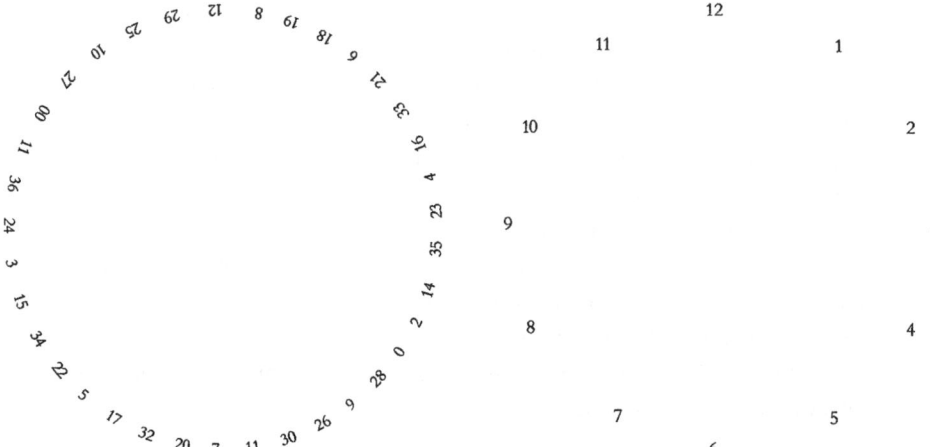

Fig. 11.1 Reprinted from *49th Parallel Psalm* by Wayde Compton (Arsenal Pulp Press, 1999) with permission of the publisher.

straddle the roles," after invoking the DJ as the conductor at the crossroads of contemporary narratives, secondary orality, and knowledge:

a hand on the texts and tomes
the keeper
spins limbs
the griot
holds in his collection the keys to corporeal
wisdom
this body of texts
these twelve-inch tables of counterclockwiseness. . .
more singles in the crates than scrolls in the ancient library
of Alexandria. (Compton 1999, 25)

Compton's *49th Parallel Psalm* closes with the section "Hear," a counterpart in the present to the earlier "Their" and equally predicated on the oral. The very last poem is "49th Parallel Psalm," which invokes again the DJ with two "parallel" circles inserted after the line, "living on the weals of steal" (see figure 11.1). Concrete poetry here remixes the wheels of steel—or turntables—themselves as the conjunction of time and chance, with a DJ Legba controlling the crossfader between the two "reinventing wheels."

The clock of the right circle is doubled by a wheel of an American roulette on the left (which, in contrast to the single-zero French wheel, uses both 0 and 00 for the bank, increasing its statistical advantage). Compton makes a few substitutions: number 1, the sign of beginning, has been replaced by two numbers 11: a doubled double. One of these takes up the place of the numbers 1 and 13, with the latter thus also missing, as is its inversion, 31. Note that in roulette, the croupier or dealer spins the wheel and the ball in opposite directions, like the DJ when scratching the "twelve-inch tables of counterclockwiseness" (Compton 1999, 25).

Turntablism thus becomes the sign and medium of the DJ Legba and of tidalectics: two circles doubling, mixing time at the crossroads between past and present, turning horizontal progression and dialectics into vertical repetition and counter-clockwiseness. The remixing of the tracks of history and time thus envision the past as accessible resource of the present, suggesting agency and another chance.

Vèvè

Compton includes a performance of turntablism and MCing on a CD that is part of *Performance Bond*. Significantly titled "The Reinventing Wheel," it offers examples of a secondary orality as remix of history, opening up to crossroads of past and future at the faultlines and interstices of its re-iteration.[7] As one line states, "The rupture is the inscription, the brokenness the tradition" (Compton 2004,103). The corresponding printed section precedes directly the section "Rune" on Vancouver's former black neighborhood, Hogan's Alley, which was erased by urban planning and a road viaduct around 1970. One of the first poems here, "Vèvè," articulates in other ways the interventionist tidalectics of "The Reinventing Wheel."

"Vèvè" is the sign in Voodoo that *invokes* Legba as the master of the crossroads, and the poem with this title is followed, toward the end of *Performance Bond*, by further historical remixes and border crossings. We find here, for instance, a photo essay that reenvisions doors under the signs of a reinvented black community, such as a "Coloured Benevolent Society," a Muslim temple, a black newspaper, and the "Pacific Negro Working Men's Association." Another remix supplements oral histories with black Vancouver residents, originally recorded by Daphne Marlatt and Carole Itter (1979) and reprinted in Compton's *Bluesprint*, with two further oral testimonies attributed to a fictive volume, *Portals: East Vancouver Oral Histories* (1972).[8] These invocations are thus prefaced by Compton's "Vèvè" itself, a dialogue that takes place on a bench "beside the Georgia Viaduct," the former site of Hogan's Alley. Two characters whose names reference modes of recording and conveyance, Digital and Analogue, discuss Brathwaite's poem equally entitled "Vèvè," and his evocation of Legba at the end of *The Arrivants*. Brathwaite here evokes Legba's sign as the ground of writing, albeit a broken one.[9]

When Analogue uses his trail mix snack food to pour a version of Legba's "Vèvè" on the broken ground of Hogan's Alley, it is eaten up by pigeons, an evanescence that prompts Digital to inquire about more permanent materials such as ink. A coyote—another incarnation of the trickster—walking by unnoticed (Compton 2004, 120), however, signals the efficacy of the Vèvè, despite its subsequent erasure. Analogue later suggests that "maybe an ephemeral language that can drift away in the wind or be eaten by birds would be able to say things we can't think of" (121). The writing of the Vèvè is ephemeral, a performance and evocation in real time, yet the vanishing result of this writing performance—if the passing coyote is any indication—has the power to invoke Legba. Analogue remarks, "It's more than language, it's sorcery or worship. It's a portal between worlds," adding later, "I don't think it's quite right to call it writing. I think what Brathwaite means is that it's the *beginning* of writing or the urge to make a new kind of language, one unique to the New World" (118–19).

It is no coincidence that Brathwaite's poem appears at the very end of a trilogy, in a section called "Beginning," just as Compton's "Vèvè" comes in the last section as preface to his remixed "portals" of Hogan's Alley. This Vèvè is thus a preface at the end that invokes Legba to grant the remix of history, passage at the border, and conveyance to the loa. The performance of writing the sign—and Compton's section title can be seen as both descriptive and performative—is a conjuring that invokes a new language with transforming powers, crossing borders from a past that elides black histories into a new history and future mediated by acts of tidalectic writing.

While the signs and materials of this performance and social aesthetics belong to diasporic archives and displacements—Voodoo, Caribbean (Bajan) exilic writing, hip hop—they are adopted and adapted here to speak to the (re-)rooting of a dispersed local history and culture. The history and culture of black British Columbia is tidalectically re/cognized by Compton's lit-hop portals. Compton's texts and performances not only cross geographical borders of the African diaspora but also reconfigure possibilities of memory that include black diasporic experience and the remixing of history and storytelling with the performative power of invocations.

Compton's sampling of resources is in many respects improvisational, but at the same time it follows certain scripts that are not indeterminate with respect to their social contexts. The terms "transcultural" and "hybrid" have to be used with a certain caution, in this respect, to speak of the encounters in historical and geographical "contact zones" orchestrated in *49th Parallel Psalm* and *Performance Bond*. The term "transculturation," originally developed by the Cuban sociologist and ethnomusicologist Fernando Ortiz in the study of Cuban culture, was used by Mary Louise Pratt in its entry into Anglophone literary studies in 1992 to denote critical selection and appropriation by subaltern social actors in the "contact zone" for contestatory or survival purposes. (The term also entered other literary fields, as well as psychology, health care, and management studies.) In many of its subsequent migratory incarnations, however, the term has tended to signify a kind of hybridity that often elides cultural specificity.

But Compton's improvisation and consumption of hip hop are circumscribed by socially identifiable tactics that offer an aesthetic that, I would argue, remains dialogic—or what he calls tidalectic—rather than dialectic. The performative moment of the circulation of the signs and relocation of archives and contexts—the moment of transcultural encounter facilitated by sound-writing technologies—does not efface their singular particularities. Compton's choices at the crossfader that connect his resources are improvisational, perhaps not so much in the real time of a sound performance as in their decisions, which are often led by the sound qualities of the signifier in the real time of writing and composition. These moments of improvisation bind the signs together, however, to make their social particularity more striking, not to subsume them under the hybrid logic of their circulation.

Notes

1. Compton also recuperates black British Columbian writing in his anthology *Bluesprint* (2001) and records oral history as a member of the Hogan's Alley Memorial Project, which is dedicated to preserving the memory of a black neighborhood in Vancouver that was erased by urban planning.

2. For Bourriaud (2005, 29), "emblematic figures" in this context are not only the DJ but also the programmer, producers of the "emergence of a new cultural configuration" that seems to answer to the demands of Guy Debord's situationist "Methods of Detournement" (1981; originally published in 1956). Debord demanded that the "literary and artistic heritage of humanity should be used for partisan propaganda purposes. . . . Any elements, no matter where they are taken from, can serve in making new combinations" (quoted in Bourriaud 2005, 29).

3. In this respect, Bourriaud's *Postproduction* (2005) rearticulates aspects of a postmodern aesthetics that emphasizes the active role of the audience and inter-

action to the point of blurring the line of producing and consuming art. Yet the "cultural" itself is marginalized here to the extent of its disappearance: any aesthetics of the transcultural one might find here seems socially fairly indeterminate. While his aesthetics of the "encounter" puts a premium on sociability, the social dimensions mediated in this "contact zone" (to use Pratt's phrase from 1991) point mainly in the direction of de-scripting and defamiliarization.

4. Lewis (1996) critiques John Cage's elision of jazz in his statements about experimental music, which emphasize spontaneity, uniqueness, indeterminacy, and "chance operations" but at the same time dismiss jazz. Jazz improvisation, however—and certainly the bebop innovators who changed U.S. music a few years before Cage made his comments about jazz—can lay claim to the central notions adduced by Cage. As part of his critique, Lewis (1996) also makes it clear that for "African-American improvisers . . . sonic symbolism is often constructed with a view toward social instrumentality as well as form." Any elision of social specificity thus would radically underdetermine such forms of improvisation. Or, as Walter Muyumba (2009, 18) puts it, "Studying how musicians communicate in jazz performance is a way of developing a more cultural music theory and a more musical culture theory."

5. For an example of a performance by Wayde Compton (with Nick Storring), see http://www.youtube.com/watch?v=4MuUirGB2Oo. Compton's collections of poetry are *49th Parallel Psalm* (1999) and *Performance Bond* (2004). He has edited the groundbreaking anthology *Bluesprint* (2001) and further commented on this corpus and his own work in *After Canaan* (2010).

6. The TISH poets—identified with the Vancouver TISH poetry newsletter launched in 1961—include Geroge Bowering, Frank Davey, Daphne Marlatt, and Fred Wah. Their influences include the Black Mountain poets Robert Creely, Robertt Duncan, and Charles Olsen.

7. See also the sound sample in Compton, "The Reinventing Wheel," http://www.horizonzero.ca/flashsite/issue8/issue8.html?lang=en&section=compton.

8. Incidentally, 1972 is Compton's year of birth.

9. "So on this ground, / write; / within the sound / of this white limestone *vèvè*, . . . / talk / of the empty roads, / vessels of your head, / claypots, shards, ruins. . . . / the Word becomes / again a god and walks among us / look, here are his rags, / here is his crutch and his satchel / of dreams; here is his hoe and his rude implements . . . / on this ground / on this broken ground" (Brathwaite 1973, 265–66).

CHAPTER 12

DEVICES OF EXISTENCE

Contact Improvisation, Mobile Performances, and Dancing through Twitter

Susan Kozel

"Devices of existence" are the mechanisms, movements, and media of life (Bourriaud 2002, 103). The expression is borrowed from Nicolas Bourriaud's writing on relational aesthetics, but in this chapter on dance improvisation and social aesthetics, the word "device" takes on several meanings that extend beyond Bourriaud. It is used as both a noun and a verb: improvisation is frequently a tool for *devising* a performance; the literal and metaphorical *devices of life* become either content or context within dance; and our *media devices* (mobile phones, computers) become vehicles for the presentation or creation of movement. Bourriaud acts as a starting point for these reflections, but his formulation of relationality is not necessarily social; nor is it particularly embodied. Jacques Rancière's (2009a) writing on aesthetics takes us further along the path toward a sensory approach to social aesthetics, and finally, the play of improvisation and intercorporeality in two unconventional dance events is addressed by a reading of Jacques Derrida's (2005) role for the anesthetic within the aesthetic, the insensible within the sensible. Rancière's framing of aesthetics as a reconfiguration of forms of perception combined with Derrida's thoughts on the anesthetic yield a way to account for the less immediate, less celebrated qualities of social aesthetic experience, such as anticipation, delay, and uncertainty, as well as the disintegration and reconstruction of memory.

Two dance events will be considered: *Small Acts* (2010) by the choreographer Ben Wright, performed at the Skånes Dansteater in Malmö, Sweden, and the IntuiTweet project (2009–2010) by Mia Keinänen, Susan Kozel, and Leena Rouhiainen occurring in the networked digital space of Twitter and Short Message Texting (SMS). My perspective on these improvisations comes from different phenomenological positions: with *Small Acts* I was a member of the audience, and with IntuiTweet I was one of the dance artists.[1] *Small Acts*, a dance performance with multiple choreographic layers, generates reflections on the transformation of relations between performer and audience, distributing and recombining the dance so that those who watch also contribute their own improvised movements to it. IntuiTweet used Twitter as the media/medium for improvisational exchanges and asked whether bodily intuition could exist within social networking. This project yielded unexpected insight into the variations of touch across distance, making it an unusual example of contact improvisation: the contact between dancers was palpable but asynchronous and dislocated. Dancers were not located in the same place or time, and movement was mediated not just by technology but by words. Motion was transferred through text messages.

This chapter enacts three theoretical shifts. The first is to consider social aesthetics not through improvisation in general, but through contact improvisation in dance. The second is to refigure contact improvisation—frequently viewed in terms of a somewhat athletic practice of leaps, supports, inversions, and falls—into a practice based on touch: touch between audience members and performers and touch between dancers through mobile technologies. The third shift is to see touch according to a phenomenological experience of contact; as something that is ceaselessly interrupted. Contact implicitly becomes "con-tact," with a hiatus in the middle of it that makes a dynamic slippage integral to the sense of touch (Derrida 2005, 229). These shifts will provide an opening for relational aesthetics to be applied to dance events and expand the notion of contact improvisation so that it might be useful for other art forms. Further, the improvisation practices illuminated in the two dance events can be seen as models for social interaction in a more general sense, the creation or re-creation of bonds between people giving rise to "new modes of confrontation or participation" (Rancière 2009a, 21).

The Intimate Bedlam of *Small Acts*

Small Acts was a performance that invited audience members to travel through all areas of the Skånes Dansteatre building in the Western Harbor district of Malmö to discover the movement of the dancers.[2] The mobility and the improvisation of this piece will be read through the actions not of the dancers but of the audience members. The notion of audience generally applied to theater and dance events implies containment and singularity (we refer to "an" audience, and it tends to be planted in numbered seats facing forward) that are not appropriate to the mobile, fluctuating group of people who visited *Small Acts*. This dance event did not occur in a theatrical space as much as it transformed the working parts of a theater into an array of public spaces; as such, we were less like audience members than like members of the public. With the assistance of maps, we journeyed through the innards of the building. We walked the backstage corridors, crowded into the workshops and wardrobe, ventured into rehearsal studios, and noticed small meeting rooms silently waiting to be animated by bodies. The only space we skirted was the black box theater itself; it remained quiet and dark.

We peered over others' shoulders to see dancers performing steps that navigated qualities between the lightness of studio movement and the weight of street movement. The dancers wore a jumbled array of outdoor clothing and shoes, exuding a sense of delight at being part of the intimate bedlam of dancing around and among 250 peripatetic members of the public. Rooms and passages of opaque plastic, illuminated by fluorescent bar lights along the floor, were built within rehearsal studios and workshops. These structures became important filtering devices as both dancers and public entered and exited like fluid pouring into and out of containers. The category of relational art is not applied as readily to dance as to other practices that stem from the visual and sculptural domains, but the dynamic and ephemeral qualities of dance, when combined with experimentation in conventions of viewing and use of space such as that which occurred with this piece, invite aesthetic formulations of relationality. *Small Acts* constructed "undecided situations" for the audience members, producing "a displacement of perception, a passage from status of spectator to that of actor, and a reconfiguration of places" (Rancière 2009a, 23–24).

Frequently it was impossible to find a place inside these crowded little rooms, and the movement had to be witnessed from outside. Watching the silhouettes of people and listening to their shuffling and breathing, it was possible to infer or imagine what might be happening inside the rooms. The process of finding the dance became a bit of a scavenger hunt: following other audience members, pursuing a dancer who dashed from one location to another down corridors or up stairs, or deciding to walk against the flow along a seemingly deserted hallway. This was a highly social event not just because of the feeling of being in a slightly chaotic and crowded public space while trying to view a performance, but because the rhythm of the experience was measured differently from more formal choreography. The improvisation of the dancers seemed to occur in between choreographic sequences and was shaped by members of the public simply by virtue of our being present and obstructing the paths of the dancers in our attempts to see what was happening. On a subtler level, the rhythm of the improvisation was affected by attempts on the part of the public to anticipate where the movement might go next. It is possible to say that anticipation is one of the modes of improvisation—in this case, anticipation on the part of the audience members, not just the performers. The state of anticipation is ambiguous. It cannot be pinned to specific senses but is powerfully affective and is crucial for dance improvisation. It is like an inhalation of breath, a moment of suspension that is not beyond the senses but is not tied explicitly to them, either. It is an enhanced state of receptivity, a breathing space where anticipation opens onto imagination and is tinged with memory.

Up to a point, Bourriaud's (2002, 18) formulation of relational aesthetics is helpful in understanding the improvisation of the audience members in *Small Acts*—for example, relational art "is a state of encounter" rather than an object as such. With *Small Acts*, it is clear that my movements through the rooms and corridors, in concert with that of other members of the public and the dancers, were the very fabric of the aesthetic experience. This piece came to being through public interaction—or improvisation—between the dancers and the public. The choreography was not a pattern of movement that could exist on its own; without those who participated as audience members it would not exist. Bourriaud continues to shed light on the experience, for it is true that the scope of the piece was more than just an encounter among people. It encompassed human interactions and a particular social context rather than a private symbolic space (14). The cultural symbolic space of the theater was inverted so that the public spaces within the theater building became private or closed off, and the normally private spaces were opened to performance. Yet if we read him more closely, it is evident that Bourriaud's focus remains largely with the art object: it may be rendered transitive, dynamic, dialogic, open-ended, and multiple, but relationality remains a structural response to an artistic ancien régime of generating static and contained artwork. "Transitivity," he writes, "is as old as the hills. It is a tangible property of the artwork. Without it, the work is nothing other than a dead object, crushed by contemplation" (26). Transitivity is the "formal disorder which is inherent to dialogue" mapped onto an object. Even his evocative explanation of form as "a lasting encounter" or a "principle of dynamic agglutination" takes its perspective from the object rather than squarely from the social, let alone from the corporeal (19–21). For him, art invents new relations "to the body" or "to the 'mysteries' of life and death," as if art and body were objects juxtaposed, rather than art's being inseparable from the experience of bodies (92).

Obviously, this is a phenomenologist's critique of Bourriaud: I cannot help but experience the world through my body. And it is equally a dancer's critique: my knowledge is corporeal, and there can be no real distinction between the sensible and the intelligible, even though they may coexist unevenly. Still, it is not desirable to dismiss Bourriaud too quickly, for he excels at the poetic encapsulation, if not at its elaboration. When he writes, "By creating and staging devices of existence including working methods and ways of being, instead of concrete objects which hitherto bounded the realm of art, the artists use time as a material" (Bourriaud 2002, 103), he provides a rough outline of a dynamic aesthetic ontology. Without heading off on too much of a tangent at this point, it is important to point out that the approach to aesthetics in this chapter is ontological, accessed by means of a variation on phenomenology. This is to say that these reflections are not concerned with formal structures of the work or its meaning as much as they reveal the dynamic ebb and flow of states of encounter of all the participants, where everyone is, in some sense, a performer. This dynamic ontology is brought to life by experimental work such as *Small Acts* and IntuiTweet.

Small Acts invited shifts in perception regarding what was expected from a dance and who was defined as a dancer. This experience was as much about glimpses of dance, and traces of dance, as it was about actually seeing dance in a standard performative mode, where sight lines are clear and movement is constructed to face forward toward a bank of seats. I arrived at a room just as the audience and dancers left, and for a moment felt I was mis-timing my choices of where to go and whom to follow. The action seemed to be eluding me. I turned the corner of a plastic-walled room just as the last person had scurried out of it in search of further dance, and my internal narratives and expectations washed over me. I am not doing this properly, I thought. I am missing something in another room. Which room? I did not know. The dance over there might be more interesting than the non-dance here. I experienced a strange numbness because I did not know how to respond to what I was sensing; then a sudden, unexpected shift in perception made the heat and residual vibrations of movement evident. I began to sense the space: dance happened here a moment ago. It was palpable, and I found myself imagining what I had just missed. In this moment my aesthetic experience coincided with Rancière's (2009a, 14) reformulation of aesthetics as a way to identify art when the border between art and not art is increasingly challenged *and*, more important, as a "redistribution of the relations between the forms of sensory experience." In other words, dance that embraces what might be called "non-dance" is art both because of its experiments with aesthetic convention and because of the impact it has on the performers and audience: it scrambles our sensory perception.[3] What seems at first like chaos or one's expectations being cruelly thwarted ("Why can I never really see what the dancers are doing?") are actually alternative orderings of senses and meaning. "Aesthetics," he writes, "is the thought of the new disorder" (13). *Small Acts* offered a glimpse into this disorder: experience of the dancers was mediated by my having to navigate cramped spaces and unexpected breaks in movement (dancers leaving the space); further, concrete sense perception (what I actually saw) collided with memory and imagination (what I thought I saw, what I might see). I did not see the dance directly, but I heard it; I sensed it kinesthetically; I anticipated, recalled, or imagined it, all while it was happening. Further, this "new disorder" of relational aesthetics is not a solitary experience. The ways we navigated, perceived, anticipated, and recollected a performance were reconfigured across multiple bodies.

Finding myself in a room recently vacated by the *Small Acts* dancers and by the cohort of audience members who had managed to squeeze in, the decision became one of staying where I was, in this room still resonating with movement, or going somewhere else to find more dance. The dance outside the room became increasingly compelling because I did not know where or what it was or which combination of dancers might reconfigure. The decision to stay where I was and to absorb the no-longer-there-yet-still-palpable dance was a crucial moment, because the dance was very much present, but differently. In the space, like a ripple on my skin, I remembered the movement I had just seen and reconstructed what I had just missed with both my memory and my imagination. I was already inventing the story of the dance that had just happened. In this way, I contributed to the aesthetic construction in which I was participating. The many disappearances of dance I experienced with *Small Acts*, either because the choreography dissolved around me and dancers left the space one by one or because I chose to abandon a room with ongoing dance, were like breaks in the moments of contact, fissures in the immediacy of the experience.

A subtler interpretation of the roles played by anticipation and recollection in this sort of distributed performance is based on the acknowledgment that one is always missing some part of the dance, that one has an awareness of what is not present. There is an absence of dance within the dance, and the sense of confusion or numbness I encountered before a burst of new sensation can be illuminated (or, some might say, rendered more confusing) by considering Derrida's role for the "anesthetic" within aesthetic experience.[4] Derrida (2005, 229) presents a phenomenological point of view, which is to say that he attempts to understand contact not just abstractly but based on an actual moment of contact or the lived experience of touch. What is revealed is that contact is suspended *in the middle of* the moment of contact; thus, an "anesthetic interruption" is embedded in the experience of contact.[5] This explains why he prefers to split the word "contact" with a hyphen, making it "con-tact." He writes that it is impossible to have contact *and* a sense (or understanding) of contact at the same time, but that we constantly slide between the two; taken from the perspective of improvisation, it is possible to say that moments of "non-contact" that confuse the senses and seem to be outside the fluidity of aesthetic experience are all part of the experience of contact.

The ripples of touch, of contact and losing contact, are rhythmic because they occur in syncopation. They occur across intervals. "Such haptical (or aesthetic in general) *différence*, which is interruption, interposition, detour of the between *in the middle* of contact, could analogically open onto what [Jean-Luc] Nancy calls a 'syncope' or what [Jean] Chrétien terms *interval*, the 'intervallic character of touch itself'" (Derrida 2005, 229). This rhythmic alternation between touch and not touching, contact and losing contact, resonates with Rancière's assertion that aesthetics is the reconfiguration of the relations among forms of sensory experience. When senses are reconfigured, they slip in and out of familiar patterns. Derrida goes on to say that there is a necessity of "insensibility within sensibility," as if the absence of sense is essential to sense. This addresses a basic but important motivation for aesthetic innovation—and, indeed, improvisation—which is that if we want to escape rigid habits that control what we see and how we move, we need to be interrupted by difference. That which is different can at first seem to be anesthetic, or nothing (229). The anesthetic or the insensible is not a deadening or an absence of sense—or, at least, not for long. It can be construed as that which is outside immediate experience, on its margins in the form of memory, anticipation, or confusion. Or it can be that which is simply not yet understood or comprehended, such as new artistic practices.

A duet between the dancers Graham Adey and Sam Denton took place in a small patch of a large studio on a layer of shredded black plastic that looked like feathers or ashes. I found myself gratefully absorbing the movement of other bodies; receiving the movement felt like being stroked. Not just how I perceived art but how I received it became relevant. By this point in the performance, I had shifted to a far more expansive and receptive mode, less goal-directed. Perception is so frequently construed as outwardly focused and evaluative, while reception involves the permission to let something in or to be lured into it. There is a difference between being drawn into a movement exchange or being kept at a remove from the internal workings of a choreography and left to admire from the outside. It must be said that there is nothing wrong with the aesthetics of virtuosity and externality, and at times this is exactly what we desire from an artistic event, but *Small Acts* fostered a version of social aesthetics that is valuable for being inclusive, for stimulating thought and community. As an aesthetic experience it provided a moment of living in the world differently and, perhaps, with more openness and delight. The suggestion that watching dance can be like being stroked or absorbing the movement of another into the fabric of one's being implies that as a member of the audience I was not just in an improvisatory relationship with the performers (whereby they moved and I moved) but that the improvisation was based on contact. Touch, as metaphor and concrete experience, was the aesthetic foundation of this experience.

This is a good point to transition to a discussion of IntuiTweet, which was in part about offering one's movement to another so that it could be embodied and owned by someone else before being released again. These two projects are variations on a theme of con-tact.

The Distributed Improvisation of IntuiTweet

IntuiTweet (2009–2010) occurs at a point of overlap between social aesthetics and social media. It was an experiment in improvisation initiated by three dancer-researchers (Mia Keinänen, Leena Rouhiainen, and me) in which we filtered moments of movement intuition through the medium of Twitter, the immensely popular social networking platform, so that they could be exchanged and transformed.[6] Before describing the details of the project, it is helpful to locate it in a broader cultural and intellectual context. IntuiTweet is part of a particular trend within digitally mediated aesthetics: artistic projects that transform modes of presentation and perception. Implied by such a transformation is "a break with the hierarchical order that determined which subjects and forms of expression were deemed worthy of inclusion in the domain of a given art" (Rancière 2009a, 10). At stake, Rancière elaborates, is not just art but also "the ways in which our world is given to perceiving itself" and the way "powers that be assert their legitimacy" (15). This is what he refers to as the regime of art: a broad compilation of politics, intelligibility, and sensibility.

The hierarchical order, to use Rancière's expression, did not manifest itself as hesitation on the part of dancers or the art world to embrace technology. Significant numbers of dancers, choreographers, programmers, and funding bodies in many countries create and support collaborative interdisciplinary work using a range of digital technologies. Twitter has been famously lambasted for being superficial, trivial, and, despite its undisputed place as a widespread social phenomenon, an enabler of people's basest desires. It is regularly used as a trope in other cultural forms, such as journalism and television programming (from comedy to drama), to indicate dumbing down and sacrificing integrity.[7] Oddly, a strong current determining what was legitimate or acceptable behavior came not from the art world but from the attitudes, codes, and conventions surrounding the use of Twitter in general. The mechanisms for conformity emerging from within the Twitter community itself constrained its creative range as much as externally imposed attitudes. In effect, the hierarchical order came from within. Despite its crowd-sourced, decentralized, and do-it-yourself principles, there is a form of Twitter etiquette that dominates (for better and for worse) its use. According to several Twitter etiquette sites, Twitter should continue to be about answering the simple question, "What are you doing?" or, in its current version, "What's happening?"[8] As one article states, "All tweets are prompted by the question 'What are you doing?' Many people don't answer the question, and others are religious about it. Does it irritate people if you don't answer the question? Sometimes. Should those people take a deep breath? Possibly."[9] Of course, social networking needs to be insulated as much as possible from insulting, threatening, and abusive behavior, but other, softer directives for appropriate conduct coincide with Rancière's concern over hierarchical orders that define expression and how a community perceives itself.[10] The shift initiated by IntuiTweet was to use Twitter not just to report what we were doing but also to explore what we were sensing or intuiting and how we were moving. This expressive mode exists in a gray zone, for Twitter etiquette tends to steer its users away from tweeting their personal states: "Your weirdly honest confession terrifies me" and "Don't just post about you, you, you. Not only is this directly against what Twitter is all about, it will get you ignored quickly."[11] Tweets are supposed to be about what you are doing, but only within a narrow band of acceptable actions and emotions; also, a lot of "re-tweeting" is expected. Further, there have been instances of vocal segments of the Twitter community being particularly condemnatory of women posting about their bodies. There were loud objections to the blogger Meghan McCain posting of a photo that revealed her cleavage ("Fellow Tweeters bullied her for showing off her bust line"[12]), and other direct and politically controversial articulations of women's bodily experiences, which would have been acceptable in other media, were loudly condemned. In 2009, Penelope Trunk was "excoriated" for tweeting about having a miscarriage while sitting in a business meeting,[13] and a year later, Angie Johnson was lambasted for chronicling how an abortion felt physically and emotionally.[14] While the content of Trunk's and Johnson's tweets is more explicit and politically sensitive than the tweets we exchanged, both women's use of social networking coincides with the phenomenological approach adopted by IntuiTweet. Collectively, these body tweets exist on a spectrum of corporeal reflection, from visceral and intimate to kinesthetic and poetic. It can be argued that, by taking a phenomenological turn and using Twitter to express and exchange what we were sensing or intuiting and how we were moving, at any given moment we were actually answering a combination of the core Twitter questions, "What is happening?" and "What are you doing?"

So what, exactly, was IntuiTweet? It took place in specifically determined improvisation periods, usually between seven and ten days. There were a limited number of primary participants (Keinänen, Rouhiainen, and me, plus up to three invited guests) and an unlimited number of followers through Twitter. With the exception of one improvisation, when we were together in Helsinki, the improvisations occurred across several countries and time zones (Russia, Finland, Norway, Denmark, France, and the United States). Our instructions were simple: we were tasked with noticing moments of movement sensation or movement *intuition* throughout our day, no matter where we found ourselves. No one really knows exactly what movement intuition is; this task was to contribute to exploring and understanding it. We translated what we noticed into a tweet of no more than 140 characters and sent it to the others using Twitter's SMS function.[15] When a tweet was received as a text message, the instructions were to improvise the movement we received, but how or when we improvised was open. We could immediately respond as though we had received an actual movement impulse—and it frequently felt like this—or we could hold on to the moment of movement and improvise a response later in the day or the next day, once we were in a different place. The other alternative was to improvise subtly, through imagination or by means of somatic response. In other words, we could enact a shift in body state rather than a repositioning of our limbs in time and space. Once this response was generated, we recoded it into a tweet and sent it off once again to join the flurry of movement messages between us. This was a crucial part of the improvisation and created an on-going movement dialogue between us. A rolling, asynchronous ebb and flow of dynamic and kinesthetic exchanges was created by converging dance improvisation and social networking.

The instructions were quite playful and game-like. For this reason, the project falls into the domain of rule-based dance improvisation at the same time that it satisfies Bourriaud's (2002, 103) criteria for relational art in that "the production of gestures wins out over the production of material things," emphasizing "the production of movement over categories." In contemporary dance history, the approaches of Yvonne Rainer and Trisha Brown, from Judson Church in the 1960s and 1970s, come to mind; there, dancers were asked to eschew technique and perform tasks such as moving awkward bed mattresses, walking, standing or speaking, and moving in repeated loops (Banes 1987). Dancers were also combined with non-dancers in happening-style events that were radical because the accepted constructions of both the dance and the dancer were questioned. Contact improvisation, which emerged out of the same era, involved sensing shifts of weight in oneself and others and reacting to the received impulses by listening to how one's body responded, then letting the movement ripple outward to influence the other bodies in the space. If we call attention to the game-like structure of Intui-Tweet, there is a distinct convergence with the ever expanding fields of game studies and game design, as well as with experiments in locative media that frequently use mobile phones' global positioning system (GPS) functions for participants to search for or create narratives. Further related cultural phenomena are the open-ended art practices of artists such as Miranda July that invite participants to follow instructions to create quirky objects or liminal experiences.[16]

Rancière's (2009a, 22) argument that relational aesthetics are characterized by "displacement and despecification of instruments, materials and apparatuses" is particularly applicable to IntuiTweet because both functions were enhanced. We de-specified the moment of improvisation into words spread across countries and time zones, and we displaced bodies from a dance studio. Additional de-specifications of dance once it is situated within the context of social networking are the liberating of this art form from young and virtuosic bodies, from the traditional evaluative gaze of the audience, and from the economic structures for production and presentation. This political and aesthetic inclusivity is characteristic of the contact improvisation ethos: "Contact Improvisation is an open-ended exploration of the kinesthetic possibilities of bodies moving through contact. Sometimes wild and athletic, sometimes quiet and meditative, it is a form open to all bodies and enquiring minds."[17] The moment of receiving a tweet, sent as SMS and announced by the usual brief phone vibration or chirp, was surprisingly kinesthetic. It felt like a touch, a stroke, or a nudge—effectively, the insertion of another's corporeal experience into my daily life. Despite being displaced from usual improvisatory contexts (the theater, the studio, or even public spaces) and displaced from the other dancing bodies, these messages triggered a range of powerful responses, revealing that networked touch is like the "tact beyond the possible" that Derrida identifies in Nancy's writing on the corpus. How is it possible that our mobile media devices can facilitate such "stroking, striking, thinking, weighing" across a distributed corpus of bodies (Derrida 2005, 66)?

Walking along a path after having emerged from a Boston underground station, I received a tweet from Leena, who was in Oslo: "Fluids passing through my legs, a sense of weight filling wide space, finally. I know I made the right decision." This caused me to experience blurred central vision and to have a strong peripheral focus. The impact was quick and involuntary to the extent that I did not craft a response but let myself shift into a responsive state, as one does when doing contact improvisation. The public path was relatively deserted, so I let myself inject a moment of dance into my more pedestrian movement, and I swerved sideways for a few steps, directly into some bushes. It was like a moment of escape. I sent the following tweet in response after my micro-improvisation: "Fluid legs made me want to walk sideways or at least to waver no more straight lines. Soft peripheral focus makes me a bad pedestrian." The exchange continued after an interval of a few minutes: "Bad pedestrian made go on all fours and crawl which I happily did in the comfort of my kitchen." I received this message while I was driving and, as if I was in the midst of an actual contact improvisation, I had a strong desire to fall on all fours myself. For obvious reasons, I could not physically react, but I was able to nurture a somatic response. I kept this sensation alive during the short drive home, and when I entered my house ten minutes later, I dropped to the floor in my kitchen to continue the improvisation. This ability to let movement responses become latent and then to release them was an unexpected result of the IntuiTweet method. The ebbs and flows of movement exchange were both concrete and immanent (not quite actualized); the movement was not just separated spatially from the original moment, but it was temporally stretched and distributed across more than one body.

Moments of improvised movement generated by our process varied in intensity—sometimes powerful and almost derailing other actions, and sometimes subtle and insinuating. A tweet arrived, and I just did not know what to do with it. I waited, slept on it, and moved around it and finally my body was comfortable improvising it. A temporal and rhythmic quality that does not exist very well in the studio or in stage performances took root: sustained inertia or protracted stillness. This was an expansion of the hiatus in con-tact, the "-" of con-tact.

My attitude toward my mobile phone shifted through this process. It was imbued with anticipated corporeal potential. Not just a device *in* motion, it became a device *for* motion. The simple sound or vibration of a received tweet, even if not retrieved then and there, could enact a shift in body state. The mobile phone might still be buried in my bag or pocket as I stood on a crowded train platform, but part of me was already aware of movement waiting to be deciphered. I was in a state of anticipation, waiting to receive. I lived in my body differently, as if the body state of the studio was filtered into my daily life. This was a distinct sensory reconfiguration that coincided with being in a state of dance while outwardly shifting very little. This was also an example of lived social aesthetics that freed art from being defined according to canons of representation or dance vocabulary and based it on a form of sensory apprehension. Echoing the earlier discussion on Twitter etiquette, this form of aesthetics is not as much a mode of doing as a mode of being (Rancière 2009a, 29).

The IntuiTweet research has not yet articulated a clear definition of movement intuition—the original research question—but in many respects we obtained a better working definition. I located movement intuition in practice and began to sense subtle variations in improvisatory content: a movement impulse was not quite the same thing as a movement sensation; a movement desire had a different temporality from a movement intuition. Each was distinct but overlapped with the others. None was more primordial, or basic, than the others, but each existed differently as a complex somatic, kinetic, and cognitive assemblage. The working definition offered here is that a movement intuition is understood by sensing what it is *not*: it is not an impulse, a sensation, or a desire. This is a highly unsatisfactory definition by most standards, but it possesses its own sort of fuzzy logic and it is, in a circular way, an intuition of what is an intuition by ruling out what is not an intuition. It is also not unlike the moment of anesthetic in the aesthetic: distinguished in terms of what it interrupts. The artistic process shifted the research goals and resulted in IntuiTweet being valuable for its contribution to conceptual, corporeal, and methodological knowledge.[18]

Improvisation as Mode of Social Interaction

I argued earlier that *Small Acts* and IntuiTweet were located in the domain of social aesthetics and that both involved a form of improvisation related to contact improvisation. The con-tact in *Small Acts* was made up of the ebbs and flows of improvisation between the movements of audience members and performers; in IntuiTweet, con-tact was fostered by movement translated into texts and transformed through a distributed network of bodies. In the final section of this chapter, I argue that these improvisation practices can also be seen as models for social interaction and that a particular construction of the body is implicated. Social interaction consists not simply of the material, gestural, and linguistic exchanges in the practice of daily life; it has the wider connotations of creating or re-creating bonds among people and gives rise to "new modes of confrontation or participation" (Rancière 2009a, 21). The improvisation central to social interaction is the crafting, moment by moment, of shared narratives and spaces using the devices of existence available to us: the mechanisms, movements, and media of life. Further, the understanding of improvisation that weaves its way through this chapter is pinned on a particular approach to embodied subjectivity: intercorporeality.

Consistent with the flow of ideas throughout this chapter, here, too, we see how Bourriaud can be used to initiate reflections on improvisation; Rancière, to clarify and ground; and Derrida, to render subtler and more complex. Bourriaud does not explicitly address improvisation but structures art in such a way that improvisation may be read into it. He locates the work of art at a "social interstice," says it is "a state of encounter," and indicates that transitivity is a "forever unfinished discursiveness" (Rancière 2009a, 16–18, 26). The bodies engaged in these discursive encounters remain implicit rather than articulated. The redistribution of the forms of sensory experience on which Rancière bases his notion of aesthetics operates through most dance forms, to greater or lesser degrees, but is most evident in contact improvisation. Nancy Stark Smith describes contact as a form of movement "based on the communication between two or more moving bodies that are in physical contact and their combined relationship to the physical laws that govern their motion—gravity, momentum, inertia." Stark Smith goes on to say that "alertness is developed in order to work in an energetic state of physical disorientation."[19] It is easy to rhapsodize about fluidity and synchronicity in contact improvisation resulting in a union of intent and motion. Considering instead the inertia and disorientation, gravity and temporality, of movement improvisation we see how touch may be varied, sporadic, and inconsistent but is all the stronger because of these qualities. In other words, we can see the role for the anesthetic in the aesthetic of contact: moments of slippage or waiting, disorientation, or searching. The experiences of *Small Acts* and IntuiTweet reveal how both improvisation and social interactions (particularly through social networking) are less about connections than they are about non-coincidence.

Once this terrain of slippage, inertia, and inconsistency is acknowledged it is valuable to turn once again to Derrida out of respect for the complexity of improvisation. Beginning with the body itself, in his reading of Merleau-Ponty, Derrida (2005, 207–8) reminds us that when my right hand touches my left, it is nothing less than the body of the other that is animated before me. This can mean that I am never fully in control or cognizant of myself, but it can also mean, in a truly networked sense, a certain dispersion of sensing. Any dancer who has performed with other dancers knows that it is as if one's proprioceptive awareness extends across all other bodies onstage; the others sense for me and with me. In terms that are uncannily relevant to the dispersed, asynchronous contact achieved through IntuiTweet, Derrida emphasizes a non-coincidence of a body with itself that "allows the articulation, conjuncture, or joining *un ajointement* (however inadequate and interruptible) between several heterogeneous sensible experiences" (350). These heterogeneous experiences in dance improvisation are the lives and bodies of the separate dancers but can at the same time be read as the tensions of sensory data and physical motion within one dancing body—impulses, sensations, knowledge, and intuition that pull in different directions within one body. The conjunctions, whether joining several people within a social network over time or joining several senses within one body in a single moment, are always inadequate and interruptible. Derrida reminds us that we are inadequate and un-identical to ourselves.

In addition to being a faithful account of the complexity of improvisation, Derrida's words are striking for depicting people linked, fallibly and disjointedly, through a technological system that itself is akin to a sensory body. We are deeply non-coincident, inconsistent, and asynchronous. Following the IntuiTweet instructions, the participants received sensory information from another heterogeneous sensible being through a distributed and de-spatialized system; this information became meaningful individually and collectively once it was enacted and shared. I suggest that our ability in IntuiTweet to integrate information that was non-identical to ourselves was due to our being deeply disrupted and non-identical within ourselves to begin with. We did not fight this state. We improvised with and through the layers of disruption. In the broad sweep of this project, the tweets with explicit movement information were less significant than the gaps between tweets—how the movement grew or developed quietly or in unexpected bursts, without our controlling or shaping it. This permits a deeper understanding of the anesthetic. It is important to see that it is not simply a binary opposite of the aesthetic but, rather, a field or event space of less consolidated, less determined, less categorizable qualities of social interaction.

Discussions of improvisation in dance do not always include considerations of the social. In improvisation, one exists in the immediacy of the present moment, but that does not mean it is clear, consistent, or context-free. Some dancers feel that improvisation happens in a state of emptiness. Cathérine Kintzler has written eloquently of the paradoxes of the void (le vide) in improvisation. She challenges the suggestion that improvisation happens in a clean, almost pure, internal corporeal space. The paradox she identifies is that the improvised dance gesture pulls away from habitual bodily movement to craft new patterns of movement at the same time that it distances itself from transcendental pretensions that actually constrain the body. Consistent with but also extending Rancière, Kintzler writes that this improvisatory act of making a void is one of shattering the immediate authority of the sensible, existing modes of being and expectations.[20] But is it social? In discourses on dance, the question arises as to whether it is possible to improvise alone. Some dancers believe we always improvise alone, and others insist we never do so, even when we are solitary. Nancy can be used to shift the perspective somewhat so we no longer expect a direct answer to the question of whether we improvise alone or not. At stake is not the singular or plural but of a state of betweenness: "The *with*, understood in terms of existence, must therefore be elaborated as a quite particular space—the word *space* being understood here in both the literal sense, since the existents are also bodies, extended beings, and in a figurative sense, which would answer the question: 'What takes place between us?'" (Nancy 2008, 119).

IntuiTweet revealed that the dance of daily life takes place between us. The focus and intensity of the engagement that dancers, accustomed to the studio, bring to the crafting of tweets using mobile phones shed light on how these devices affect and transform our expressive and corporeal behavior beyond the studio. *Small Acts* foregrounded the collective practices of movement, perception, and constructions of narrative of a particular community. Embedded in these examples is a definition of the social that is innately intercorporeal. This follows a basic phenomenological perspective informed by the late writings of Merleau-Ponty in which the relation between people is not construed in terms of the self or identities as much as it is about intercorporeality, a field of multiple embodied exchanges (Diprose 2002; Kozel 2007; Merleau-Ponty 1968). The boundaries between bodies are inherently fluid, and each person is taken to be a multiply sensed incarnate being perpetually engaged in a dance between subject and object, between one being and another. An emphasis on intercorporeality does not eschew politics and the social for, following Merleau-Ponty, perception, agency, and subjectivity in general take place as a body opened up to the bodies of others.

Like the dancers in IntuiTweet, the body is porous: receiving impulses from others, being derailed by others to greater or lesser degrees, and reformulating the traces of others into new transmissions or relations. It is because the body is constituted in relation to others that it is ambiguous, opened to the world and to others, and so can act at all. Rosalyn Diprose explains intercorporeality in Merleau-Ponty based on an understanding of the self as "a lived body ambiguously caught between subject and object" (Merleau-Ponty 1968, 69). In other words, I am who I am because you exist. The "I" and "you" lose further distinction in intercorporeality when the Merleau-Pontian relation of reversibility is recognized to occur in the most fundamental sensory engagement with the world. Each of us is already permeated by otherness; even when we touch the world we are touched in return, we see and are seen, we listen as we speak. These ever more fragmentary moments of sliding between being-subject and being-object are how we exist in the world. These are fundamentally improvisational in that I am forever acting *and* responding, without really having a starting point in one or the other modality. These moments are also fundamentally relational.

Returning, at the end of this chapter, to the devices of existence: improvisation is one way to navigate the world. The argument is ontological in that it refers to a state of being in the world; it is experiential in that it refers to concrete sensory engagement with others; and it is haptic in that it is based on touch. We are not left to our own devices as much as we participate in the devising of our worlds. A message we can take from relational aesthetics is that the beginnings of a path, a formula, a game, or a story may be given to us by an artist or a choreographer, but we are expected to take it from there and improvise. Improvisation, even when it is crisp, fluid, or truly inspired, is still a play across the hiatus of con-tact. To use another set of metaphors, it is messy. It slips and slides; it lingers or ends before it has fully started; it glides in and out of shadow; it gets distracted. It becomes tired and sad and has moments of unruly joy. It spirals off in leaps of fancy. It hurts and needs comfort. The implication of this disruption of space, time, and materiality is that any encounter with otherness in all of its forms—whether another person, a sound, a movement, or an unexpected event—invites a moment of improvisation. Improvisation is a mode of social interaction.

Notes

The research and artistic practice that contributed to this chapter was supported in part by a residency at La Chartreuse (Avignon, France) and the ACCR (The European Network of Cultural Centres, http://www.accr-europe.org). I thank Mia Keinänen and Leena Rouhiainen, my collaborators on the IntuiTweet project, and emphasize that I do not speak for them but gratefully build on our work together. I also thank Åsa Söderberg of the Skånes Dansteater for clarification and photos.

1. This chapter does not contain an explicit account of phenomenology as a methodology. An extensive discussion of this approach to phenomenology, based on the late writings of Merleau-Ponty and not the Husserlian transcendental version, is in Kozel 2007. For related discussions of methodology in relation to research in performance and media, see Kozel 2010a, 2010b.

2. Ben Wright created the original version of *Small Acts* in 2008 as a quintet for stage and live piano for his U.K. company Bgroup. In 2010, Wright reinvented the work for Skånes Dansteater (http://www.skanesdansteater.com), dissecting the structure of the original piece and dividing it among thirteen performers and twenty-two areas of the company's building. He inserted new movement material developed collaboratively with Skånes Dansteater's dancers and the score, consisting of several piano miniatures by the British composer Howard Skempton, was recorded and played back over an assortment of loudspeakers. The design of the performance areas was enhanced by Jens Sethzman's temporary light structures, and costumes were designed by Theo Clinkard.

3. "Non-dance" is an appropriately underdefined notion. In dance scholarship, it can be located outside an "exhausted" artform (Lepecki 2006) and in convergences between dance and other art forms, such as circus. In practice, it can take the form of the pared-down, repetitive choreographic work of Jérome Bel, which is about the frailty of the body rather than the dance (http://www.jeromebel.fr), or Ivana Müller's conceptual approach to choreography, by which she produces movement without moving (www.dance-tech.net). Non-dance exposes or transcends the borders of conventionally defined dance. Relating to non-dance, I have reflected on the mobile narratives of IntuiTweet as contra-choreography in Kozel 2013.

4. I translate *phénoménalité esthésique* as "aesthetic experience" for simplicity (Derrida 2005, 229).

5. This is very like the argument for the touching-touched in Merleau-Ponty (1968).

6. IntuiTweet was part of a larger initiative called Intuition in Creative Processes, a Helsinki-based collaboration between dance researchers associated with the Theatre Academy (Leena Rouhiaine, Mia Keinänen) and designers from the Media Lab of the University of Arts and Design (Samu Mielonen, Asta Raami). This project was supported by the Academy of Finland.

7. On April Fool's day of 2009, the *Guardian* ironically "reported" that it would cease print publication in favor of disseminating all news via Twitter: RioPalof, "Twitter Switch for Guardian, after 188 Years of Ink," March 31, 2009, http://www.guardian.co.uk/media/2009/apr/01/guardian-twitter-media-technology. Twitter is seen as an ego-based exercise on the part of those who think they are "fascinating": Margaret Mason, "Writing My Twitter Etiquette Article: 14 Ways to Use Twitter Politely," August 15, 2008, http://www.themorningnews.org/archives/the_thoughtful_user_guide/writing_my_twitter_etiquette_article_14_ways_to_use_twitter_politely.php. Some journalists defend Twitter from accusations of superficiality: Claire Cain Miller, "Putting Twitter's World to Use," April 13, 2009, http://www.nytimes.com/2009/04/14/technology/internet/14twitter.html?dlbk.

In the broader context of WikiLeaks, "engagement on social networking sites is frantic but shallow," John Kampfner, "WikiLeaks Turned the Tables on Governments, but the Power Relationship Has Not Changed," *The Guardian*, January 17, 2011, http://www.guardian.co.uk/media/2011/jan/17/wikileaks-governments-journalism?CMP=twt_fd.

8. PBworks, "Twitter Fan Wiki," last edited 2010, http://twitter.pbworks.com/w/page/1779812/Hashtag. The shift to "What's happening?" occurred in November 2009.

9. Mason, "Writing My Twitter Etiquette Article."

10. The motivation to reveal these attitudes and to push at their edges echoes a social anthropologist's sensitivity to "unspoken assumptions and implicit forms of knowledge and belief" (Born 2005, 14) in combination with an artist's desire to critique and create something new on the basis of this sensitivity.

11. Lindsay Cutler, "Nine Essentials of Twitter Etiquette," Nerve.com, April 15, 2010, http://www.nerve.com/dispatches/cutler/nine-essentials-of-twitter-etiquette. An additional source, at http://www.webdoctus.com/2010/01/complete-guide-to-twitter-etiquette, is no longer accessible.

12. Hilary Moss, "Meghan McCain's Cleavage-Covering Style: Nothing to See Here! (Photos)," *Huffington Post*, March 18, 2010, http://www.huffingtonpost.com/2009/10/19/meghan-mccains-cleavage-c_n_326308.html.

13. "After a few days of being excoriated for those three sentences dashed off in the middle of a meeting, Trunk addressed the controversy in a new blog post: 'Not only have bloggers written whole posts about the disgustingness of it,

but 70 people unfollowed me, and people actually came to my blog and wrote complaints about the twitter on random, unrelated posts'": Tracy Clark-Flory, "Tweeting a Miscarriage," Salon.com, September 26, 2009, http://www.salon.com/life/broadsheet/feature/2009/09/26/miscarriage_tweet. It was also picked up by CNN and she was asked why she was being so personal: Jessica Goldberg, "A TMI Tweet about Work, Wisconsin and a Woman's Right to Choose," TheFrisky.com, October 1, 2009, http://www.thefrisky.com/post/246-a-tmi-tweet-about-work-wisconsin-and-a-womans-right-to-choose.

14. See Jessica Wakeman, "'I'm Live-Tweeting My Abortion.'" TheFrisky.com, February 24, 2010, http://www.thefrisky.com/post/246-im-live-tweeting-my-abortion-on-twitter. It is worth indicating that it is impossible to assess what percentage of Twitter users made up the vocal community of objectors.

15. This function has been largely disabled in the interests of Twitter supporting smart phones with Wi-Fi access rather than facilitating continued usage by standard mobile phones. This is an unfortunate part of Twitter's business strategy, because it means users without smart phones (the majority of the population) can interface only via their computers, not via their mobile phones.

16. See http://www.learningtoloveyoumore.com. Some of her instructions are, "Feel the news" and "Make a portrait of your friend's desires."

17. From Ray Chung workshop announcement, London, 2009, http://www.contactquarterly.com/cq/webtext/resource.html (no longer accessible).

18. "About Contact Improvisation (CI)," Contact Quarterly, 2011, http://www.contactimprov.net/about.html. For a discussion of the method to emerge from this project, called the Intuitive Imagination method, see Kozel 2010a.

19. Stark Smith speaking for herself and for Steve Paxton's approach to contact improvisation; see "About Contact Improvisation (CI)."

20. Catherine Kintzler, "La danse: L'improvisation et les paradoxes du vide (Première partie)," blog post, 2009, http://www.mezetulle.net/article-30667877.html.

CHAPTER 13

THE DRAMATURGY OF SPONTANEITY

Improvising the Social in Theater

Zoë Svendsen

It seemed fitting that these good improvisations so often
began in the blurred space between lunch break and
performance, between the everyday and the fantastic.
—Tim Etchells (1999, 52)

This is how Tim Etchells, artistic director of Forced Entertainment, the
quintessential postmodern British experimental theater company, sums up
the alchemical interaction between sociability and aesthetics at the heart
of theatrical experimentation.[1] The "between" is the subject of this chapter,
which will explore the multifaceted ways in which social relations are revealed or reconfigured by being placed in the service of aesthetic practice,
"between the everyday and the fantastic," in the contemporary making of
theater in Britain.

Most works for the theater depict social relations at the level of narrative,
focusing on family, friendship groups, or other power structures. Further,
the making of the modern theater, from Schiller through Brecht to the happenings of the 1960s, has frequently been motivated by a desire for social
change (Kershaw 1992; Rancière 2009b). Nevertheless, the social relations
specifically produced within and by the conventional spatial codes of the
theater itself are rarely remarked on by theater scholars. These conventions
form the backdrop to this discussion of the place of improvisation within
dramaturgical practice in theater, which argues that theatrical aesthetics
frequently rely on an oscillation between improvisation in the moment and

prearranged composition, resulting in performance dramaturgies that seek to imply spontaneity while nevertheless firmly structuring audiences' experience. The theatrical aesthetics described in this chapter thereby problematize the assertion of a "relational" aesthetics as a distinct—and recent—category of art (Bourriaud 2002). That is, I argue that the use of social relations as a tool in the production of aesthetics is not merely a recent phenomenon, as implied by the rhetoric of relational aesthetics. Instead, this chapter examines how questions of the social are key to understanding the operations of theatricality within any given historical moment. To do so, I examine the influence of modernist aesthetics—against which Nicolas Bourriaud defines relational aesthetics—on theater. This leads to a discussion of how the discourse of theatrical improvisation functions in this context, and how it offers a space for acknowledging social practice.

Three distinct works in which I have been involved as a director, dramaturg, or writer will then illustrate varying ways in which the sociability of improvisational practice can be placed in service of aesthetic structures: *Discombobulator* (2009–10), an interdisciplinary performance that incorporated dance, live composition of electronic music, and video; *Four Men and a Poker Game* (2008), an adaptation of Brecht's short story; and *3rd Ring Out: Rehearsing the Future* (2010–11), a multimedia audience-interactive performance. Each incorporates a response to the conventional organization of social relations in theater, and each differently demonstrates how the conflicting histories of modern aesthetics and the social in theater might be brought into dialogue.

Aesthetics against the Social in Modernism

In theater, the reminder through the incursion of the social through the presence of the audience that art's putative autonomy is a cultural construct returns over and over to disturb the sovereignty of the work. This is the ground of modernist antagonism to theater and becomes no less than a call to arms in defense of art in Michael Fried's widely cited formulation:

> The success, even the survival, of the arts has come increasingly to depend on their ability to defeat theatre. This is perhaps nowhere more evident than within theatre itself, where the need to defeat what I have been calling theater has chiefly made itself felt as the need to establish a drastically different relation to its audience. (The relevant texts are, of course, Brecht and Artaud.) For theatre has an audience—it exists *for one*—in a

way other arts do not; in fact, this more than anything else is what modernist sensibility finds intolerable in theatre generally. (Fried 1967, 163;
emphasis added)

What Fried (1980, 109) calls "theater" is the acknowledgment of co-presence
in the structural relation between artwork and audience. In his later full-
length work, *Absorption and Theatricality*, Fried uses the term "absorption"
in opposition to theatricality. He terms any invitation by an artwork to a social relation in the viewer's present, "theatricality." He makes extensive use
of the eighteenth-century French theorist Denis Diderot's writings on painting to suggest that the primary condition of possibility for absorption is non-
reciprocity between the expressivity of the artwork and its reception by the
viewer. Implicit in Fried's argument is the notion that an artwork's "awareness" of being spectated lays bare in an embarrassing way the relationship of
service between the product and the consumer of that product. Fried quotes
Diderot at length on a painting depicting Susanna and the Elders: the nude
subject remains modest not only because she hides herself from the other
figures depicted but, crucially, because the painting is composed to make it
clear that the subject does not "know" that her nakedness is being revealed
to the viewer of the painting (96–97). On this view, the artwork remains autonomous only as long as the social relations in the here and now that bring
it into being are sublimated or denied.

However, attending to the aesthetic practices of the theater of "Western
industrial or post-industrial modernity" (Ridout 2006, 6) reveals their specifically *social* character, belying the distinction between aesthetics and social relations posited by Fried. One of the reasons that theater consistently
fails to live up to the attempts of practitioners to dispense with any ac-
knowledgement of social interaction in the here and now is that it is in the
nature of theater to be *real* as well as representational: "[Theater] is really
a language whose words consist to an unusual degree of things that are
what they seem to be. In theater, image and object, pretense and pretender,
sign-vehicle and content, draw unusually close. . . . In the theatre light is
brightness pretending to be brightness, a chair is a chair pretending to be
another chair, and so on" (States 1985, 20). Using this at once doubleness of
theatricality, contemporary theater increasingly acknowledges its capacity
not only for representing social relations, but also for shaping the sociality
of the occasion. In these moments, we hover between experiencing the stage
as itself and as a signifier. Joe Kelleher and Nicholas Ridout (2007, 104) suggest that exploitation of this both-and feature of theatricality lies at the

heart of the operations of the contemporary Italian director Romeo Castel-lucci's theater. "Then, everything became very clear," they write. "The veils had been lifted, and we looked straight into the wide open space of a marble box in which every action seemed to have its own proper name and to need no explanation. In English, there is a phrase with which one can signal one's approval of this kind of straight-talking: calling a spade a spade. Suddenly, this theatre seemed to be presenting spades as spades. Each action of the episode took place, as it were, in broad daylight."

Nevertheless, while embodied performance provides an ideal ground for explorations of aesthetics beyond Friedian high modernism, and has been embraced in contemporary art discourse as such, the history of the nineteenth-century and twentieth-century theater was one of social prac-tices designed to corral an audience toward the type of absorbed attention that Fried cited much later as a precondition of aesthetic experience. Au-gust Strindberg (2008), the late nineteenth-century Swedish playwright and theorist, developed a program for an "intimate theater" that is exem-plary for modernist theatrical works that display a desire for independence from their audiences. Strindberg's aim to diminish sociability in the theater of his time—with techniques such as darkness in the auditorium, banning boxes and applause during performances, and stopping actors from direct-ing their lines specifically to the audience—was directly linked to the belief that such interaction would be detrimental to absorbed attention, allow-ing an audience to "escape from the suggestive influence of the dramatist-hypnotist" (68–69). Such absorption involves a self-forgetting, an immer-sion in the time posited by the fictional realm in place of real physical time (Fried 1980). In this, paradoxically, the audience enters the theater to leave the present moment of the social behind—or, at least, relegate it to periph-eral vision. In a standard proscenium arch or end-on space, everything out-side the triangle inscribed in space by the gaze trained on the theatrical scene—with the eye at the apex—is excluded. Absorption in the onstage action within the literal and metaphorical frame of theatrical representation dissolves the social position from which the subject is seeing.

The "small stage and a small auditorium" were particularly important in the founding of Strindberg's "intimate theater" as a solution to the funda-mental problem of realism in large spaces. To be seen and heard, the scale of the actors' gestures and vocal projection must be commensurate with the size of the whole theater space and not the size of the imagined space of the fiction. Therefore, a large space is always overtly "for" the audience rather than apparently independent of it. This concern with how the relationship between actor and audience might disturb Strindberg's (2008, 66) desired illusion of artistic autonomy extends to disciplining not only the audience but also the actors: "I do fervently wish that vital scenes should not be performed next to the prompter's box, as duets designed to elicit applause, but rather located to that part of the stage the action dictates."

The trend throughout the mid-twentieth century in Britain was generally toward designing theaters and encouraging audience behavior to set social interaction aside in the focus on mimetic action onstage (Rebellato 1999; Shepherd and Womack 1996; Wiles 2003). The changing behavioral code for theater reception corresponded with a shift in the class base of theatergoing audiences from working class to middle class in the early to mid-century (Shepherd and Womack 1996). Dan Rebellato identifies a particular moment in which the cultural dominance of this theater was cemented: in the attitude of the directors, writers, and actors at the Royal Court to its audience in the 1950s and 1960s. No longer regarded as "patrons," who were "exercising an assumed right because that role made them the arbiters of taste" (Kershaw 2004, 299), Rebellato (1999, 111–13) convincingly demonstrates how audiences at the Royal Court were treated as "clients," assumed to lack a specialist knowledge that would enable them to make valid judgments—the dark side of the Royal Court's championing of the artist's "right to fail." In the case of the Royal Court, the text of the play rather than any given production was regarded as the artistic object (101–2). The elision of the "literary" play and its theatrical production allowed for an ideological unity of the artwork that was, however, threatened if the audiences' presence had to be taken into account: "The Royal Courtiers wanted their unique and self-present moments of pure expressivity to be seen—in other words, they wanted an audience—but if an audience is required, how can the 'original' object be complete? A theater that requires an audience's approval locates that audience on the interior of its texts, allows it to mark an absence within the text, requiring completion and confirmation. . . . But if that text is already complete, the audience is exiled to a position of pure exteriority, leaving the integrity of the text intact" (110–11).

The Court's founder, George Devine, commented that "the Royal Court ideal is to be likened to an art gallery or a literary magazine" (Rebellato 1999, 113), explicitly allying the Court with other arts that traditionally focused on individual genius rather than creative collaboration. Devine's aspiration to emulate such artistic practices, which privilege individual authorship and artistic autonomy, offers a direct denial of the permeability of social and aesthetic practices specific to theater.

The conventions of the modern theater are directly related to attempts to deny the sociality of the theatrical event. These conventions include sitting in the dark in rows facing the stage, in silence, with minimum interference from other spectators in the aural or visual field. Nevertheless, over the course of the twentieth century innumerable companies, performances, and events have formulated methods to overcome these conventions, seeking a mode of theater that does not separate stage and audience. From the anti-institutional avant-garde practices of Surrealists, Dadaists, and Futurists, to Brechtian epic, to the socialist theater companies that took theater directly "to the people" in Britain of the 1960s and 1970s (Kershaw 1992), theater makers consistently have sought some form of direct social engagement with audiences. In some cases, the shift toward an acknowledgment of the sociality of the occasion is manifested in a move toward performances that return the job of framing the event to the audience by offering a spatial dramaturgy that allows audience members to wander at will through a series of arenas in which a loose narrative is being generated. In the production of *Faust* by the British performance company Punchdrunk in 2007, for example, a several-story warehouse offered multiple opportunities to chose how to experience the performance. As spectators, we "know" that a representation of the story of Faust is taking place somewhere in the building, but we are not always there to see it.

In coining the phrase "relational aesthetics" in the late 1990s, Bourriaud offered a rubric within aesthetic theory for the categorization of works that saw social relations as material from which the very artwork could be constructed, laying claim to the practicing of social relations *as* art in the broadest possible sense. The aesthetics of autonomous art, as represented by Fried and other modernists, such as Clement Greenberg (1993), correspond to what Bourriaud (2002, 14) delineates as the "assertion of an independent and *private* symbolic space," where the term "private" is equated with the individual imagination. It is against this "private symbolic" realm that Bourriaud defines the openly socially participatory function of "relational aesthetics." Yet the naming under a single rubric of a multiplicity of practices that encode different formulations of social relations has been rightly criticized for suggesting that in the context of standardized practices in late capitalism, attention to social relations is *in itself* a positive, political act (Bishop 2004). Further, whether due to the failure to overcome or the refusal to deny social contingency, theater aesthetics could be said to have been always already relational, always rehearsing the possibility of social communities.

Improvisation in Theater

Improvisation plays a key role in the history of theater as a socially oriented practice. Some go as far as to describe all acting as in some way a process of improvisation (Frost and Yarrow 1990, 1), while the contemporary philosopher David Velleman (2009) has used improvisation in acting as a model for considering moral action. Perhaps it is the difficulty of defining the boundaries of improvisation within established theater practice that accounts for the lack of theoretical writing on theatrical improvisation when compared with musical improvisation. Most often discussed in the context of "how-to" practical handbooks, the idea of improvisation in theater is consistently allied, often implicitly, with sociability (Frost and Yarrow 1990; Nachmanovitch 1990; Spolin 1973).

The definition of "improvisation" given by Anthony Frost and Ralph Yarrow (1990, 1) encodes the commonly assigned attributes of the activity: of spontaneity, the foregrounding of the human, and the alertness to the specific moment in space and time of the performance; "the skill of using bodies, space, all human resources, to generate a coherent physical expression of an idea, a situation, a character (even, perhaps, a text); to do this spontaneously, in response to the immediate stimuli of one's environment, and to do it *à l'improviste*: as though taken by surprise, without preconceptions." The success of improvisation on these terms is equated with an Artaudian infusion of life into art: "Where improvisation is most effective, most spontaneous, least 'blocked' by taboo, habit or shyness, it comes close to a condition of integration with the environment or context" (2). Theater practices that focus on improvisation as the primary condition of performance have often sought to dissolve the division between performers and audiences, encouraging participation from spectators: from Ken Campbell's "improvathons" to Keith Johnstone's "Theatresports" (1999).[2] The director, teacher, and actor Viola Spolin of Chicago was one of the earliest practitioners in the twentieth century to formalize game playing into a system for theatrical creativity. Having trained as a settlement worker at Neva Boyd's Group Work School in Chicago in the 1920s, Spolin developed theatrical improvisation techniques as part of her work as a drama supervisor in the late 1930s for the Chicago branch of the Works Progress Administration's Recreational Project (Robinson et al. 1989). Spolin's (1973, 4) stated aim was to help "both teacher and student find personal freedom." Her procedural guide espouses a humanist credo that is common to much discussion of theatrical improvisation as emancipatory and productive of selfhood. Like Frost and Yarrow, Spolin privileges the impression of spontaneity fostered by improvisational action: "Through spontaneity we are re-formed into ourselves. It creates an explosion that for the moment frees us from handed-down frames of reference, memory choked with old facts and information and undigested theories and techniques of other peoples' findings. . . . The intuitive can only respond in immediacy—right now. It comes bearing its gifts in the moment of spontaneity, the moment when we are freed to relate and act, involving ourselves in the moving, changing world around us" (4). From the vantage point of the present, statements such as this (see also Crickmay and Tufnell 1990; Polsky 1998) mystify improvisation's relation to the social (Mermikides and Smart 2010), disregarding the many pressures brought to bear on any occasion of apparent immediacy. Nevertheless, what is revealed by such descriptions of spontaneity is the orientation of attention in time toward the present: "Attention is focused on the moment when things take shape" (Frost and Yarrow 1990, 2; see also Crickmay and Tufnell 1990). The "community" that is thereby established, however temporarily, is generated through interaction in the present.

However, the orientation of participants' attention is trained not on the sociality of the occasion but on the co-production of a (temporal) construction that is not conceived of as social: the theatrical event. Co-attending in this way to construction requires listening and reciprocity, practices that are highly valued within social paradigms in Western culture. In her research on jazz, Ingrid Monson (1996, 73) has examined in detail how metaphors used by jazz musicians point to the parallels between social and aesthetic practice through their use of terms such as "talking," "conversation," and "saying something" as common designations for "good improvisation." These terms actively emphasize the "interpersonal, face-to-face quality of improvisation" (78). Monson's examples suggest how notions of spontaneity are reciprocally related to perceptions of (lack of) effort required in improvising together (80), while pointing to the effort required to set up the conditions in which such spontaneity becomes possible:

> Nearly every musician who talked to me mentioned the importance of listening in good ensemble playing. Listening in an active sense—being able to respond to musical opportunities or to correct mistakes—is implicit in the way that musicians use this term. . . . Listening affects what musicians

decide to play at a particular moment. . . . This spontaneity is absolutely central in the jazz improvisational aesthetic. (Monson 1996, 84)

The importance of listening—of paying attention to one another—is mirrored in the discourse of improvisation in theater. The director and teacher Chris Johnston (2006) prefaces his guide to improvisation by quoting Miles Davis: "Play what you hear, not what you know." Tina Bicât and Chris Baldwin (2002, 7) suggest as a prerequisite for collaborative devising the injunction that "each member of the company must listen and talk to the others with trust and attention," to enable them to be "sensitive to the dynamics of intense collaborative group work."

Spontaneity is here equated with the social present; stories of emancipation through improvisation and stories of improvisation as equivalent not to "art" but to "life" both trade on the same binary of art as autonomous and improvisation as heteronomous—that is, a social act. The values attributed to "liveness" often entail that the uniqueness of any given performance is emphasized over that which is repeated (Auslander 1999). Indeed, the idea that performance is unrepeatable, ephemeral, and exclusively shared by those present at the time connects with performance art's emphasis on entropy (R. Ferguson 1998) and with Peggy Phelan's (1993, 146) famous claim that "performance's being becomes itself through disappearance," leaving "no visible trace" and thereby evading commodification.[3] Although Phelan's ontology of performance allows for the radical contingency of such structuring—that is, the ever present awareness in performance that *it could go wrong*, it underplays the desire inherent in many performances, not only in theater but also in performance art—that *it should go right*. The work to make performances repeatable is not merely the result of theater's compromise with a capitalist economy (Rebellato 2006; Ridout 2006). It also implies an attempt to wrest a precarious stability for temporally contingent artistic practice in the face of inevitable entropy.

Although from the perspective of practice I would therefore contest the privileging of the ephemeral in performance, like many other theater makers I can remember moments of extraordinary improvisation in rehearsal—moments that could be reenacted or reconstructed but never with the same degree of affect. From long-running West End plays to internationally franchised musicals, there are significant—and commercially dominant—parts of the theater sector that are distinctly more focused on product than process (Rebellato 2009, 39–46). Improvisation in theater has long been key to countering performance art's charge of the deadliness of theater, supposedly brought about by the commodification of the event and resulting in a "Mc-Theater" (39).

There is, on the other hand, a fine line between improvisation as constructed within a performance aesthetic, thereby implying spontaneity, freedom, and non-repeatable liveness, and the threat of a collapse of the construct into sociality. This is illustrated by the description provided on the British theater company Forced Entertainment's website of the performance *Bloody Mess* in 2004. Forced Entertainment has long challenged the "rules" of dramatic theater, yet the company tacitly relies on social rules for how audience members have become used to engaging with theatrical performance: keeping still and quiet to enable absorption in the moment, not interacting with the scene played before them, and so on. The description of *Bloody Mess* enacts the performance's rejection of dramatic structure by merely listing its components, working by accumulation:

> A strobe light flickers, pointed at the ground. A pair of clowns in smeared make-up start an ugly fight that threatens to take over the stage. . . . A delinquent cheerleader dances and yells. A woman weeps in a fit of operatic grief then stops, changes costume and starts again. The strains of Deep Purple or maybe Black Sabbath blast from the [public address system] only to be replaced by the Bach Cello Suites. A bloke starts to tell the history of the world from the Big Bang onwards but is quickly interrupted. A sound check. An interview. A seductive monologue. Rock-gig roadies creep across the stage—bringing disco lights, new speakers and a microphone that no one really wants.[4]

What we see at work here is representation destabilized; the notion of a precise and repeatable dramaturgy, destabilized; and a revelation of the being here and now of performance, of the potential for failure. Yet the provocative note at the end of the text is less, or more, than a joke: "Genuine audience members only. No drunks. No timewasters." Only the performers, and not the audience, are allowed to improvise. If the audience members are as cavalier with the social rules of theater as Forced Entertainment are in their testing of traditions of representation, mimesis, and narrative, then the edifice collapses into a "real" mess. It is a condition of the aesthetic of performance that its contingency is held up to view—contained within the geometric frame of representation. For Forced Entertainment, if the audience were actually to join in, the performance would no longer be art.

The pleasure taken in the live, the improvised, is partially relief from the effort of construction, and partly an acknowledgment of the precariousness of any attempt to create a stable structure. Overt improvisation can further operate as a tacit (and sometimes delusional) claim that we are all "in it together." Some twentieth-century theater architects have sought a balance between an aesthetics of distance and an appreciation of the social dimension of theatergoing. In this they conceptualize the former as an "other" to the latter, each with its distinct form of spatial operation, in which architectural features that enable social interaction require defending against the hegemony of architectures that focus attention solely on the stage (Leacroft 1949; Mackintosh 1993).[5] It is therefore not as an "other" to but as constitutive *of* theater aesthetics that improvisational practices have particular force within the creation of rehearsed structures. As Monson demonstrates, certain kinds of social engagement are a prerequisite of the aesthetics of improvisation. Improvisation is enabled through a complex interaction among social principles, harnessed for aesthetic production, which effect the conditions of possibility for attention to be focused on invention in the moment. The discourse valorizes spontaneity, yet habit, genre expectations, and a shared language of improvisational techniques all feature as the building blocks of potentiality in the creative present, whether or not they are acknowledged as such (Heddon and Milling 2006).

Case Study I: *Discombobulator*

A first example of an integrated practice of sociability and aesthetics in performance work in which I have been involved as dramaturg and director was specifically organized around, and thereby commented on, the conventions of the theater of modernity in which the audience is imagined as silent—if not altogether absent. *Discombobulator* (2009–10) illustrated how, in theatrical performance, improvisation is often dependent on containment within a structured frame and is produced spatially and temporally through implicit, and sometimes explicit, rules.[6] The pleasure is partially determined by the recognition that improvisation functions like a riff, a flourish of spontaneous invention that plays on a preordained structure, rather than a collapse into the time scale and improvisational nature of life. *Discombobulator* used the conventions of a proscenium arch theater space—notably, the pictorialism of audiences' orientation to a framed scene, the darkness of the auditorium, and the convention of staying silent. Both dance and music were partially improvised, with movement within a specific sphere of light triggering electronic music through the use of motion-capture technology. The music produced thereby was then manipulated and recomposed live. Simultaneously, the music gave signals to the dancer, Ben Duke, within the schema of the storytelling. As a result, the improvisation within each element became reciprocally related and, due to the simplicity of binding sound directly to movement, potentially indiscernible to an audience *as* improvisation. Invention here was overtly delimited by a set of pre-agreed parameters for what constitutes aesthetic practice.

Discombobulator thereby offered a short theatrical essay on agency and lack of it, in which by means of motion capture technology, a dancer appeared to dance into existence a vast backdrop image of a virtual world that would start to disappear again whenever he stopped moving. Duke's improvised movements also generated the watery sounds that opened the performance. The dancer appeared to discover his agency through the generation of sound, concurrently with the audience. His naïve testing, pleasure, and confusion—in relation to the apparent sonic responsiveness of the air around him—produced ripples of laughter in the audience in an age-old technique that is familiar from clowning traditions. The virtual world, displayed on a backdrop covering the entirety of the back of the stage, appeared to imply a paradise beyond an old, broken-down house façade, with a door that would disappear whenever Duke moved out of the light and toward it. Once his efforts had apparently "fixed" the image, virtual versions of the dancer began to appear. Sometimes the virtual figure would appear to interact with the real figure; then it would be multiplied into three virtual versions, each of which turned and stared at the real figure.[7]

Improvisation was used to imply entrapment within an aesthetic structure—the live struggling against the machinery of the theater. *Discombobulator* offered a direct response to the particular space in which it was first performed: the Teatro Piccolo Arsenale in Venice,[8] a cavernous hall into which a traditional proscenium arch, a pictorially orientated space, had been built. Castellucci describes the "violence" of such purpose-built theaters when discussing the Municipal Theater in Marseille: "The relation to the public is very hard and violent because it is obliged to offer up 'spectacle'; everything is prepared in such a way that something has to happen. There is coercion; there is a relationship of violence in this waiting for the 'spectacle.' . . . There is no possibility of passage or circulation between the audience and the stage, there's a clear separation" (quoted in Kelleher and Ridout 2007, 204). *Discombobulator* used the "violence" of a space that holds every action up as "spectacle" as the frame for an interactive mechanism that then thematized the limitations of human agency. Within this framework, the improvised appeal to the audience achieved a poignancy that was both comforting and impotent. The tension between the pre-structured and the improvised resulted in a final sequence of frenzied movement that ultimately brought physical collapse. The live body fought the machine-like mechanism of theater and lost.

Case Study II: *Four Men and a Poker Game*

In addition to being used to destabilize performance, this doubleness of theater — which plays both on presence (in the theater, in social time) and on aesthetic distance (the bridge to a fictional realm) — can also be harnessed to use social relations among the audience members to reinforce the aesthetic construct. This was the case with *Four Men and a Poker Game* by Brecht, a short story I adapted and directed for the stage with the composer and musician David Paul Jones.[9] The story itself is a parable of capitalism figured through four champion swimmers playing poker on a ship from Havana to New York. The harnessing of pre-established social relations to aesthetic effect was predicated on a reconfiguration of the spatial relationship between audience and performers, away from the conventional form used in *Discombobulator.* The performance setting of the story was a backroom bar; the audience sat at small tables throughout the space, with a passageway left for the Glaswegian actor David McKay to use as he moved among the audience. Jones played his own score, which was largely pre-composed but allowed space for musical improvisation. The composition was tightly enmeshed in the rhythm of the performance as a whole, at times appearing to take the story to a more abstract level. The story itself was told by McKay rather than acted out, but this telling was situated quasi-dramatically, in that the audience were "cast" as punters in the bar, listening to a man telling a story to live piano. This gentle fiction established the situation of storytelling in which the audience participated, providing a framework for listening.

The performance relied both on the maintenance of the social rules governing audiences' behavior that apply in standard theater spaces, but not in bars (i.e., that the audience would not move about or talk to one another and would attend to the story), and on the capacity of small improvised acts of engagement between the performer and individual audience members to elide the actual space and time of the theater with the fictional realm indicated. Improvised interaction included the preamble to the telling of the story, additional invented text delivered to individual audience members, and the deliberate making of eye contact. The improvisation both established the fiction of the bar and made the telling of the story occur not in some fictional other time but in the here and now.

Improvisation in performance can collapse the distance implicitly posited by the aesthetic structure between the time frame of the fiction and the actual time of experiencing in the theater. The concentration of the actor and the audience is aligned, in concert, focused on the present moment rather than on memory or reconstruction. This is facilitated by a turn to the social relations of the theater within the aesthetic frame, performed through a sleight of hand that reconfigures social time *as* aesthetic time. Nevertheless, in the schema of *Four Men and a Poker Game*, it soon became clear that the audience would not be coerced into interacting as co-performers, for the here-and-now set-up for the storytelling functioned merely as a holding place for a move into an imaginative realm that was created almost entirely aurally. Indeed, the social proximity of strangers in a formation at once familiar from a social perspective (a bar) and unfamiliar from a theatrical perspective (other spectators were always directly in each audience member's visual frame) provided encouragement to retreat into the private imaginative realm generated by the focus of the storytelling. The lighting shifted in the course of the performance, from lighting the audience strongly—emphasizing the sociability of the space—to isolating the actor in light, with the audience now in shadow, as the grip of the mental projection created by the story took hold.

This interplay between the social and the fictional did, however, foreground the vulgar reality of the monetized relation between performer and audience (cf. Rebellato 2006; Ridout 2006). The audience pays and the performers perform—the story will be told from start to finish. The decision to insert a break in the storytelling about a third of the way through not only paid homage to Brecht in its disruption of any absorption in the imagined world of the story, but also acted as a reminder of the contingency of performance. This disruption took the form of a cigarette break—for the actor but not for the audience. Jones stopped playing the piano, and McKay left the playing space to smoke a cigarette, which he had to do outside due to smoking regulations. About half of the audience could see what McKay was doing and almost invariably would discuss this loudly enough for the other half of the audience to know what was happening. In his review in the *Herald*, the critic Neil Cooper identified this moment as interrupting "the flow."[10] As intended, it did not "work" aesthetically; instead, it disrupted (and revealed) the service culture that underlies social expectations of performance. (During one performance in Glasgow, someone muttered loudly about not having paid for a ticket to wait while the actor had a fag break.) It further served the performance by offering a semblance of spontaneity for the rest of the performance and infusing the aesthetic construction with a fragility or non-inevitability that shored up the tension of the storytelling. This playfulness is fundamental to the experience of improvisation—the knowledge that it *could* be different, that what is being performed is contingent on the moment at hand.

Case Study III: *3rd Ring Out*

3rd Ring Out: Rehearsing the Future (2010–11) goes much further than the previous two examples in playing on the porousness of social and aesthetic relations.[11] It works from the premise of the apparently relational toward an immersion in a fictive scenario that functions in line with the aesthetics of tradition that Bourriaud terms "private, symbolic." *3rd Ring Out* is at once a performance, a game, a simulation, and an artistic event, eliding artistic and social practice in the production of an emergency planning–style rehearsal for a climate-changed future. It takes place in two shipping containers, the interiors of which resemble smart emergency planning cells. Split into groups and ushered into separate containers, spectators experience an interactive simulation of events that unfold as a result of climate change; the scenarios are led by two performers who play "team leaders." At key points, the audience members vote on decisions that then affect the course of the narrative. The performance toured to five locations in the United Kingdom in the spring of 2010; in each location, the scenario was adapted so that the narrative was specific to, and offered an accurate projection of the future of, each city in which it was performed. The fictional scenario took the audience forward into a future of global warming, from now until 2033, exploring the potential human consequences of climate change. It used scientific research to imagine how the world might be altered and what impact this might have on the United Kingdom. The production offered an interlinked web of potential catastrophes with far-reaching geopolitical consequences, such as mass migration and competition for resources.

The act of watching and interacting with the performance could be understood as itself a social practice, in the form of an exercise or rehearsal of the sorts of ethical dilemmas that might arise on the basis of problems caused by a destabilized climate. The project had a rather different genesis from its current focus on climate change. It emerged from a series of investigations into rehearsing for disaster, which began with looking at Cold War models of exercises that tested civic administration systems for post-apocalyptic governance, and moved on to explore contemporary emergency-planning procedures, including plans for dealing with terrorism. The research also encompassed interviews with people experienced in rehearsing responses to nuclear attack.

A major influence on *3rd Ring Out* is *Stages of Emergency*, in which the theater historian Tracy Davis explores Cold War nuclear exercises through the paradigm of rehearsal and performance. Davis's discussion of how these procedural rehearsals extend into everyday life in the present was an important catalyst for the project. Davis (2007, 2) suggests that civil defense has been "resurrected as homeland security"—that is, "Our small gestures—globalized through compliance at foreign airports and corporate offices, on public transport and in gatherings of all kinds—occur on a massive scale and are habituated into routines. . . . The mantra of the 'what-if' keeps the gestures fresh." Davis here extends the concept of "rehearsal" beyond the specialized functions of emergency planning, suggesting how such practices now suffuse everyday life, with their function as rehearsal rendered invisible. This characterization of such practices, in combination with our research for the project, had powerful implications for both the structure of *3rd Ring Out* and its politics. First, Davis's point reveals how these procedures can be construed as rehearsals for civil obedience. Anyone who flies regularly or visits public institutions in London or New York is well versed in obeying instructions to remove items of clothing, open bags for searching, and so on, regardless of any opinion on the part of the individuals searching and being searched as to the point or the efficacy of these actions.

What this suggests is that "belief" as such is not important in relation to such rehearsals; rather, what matters is compliance. This was precisely the most surprising and intriguing aspect of the research into Cold War exercises for *3rd Ring Out*: the interviewees who had participated in such rehearsals often did so regardless of their beliefs in the efficacy or otherwise of the exercise—or, indeed, their perception of the likelihood of the outbreak of nuclear war.[12] It also seems clear that, from American "duck and cover" procedures for schoolchildren in the 1950s to British "protect and survive" leaflets in the 1980s, it was widely believed that these activities would not adequately respond to the catastrophe unleashed by a nuclear bomb. Davis (2007, 10) quotes a director of the U.S. Federal Civil Defense Administration, who told Canadian officials in 1955 about his conviction that, having seen footage of a test of the new hydrogen bomb, "'Duck and Cover' [is] dead. You don't duck from the explosion of a nuclear weapon, you die, that's all." However, this lack of belief in its efficacy did not prevent participants from taking the rehearsal itself seriously. The "if" of the "what-if" did not need to be particularly stable to—as Davis puts it—"keep the gesture fresh." Whether you pass through airport security and mentally mock the inadequacy of the procedure, see it cynically or paranoically as a fear-mongering exercise on the part of governments, or believe wholeheartedly in its capacity to deter terrorists is irrelevant as long as you comply.

Returning to *3rd Ring Out*, this observation remains an important structural point, but one that can be framed in a more positive light. *3rd Ring Out* grafts the kinds of compliance afforded by theater etiquette onto the compliance required for the participation in such rehearsals. Aided by the "as-if" symbolic space of performance, the emphasis on practicing, rather than believing, sets to one side a technical debate over likelihood and probability that continues to choke popular discussions of climate change. Instead, the practicing focuses on the relationship between procedure and action: by voting, the audience participates in the ethics of decision making. Even if as an audience member you are simply obeying instructions, at the very least you will have rehearsed your attitude to the rehearsal—dystopian, utopian, or merely cynical.

Furthermore, and returning to the question of improvisation in performance, from discussion with emergency planners it seems that the most effective exercises are not those that prescribe precise courses of action, but those that are effectively guidance notes for improvisation. The scenarios provided to the civil servant "players" of nuclear war exercises look uncannily like the sort of instructions provided to actors when improvising a scene in rehearsal. The methodology of Katie Mitchell, a former associate director of London's National Theatre, suggests that actors require a certain set of tools to be able to improvise well. In relation to the scene at hand, they need to know what their aim is, what the situation is (this includes the setting and the relationship with one another in the scene), how long they have, and where they are (Velleman 2009). These are precisely the elements provided to civil servants in briefing documents for nuclear exercises: instructions for improvisation.[13]

In the blurred space "between the everyday and the fantastic" (Etchells 1999, 52), it is clear that it is the underlying conditions for improvisation that are key to its artistic efficacy. For 2011, one of the containers was converted into an installation and conversation space—a "strategy" cell—while performances took place in what was now characterized as the "emergency" cell.[14] While the performance "rehearses" short-term responses to an emergency, the installation improvised strategies for alternative, and sustainable, futures. The installation also offered a discursive space that was more explicitly "relational" than the performance. The opportunity to respond immediately to the provocations offered by the performance by suggesting ideas for the future of the city was welcomed by audiences at the Watford Imagine Festival and the Edinburgh Fringe Festival 2011.[15] What became clear in the Watford iteration of the installation was that an invitation to the audience members to improvise is not sufficient. The reliance of improvisational practices on pre-structured relationships was revealed by a general habitual recourse on the part of the audience to opinion poll–type responses to the question of a better future, from "more police on the high street" to "more hospitals." In the absence of an explicit "art" structure, the social relations reproduced borrowed from think tank or Council consultation–type events. The challenge for this aspect of *3rd Ring Out* became to harness the patent enthusiasm for being offered a forum for response (hundreds of responses were gathered in Watford) to an alternative practice that moved into less familiar and more creative territory. To this end, for the Edinburgh performances, seven artists from the city or nearby were invited to respond to suggestions made by the public for the city's future. Their creation of a network of consequences integrated the suggestions from the public into a comprehensive and imaginatively appealing projection for Edinburgh's future.[16]

While the response to the installation revealed a hunger for community engagement, *3rd Ring Out* problematizes the simple equation of participation with community that is explicit in Bourriaud's concept of relational aesthetics. An apparent community within the performance is established through the performers' continuous acknowledgment of the twelve audience-participants, intensified by their physical proximity in the small space of the shipping container, sitting around a shared table. However, the anonymous voting disrupts the chimera of consensus that participatory theater can foster. While the codes of dialogue among strangers might soften or disguise disagreement in the desire for a polite and ultimately impersonal consensus, the requirement to make a private decision for each vote, which then may or may not reflect the majority view, opens up the possibility of dissent. The voting outcomes repeatedly acknowledge that groups of people who experience performances together are not communities that express a joint identity. This was felt particularly acutely by some audience members in response to the question within the scenario of whether to accept refugees. Participants would share anecdotes of their shock when the majority of others at the same performance, for example, voted against refugees, a difference of opinion that implied a rift in a socially liberal consensus about human rights and that therefore challenged preconceptions about the values held by their fellow theatergoers. *3rd Ring Out* not only did not promise an emancipatory community politics or indulge in fantasies of the audience as a collective social body, but it demonstrated the fallacy promulgated by Bourriaud of assuming that such vague goodwill, constructed from the etiquette governing behavior in theaters (or, indeed, in art galleries), can ultimately be equated with genuine community.

Notes

1. See http://www.forcedentertainment.com/. Accessed July 15, 2016.

2. See http://www.guardian.co.uk/stage/2005/dec/22/theatre2. Accessed July 15, 2016.

3. For an excellent and succinct account of the historical antagonism between theater studies and performances studies, see Ridout, 2006, esp. 5–10.

4. See http://www.forcedentertainment.com/project/bloody-mess/. Accessed July 15, 2016.

5. After the brief hegemony of proscenium arch and end-on spatial configurations in the mid-twentieth century theater, shifts toward more "inclusive" spaces in the twenty-first century include the building of the Royal Shakespeare Company's new theater at Stratford-upon-Avon, modeled architecturally on a Renaissance courtyard theater, which both privileges interaction with the audience and satisfies a trend towards the historical "authenticity" fostered particularly at the reconstructed Globe Theatre in London. Both of these refer back to earlier historical periods in which engagement between audiences and the stage were the norm. The architecturally flexible Young Vic in London, built in 1970 as a temporary space and refurbished permanently in 2004–2006, is another example of a socially "inclusive" space, while the majority of London fringe theaters offer alterable seating and an undeniable social proximity.

6. *Discombobulator* was a fifteen-minute-long interdisciplinary piece made over ten days for a workshop performance at the Contemporary Music Festival of the Venice Biennale 2009. It was performed in London at the Purcell Rooms in 2010 as part of the annual international dance festival, Dance Umbrella.

7. See http://www.southbankcentre.co.uk/find/dance-performance/tickets/ben-duke-will-duke-dario-palermo-zoë-svendsen-53908. Accessed July 15, 2016.

8. See http://www.labiennale.org/en/dance/venues/teatro_piccolo_arsenale.html. Accessed July 15, 2016.

9. *Four Men and a Poker Game*, adapted and directed by Zoë Svendsen from a translation by John Willet of Brecht's short story "Four Men and a Poker Game," with music composed by David Paul Jones; performed by David McKay at Northern Stage, Newcastle, and The Tron, Glasgow, November 2008.

10. Neil Cooper, "Four Men and a Poker Game, Tron Theatre, Glasgow," *Herald Scotland*, November 21, 2008, http://metisarts.co.uk/four-men-and-a-poker-game/. Accessed July 15, 2016.

11. *3rd Ring Out* toured the United Kingdom in May–July 2010, performing at the Norfolk and Norwich Festival; in Newcastle, in association with Northern Stage; in Cambridge, in association with the Junction; at the Pulse Festival in Ipswich; and at the Greenwich and Docklands International Festival in London. In 2011, a new version of *3rd Ring Out* was presented at the Watford Imagine Festival and at the Edinburgh Fringe Festival.

12. All the interviews are gathered on the Internet under http://www.thebunkerproject.info. Accessed July 15, 2016.

13. For extensive examples of nuclear exercise briefing documents, see British National Archives, HO322/309, LAB12/1028, LAB12/1019; Cambridge Library Local Studies Collection, W12-0702F/C45.8.

14. See http://www.3rdringout.com/strategy-cell/. Accessed July 15, 2016.

15. *3rd Ring Out* was performed six times a day, with the installation open to the public for eight hours on June 24–28, 2011, at the Watford Imagine Festival. It was then presented at the Edinburgh Fringe Festival, situated on the Grassmarket, August 18–28, 2011.

16. The work of the seven artists is archived at http://www.3rdringout.com/blog/. Accessed July 15, 2016.

REFERENCES

Abowd, Gregory D., Elizabeth D. Mynatt, and Tom Rodden. 2002. "The Human Experience." *IEEE Pervasive Computing* (January–March): 48–57.

"A Brief History of the Music Department." http://www.mills.edu/academics/undergraduate/mus/history.php.

Abrahamson, Eric, and David H. Freedman. 2006. *A Perfect Mess: The Hidden Benefits of Disorder—How Crammed Closets, Cluttered Offices, and On-the-Fly Planning Make the World a Better Place.* London: Weidenfeld and Nicolson.

Abrams, Muhal Richard, and John Shenoy Jackson. 1973. "Association for the Advancement of Creative Musicians." *Black World* (November): 72–74.

Adlington, Robert. 2008. "Organizing Labor: Composers, Performers, and 'the Renewal of Musical Practice' in the Netherlands, 1969–72." *Musical Quarterly* 90, nos. 3–4:539–77.

———, ed. 2009. *Sound Commitments: Avant-garde Music and the Sixties.* Oxford: Oxford University Press.

———. 2013a. *Composing Dissent: Avant-Garde Music in 1960s.* Amsterdam: Oxford University Press.

———, ed. 2013b. *Red Strains: Music and Communism outside the Communist Bloc.* Oxford: Oxford University Press.

Adorno, Theodor. 2002a. *Essays on Music.* Edited by Richard Leppert. Translated by Susan Gillespie. Berkeley: University of California Press.

———. 2002b. "On Popular Music." *Studies in Philosophy and Social Science* 9 (1941): 17–48.

Ake, David. 2002. *Jazz Cultures.* Berkeley: University of California Press.

Alberro, Alexander, and Blake Stimson. 2009. *Institutional Critique: An Anthology of Artists' Writings.* Cambridge, MA: MIT Press.

Altman, Rick. 1981. *Genre: The Musical; A Reader.* London: Routledge.

———. 1987. *The American Film Musical.* Bloomington: Indiana University Press.

———. 1996. "Cinema and Genre." In *The Oxford History of World Cinema,* edited by Geoffrey Nowell-Smith, 276–85. Oxford: Oxford University Press.

Anderson, Benedict. 1983. *Imagined Communities: Reflections on the Origin and Spread of Nationalism.* London: Verso.

Atik, Yaakov. 1994. "The Conductor and the Orchestra: Interactive Aspects of the Leadership Process." *Leadership and Organization Development Journal* 15 (1): 22–28.

Attali, Jacques. 1985. *Noise: The Political Economy of Music*. Manchester: Manchester University Press.

Aumont, Jacques, and Michel Marie. 2007. *Dictionnaire théorique et critique du cinéma*. Paris: Armand Colin.

Auslander, Philip. 1999. *Liveness: Performance in a Mediatized Culture*. London: Routledge.

———. 2013. "Jazz Improvisation as a Social Arrangement." In *Taking It to the Bridge: Music as Performance*, edited by Nicholas Cook and Richard Pettengill, 52–69. Ann Arbor: University of Michigan Press.

Austin, John. 1996. "The Province of Jurisprudence Determined and the Uses of the Study of Jurisprudence." In *The Philosophy of Law: Classic and Contemporary Readings with Commentary*, edited by Frederick Schauer and Walter Sinnott-Armstrong, 32–39. New York: Oxford University Press.

Baas, Jacquelynn, ed. 2011. *Fluxus and the Essential Questions of Life*. Chicago: University of Chicago Press.

Bailey, Derek. 1992. *Improvisation: Its Nature and Practice in Music*. London: British Library National Sound Archive.

Balsamo, Anne. 2011. *Designing Culture: The Technological Imagination at Work*. Durham, NC: Duke University Press.

Banes, Sally. 1987. *Terpsichore in Sneakers*. Middletown, CT: Wesleyan University Press.

Barg, Lisa. 2013. "Queer Encounters in the Music of Billy Strayhorn." *Journal of the American Musicological Society* 66 (3): 721–824.

Barry, Andrew. 2013. *Material Politics: Disputes along the Pipeline*. West Sussex, UK: John Wiley and Sons.

Barry, Andrew, and Nigel Thrift. 2007. "Gabriel Tarde: Imitation, Invention and Economy." *Economy and Society* 36 (4): 509–25.

Bateson, Gregory. 1979. *Mind and Nature: A Necessary Unity*. New York: E.P. Dutton.

Baumes, Ben. 2005. "What Else Can This Thing Do? An Interview with Kenneth Goldsmith on Radio Practices." *Repellent Magazine*. http://epc.buffalo.edu/authors/goldsmith/repellent_interview.html.

BAVO [Gideon Boie and Matthias Pauwels]. 2007. "The Murder of Creativity in Rotterdam: From Total Creative Environments to Gentripunctural Injections." In *Mycreativity Reader: A Critique of Creative Industries*, edited by Geert Lovink and Ned Rossiter, 156–66. Amsterdam: Institute of Network Cultures.

Bazin, André. 1967. *What Is Cinema?* Vol. I. Translated by Hugh Gray. Berkeley: University of California Press.

Becker, Howard. 1963. *Outsiders: Studies in the Sociology of Deviance*. New York: Free Press.

Begbie, Jeremy S. 2000. *Theology, Music and Time*. Cambridge: Cambridge University Press.

Behrman, David. 1976. *On the Other Ocean*. Lovely Music CD 1041, 1976. Compact disc.

Benjamin, Walter. 1969. "The Work of Art in the Age of Mechanical Reproduction." In *Illuminations*. Translated by Harry Zohn, 217–52. New York: Schocken.

———. 1999. *The Arcades Project*. Edited by Rolf Tiedemann, translated by Howard Eiland and Kevin McLaughlin. Cambridge, MA: Harvard University Press.

Bennett, Jane. 2010. *Vibrant Matter: A Political Ecology of Things*. Durham, NC: Duke University Press.

Benson, Bruce Ellis. 2003. *The Improvisation of Musical Dialogue: A Phenomenology of Music*. Cambridge: Cambridge University Press.

Bergala, Alain. 2006. *Godard au travail*. Paris: Cahiers du Cinéma.

Berliner, Paul. 1994. *Thinking in Jazz: The Infinite Art of Improvisation*. Chicago: University of Chicago Press.

Bernstein, Charles. 1986. *Content's Dream: Essays 1975–1984*. Los Angeles: Sun and Moon.

———. 1992. "Optimism and Critical Excess." In *A Poetics*. Cambridge, MA: Harvard University Press.

Bernstein, David W. 2008. *The San Francisco Tape Music Center: 1960s Counterculture and the Avant-Garde*. Berkeley: University of California Press.

Bicât, Tina, and Chris Baldwin, eds. 2002. *Devised and Collaborative Theatre: A Practical Guide*. Marlborough, UK: Crowood.

Bird, Charles S., and Mamadou Kante. 1977. *An Ka Bamanankan Kalan: Intermediate Bambara*. Bloomington: Indiana University Linguistics Club.

Bischoff, John. 1991. "Software as Sculpture: Creating Music from the Ground Up." *Leonardo Music Journal* 1 (1): 37–40.

Bischoff, John, Rich Gold, and Jim Horton. 1978. "Music for an Interactive Network of Microcomputers." *Computer Music Journal* 2 (3): 24–9.

Bishop, Claire. 2004. "Antagonism and Relational Aesthetics." *October* 110: 51–79.

———. 2005. "The Social Turn: Collaboration and Its Discontents." *Artforum* 44 (6): 178–83.

———. 2006. *Participation*. London: Whitechapel.

———. 2012. "Participation and Spectacle: Where Are We Now?" In *Living as Form: Socially Engaged Art from 1991–2011*, edited by Nato Thompson, 34–45. Cambridge, MA: MIT Press.

Blacking, John. 1974. *How Musical Is Man?* Seattle: University of Washington Press.

Bloom, Harold. 1973. *The Anxiety of Influence: A Theory of Poetry*. New York: Oxford University Press.

Bluttal, Steven, ed. 2006. *Andy Warhol "Giant" Size*. London: Phaidon.

Boal, Augusto. 1998. *Legislative Theatre: Using Performance to Make Politics.* Translated by Adrian Jackson. London: Routledge.

Bogle, Donald. 2001. *Toms, Coons, Mulattoes, Mammies, and Bucks: An Interpretive History of Blacks in American Films.* New York: Continuum.

———. 2005. *Bright Boulevards, Bold Dreams: The Story of Black Hollywood.* New York: Random House.

Bök, Christian. 2002. *Pataphysics: The Poetics of an Imaginary Science.* Evanston, IL: Northwestern University Press.

———. 2005. "A Silly Key: Some Notes on *Soliloquy* by Kenneth Goldsmith." *Open Letter* 12 (7): 65–76.

———. 2006. "Aleatory Writing: Notes toward a Poetics of Chance." *Public* 33: 24–33.

Boland Jr., Richard J., and Fred Collopy. 2004. "Design Matters for Management." In *Managing as Designing*, edited by Richard Boland Jr. and Fred Collopy, 3–18. Stanford, CA: Stanford University Press.

Bolt Rasmussen, Mikkel. 2009. "The Politics of Interventionist Art: The Situationist International, Artist Placement Group, and Art Workers' Coalition." *Rethinking Marxism* 21 (1): 34–49.

Boon, Marcus. 2010. *In Praise of Copying.* Cambridge, MA: Harvard University Press.

Borges, Jorge Luis. 1964. *Labyrinths: Selected Stories and Other Writings.* Edited by Donald A. Yates and James E. Irby. New York: New Directions.

Born, Georgina. 1993a. "Afterword." In *Rock and Popular Music: Politics, Policies, Institutions*, edited by Tony Bennett, Lawrence Grossberg, John Shepherd, and Graeme Turner, 266–93. London: Routledge.

———. 1993b. "Understanding Music as Culture: Contributions from Popular Music Studies to a Social Semiotics of Music." In *Tendenze e metodi nella ricerca musicologica*, edited by Raffaele Pozzi, 211–28. Florence: Olschki.

———. 1995. *Rationalizing Culture: IRCAM, Boulez and the Institutionalization of the Musical Avant-Garde.* Berkeley: University of California Press.

———. 2004. *Uncertain Vision: Bert, Dyke, and the Reinvention of the BBC.* London: Secker and Warburg.

———. 2005. "On Musical Mediation: Ontology, Technology and Creativity." *Twentieth-Century Music* 2 (1): 7–36.

———. 2009. "Listening, Mediation, Event: Anthropological and Sociological Perspectives." *Journal of the Royal Musical Association* 134 (1): 79–89.

———. 2010a. "For a Relational Musicology: Music and Interdisciplinarity, beyond the Practice Turn." *Journal of the Royal Musical Association* 135 (2): 205–43.

———. 2010b. "On Tardean Relations: Temporality and Ethnography." In *The Social after Gabriel Tarde: Debates and Assessments*, edited by Matei Candea, 232–49. London: Routledge.

———. 2010c. "The Social and the Aesthetic: For a Post-Bourdieuian Theory of Cultural Production." *Cultural Sociology* 4 (2): 171–208.

————. 2011. "Music and the Materialization of Identities." *Journal of Material Culture* 16 (4): 1–13.

————. 2012. "Music and the Social." In *The Cultural Study of Music: A Critical Introduction*, 2nd ed., edited by Martin Clayton, Trevor Herbert, and Richard Middleton, 261–74. London: Routledge.

————. 2013a. "Drifting, Merging and Bifurcating: Institutional and Ontological Politics in Digital Art Musics in the UK." Paper presented at Music, Digitisation, Mediation: Towards Interdisciplinary Music Studies, Oxford University.

————. 2013b. "Introduction." In *Music, Sound and Space: Transformations of Public and Private Experience*, edited by Georgina Born, 1–69. Cambridge: Cambridge University Press.

————. 2013c. "Music: Ontology, Agency, and Creativity." In *Distributed Objects: Meaning and Mattering after Alfred Gell*, edited by Liana Chua and Mark Elliot, 130–54. Oxford: Berghahn.

————. 2014. "Refraction and Protention: Aesthetic-and-Social Dynamics in the Framing of Audience—5 Optics." Paper presented at Politics of Framing and Staging: Performance as Paradigm, Centre for Research in the Arts, Social Sciences, and Humanities, University of Cambridge.

Born, Georgina, and Andrew Barry. 2010. "Art-Science: From Public Understanding to Public Experiment." *Journal of Cultural Economy* 3 (1): 103–19.

Born, Georgina, and David Hesmondhalgh. 2000. "Introduction." In *Western Music and Its Others: Difference, Representation, and Appropriation in Music*, edited by Georgina Born and David Hesmondhalgh, 1–58. Berkeley: University of California Press.

Bourdieu, Pierre. 1977. *Outline of a Theory of Practice*. Translated by Richard Nice. New York: Cambridge University Press.

————. 1984. *Distinction: A Social Critique of the Judgment of Taste*. London: Routledge.

————. 1990. "Structures, Habitus, Practices." In *Outline of a Theory of Practice*, 52–65. Stanford, CA: Stanford University Press.

————. 1993. "The Field of Cultural Production." In *The Field of Cultural Production: Essays on Art and Literature*, edited by Randal Johnson, 29–73. New York: Columbia University Press.

Bourdieu, Pierre, and Hans Haacke. 1995. *Free Exchange*. Cambridge: Polity.

Bourriaud, Nicolas. 2002. *Relational Aesthetics*. Dijon, FR: Les Presses du Reel.

————. 2005. *Postproduction: Culture as Screenplay: How Art Reprograms the World*. New York: Lukas and Sternberg.

Bowen, José A. 1993. "The History of Remembered Innovation: Tradition and Its Role in the Relationship between Musical Works and Their Performances." *Journal of Musicology* 11 (2): 139–73.

Brackett, David. 2005. "Questions of Genre in Black Popular Music." *Black Music Research Journal* 25 (1/2): 73–92.

————, ed. 2009. *The Pop, Rock, and Soul Reader: Histories and Debates*. 2nd ed. New York: Oxford University Press.

———. 2016. *Categorizing Sound: Genre and 20th-Century Popular Music.* Berkeley: University of California Press.

———. 2014. "Popular Music Genres: Aesthetics, Commerce and Identity." In *The SAGE Handbook of Popular Music Studies,* edited by Andy Bennett and Steve Waksman. Thousand Oaks, CA: SAGE.

Brathwaite, Edward. 1973. *The Arrivants: A New World Trilogy.* Oxford: Oxford University Press.

Broneck, Kathy. 2002. "Graphical User Interface." In *Encyclopedia of New Media: An Essential Reference to Communication and Technology,* edited by Steve Jones, 207–9. Thousand Oaks, CA: SAGE.

Brooks, William. 1982. "On Being Tasteless." *Popular Music* 2: 9–18.

Buchloh, Benjamin H. D. 1990. "Conceptual Art 1962–1969: From the Aesthetic of Administration to the Critique of Institutions." *October* 55 (Winter): 105–43.

Bürger, Peter. 1984. *Theory of the Avant-Garde.* Translated by Michael Shaw. Manchester: Manchester University Press.

Burrows, Jared. 2004. "Musical Archetypes and Collective Consciousness: Cognitive Distribution and Free Improvisation." *Critical Studies in Improvisation* 1 (1). http://www.criticalimprov.com/article/view/11/35.

Cameron, Kim S. 2003. "Organizational Transformation through Architecture and Design: A Project with Frank Gehry." *Journal of Management Inquiry* 12 (1): 88–92.

Campbell, Keith W., Amy B. Brunell, and Joshua D. Foster. 2004. "Sitting Here in Limbo: Ego Shock and Posttraumatic Growth." *Psychological Inquiry* 15 (1): 22–26.

Candea, Matei, ed. 2010. *The Social after Gabriel Tarde: Debates and Assessments.* London: Routledge.

Capdenac, Michel. 1961. *Lettres françaises* (September 14).

Carastathis, Anna. 2010. "Fanon on Turtle Island: Revisiting the Question of Violence." In *Fanon and the Decolonization of Philosophy,* edited by Elizabeth A. Hoppe and Tracey Nicholls, 77–102. Lanham, MD: Lexington.

Cardew, Cornelius. 1971. "Towards an Ethic of Improvisation." In *Treatise Handbook, Including Bun no. 2 and Volo solo.* London: Edition Peters. http://www.ubu.com/papers/cardew_ethics.html.

Carles, Phillipe, and Jean-Louis Comolli. 1971. *Free Jazz/Black Power.* Paris: Gallimard Education.

Carlson, Marvin A. 1989. *Places of Performance: The Semiotics of Theatre Architecture.* Ithaca, NY: Cornell University Press.

Caux, Daniel. 1969. "A.A.C.M. Chicago." *Jazz Hot* 254 (October): 16–19.

Chadabe, Joel. 1997. *Electric Sound: The Past and Promise of Electronic Music.* Upper Saddle River, NJ: Prentice Hall.

Chandler, Annmarie, and Norie Neumark, eds. 2005. *At a Distance: Precursors to Art and Activism on the Internet.* Cambridge, MA: MIT Press.

Citron, Marcia J. 1993. *Gender and the Musical Canon.* Champaign: University of Illinois Press.

Clooney, Rosemary. 1999. *Girl Singer: An Autobiography.* New York: Broadway.

Cochrane, Richard. 2000. "Playing by the Rules: A Pragmatic Characterization of Musical Performance." *Journal of Aesthetics and Art Criticism* 58 (2): 135–41.

Collet, Jean. 1963. *Télérama* 716 (October 6).

Comaroff, Jean, and John Comaroff. 1991. *Of Revelation and Revolution, Vol. I, Christianity, Colonialism, and Consciousness in South Africa.* Chicago: University of Chicago Press.

———. 1997. *Of Revelation and Revolution: The Dialectics of Modernity on a South African Frontier.* Chicago: University of Chicago Press.

Compton, Wayde. 1999. *49th Parallel Psalm.* Vancouver, BC: Advance Editions.

———, ed. 2001. *Bluesprint: Black British Columbian Literature and Orature.* Vancouver, BC: Arsenal Pulp.

———. 2003a. "Culture at the Crossroads: Voodoo Aesthetics and the Axis of Blackness in Literature of the Black Diapora." *Matatu: Journal for African Culture and Society* 27/28:481–513.

———. 2003b. "The Reinventing Wheel: On Blending the Poetry of Cultures through Hip Hop Turntablism." *HorizonZero* 8. http://www.horizonzero.ca/flashsite/issue8/issue8.html?lang=enandsection=compton.

———. 2004. *Performance Bond.* Vancouver, BC: Arsenal Pulp.

———. 2010. *After Canaan: Essays on Race, Writing, and Region.* Vancouver, BC: Arsenal Pulp.

Cook, Nicholas. 1999. "At the Borders of Musical Identity: Schenker, Corelli, and the Graces." *Music Analysis* 18 (2): 179–233.

———. 2004a. "In Praise of Symbolic Poverty." In *Managing as Designing,* edited by Richard J. Boland Jr. and Fred Collopy, 85–89. Stanford, CA: Stanford University Press.

———. 2004b. "Making Music Together, or Improvisation and Its Others." *The Source: Challenging Jazz Criticism* 1: 5–25.

———. 2014. *Beyond the Score: Music as Performance.* New York: Oxford University Press.

Coote, Jeremy, and Anthony Shelton, eds. 1992. *Anthropology, Art, and Aesthetics.* Oxford: Clarendon.

Craft, Alastair. 2008. "The Role of Culture in Music Information Retrieval: A Model of Negotiated Musical Meaning, and Its Implications in Methodology and Evaluation of the Music Genre Classification Task." PhD diss., Goldsmiths, University of London.

Cresswell, Tim. 2006. *On the Move: Mobility in the Western World.* New York: Routledge.

Crickmay, Chris, and Miranda Tufnell. 1990. *Body Space Image: Notes towards Improvisation and Performance.* London: Dance Books.

Cross, Ian. 2006. "Four Issues in the Study of Music in Evolution." *World of Music* 48 (3): 55–63.

Dance, Stanley. 1970. *The World of Duke Ellington.* New York: Da Capo.

Darlington, W. A. 1922. *Through the Fourth Wall*. London: Chapman and Hall.

Davidson, Jane, and James Goode. 2002. "Social and Musical Co-ordination between Members of a String Quartet: An Exploratory Study." *Music Psychology* 30 (2): 186–201.

Davis, Tracy C. 2007. *Stages of Emergency: Cold War Nuclear Civil Defense*. Durham, NC: Duke University Press.

Day, Timothy. 2000. *A Century of Recorded Music: Listening to Musical History*. New Haven, CT: Yale University Press.

de Baecque, Antoine. 2009. *La nouvelle vague: Portrait d'une jeunesse*. Paris: Flammarion.

de Certeau, Michel. 1988. *The Practice of Everyday Life*. Translated by Steven Rendall. Berkeley: University of California Press.

Debord, Guy. 1981. "Methods of Detournement." In *Situationist International Anthology*. Edited and translated by Ken Knabb. Berkeley, CA: Bureau of Public Secrets.

DeLanda, Manuel. 2006. *A New Philosophy of Society: Assemblage Theory and Social Complexity*. London: Continuum.

———. 2008. "Deleuze, Materialism and Politics." In *Deleuze and Politics*, edited by Ian Buchanan and Nicholas Thoburn, 160–77. Edinburgh: Edinburgh University Press.

Deleuze, Gilles. 1988. *Foucault*. Translated by Séan Hand. London: Athlone.

———. 2001. *Pure Immanence: Essays on a Life*. Introduction by John Rajchman, translated by Anne Boyman. New York: Zone.

Deleuze, Gilles, and Félix Guattari. 1987. *A Thousand Plateaus: Capitalism and Schizophrenia*. Translated by Brian Massumi. Minneapolis: University of Minnesota Press.

DeMicheal, Don. 1998. "John Coltrane and Eric Dolphy Answer the Jazz Critics." In *The John Coltrane Companion: Five Decades of Commentary*, edited by Carl Woideck, 109–17. New York: Schirmer.

Denis, Paul. 1943. "The Negro Makes Advances: Edging into Radio, Films; Bigger than Ever in Music; and despite Many Obstacles." *Billboard* (January 2): 28.

DeNora, Tia. 2003. *After Adorno: Rethinking Music Sociology*. Cambridge: Cambridge University Press.

———. 2010. *Music in Everyday Life*. Cambridge: Cambridge University Press.

Derrida, Jacques. 1980. "The Law of Genre." Translated by Avital Ronell. In *Critical Inquiry* 7 (1): 55–81.

———. 2005. *On Touching: Jean Luc Nancy*. Stanford, CA: Stanford University Press.

DeVeaux, Scott. 1988. "Bebop and the Recording Industry: The 1942 AFM Recording Ban Reconsidered." *Journal of the American Musicological Society* 41 (1): 126–65.

———. 1991. "Constructing the Jazz Tradition: Jazz Historiography." *Black American Literature Forum* 25 (3): 525–60.

————. 1997. *The Birth of Bebop: A Social and Musical History*. Berkeley: University of California Press.

Dewdney, A. K. 1987. "Computer Recreations: Diverse Personalities Search for Social Equilibrium at a Computer Party." *Scientific American* (September): 112–15.

Diprose, Rosalyn. 2002. *Corporeal Generosity: On Giving with Nietzsche, Merleau-Ponty, and Levinas*. Albany: State University of New York Press.

Dixon, Melvin. 2000. "A Conversation with Melvin Dixon." Interviewed by Jerome de Romanet. *Callaloo* 23 (1): 84–109.

Dodd, Julian. 2007. *Works of Music: An Essay in Ontology*. Oxford: Oxford University Press.

Douchet, Jean. 1998. *Nouvelle vague*. Vanves, FR: Hazan.

Dourish, Paul. 2004. "What We Talk about When We Talk about Context." *Personal and Ubiquitous Computing* 8 (1): 19–30.

Downey, Anthony. 2007. "Towards a Politics of (Relational) Aesthetics." *Third Text* 21 (3): 267–75.

DuCille, Ann. 1997. "The Shirley Temple of My Familiar." *Transition* 73: 10–32.

Dufrenne, Mikel. 1989. *The Phenomenology of Aesthetic Experience*. Translated by Edward S. Casey. Evanston, IL: Northwestern University Press.

Dworkin, Craig Douglas. 2007. "The Imaginary Solution." *Contemporary Literature* 48 (1): 29–60.

Dworkin, Craig Douglas, and Kenneth Goldsmith, eds. 2011. *Against Expression: An Anthology of Conceptual Writing*. Evanston, IL: Northwestern University Press.

Edwards, Brent Hayes. 2004. "The Literary Ellington." In *Uptown Conversations: The New Jazz Studies*, edited by Robert G. O'Meally, Brent Hayes Edwards, and Farah Jasmine Griffin, 326–56. New York: Columbia University Press.

Egen, Daniel. 2010. *America's Film Legacy: The Authoritative Guide to the Landmark Movies in the National Registry*. New York: Continuum.

Eliot, T. S. 1957. "Poetry in the Eighteenth Century." In *The Pelican Guide to English Literature 4: From Dryden to Johnson*, edited by Boris Ford, 271–77. Harmondsworth, UK: Penguin.

Ellington, Duke. 1972. *Music Is My Mistress*. New York: Oxford University Press.

Engels, Friedrich. 1972. *The Origin of the Family, Private Property and the State*. New York: Pathfinder.

Ennis, Philip. 1992. *The Seventh Stream: The Emergence of Rocknroll in American Popular Music*. Hanover, NH: Wesleyan University Press.

Epp, Roger. 2008. *We Are All Treaty People: Prairie Essays*. Edmonton: University of Alberta Press.

Erenberg, Lewis. 1998. *Swingin' the Dream: Big Band Jazz and the Rebirth of American Culture*. Chicago: University of Chicago Press.

Esquenazi, Jean-Pierre. 2004. *Godard et la société française des années 1960*. Paris: Armand Colin.

———. 2007. *Sociologie des oeuvres*. Paris: Armand Colin.

Etchells, Tim. 1999. *Certain Fragments: Contemporary Performance and Forced Entertainment*. London: Routledge.

Fanon, Frantz. 1963. *The Wretched of the Earth: A Negro Psychoanalyst's Study of the Problems of Racism and Colonialism in the World Today*. Translated by Constance Farrington. New York: Grove.

Feigelson, Kristian, and Adeline Lamberbourg. 2009. "La fabrique filmique: Les coulisses des tournages." In *Cinéma et stratégi: Économie des interdépendances*, 103–12. Edited by Laurent Créton. *Théorème* 12.

Feld, Steven. 1982. *Sound and Sentiment: Birds, Weeping, Poetics, and Song in Kaluli Expression*. Philadelphia: University of Pennsylvania Press.

———. 1984. "Sound Structure as Social Structure." *Ethnomusicology* 24 (3): 383–409.

———. 1988. "Aesthetics as Iconicity of Style, or 'Lift-Up-Over Sounding': Getting into the Kaluli Groove." *Yearbook for Traditional Music* 20: 74–113.

———. 1994. "Aesthetics as Iconicity of Style." In *Music Grooves: Essays and Dialogue*, 109–96. Chicago: University of Chicago Press.

———. 1996. "Waterfalls of Song: An Acoustemology of Place Resounding in Bosavi, Papua New Guinea." In *Senses of Place*, edited by Steven Feld and Keith Basso, 91–135. Santa Fe, NM: Schools of American Research Press.

Ferguson, Roderick A. 2004. *Aberrations in Black: Toward a Queer of Color Critique*. Minneapolis: University of Minnesota Press.

Ferguson, Russell, ed. 1998. *Out of Actions: Between Performance and the Object 1949–1979*. New York: Thames and Hudson.

Fischlin, Daniel. 2009. "Improvisation and the Unnameable: On Being Instrumental." *Critical Studies in Improvisation* 5 (1). http://www.criticalimprov.com/article/view/1121/1638.

Fischlin, Daniel, and Ajay Heble, eds. 2004. *The Other Side of Nowhere: Jazz, Improvisation, and Communities in Dialogue*. Middletown, CT: Wesleyan University Press.

Fischlin, Daniel, Ajay Heble, and George Lipsitz. 2013. *The Fierce Urgency of Now: Improvisation, Rights, and the Ethics of Co-Creation*. Durham, NC: Duke University Press.

Florida, Richard L. 2012. *The Rise of the Creative Class, Revisited*. Kindle Edition. New York: Basic.

Floyd Jr., Samuel A. 1991. "Ring Shout! Literary Studies, Historical Studies, and Black Music Inquiry." *Black Music Research Journal* 11 (2): 49–70.

Fornäs, Johan. 1994. "Karaoke: Subjectivity, Play and Interactive Media." *Nordicom Review* 15 (1): 87–103.

Foster, Hal. 1995. "The Artist as Ethnographer?" In *The Traffic in Culture: Refiguring Art and Anthropology*, edited by George Marcus and Fred Myers, 302–9. Berkeley: University of California Press.

———. 2006. "Chat Rooms." In *Participation*, edited by Claire Bishop, 190–95. London: Whitechapel.

Foucault, Michel. 1972. *The Archaeology of Knowledge and the Discourse on Language.* New York: Pantheon.

———. 1977a. "Nietzsche, Genealogy, History." In *Language, Counter-Memory, Practice: Selected Essays and Interviews by Michel Foucault.* Edited by Donald F. Bouchard, translated by Donald F. Bouchard and Sherry Simon, 139–64. Ithaca, NY: Cornell University Press.

———. 1977b. "Theatrum Philosophicum." In *Language, Counter-Memory, Practice,* edited by Donald F. Bouchard, translated by Donald F. Bouchard and Sherry Simon, 165–96. Ithaca, NY: Cornell University Press.

———. 1979. *Discipline and Punish: The Birth of the Prison.* New York: Vintage.

———. 1982. "The Subject and Power." *Critical Inquiry* 8 (4): 777–95.

Fournier, Christiane. 1958. *Nos enfants sont-ils des monstres?* Paris: Lib. Arthème Fayard.

Frank, Thomas. 1997. *The Conquest of Cool: Business Culture, Counterculture, and the Rise of Hip Consumerism.* Chicago: University of Chicago Press.

Fraser, Andrea. 2005. "From the Critique of Institutions to an Institution of Critique." *Artforum* 44 (1): 278–85.

Freedman, Marvin. 1940. "Black Music's on Top; White Jazz Stagnant." *Down Beat* (April 1): 7, 20.

Freire, Paulo. 2000. *Pedagogy of the Oppressed.* Translated by Myra Bergman Ramos. New York: Bloomsbury.

Fried, Michael. 1967. "Art and Objecthood." In *Art and Objecthood: Essays and Reviews,* 148–72. Chicago: University of Chicago Press.

———. 1980. *Absorption and Theatricality.* London: University of California Press.

Friedman, Ken, ed. 1998. *The Fluxus Reader.* West Sussex, UK: Academy Editions.

Friedwald, Will. 1996. *Jazz Singing: America's Great Voices from Bessie Smith to Bebop and Beyond.* New York: Da Capo.

Frith, Simon. 1998. *Performing Rites: On the Value of Popular Music.* Cambridge, MA: Harvard University Press.

Frost, Anthony, and Ralph Yarrow. 1990. *Improvisation in Drama.* Basingstoke, UK: Macmillan.

Frow, John. 2005. *Genre.* London: Routledge.

Gabbard, Krin. 1996. *Jammin' at the Margins: Jazz and the American Cinema.* Chicago: University of Chicago Press.

Gaonkar, Dilip, and Elizabeth Povinelli. 2003. "Technologies of Public Forms: Circulation, Transfiguration, Recognition." *Public Culture* 15 (2): 385–97.

Gatens, Moira, and Genevieve Lloyd. 2002. *Collective Imaginings: Spinoza, Past and Present.* London: Routledge.

Gates, Henry Louis. 1988. *The Signifying Monkey: A Theory of African American Literary Criticism.* Oxford: Oxford University Press.

Gauthier, Guy. 2002. "Jean Rouch, Gourou Nouvelle Vague." *Cinémaction* 104, *Flashback sur la Nouvelle Vague* special issue. Paris: Corlet Télérama.

Gehry, Frank. 2004. "Reflection on Designing and Architectural Practice." In

Managing as Designing, edited by Richard J. Boland Jr. and Fred Collopy, 19–35. Stanford, CA: Stanford University Press.

Gendron, Bernard. 2002. *Between Montmartre and the Mudd Club: Popular Music and the Avant-Garde*. Chicago: University of Chicago Press.

Gennari, John. 2006. *Blowin' Hot and Cool: Jazz and Its Critics*. Chicago: University of Chicago Press.

Giddens, Anthony. 1984. *The Constitution of Society: Outline of the Theory of Structuration*. Cambridge: Polity.

Gilroy, Paul. 1993. *The Black Atlantic: Modernity and Double Consciousness*. Cambridge, MA: Harvard University Press.

———. 2000. *Against Race: Imagining Political Culture beyond the Color Line*. Cambridge, MA: Harvard University Press.

Goehr, Lydia. 1992. *The Imaginary Museum of Musical Works: An Essay in the Philosophy of Music*. Oxford: Clarendon.

Goffman, Erving. 1959. *The Presentation of Self in Everyday Life*. New York: Doubleday.

———. 1967. *Interaction Ritual: Essays in Face-to-Face Behavior*. New York: Pantheon.

———. 1986. *Frames Analysis: An Essay on the Organization of Experience*. Boston: Northeastern University Press.

Gold, Rich. 1993a. "Art in the Age of Ubiquitous Computing." *American Art* 7 (4): 2–11.

———. 1993b. "This Is Not a Pipe." *Communications of the ACM* 36 (7): 72.

———. 2007. *The Plenitude: Creativity, Innovation, and Making Stuff*. Cambridge, MA: MIT Press.

———. 2008. *The Plenitude: Design and Engineering in the Era of Ubiquitous Computing*. Cambridge, MA: MIT Press. http://cygnuscon.files.wordpress .com/2013/02/the-plenitude.pdf.

Goldsmith, Kenneth. 1999. "Near the Edge and Off the Page: Blurring the Boundaries between Composition and Improvisation at the End of the Century." *Pulse! Magazine* 180 (April).

———, ed. 2004. *I'll Be Your Mirror: The Selected Andy Warhol Interviews: 1962–1987*. New York: Carroll and Graf.

———. 2011a. "My Career in Poetry; or, How I Learned to Stop Worrying and Love the Institution." *Enclave Review* (Spring): 7–9.

———. 2011b. *Uncreative Writing: Managing Language in the Digital Age*. Kindle Edition. New York: Columbia University Press.

———. 2011c. "Unedited Transcript: Kenneth Goldsmith." Interviewed by Marcus Boon. *BOMB* 117. http://bombsite.com/issues/117/articles/6071.

———. 2013a. "Re: [conceptual-writing] blast from the past: Kenny's prose as a business guy." Email to the Conceptual Writing list in response to Darren Wershler, December 24, 4:24 pm. http://groups.yahoo.com/neo/groups /conceptual-writing/info. Restricted.

———. 2013b. *Seven American Deaths and Disasters*. Brooklyn, NY: PowerHouse.

Govan, Emma, Helen Nicholson, and Katie Normington. 2007. *Making a Performance: Devising Histories and Contemporary Practices*. London: Routledge.

Gracyk, Theodore. 1996. *Rhythm and Noise: An Aesthetics of Rock*. Durham, NC: Duke University Press.

Gratton, Peter. 2010. "Sovereign Violence, Racial Violence." In *Fanon and the Decolonization of Philosophy*, edited by Elizabeth A. Hoppe and Tracey Nicholls, 103–14. Lanham, MD: Lexington.

Gray, Herman. 2003. "Transcommunality: Politics, Culture, and Practice." In John Brown Childs, *Transcommunality: From the Politics of Conversion to the Ethics of Respect*, 197–210. Philadelphia: Temple University Press.

Greenberg, Clement. 1993. *The Collected Essays and Criticism, Volume 4: Modernism with a Vengeance, 1957–1969*, edited by John O'Brian. Chicago: University of Chicago Press.

Guerrero, Ed. 1993. *Framing Blackness: The African American Image in Film*. Philadelphia: Temple University Press.

Gushee, Lawrence. 1998. "The Improvisation of Louis Armstrong." In *In the Course of Performance: Studies in the World of Musical Improvisation*, edited by Bruno Nettl with Melinda Russell, 291–334. Chicago: University of Chicago Press.

Hagberg, Garry. 2016. "Playing as One: Ensemble Improvisation, Collective Intention, and Group Attention." In *The Oxford Handbook of Critical Improvisation Studies*, edited by George E. Lewis and Benjamin Piekut, 481–99. Oxford: Oxford University Press.

Hagstrom-Miller, Karl. 2010. *Segregating Sound: Inventing Folk and Pop Music in the Age of Jim Crow*. Durham, NC: Duke University Press.

Hajdu, David. 1996. *Lush Life: A Biography of Billy Strayhorn*. New York: Farrar, Straus and Giroux.

———. 1999. "A Jazz of Their Own." *Vanity Fair* (May): 188–96.

Hall, Stuart. 1992. "What Is This 'Black' in Black Popular Culture?" In *Black Popular Culture*, edited by Gina Dent, 21–36. Seattle: Bay Press.

Hanslick, Eduard. 1986. *On the Musically Beautiful: A Contribution Towards the Revision of the Aesthetics of Music*. Translated by Geoffrey Payzant. Indianapolis, IN: Hackett.

Harper, Phillip Brian. 1996. *"Are We Not Men?": Masculine Anxiety and the Problem of African American Identity*. New York: Oxford University Press.

Harvie, Jen, and Andy Lavender, eds. 2010. *Making Contemporary Theatre: International Rehearsal Processes*. Manchester: Manchester University Press.

Heble, Ajay. 2000. *Landing on the Wrong Note: Jazz, Dissonance, and Critical Practice*. New York: Routledge.

Heddon, Deirdre, and Jane Milling. 2006. *Devising Performance: A Critical History*. Basingstoke, UK: Palgrave Macmillan.

Hennion, Antoine. 1993. *La passion musicale: Une sociologie de la médiation*. Paris: Métailié.

———. 2001. "Music Lovers: Taste as Performance." *Theory, Culture and Society* 18 (5): 1–22.

———. 2003. "Music and Mediation: Toward a New Sociology of Music." In *The Cultural Study of Music: A Critical Introduction*, edited by Martin Clayton, Trevor Herbert, and Richard Middleton, 80–91. London: Routledge.

Hesmondhalgh, David. 2005. *Understanding Media: Inside Celebrity*. New York: Open University Press.

Higgins, Hannah. 2002. *Fluxus Experience*. Berkeley: University of California Press.

Hobbes, Thomas. 2007. "The Leviathan" (excerpt). In *Ethical Theory: Classical and Contemporary Readings*, 5th ed., edited by Louis P. Pojman, 326–35. Belmont, CA: Thomson Wadsworth.

hooks, bell. 1989. "'when i was a young soldier for the revolution': coming to a voice." In *Talking Back: Thinking Feminist, Thinking Black*. Cambridge, MA: South End Press.

———. 1990. *Yearning, Race, Gender, and Cultural Politics*. Cambridge, MA: South End.

———. 1992. *Black Looks: Race and Representation*. New York: Routledge.

———. 1994. *Outlaw Culture: Resisting Representations*. New York: Routledge.

———. 1995a. *Art on My Mind: Visual Politics*. New York: New Press.

———. 1995b. *Killing Rage: Ending Racism*. New York: Henry Holt.

———. 2000. *Where We Stand: Class Matters*. New York: Routledge.

———. 2008. "Feminist Politics: Where We Stand." In *Women's Voices, Feminist Visions: Classic and Contemporary Readings*, 4th ed., 40–42. New York: McGraw-Hill.

———. 2009. *Belonging: A Culture of Place*. New York: Routledge.

Horne, Lena, and Richard Schickel. 1986. *Lena*. New York: Limelight.

Horton, Jim. 1999. "Unforeseen Music: The Autobiographical Notes of Jim Horton." *Leonardo Music Journal Online* 9. http://leonardo.info/lmj/horton.html.

Howland, John. 2009. *Ellington Uptown: Duke Ellington, James P. Johnson, and the Birth of Concert Jazz*. Ann Arbor: University of Michigan Press.

Hubbs, Nadine. 2004. *The Queer Composition of America's Sound: Gay Modernists, American Music and National Identity*. Berkeley: University of California Press.

Huhtamo, Erkki. 1999. "From Cybernation to Interaction: A Contribution to an Archaeology of Interactivity." In *The Digital Dialectic: New Essays on New Media*, edited by Peter Lunenfeld, 96–110. Cambridge, MA: MIT Press.

Hutcheon, Linda. 1988. *A Poetics of Postmodernism: History, Theory, Fiction*. New York: Routledge.

"In Memory: Rich Gold (1950–2003)." 2003. *Leonardo* 36 (3): 253–54.

Ingold, Tim. 1996. "Aesthetics Is a Cross-Cultural Category." In *Key Debates in Anthropology*. London: Routledge.

Jarry, Alfred. 1996. *Exploits and Opinions of Dr. Faustroll, Pataphysician.* Translated by Simon Watson Taylor. Boston: Exact Change.

Johnson, Bruce. 2002. "Jazz as Cultural Practice." In *The Cambridge Companion to Jazz,* edited by Mervyn Cooke and David Horn, 96–113. Cambridge: Cambridge University Press.

Johnson, James. 1995. *Listening in Paris: A Cultural History.* Berkeley: University of California Press.

Johnston, Chris. 2006. *The Improvisation Game: Discovering the Secrets of Spontaneous Performance.* London: Nick Hern.

Johnstone, Keith. 1979. *Impro: Improvisation and the Theatre.* London: Faber and Faber.

———. 1999. *Impro for Storytellers: Theatresports and the Art of Making Things Happen.* London: Faber and Faber.

Jones, Leroi [Amiri Baraka]. 1963. *Blues People: Negro Music in White America.* New York: William Morrow.

Kalar, Brent. 2006. *The Demands of Taste in Kant's Aesthetics.* London: Continuum.

Kallberg, Jeffrey. 1996. *Chopin at the Boundaries: Sex, History, and Musical Genre.* Cambridge, MA: Harvard University Press.

Kaufman, Jason. 2007. "So Bad It's Good." *Contexts* 6 (Fall): 81–4.

Keil, Charles. 1966. *Urban Blues.* Chicago: University of Chicago Press.

Kelleher, Joe, and Nicholas Ridout, eds. 2007. *The Theatre of Societas Raffaello Sanzio.* London: Routledge.

Kernfeld, Barry. 1995. *What to Listen for in Jazz.* New Haven, CT: Yale University Press.

Kershaw, Baz. 1992. *The Politics of Performance: Radical Theatre as Cultural Intervention.* London: Routledge.

———, ed. 2004. *The Cambridge History of British Theatre, Volume 3, since 1895.* Cambridge: Cambridge University Press.

Kester, Grant H. 2004. *Conversation Pieces: Community and Communication in Modern Art.* Berkeley: University of California Press.

Kivy, Peter. 1993a. "Platonism in Music: A Kind of Defense." In *The Fine Art of Repetition: Essays in the Philosophy of Music,* 35–58. Cambridge: Cambridge University Press.

———. 1993b. "Platonism in Music: Another Kind of Defense." In *The Fine Art of Repetition: Essays in the Philosophy of Music,* 59–74. Cambridge: Cambridge University Press.

———. 2009. *Antithetical Arts: On the Ancient Quarrel between Literature and Music.* Oxford: Oxford University Press.

Knight, Arthur. 2002. *Disintegrating the Musical: Black Performance and American Musical Film.* Durham, NC: Duke University Press.

Kofsky, Frank. 1970. *Black Nationalism and the Revolution in Music.* New York: Pathfinder.

———. 1998 (1970). *John Coltrane and the Jazz Revolution of the 1960s* [origi-
nally published as *Black Nationalism and the Revolution in Music*]. New York:
Pathfinder.

Kolodin, Irving. 1941. "The Dance Band Business: A Study in Black and White."
Harper's Magazine (June): 78–82.

Kostelanetz, Richard. 1988. *Conversing with Cage*, 2nd ed. New York: Limelight.

Kozel, Susan. 2007. *Closer: Performance, Technologies, Phenomenology*. Cambridge, MA: MIT Press.

———. 2010a. "Intuitive Improvisation: A Phenomenological Method for Dance
Experimentation with Mobile Digital Media." *Studia UBB Philosophia* 3:
71–80. http://www.studia.ubbcluj.ro/download/pdf/557.pdf.

———. 2010b. "The Virtual and the Physical: A Phenomenological Approach to
Performance Research." In *The Routledge Companion to Research in the Arts*.
Edited by Michael Biggs and Henrik Karlsson, 204–22. London: Routledge.

———. 2013. "Collective Corporeality: Listening to the Body through Twitter."
In *Digital Storytelling and Mobile Media: Narrative Practices with Locative Technologies*. Edited by Jason Farman, 79–94. London: Routledge.

Krukowski, Damon. 2008. "Free Verses: Kenneth Goldsmith and UbuWeb." *Artforum* (March). http://epc.buffalo.edu/authors/goldsmith/artforum.html.

Latour, Bruno. 2005. *Reassembling the Social: An Introduction to Actor Network
Theory*. Oxford: Oxford University Press.

Lautréamont, Comte de. 1994. *Maldoror and The Complete Works of the Comte de
Lautreamont*. Translated by Alexis Lykiard. Cambridge, MA: Exact Change.

Law, John, and John Urry. 2004. "Enacting the Social." *Economy and Society*
33 (3): 390–410.

Layton, Robert. 1991. *The Anthropology of Art*. Cambridge: Cambridge University Press.

Leacroft, Richard. 1949. *Civic Theatre Design*. London: D. Dobson.

Lehmann, Andreas, and Reinhard Kopiez. 2010. "The Difficulty of Discerning
between Improvised and Composed Music." *Musicae Scientiae*, special issue:
113–29.

Lehmann, Hans Thies. 2006. *Postdramatic Theatre*. Translated by Karen Jürs-
Munby. London: Routledge.

Lepecki, Andre. 2006. *Exhausting Dance*. London: Routledge.

Levinson, Jerrold. 1990a. "What a Musical Work Is." In *Music, Art, and Metaphysics*, 63–88. Ithaca, NY: Cornell University Press.

———. 1990b. "What a Musical Work Is, Again." In *Music, Art, and Metaphysics*,
215–65. Ithaca, NY: Cornell University Press.

Lewis, Eric. 2007. "Ontology, Originality and the Musical Work: Copyright Law
and the Status of Samples." In *Meredith Lectures 2006: Intellectual Property at
the Edge: New Approaches to IP in a Transsystemic World*, edited by the Faculty
of Law, McGill University, 169–206. Montreal: Yvon Blais.

Lewis, George E. 1996. "Improvised Music after 1950: Afrological and Eurological Perspectives." *Black Music Research Journal* 16 (1): 91–122.

———. 1998. "Singing Omar's Song: A (Re)construction of Great Black Music." *Lenox Avenue* 4: 69–92.

———. 2000. "Too Many Notes: Computers, Complexity and Culture in Voyager." *Leonardo Music Journal* 10:33–39.

———. 2003. "The Secret Love between Interactivity and Improvisation, or Missing in Interaction: A Prehistory of Computer Interactivity." In *Improvisation V: 14 Beiträge*, edited by Walter Fähndrich, 193–203. Winterthur: Amadeus.

———. 2004. "Improvised Music after 1950: Afrological and Eurological Perspectives." In *The Other Side of Nowhere: Jazz, Improvisation, and Communities in Dialogue*, edited by Daniel Fischlin and Ajay Heble, 131–72. Middletown, CT: Wesleyan University Press.

———. 2007. "Mobilitas Animi: Improvising Technologies, Intending Chance." *Parallax* 13 (4): 108–22.

———. 2008. *A Power Stronger than Itself: The AACM and American Experimental Music*. Chicago: University of Chicago Press.

———. 2009. "The Condition of Improvisation." Paper presented at the Fourth Annual Festival/Conference of the International Society for Improvised Music, University of California, Santa Cruz, December. http://www .improvisedmusic.org/writings/Lewis.UCSC.keynote.v3.pdf.

Lipsitz, George. 1994. *Dangerous Crossroads: Popular Music, Postmodernism and the Poetics of Place*. London: Verso.

Liu, Alan. 2004. *The Laws of Cool: Knowledge Work and the Culture of Information*. Chicago: University of Chicago Press.

Lomax, Alan. 1962. "Song Structure and Social Structure." *Ethnology* 1, no. 4:425–51.

Long, Nicholas, and Henrietta Moore. 2012a. *Sociality: New Directions*. Oxford: Berghahn.

———. 2012b. "Sociality Revisited: Setting a New Agenda." *Cambridge Anthropology* 30 (1): 40–47.

Lorand, Ruth. 1989. "Free and Dependent Beauty: A Puzzling Issue." *British Journal of Aesthetics* 29 (1): 32–40.

MacKinnon, Catharine. 1983. "Feminism, Marxism, Method, and the State: Toward Feminist Jurisprudence." *Signs: Journal of Women in Culture and Society* 8 (4): 635–58.

Mackintosh, Iain. 1993. *Architecture, Actor and Audience*. London: Routledge.

Magee, Jeffrey. 1999. "Fletcher Henderson, Composer: A Counter-Entry to the 'International Dictionary of Black Composers.'" *Black Music Research Journal* 19 (1): 61–70.

Manning, Susan. 2004. *Modern Dance, Negro Dance: Race in Motion*. Minneapolis: University of Minnesota Press.

Manovich, Lev. 2001. *The Language of New Media*. Cambridge, MA: MIT Press.

Marie, Laurent. 2005. *Le cinéma est à nous. Le PCF et le cinéma français de la libération à nos jours*. Paris: L'Harmattan.

Marlatt, Daphne, and Carole Itter, eds. 1979. *Opening Doors: Vancouver's East End*. Victoria, BC: Aural History Program.

Martin, Stewart. 2007. "Critique of Relational Aesthetics." *Third Text* 21 (4): 369–86.

McClary, Susan. 1991. *Feminine Endings: Music, Gender, and Sexuality*. Minneapolis: University of Minnesota Press.

McGonigal, Jane Evelyn. 2006. "This Might Be a Game: Ubiquitous Play and Performance at the Turn of the Twenty-First Century." PhD diss., University of California, Berkeley.

McKay, George. 2005. *Circular Breathing: The Cultural Politics of Jazz in Britain*. Durham, NC: Duke University Press.

Meintjes, Louise. 2003. *Sound of Africa! Making Music Zulu in a South African Studio*. Durham, NC: Duke University Press.

Merleau-Ponty, Maurice. 1968. *The Visible and the Invisible*. Translated by Alphonso Lingis. Evanston, IL: Northwestern University Press.

Mermikides, Alex, and Jackie Smart, eds. 2010. *Devising in Process*. Basingstoke, UK: Palgrave Macmillan.

Metzger, Gustav. 1972. "A Critical Look at Artist Placement Group." *Studio International* 940: 4–5.

Miller, Paul. 2004. *Rhythm Science*. Mediawork Pamphlet Series. Cambridge, MA: Mediawork/MIT Press.

Monson, Ingrid. 1996. *Saying Something: Jazz Improvisation and Interaction*. Chicago: University of Chicago Press.

———. 2002. "Jazz Improvisation." In *The Cambridge Companion to Jazz*, edited by Mervyn Cooke and David Horn, 114–32. Cambridge: Cambridge University Press.

———. 2007. *Freedom Sounds: Civil Rights Call Out to Jazz and Africa*. Oxford: Oxford University Press.

Möntmann, Nina, ed. 2006. *Art and Its Institutions: Current Conflicts, Critique and Collaborations*. London: Black Dog.

Morphy, Howard, and Morgan Perkins, eds. 2006. *The Anthropology of Art: A Reader*. Oxford: Blackwell.

Mouffe, Chantal. 2000. "Hegemony and New Political Subjects: Toward a New Concept of Democracy." Translated by Stanley Gray. In *Readings in Contemporary Political Sociology*, edited by Kate Nash, 295–309. Oxford: Blackwell.

Mullin, Donald C. 1970. *The Development of the Playhouse: A Survey of Theatre Architecture from the Renaissance to the Present*. Berkeley: University of California Press.

Mumma, Gordon. 1967. "Creative Aspects of Live Performance Electronic Music Technology." Audio Engineering Society, Papers of the 33rd National Convention, http://brainwashed.com/mumma/creative.htm.

Murphy, John. 1999. "Patron's Statement for 'When Attitudes Become Form.'" Reprinted in *Conceptual Art: A Critical Anthology*, edited by Alexander Alberro and Blake Stimson, 127–28. Cambridge, MA: MIT Press.

"Music at Mills: An Illustrious Musical History." http://musicnow.mills.edu /music_at_mills_history.php.

Muyumba, Walton M. 2009. *The Shadow and the Act: Black Intellectual Practice, Jazz Improvisation, and Philosophical Pragmatism.* Chicago: University of Chicago Press.

Nachmanovitch, Stephen. 1990. *Free Play: Improvisation in Life and Art.* New York: Jeremy P. Tarcher/Putnam.

Nancy, Jean-Luc. 2008. "The Being-with of the Being-There." In *Rethinking Facticity,* edited by François Raffoul and Eric Sean Nelson, 113–28. Albany: State University of New York Press.

Neale, Stephen. 1980. *Genre.* London: British Film Institute.

———. 1990. "Questions of Genre." In *Approaches to Media: A Reader,* edited by Oliver Boyd-Barrett and Chris Newbold, 460–72. London: Arnold.

Nettl, Bruno, and Melinda Russell, eds. 1998. *In the Course of Performance: Studies in the World of Musical Improvisation.* Chicago: University of Chicago Press.

Nicholls, Tracey. 2010. "Opening up the Academy: Fanon's Lessons for Inclusive Scholarship." In *Fanon and the Decolonization of Philosophy,* edited by Elizabeth A. Hoppe and Tracey Nichols, 19–36. Lanham, MD: Lexington.

Nicholson, Stuart. 1999. *Reminiscing in Tempo: A Portrait of Duke Ellington.* Hanover, NH: Northeastern University Press.

Niedzviecki, Hal. 2004. *Hello, I'm Special: How Individuality Became the New Conformity.* Toronto: Penguin Canada.

Nooshin, Laudan. 2003. "Improvisation as 'Other': Creativity, Knowledge and Power—The Case of Iranian Classical Music." *Journal of the Royal Musical Association* 128 (2): 242–96.

North, Michael. 2001. "Visual Histories: The Year as Literary Period." *Modern Language Quarterly* 62 (4): 407–24.

Okin, Susan Moller. 1999. *Is Multiculturalism Bad for Women?* Princeton, NJ: Princeton University Press.

Oliver, Michael, ed. 1999. *Settling the Score.* London: Faber.

"Open the Door, Richard, and Let All the Lawyers In." 1947. *Billboard* (January 25): 18.

Ortner, Sherry B. 1996. *Making Gender: The Politics and Erotics of Culture.* Boston: Beacon.

Osborne, Peter. 2013. *Anywhere or Not at All: Philosophy of Contemporary Art.* London: Verso.

Oswald, John. 2006. "Bettered by the Borrower: The Ethics of Musical Debt." In *Audio Culture: Readings in Modern Music,* edited by Christopher Cox and Daniel Warner, 131–38. New York: Continuum International.

Paddison, Max. 1993. *Adorno's Aesthetics of Music.* Cambridge: Cambridge University Press.

Pashenkov, Nikita. 2002. "Optical Turntable as an Interface for Musical Performance." Master's thesis, Program in Media Arts and Sciences, Massachusetts

Institute of Technology, Cambridge. http://dspace.mit.edu/bitstream/handle/1721.1/62364/50783881.pdf.

Patton, Paul. 2000. *Deleuze and the Political*. London: Routledge.

Peck, Jamie. 2005. "Struggling with the Creative Class." *International Journal of Urban and Regional Research* 29 (4): 740–70.

Pellegrinelli, Lara. 2008. "Separated at 'Birth': Singing and the History of Jazz." In *Big Ears: Listening for Gender in Jazz Studies*, edited by Nicole Rustin and Sherrie Tucker, 31–47. Durham, NC: Duke University Press.

Penny, Simon. 1995. "The Pursuit of the Living Machine." *Scientific American* (September): 216.

———. 2016. "Improvisation and Interaction, Canons and Rules, Emergence and Play." In *The Oxford Handbook of Critical Improvisation Studies*, Volume II, edited by George E. Lewis and Benjamin Piekut, 401–423. New York: Oxford University Press.

Perlman, Marc. 1998. "The Social Meanings of Modal Practices: Status, Gender, History, and *Pathet* in Central Javanese Music." *Ethnomusicology* 42 (1): 45–80.

Perloff, Marjorie. 2008. "Unoriginal Genius: Walter Benjamin's *Arcades* as Paradigm for the New Poetics." *Études Anglaises* 61 (2): 229–52.

Peters, Gary. 2009. *The Philosophy of Improvisation*. Chicago: University of Chicago Press.

Phelan, Peggy. 1993. *Unmarked: The Politics of Performance*. London: Routledge.

Pickering, Andrew. 2010a. *The Cybernetic Brain: Sketches of Another Future*. Chicago: University of Chicago Press.

———. 2010b. "Material Culture and the Dance of Agency." In *The Oxford Handbook of Material Culture Studies*, ed. Dan Hicks and Mary Carolyn Beaudry, 191–208. Oxford: Oxford University Press.

Polley, Paula, and Sam Nelson. 1986. *A Computer Owner's Guide to the Care of and Communication with Little Computer People: Instructions for the Commodore Amiga and Atari ST*. Mountain View, CA: Activision.

Polsky, Milton E. 1998. *Let's Improvise: Becoming Creative, Expressive and Spontaneous through Drama*. London: Prentice Hall.

Porter, Eric. 2002. *What Is This Thing Called Jazz? African American Musicians as Artists, Critics, and Activists*. Berkeley: University of California Press.

Post, Steve. 1993. "Son of Playlist: The Decline and Fall of Commercial Free-Form Radio." In *Radiotext(e)*, edited by Neil Strauss, 106–13. New York: Semiotext(e).

Puchner, Martin. 2002. *Stage Fright: Modernism, Anti-theatricality, and Drama*. Baltimore.MD: Johns Hopkins University Press.

Rabinow, Paul. 2003. *Anthropos Today: Reflections on Modern Equipment*. Princeton, NJ: Princeton University Press.

Rabinowitch, Tal-Chen. 2010. "Long-Term Musical Group Interaction Has a Positive Effect on Empathy in Children." Paper presented at the Annual Conference of the Society for Education, Music and Psychology Research, University of Leeds, September.

Radano, Ronald. 2003. *Lying up a Nation: Race and Black Music*. Chicago: University Press of Chicago.

Rancière, Jacques. 2004. *The Politics of Aesthetics: The Distribution of the Sensible*. Translated by Gabriel Rockhill. London: Continuum.

———. 2009a. *Aesthetics and Its Discontents*. Translated by Steven Corcoran. Cambridge: Polity.

———. 2009b. *The Emancipated Spectator*. London: Verso.

Rasmussen, Chris. 2010. "'The People's Orchestra': Jukeboxes as the Measure of Popular Musical Taste in the 1930s and 1940s." In *Sound in the Age of Mechanical Reproduction*, edited by David Suisman and Susan Strasser, 181–98. Philadelphia: University of Pennsylvania Press.

Reason Myers, Dana. 2002. "The Myth of Absence: Representation, Reception and the Music of Experimental Women Improvisers." PhD diss., University of California, San Diego.

Rebellato, Dan. 1999. *1956 and All That: The Making of Modern British Drama*. London: Routledge.

———. 2006. "The Theatre Is Not Local: Borges's Birds and the Otherwhere of Theatre." Paper presented at IFTR/FIRT, University of Helsinki, Finland, August.

———. 2009. *Theatre and Globalization*. Basingstoke, UK: Palgrave Macmillan.

Ridout, Nicholas. 2006. *Stage Fright, Animals, and Other Theatrical Problems*. Cambridge: Cambridge University Press.

Roads, Curtis. 1985. "Improvisation with George Lewis." In *Composers and the Computer*, edited by Curtis Roads, 75–80. Los Altos, CA: William Kaufman.

Robinson, Alice M., Vera Mowry Roberts, and Milly S. Barranger, eds. 1989. *Notable Women in American Theatre: A Biographical Dictionary*. New York: Greenwood.

Rodenbeck, Judith. 2011. *Radical Prototypes: Allan Kaprow and the Invention of Happenings*. Cambridge MA: MIT Press.

Rose, Tricia. 1994. *Black Noise: Rap Music and Black Culture in Contemporary America*. Middletown, CT: Wesleyan University Press.

Rowan, Dean C. 2004. "Modes and Manifestations of Improvisation in Urban Planning, Design, and Theory." *Critical Studies in Improvisation* 1 (1). http://www.criticalimprov.com/article/view/10/33.

Rustin, Nichole and Sherrie Tucker. 2008. *Big Ears: Listening for Gender in Jazz Studies*. Durham, NC: Duke University Press.

Rutten, Kris, An van Dienderen, and Ronald Soetaert. 2013. "Revisiting the Ethnographic Turn in Contemporary Art." *Critical Arts* 27 (5): 459–73.

Saal, Ilka. 2007. *New Deal Theater: The Vernacular Tradition in American Political Theater*. New York: Palgrave Macmillan.

Salter, Chris. 2010. *Entangled: Technology and the Transformation of Performance*. Cambridge, MA: MIT Press.

Sansom, Matthew. 2001. "Imaging Music: Abstract Expressionism and Free Improvisation." *Leonardo Music Journal* 11: 29–34.

Scarré, Geoffrey. 1981. "Kant on Free and Dependent Beauty." *British Journal of Aesthetics* 21 (4): 351–62.

Schneider, Arnd, and Christopher Wright. 2006. *Contemporary Art and Anthropology.* Oxford: Berg.

———. 2010. *Between Art and Anthropology: Contemporary Ethnographic Practice.* Oxford: Berg.

Schubert, Hannelore. 1971. *The Modern Theatre: Architecture, Stage Design, Lighting.* London: Pall Mall.

Schutz, Alfred. 1964. "Making Music Together." In *Collected Papers II: Studies in Social Theory,* edited by Arvid Brodersen, 159–78. The Hague: Martinus Nijhoff.

Scruton, Roger. 1997. *The Aesthetics of Music.* Oxford: Oxford University Press.

Sennett, Richard. 2002. *The Fall of Public Man.* London: Penguin.

Sewell Jr., William H. 1992. "A Theory of Structure: Duality, Agency and Transformation." *American Journal of Sociology* 98 (1): 1–22.

Shepherd, Simon, and Peter Womack. 1996. *English Drama: A Cultural History.* Oxford: Blackwell.

Skinner, Ryan. 2015. *Bamako Sounds: The Afropolitan Ethics of Malian Music.* Minneapolis: University of Minnesota Press.

Skrebowski, Luke. 2009. "Systems, Contexts, Relations: An Alternative Genealogy of Conceptual Art." PhD diss., Middlesex University.

Slater, Howard. 2001. "The Art of Governance: The Artist Placement Group 1966–1989." *Variant* 11.

Small, Christopher. 1998. *Musicking: The Meanings of Performing and Listening.* Hanover, NH: University Press of New England and Wesleyan University Press.

Smith, Julie Dawn. 2004. "Playing Like a Girl: The Queer Laughter of the Feminist Improvising Group." In *The Other Side of Nowhere: Jazz, Improvisation, and Communities in Dialogue,* edited by Daniel Fischlin and Ajay Heble, 224–43. Middletown, CT: Wesleyan University Press.

Smith, Wadada Leo. 1973. *notes (8 Pieces) source a new | world music: creative music.* Self-published.

Smith, R. J. 2004. "Richard Speaks! Chasing a Tune from the Chitlin Circuit to the Mormon Tabernacle." In *This Is Pop: In Search of the Elusive at Experience Music Project,* edited by Eric Weisbard, 75–89. Cambridge, MA: Harvard University Press.

Solis, Gabriel, and Bruno Nettl, eds. 2009. *Musical Improvisation: Art, Education, and Society.* Urbana: University of Illinois Press.

Somerville, Siobhan B. 2000. *Queering the Color Line: Race and the Invention of Homosexuality in American Culture.* Durham, NC: Duke University Press.

Southern, Eileen. 1997. *Music of Black Americans: A History.* 3rd ed. New York: W. W. Norton & Company.

Spivak, Gayatri Chakravorty. 1979. "Explanation and Culture: Marginalia." *Humanities in Society* 2 (3): 201–21.

Spolin, Viola. 1973. *Improvisation for the Theatre: A Handbook of Teaching and Directing Techniques*. London: Pitman.

Stallybrass, Peter. 2007. "'Against Thinking': Responses to Ed Folsom, 'Database as Genre: The Epic Transformation of Archives.'" *Proceedings from the Modern Literary Association* 122 (5): 1580–7.

Stanbridge, Alan. 2008. "From the Margins to the Mainstream: Jazz, Social Relations, and Discourses of Value." *Critical Studies in Improvisation* 4 (1). http://www.criticalimprov.com/article/download/361/959.

Stanyek, Jason, and Benjamin Piekut. 2010. "Deadness: Technologies of the Intermundane." *TDR: The Drama Review* 54 (1): 14–38.

States, Bert O. 1985. *Great Reckonings in Little Rooms*. Berkeley: University of California Press.

Stein, Gertrude. 1935. "Plays." In *Writings and Lectures 1911–1945*, edited by Patricia Meyerowitz, 59–83. London: Owen.

Steinbeck, Paul. 2008. "'Area by Area the Machine Unfolds': The Improvisational Performance Practice of the Art Ensemble of Chicago." *Journal of the Society for American Music* 2 (3): 397–427.

Stephens, Vincent. 2008. "Crooning on the Fault Lines: Theorizing Jazz and Pop Vocal Singing Discourses in Rock." *American Music* 26 (2): 156–95.

Sterne, Jonathan. 2003. *The Audible Past: Cultural Origins of Sound Reproduction*. Durham, NC: Duke University Press.

Stewart, Jesse. 2010. "DJ Spooky and the Politics of Afro-Postmodernism." *Black Music Research Journal* 30 (2): 337–61.

Stewart, John L. 1991. *Ernst Krenek: The Man and His Music*. Berkeley: University of California Press.

Stratemann, Klaus. 1992. *Duke Ellington: Day by Day and Film by Film*. Copenhagen: JazzMedia.

Strathern, Marilyn. 1988. *The Gender of the Gift: Problems with Women and Problems with Society in Melanesia*. Berkeley: University of California Press.

———. 1990. "The Concept of Society Is Theoretically Obsolete." In *Key Debates in Anthropology*, edited by Tim Ingold, 60–66. London: Routledge.

Straw, Will. 1991. "Systems of Articulation, Logics of Change: Communities and Scenes in Popular Music." *Cultural Studies* 5 (3): 368–88.

———. 2010. "The Circulatory Turn." In *The Wireless Spectrum: The Politics, Practices and Poetics of Mobile Media*, edited by Barbara Crow, Michael Longford, and Kim Sawchuk, 17–28. Toronto: University of Toronto Press.

Strindberg, August. 2008. "Preface." In *Miss Julie and Other Plays*, translated by Michael Robinson, 56–68. Oxford: Oxford University Press.

Suchman, Lucy. 2007. *Human-Machine Reconfigurations: Plans and Situated Actions*. 2nd ed. Cambridge: Cambridge University Press.

Taylor, Timothy D. 1998. "Moving in Decency: The Music and Radical Politics of Cornelius Cardew." *Music & Letters* 79 (4): 555–76.

Theberge, Paul. 1997. *Any Sound You Can Imagine: Making Music/Consuming Technology*. Middletown, CT: Wesleyan University Press.

Thoburn, Nicholas. 2003. *Deleuze, Marx and Politics*. London: Routledge.

Thomas, Nicholas. 1991. *Entangled Objects: Exchange, Material Culture, and Colonialism in the Pacific*. Cambridge, MA: Harvard University Press.

Thompson, Nato, ed. 2012. *Living as Form: Socially Engaged Art from 1991–2011*. Cambridge, MA: MIT Press.

Tinkcom, Matthew. 2002. *Working Like a Homosexual: Camp, Capital, Cinema*. Durham, NC: Duke University Press.

Tolmie, Peter, James Pycock, Tim Diggins, Allan MacLean, and Alain Karsenty. 2002. "Unremarkable Computing." Paper presented at the Conference on Human Factors in Computing Systems, Minneapolis.

Tucker, Mark, ed. 1993. *The Duke Ellington Reader*. New York: Oxford University Press.

Tucker, Sherrie. 2000. *Swing Shift: "All-Girl" Bands of the 1940s*. Durham, NC: Duke University Press.

Turino, Thomas. 2008. *Music as Social Life: The Politics of Participation*. Chicago: University of Chicago Press.

Turkle, Sherry. 2012. *Alone Together: Why We Expect More from Technology and Less from Each Other*. New York: Basic.

Vaidhyanathan, Siva. 2001. *Copyrights and Copywrongs: The Rise of Intellectual Property and How It Threatens Creativity*. New York: New York University Press.

Valiquet, Patrick. 2014. "'The Digital is Everywhere': Negotiating the Aesthetics of Digital Mediation in Montreal's Electroacoustic and Sound Art Scenes." PhD diss., Oxford University.

van de Leur, Walter. 2002. *Something to Live for: The Music of Billy Strayhorn*. New York: Oxford University Press.

Varda, Agnès. 1994. "Varda par Agnès." *Cahiers du Cinéma*.

Velleman, J. David. 2009. *How We Get Along*. Cambridge: Cambridge University Press.

Wald, Elijah. 2009. *How the Beatles Destroyed Rock 'n' Roll: An Alternative History of American Popular Music*. New York: Oxford University Press.

Walker, John A. 2002. *Left Shift: Radical Art in 1970s Britain*. London: I. B. Tauris.

Wallace, Michelle. 1998. *Black Popular Culture*. Edited by Gina Dent. New York: New Press.

Wallis, Brian. 1995. "Review of bell hooks, *Art on My Mind: Visual Politics*." *Art in America* 83 (12): 25–26.

Walser, Robert, ed. 1999. *Keeping Time: Readings in Jazz History*. Oxford: Oxford University Press.

Walton, Kendall. 1970. "Categories of Art." *Philosophical Review* 79: 334–67.

Watkin, David. 1996. "Corelli's Op. 5: 'Violino e violone o cimbalo'?" *Early Music* 24 (4): 645–63.

Weber, Max. 1946. "Politics as a Vocation." In *From Max Weber: Essays in Sociology*, edited and translated by Hans Heinrich Gerth and C. Wright Mills, 77–128. New York: Oxford University Press.

———. 1978. *Economy and Society: An Outline of Interpretive Sociology.* Vol. I. Berkeley: University of California Press.

Weiser, Mark. 1993. "Some Computer Science Issues in Ubiquitous Computing." *Communications of the ACM* 36 (7): 75–84.

Weiser, Mark, Rich Gold, and John Seely Brown. 1999. "The Origins of Ubiquitous Computing Research at PARC in the Late 1980s." *IBM Systems Journal* 38 (4): 693–96.

Wiles, David. 2003. *A Short History of Western Performance Space.* New York: Cambridge University Press.

Willard, Patricia. 1999. "Dance: The Unsung Element of Ellingtonia." *Antioch Review* 57 (3): 402–14.

Wolf, Jaime. 1999. "No Hits, All the Time." *New York Times Magazine*, April 11. http://www.nytimes.com/library/magazine/home/041199wolf.html.

Wolff, Christian. 1964. "For 1, 2, or 3 People." New York, London, Frankfurt, and Leipzig: C.F. Peters. Music score.

Wright, Will. "Will Wright: A Chat about 'The Sims' and 'SimCity'" CNN.com, January 20, 2000, http://www.cnn.com/chat/transcripts/2000/1/wright/index.html.

Zak III, Albin. 2001. *The Poetics of Rock: Cutting Tracks, Making Records.* Berkeley: University of California Press.

———. 2010. *I Don't Sound Like Nobody: Remaking Music in 1950s America.* Ann Arbor: The University of Michigan Press.

Žižek, Slavoj. 1989. *The Sublime Object of Ideology.* London: Verso.

———. 1997. *The Plague of Fantasies.* London: Verso.

———, ed. 2006. *The Parallax View.* Cambridge, MA: MIT Press.

———. 2008. *Violence: Six Sideways Reflections.* New York: Picador.

Zuckert, Rachel. 2007. *Kant on Beauty and Biology: An Interpretation of the "Critique of Judgment."* Cambridge: Cambridge University Press.

CONTRIBUTORS' BIOGRAPHIES

LISA BARG teaches at the Schulich School of Music at McGill University. Her research and teaching focus on the intersection of race, gender, and sexuality in twentieth-century music, modernism, jazz, and popular music. She has published articles in *American Music, Journal of the Society of American Music, Journal for the American Musicological Society, Musical Quarterly, Black Music Research Journal,* and *Women and Music.* She is currently finishing a book, *Day Dream: Billy Strayhorn, Queer History and Midcentury Jazz.* An article from that project, "Queer Encounters in the Music of Billy Strayhorn," was awarded the Philip Brett Award for excellence in LGBTQ musicology in 2015.

GEORGINA BORN trained as an anthropologist and performed as an improvising cellist and bass guitarist with groups that include Henry Cow, the Feminist Improvising Group (FIG), Derek Bailey's Company, and Mike Westbrook's Orchestra. She is Professor of Music and Anthropology at Oxford University and Professorial Fellow of Mansfield College. In 2014, she was the Bloch Visiting Professor in Music at the University of California, Berkeley, and from 2013 to 2015, she was the Schulich Visiting Chair in Music at McGill University. Born researches cultural production, including major Western cultural institutions. She has also written on television, software, art-science, and interdisciplinarity. She directs the research program Music, Digitization, Mediation: Towards Interdisciplinary Music Studies, which is funded by the European Research Council. Her recent books are *Interdisciplinarity* (with Andrew Barry; 2013) and *Music, Sound and Space* (2013). She is a Fellow of the British Academy and of Academia Europaea.

DAVID BRACKETT teaches at the Schulich School of Music of McGill University, where he specializes in the history of popular music, jazz, and contemporary classical music. In addition to more than forty journal articles, book chapters, and book reviews, he has published three books: *Interpreting Popular Music* (1995) and *The Pop, Rock, and Soul Reader: Histories and Debates* (2005). His latest book, *Categorizing Sound: Genre and Twentieth-Century Popular Music* (2016), analyzes the conditions necessary for the emergence and perpetuation of the categories that are central to the classification of popular music.

NICHOLAS COOK is the 1684 Professor of Music at the University of Cambridge. His books range from *Music: A Very Short Introduction*, which has appeared in fifteen languages, to *The Schenker Project: Culture, Race, and Music Theory in Fin-de-siècle Vienna*, which won the Society for Music Theory's Wallace Berry Award in 2010. His latest book is *Beyond the Score: Music as Performance* (2013). Currently, he is a British Academy Wolfson Research Professor, working on a project titled "Musical Encounters: Studies in Relational Musicology." He is a Fellow of the British Academy and of Academia Europaea.

MARION FROGER is Professor of Cinema Studies at the University of Montreal. Her research is concerned with the place of cinema within the formation of the social bond. It addresses how cinema reveals subtle features of forms of sociability within particular contexts (those of France and Quebec) and the different sorts of social imaginary conveyed by films. She has published, among other books, *Le cinéma à l'épreuve de la communauté: La production de l'ONF 1960–1980*, which won the Prix du Canada in Sciences Sociales in 2011. In 2013–14, she held the chair in Contemporary Quebec Studies at the Université Sorbonne-Nouvelle in Paris. She is a member of the scientific committee of the Centre de Recherches Intermédiales sur les Arts, les Lettres et les Techniques and a research fellow at the Centre d'études et de recherches internationals of the University of Montreal. She has edited the journal *Intermédialités/Intermediality* since 2013.

SUSAN KOZEL works at the convergence between dance and digital media. She combines movement practices such as improvisation and somatics with philosophical writing on affect and phenomenology. She is a professor at the School of Art and Culture of Malmö University in Sweden, project leader of the interdisciplinary research project Living Archives, and a member of the Advisory Board of the Swedish National School for Artistic Research. Her publications include *Closer: Performance, Technologies and Phenomenology* (2007) and *Mobile Choreographies: Affect and Encryption in the Performance of Mobile Media* (forthcoming). Recent shorter scholarly writings addressed topics of augmented reality, somatic materialism, and bodily expression in electronic music. Her current artistic research explores affect using mobile devices, while previous performances and installations spanned a wide range of responsive technologies from motion capture to wearables.

ERIC LEWIS is Associate Professor of Philosophy at McGill University, where he is also the Director of the Institute for the Public Life of Art and Ideas. He is the author of *The Video Art of Sylvia Safdie* (2013) and *Alexander of Aphrodisias on Book 4 of Aristotle's Meteorlogica* (1996). His research focuses on the philosophy of improvised arts; he has also written on improvisation and copyright law, feminist theory, visual art, and new media art. He leads a research team on improvisation, disabilities, and new technologies and runs an improvised new media art residency program. He is currently completing a manuscript entitled

Intents and Purposes: Towards a Philosophy of Afrological Aesthetics. He is also an active improviser playing both trumpet and electronics.

GEORGE E. LEWIS is the Edwin H. Case Professor of American Music at Columbia University and a Fellow of the American Academy of Arts and Sciences. He has been a member of the Association for the Advancement of Creative Musicians (AACM) since 1971, and his widely acclaimed *A Power Stronger than Itself: The AACM and American Experimental Music* (2008) received the American Book Award and the American Musicological Society's first Music in American Culture Award. His creative work as a composer, improviser, and computer/installation artist is documented in more than 140 recordings. He and Benjamin Piekut are co-editors of the *Oxford Handbook of Critical Improvisation Studies* (2016).

INGRID MONSON is the Quincy Jones Professor of African American Music at Harvard University, where she holds a joint appointment in the Department of Music and Department of African and African American Studies. She is a noted jazz scholar and ethnomusicologist with a lifelong interest in the relationships among music, race, aesthetics, and politics. Her most recent book, *Freedom Sounds: Civil Rights Call Out to Jazz and Africa* (2007), addresses these issues in the jazz world of the 1950s and 1960s. She is also the author of *Saying Something: Jazz Improvisation and Interaction* (1996), which addresses the interactive and communal dimensions of jazz improvisation as a musical process. She is currently working on the book *Kenedougou Visions*, about the Malian balafonist Neba Solo, and a series of essays on aesthetics and the body.

TRACEY NICHOLLS is Associate Professor of Philosophy at Lewis University, Romeoville, Illinois; co-director of the Women's Studies Program; and research associate with the Improvisation, Community, and Social Practice project. She is the author of *An Ethics of Improvisation: Aesthetic Possibilities or a Political Future* (2012), based on her dissertation. Her work in social and political philosophy contributes to discourses about privilege and marginalization in decolonization theory, feminist theory, and peace studies. Her current book project, *Places We Come From; Places We Call Home*, explores social possibilities embedded in postcolonial conceptions of belonging and national identity, and she is planning a book-length consideration of how an ethics of improvisation can support "culture-jamming" efforts to dismantle rape culture.

WINFRIED SIEMERLING is Professor of English at the University of Waterloo and an associate of the W. E. B. Du Bois Institute at Harvard University. His most recent monograph is *The Black Atlantic Reconsidered: Black Canadian Writing, Cultural History, and the Presence of the Past* (2015). Earlier books include *Canada and Its Americas: Transnational Navigations* (2010), *The New North American Studies: Culture, Writing, and the Politics of Re/Cognition* (2005), *Cultural Difference and the Literary Text* (1996–97), *Writing Ethnicity* (1996), and *Discoveries of the Other* (1994). He is a contributor to *The Oxford Handbook of the African American Slave Narrative* (2014) and *The Cambridge History of Postcolonial Literature* (2012) and a co-researcher in the International Institute for Critical Studies in Improvisation: A Partnered Research Institute (2013–20), funded by the Social Sciences and Humanities Council of Canada.

WILL STRAW is Professor in the Department of Art History and Communications Studies at McGill University. He is the author of *Cyanide and Sin: Visualizing Crime in '50s America* (2006) and the co-editor of *Circulation and the City: Essays on Urban Culture* (2010), *Aprehendiendo al delincuente: Crimen y medios en América del norte* (2011), *Cambridge Companion to Pop and Rock* (2001), and fifteen more volumes in cultural and media studies. He is the author of more than 150 articles on urban culture, cinema, music, and media. He has directed collaborative research projects on Media and Urban Life in Montreal and The Urban Night as Interdisciplinary Object. His current research focuses on the relationship between conceptualizations of cultural scene and the culture of night in cities.

ZOË SVENDSEN holds a lectureship in Drama and Performance in the English Faculty, University of Cambridge. As the director of METIS in London, she is involved in creating interdisciplinary projects that explore contemporary political issues. As a dramaturg, Svensden has collaborated on contemporary productions of classic texts, including *Arden of Faversham*, *Miss Julie*, *Edward II*, *Measure for Measure*, and *The Changeling*. She is an artistic associate at the New Wolsey Theatre and associate artist with the Company of Angels, for which she has translated several plays from German. She is currently the affiliated artist at the Max-Planck-Institute for the History of Science in Berlin and is an honorary research fellow at Birkbeck College, University of London's Centre for Contemporary Theatre.

DARREN WERSHLER is the Concordia University Research Chair in Media and Contemporary Literature and the co-founder and co-coordinator of the Concordia Media History Research Centre. He is the author or co-author of twelve books, including, most recently, *Guy Maddin's My Winnipeg* (2009), *The Iron Whim: A Fragmented History of Typewriting* (2005), *Free as in Speech and Beer: Open Source, Peer-to-Peer, and the Economics of the Online Revolution* (2002), and *Nicholodeon: A Book of Lowerglyphs* (1997).

INDEX

Abrams, Muhal Richard, 149
abstract expressionism, 11–12, 17
action painting, 11–12
Activision, 103, 108
Adorno, Theodor, 29n12, 29–30n14, 42, 65, 73, 123, 232n18
African American: improvisation, 46, 50–51; jazz, 80, 115; music, 117–18, 120–21, 124–25, 130
agency, 299; nonhuman, 99–100, 105; and subjectivity, 101
algorithmic symbolism (AS), 103–4
AMM, 48–49
"Anal Magic with Kenny G," 160, 173–74
Anderson, Cat, 190–92
Anderson, Edmund, 196, 210n22
Anderson, Ivie, 187, 196
anesthetic, 268, 274, 281–83
anticipation: as mode of improvisation, 271, 273–74, 280
architecture, 218–19; and social relationships, 67–69
Armstrong, Louis, 63, 141, 214
arranging, 20, 187–88; relationship to composition, 187–89
art: and agency, 221; anthropology of, 5–6; anti-aesthetic, 6–7; conceptual, 6, 36; contemporary, 34, 39; vs. craft, 218–19; democratization of, 217; as emancipatory, 82–83, 200; expansive definition of, 5; as

functionless, 3; legislative, 38; participatory, 7, 35–36; politics of, 214–15; postconceptual, 29nn11–12; process, 168; relational, 35–36, 99–100, 103, 105, 270–71, 278; role in black communities, 215–21; socially engaged, 13, 37–39, 41; and social identity, 213; as social relations, 293; and spirituality, 222; as transformative, 220
Art Ensemble of Chicago (AEC), 13, 52–53, 55, 135–37, 139–40, 150–56, 157n1
Arthur Freed Unit, 186, 199–200, 202, 209n5, 211n27
artificial intelligence (AI), 91, 99–100, 104, 109n10
Artist Placement Group (APG), 13, 34–37
Art on My Mind, 213–14, 216–17, 219, 221
Association for the Advancement of Creative Musicians (AACM), 13, 51–53, 135–36, 139, 148–50, 157n2, 158n6; and black radical politics, 18, 154–56; as challenging genre, 18, 156–57; in Paris, 136, 140–45, 153–54, 157–58n3, 159nn18–19
audience, 24, 35, 278–79, 290–94, 297–98; as improviser, 269, 271; mobility of, 269; as participant, 269–74, 289, 300–305; role of, 45, 82

computer music, 16, 90n3, 91–96; composition of, 96; humanization of, 16, 96; influences on, 100; and performativity, 95–98

contact improvisation, 23–24, 269, 273–75, 278–79, 281–82

Cooper, Lindsay, 55–56

copyright, 59–60, 63, 134n25

Corelli, Arcangelo, 14, 62–63

corporeality, 23–24, 125, 268, 281, 284

Craft, Robert, 71–72

Crane, David, 16, 103

creativity: and business, 166–68; corporate, 177; and neoliberalism, 166

cybernetics, 16, 91, 100–102, 108

dance, 23–24, 203–7, 245, 268–85. *See also* contact improvisation.

Davis, Miles, 196

decolonization, 141, 214–29, 230n8

Deleuze, Gilles, 36–37, 44, 58n1, 165

Derrida, Jacques, 24, 144, 153, 156, 158n10, 268–69, 274, 279, 281–82

Devine, George, 25, 292

diaspora: African, 23, 80, 82, 136, 140–41, 255–266, 266n1, 267n5

Discombobulator, 25, 289, 298–300, 306n6

DJ, 19, 171, 178, 256, 262–63, 266n2; Kenneth Goldsmith as, 160–61, 170–77

"DJ," 260, 262–64

Duchamp, Marcel, 7, 37

Dudamel, Gustavo, 75

Dunham Dance Company, 203–4

Dunham, Katherine, 203–4, 211–12nn32–34

Edens, Roger, 202, 209n5, 211n30

Edinburgh Fringe Festival, 305, 307n11, 307n15

Ellington, Duke, 20, 49, 114–16, 121, 141, 183–84, 186–87, 194, 204–5, 209n7, 209n10, 209nn19–22, 211n30, 211–12n32, 212n34, 212n36,

214; collaboration with Billy Strayhorn, 193–95, 207, 210n21; collaboration with Rosemary Clooney, 183–84, 207

Ellington Orchestra, 183–85, 188, 196, 202–3, 210n23, 212n34

embodiment, 4, 172, 268, 275

empractise, 11, 29n13, 41, 54, 58n2

Etchells, Tim, 288, 304

"ethic of love," 214, 219–25

Eurological: 256

Fanon, Frantz, 225, 227–28, 231n16

Favors, Malachi, 135, 139

feminism, 56, 58n5

Feminist Improvising Group (FIG), 13, 53–57; and queer politics, 55–57

Ferrer, José, 185, 194, 209nn15–16

film. *See* cinema.

Fitzgerald, Ella, 187, 193

"Flamingo," 187, 195–207, 210nn22–23, 211n25, 211n28, 211–12n32

Fletcher, Dusty, 127, 133n24

Florida, Richard, 161, 165–67, 169–70, 177

Fluxus, 6–8, 28n8, 37, 168

49th Parallel Psalm, 255, 259–63, 266

Forced Entertainment, 288, 297

Four Men and a Poker Game, 25, 289, 300–302, 306n9

free improvisation, 12, 30n17, 61, 91, 94, 99, 117, 160

Gehry, Frank, 67–69, 74

gender, 185–186, 195; politics of, 277

Godard, Jean-Luc, 22, 233–48, 248–49n1, 249n5, 249–50n8

Gold, Rich, 16, 93–94, 102–3, 106–8, 109n6, 109n14

Goldsmith, Kenneth [Kenny G], 19, 160–78; as DJ, 160–61, 170–77; improvisations of, 160–62; music criticism of, 163, 178

Gonzalez-Torres, Felix, 217, 222

Gorelick, Kenneth [Kenny G], 176–77

great black music, 135–57; as genre, 156–57, 159n20
"Grievin'," 189–95, 197, 209n10

Hagberg, Garry, 47–48
Hanning, Jens, 35–36
happenings, 6–8, 28n8, 288
Hawkins, Erskine, 116, 120–25, 129, 133n17
Henry Cow, 55–56
hip hop, 23, 84, 89, 231–32n17, 255, 257–62, 265–66; as memory, 259–60
Hodges, Johnny, 189, 207
Hogan's Alley, 264–65, 266n1
Holiday, Billie, 193, 209n13
hooks, 21, 141–43, 213–29; art criticism of, 21; identity, 213; on improvisation, 219; misrepresentations of, 226–27, 231n15; on music, 216
Horne, Lena, 186, 197, 202, 209n5, 211n30
Horton, Jim, 93–96, 99–100, 102
humanism, 16, 178, 225–27, 295; anti-, 34–35, 44; post-, 99
Hume, David, 1–2
hybridity, 140–42; cultural, 225, 229, 266

"I'm Checkin' Out, Goom-Bye," 189, 195, 209n10
improvisation: African American, 46, 50–51; Afrological, 98, 209n6, 256; in art criticism of bell hooks, 219; autonomy in, 145–50, 159n14; business and, 166–69; and community, 89, 234; with computers, 16, 96; as contested ground, 10–11; and dramaturgical practice, 25; as emancipatory, 82–83; free, 12, 30n17, 61, 91, 94, 99, 117, 160; and freedom, 160–61, 163–64; and genre, 118; group, 10; impure, 161, 171; and intercorporeality, 23; and intimacy, 20, 193, 195, 246–48; meanings of, 26; and memory,

164–65; neoliberal formulation of, 166–69; in New Wave film, 22, 233–45, 250–51n16; patterns in, 61–62; and political action, 14–15, 29–30n14, 41, 214, 219; and power, 160–61; as practice of resistance, 50; process of, 61; romanticization of, 15; scripted, 171; as social act, 269, 281–85, 293, 296; as social practice, 9–11, 29–30n14, 41, 47–49, 66–67; solos in, 123–24; theatrical, 25–26, 288–89, 294–306; tradition within, 117; transcultural, 256, 265–66; uncreative, 170, 174, 177; as unforeseen, 98–99; and work performance, 14
interactivity, 91–108
intimacy: and improvisation, 20, 193, 195, 246–48
IntuiTweet, 23–24, 269, 272, 275–84, 285n3, 286n6

Jackson, John Shenoy, 149
Jarman, Joseph, 135, 137, 145, 150–52, 156, 159n18
jazz, 114–17, 130–31, 232n18, 233, 259, 267n4, 295: and action painting, 11–12; commodification of, 228; composition in, 64; free, 45, 55, 59, 74–75, 137, 225, 227; impact of historical events on, 78–79; improvisation, 47, 61–62, 69; as intentional, 11–12; mythologization of, 60; vs popular music, 18; and race, 80–81, 115; vs Western art music, 73–74; women in, 53–55, 83, 196
Jeffries, Herb, 196–97, 200–5, 208, 210n22
Jenkins, Leroy, 135–36, 140, 148
Johnstone, Keith, 164, 294
jukeboxes, 122, 126–27, 202
Jump for Joy, 196, 202–3

Kant, Immanuel, 1–3, 27n1, 28n7, 98, 164, 213, 231n12

Kaye, Sammy, 126
Keinänen, Mia, 269, 275–281, 286n6
Kenny G. *See* Goldsmith, Kenneth, for the radio DJ, or Gorelick, Kenneth, for the saxophonist.
Keyboard Input Module (KIM-1), 93, 95, 103
King, Martin Luther, Jr., 222–25
Krenek, Ernst, 72–73, 77n2

lead sheets: vs scores, 62–63
League of Automatic Music Composers, 93–107, 109n5
Legba, 259–65
Little Computer People (LCP), 16, 103–8, 109n14, 109n19
liveness, 95, 97–98, 234, 296–97

Mali, 15, 83–89
Mars Club, 194–95, 209n17
Martin, Freddy, 126, 129
"MC" 259–62
mechanical reproduction, 118–20, 132n13
memory, 258–59, 268, 271–74; hip hop as, 259–60
Message to Our Folks, 136–37, 139–40, 150–52
Methodfive Inc., 168–69
Metro-Goldwyn-Mayer (MGM), 186, 199, 200, 210n22, 211n27–30, 212n38
microcomputers, 92, 95, 104, 109n6
microsocialities, 13, 36, 42–57, 75, 78, 81; of performance, 43–53, 57
Miller, Glenn, 116, 120–24, 126, 129, 133n22
Miller, Mitch, 183, 208n1
Miller, Paul (DJ Spooky), 171
Mills College, 92–95, 99
Mingus, Charles, 62, 84
Minnelli, Vincente, 186–87, 202, 211n27
minstrelsy, 114, 125, 128
Mitchell, Roscoe, 52, 93, 135, 151

movement intuition, 24, 275–81
Mozart, Amadeus, 63–65, 69–70, 75
multitrack recording, 71, 185, 210n18
Mumma, Gordon, 93, 97, 101
music: in academia, 42; as assemblage, 44; as inherently social, 73, 76; microsocialities of, 43–50, 52; social mediation of, 41–43
Musicolour, 100–102

Neba Solo, 83–88
network music, 95–96, 109n6
New Musicology, 12, 65
New Wave, 21–22, 233–48; characterization of, 243; community of, 242; improvisation in, 233–45, 250–51n16
Nicols, Maggie, 55–56
notation: in Western Art Music, 60–65, 69, 74
notes (8 pieces), 145, 147
Nouvelle Vague. *See* New Wave.
novelty recordings, 18, 123, 125–29, 183, 193

ocularcentricity, 59, 63–66, 71
Oliveros, Pauline, 93, 101
"Open the Door, Richard!," 18, 114–16, 119, 126–29
orality, 59, 63, 124, 257–59, 261–264, 266n1

Panorams, 202, 211n31
Papua New Guinea, 81
Paris: AACM in, 18, 135–57
Parker, Charlie "Bird," 3, 30n19, 50–51, 139
"Passion Flower," 189, 194, 207
pataphysics, 173, 176
Performance Bond, 255, 259, 264, 266, 267n5
Perkis, Tim, 93, 95
Peter B. Lewis Building, 67–69
photography, 119, 230n5; role in black art production, 217–18

swing, 113–21, 124–26, 130–31, 133n17, 188, 190, 196, 207

Tchaikovsky, Pyotr, 72–73
Terrain Reader, 102–3
theatre, 288–306; doubleness of, 25, 290; intimate, 291.
3rd Ring Out: Rehearsing the Future, 25–26, 289, 302–6, 307nn11–16
tidalectics, 259–62, 264–66
Tin Pan Alley, 80, 121
Townsend, Irving, 184–85, 194, 208n2, 209n10
transcultural improvisation, 23, 255–66, 266–67n3
Traoré, Souleymane, 83–88
Truffaut, François, 236–38, 241–44, 249nn5–6, 249–50nn8–10
"Turkish Jokes," 35–36
turntablism, 23, 255–56, 258, 261–64
"Tuxedo Junction," 116, 119–24, 127, 129, 133n17
Twitter, 23–24, 269; improvisation with, 275–83, 286n7, 286–87nn13–15

ubiquitous computing, 93, 106–8
Ubuweb, 161, 163, 169, 172–74

Vadim, Roger, 237–38, 241, 249–50nn8–9
venues: role in performance, 24–25, 270–71, 298, 301, 306n5
"Vèvè," 264–65, 267n9

Warhol, Andy, 161, 165, 168, 170
Watford Imagine Festival, 305, 307n11, 307n15
Webern, Anton, 71–72, 92
Western art music (WAM), 59–67, 118, 153; attack on, 155; improvisation in, 64; mythologization of, 60, 74; notation in, 60–65, 69, 74; and social interaction, 67–74
Williams, Cathy, 55–56
WFMU, 19, 160–61, 170–76
women: experience in music, 53–55, 83; in jazz, 196
Wright, Ben, 268, 285n2

Xerox Palo Alto Research Centre (PARC), 93, 104, 106, 108

Your Hit Parade, 113–15

Zorn, John, 49, 163, 176–77
Zorn, Jonathan, 176–77

Printed and bound by CPI Group (UK) Ltd, Croydon, CR0 4YY

26/02/2024

14458975-0004